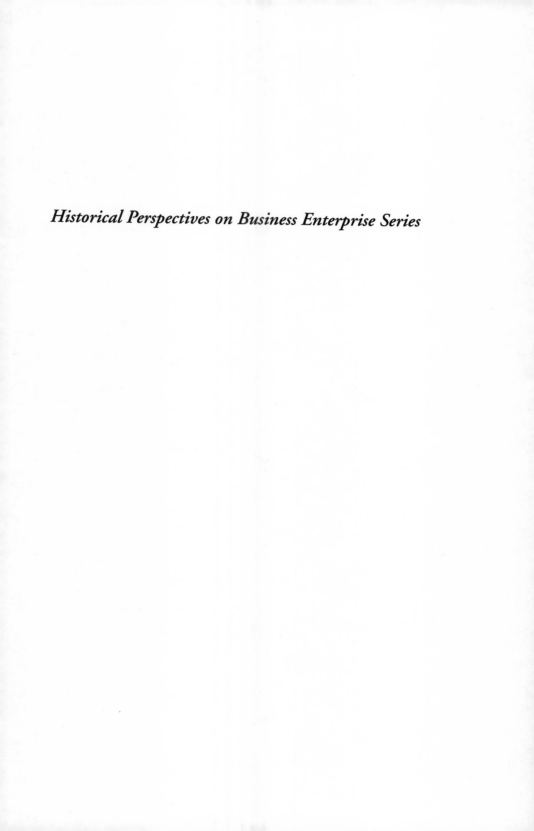

Historical Perspectives on Business Enterprise Series

Airline Executives and Federal Regulation

*Case Studies in American Enterprise from
the Airmail Era to the Dawn of the Jet Age*

Edited by W. DAVID LEWIS

Ohio State University Press

Columbus

Library of Congress Cataloging-in-Publication Data

Airline executives and federal regulation : case studies in American enterprise from the airmail era to the dawn of the jet age / edited by W. David Lewis.
     p. cm. — (Historical perspectives on business enterprise series)
    Includes bibliographical references and index.
    ISBN 0-8142-0833-9
    1. Aeronautics, Commercial—United States—Biography. 2. Executives—United States—Biography. 3. Aeronautics, Commercial—United States—Government policy. I. Lewis, W. David (Walter David), 1931– II. Series.

HE9803.A3 A365 2000
387.7'1—dc21
                                    99-054308

Text and jacket design by Diane Gleba Hall.
Type set in Adobe Garamond by Nighthawk Design.
Printed by McNaughton & Gunn.

9 8 7 6 5 4 3 2 1

Contents

Preface

IN AIRLINE REGULATION, AS IN EVERY OTHER subject within its majestic sweep, history has a human face. Most studies of airline regulation have been written by economists, yielding valuable insight into the interplay between government and market forces. Such studies, however, are not primarily people oriented. They pay little attention to the personalities involved in the complex process by which the laws of supply and demand coexist with the dreams and ambitions of strong-minded individuals with a rich blend of egos, temperaments, drives, and talents. Such a task is best suited to historians, which provides the rationale for this book. The essays it contains are case studies, building on a well-established tradition of business historiography that focuses on the lives and activities of specific entrepreneurs.

The volume resulted from a discussion with two business historians, Mansel Blackford and Austin Kerr, of Ohio State University, who subscribe to the ideas I have just mentioned. Our conversation occurred during a research trip to Columbus, Ohio. It took place soon after the publication of my book *Sloss Furnaces and the Rise of the Birmingham District: An Industrial Epic* (Tuscaloosa: University of Alabama Press, 1994), about which Blackford had written a highly favorable review. The central figure in that study is a southern entrepreneur, Joseph Bryan, who was born into the Virginia plantation aristocracy and played a major role in the South's industrial development after the Civil War. Applying lessons he had learned from a patrician agricultural background, Bryan built the Sloss-Sheffield Steel and Iron Company of Birmingham, Alabama, into one of the world's largest manufacturers of foundry pig iron. Some of Bryan's attitudes and policies were rooted in convictions about racial matters that are rightly abhorred by modern readers. Nevertheless, by the standards of his day he was a man of monumental integrity whose strongly conservative orientation undergirded a patient, step-by-step style of business leadership that was well-suited to the growth of the firm he headed. Today a statue of him in Richmond's Monroe Park bears on its pedestal the statement, "The character of the citizen is the strength of the state."

Character is a subject with which historians can, and should, grapple. A dictionary definition of character states that it has to do with "the attributes or features that make up and distinguish the individual." Character involves not merely the presence or absence of rectitude but a constellation of traits and habits that emerge out of a human being's personal experience. Much of the discussion that took place among Blackford, Kerr, and myself concerned the role played by human character as a key variable in the history of business enterprise.

Throughout my career I have studied the interaction between technology and entrepreneurship in two main areas, commercial aviation and the iron and steel industry. Having finished my book on Sloss Furnaces, I was moving back into aviation by writing a biography of Edward V. ("Eddie") Rickenbacker, a national hero who built Eastern Air Lines into one of the most profitable carriers in the American sky before a series of blunders, connected partly with his fierce opposition to federal regulation, ultimately forced him into retirement. As my conversation with Blackford and Kerr switched from Bryan to Rickenbacker, it became clear that a book of case studies devoted to significant pioneers in American commercial aviation, persons whose character was shaped to some degree by their experiences with federal regulation, would be a worthwhile project. Having an excellent model already in mind, I agreed to undertake it.

That model was supplied by William M. Leary's *Aviation's Golden Age: Portraits from the 1920s and 1930s* (Iowa City: University of Iowa Press, 1989). In that important work, eight historians, including Leary himself, examined the contributions made to the development of American aviation by such persons as Henry Ford, Daniel and Harry Guggenheim,

Admiral William A. Moffett, General Benjamin Foulois, and Herbert Hoover. Each essay in Leary's book is scholarly and well-documented but was written for both specialists and nonspecialists. Sensitively edited by Leary, the book makes a solid contribution to understanding the development of American aviation in a crucial phase of its development.

I am also heavily indebted to another of Leary's many contributions to the history of flight. Several years after editing *Aviation's Golden Age*, Leary organized and edited *The Airline Industry* (New York: Facts on File, 1994), part of the *Encyclopedia of American Business History and Biography*, published by Bruccoli Clark Layman Books. Leary's pioneering work consists of 157 essays, mostly biographical but in some cases dealing with specific airlines or important pieces of legislation, written by 38 historians. It is the best indication in existence that the scholarly study of American commercial aviation has reached a state of maturity that is highly gratifying to those who have worked diligently to build it into an academic discipline. The fact that seven of the eight executives featured in the present volume were the subject of essays by the same historians in *The Airline Industry* (the sole exception, Robert F. Six, is covered by a scholar who also contributed to that book) testifies to the debt I owe Leary, a longtime friend and colleague who gave freely of his time and advice at every stage of my project. My gratitude to him is boundless.

In choosing subjects for the case studies that make up the present book, I wanted to strike a proper balance among executives representing various categories of airlines: large, medium-sized, and small; scheduled and unscheduled. Although large trunklines like American, Eastern, Continental, and Northwest are represented by half of the essays, I also selected smaller firms like Pennsylvania Central, Mohawk, and National, and one nonscheduled carrier, Transocean.

I also avoided selecting only executives known to have difficult or adversative relationships with federal regulators. Some of the case studies presented here—my own essay on Rickenbacker, for example—do involve strong elements of conflict. Others, however, including Roger E. Bilstein's essay on C. R. Smith (American Air Lines) and Michael H. Gorn's study of Robert F. Six (Continental Airlines), deal with business leaders who wholeheartedly accepted government regulation and thrived under it. One chapter, in which William F. Trimble recounts the experience of George R. Hann (Pennsylvania Central Airlines), concerns a pioneering figure who benefited from government intervention early in his career, suffered from it later, and ultimately figured in the development of a company (Capital Air Lines) that moved its corporate headquarters to Washington because it needed to be as close as possible to the federal regulators on whom its welfare depended. Another case study, Roger D. Launius's account of the tragic career of Orvis Nelson (Transocean Air Lines), discusses an entrepreneur who desperately wanted to be an accepted member of a heavily regulated industry and was driven into bankruptcy because he could not join the club. Yet another essay, by George E. Hopkins on George T. Baker (National Airlines), discusses the career of a swashbuckling executive whose firm survived mainly because of antipathy by regulators toward a more powerful captain of industry, Rickenbacker. William M. Leary's analysis of Robert E. Peach (Mohawk Airlines) reveals the poignant experience of a hard-driving figure who adroitly navigated turbulent regulatory seas but was finally overwhelmed by his own pursuit of growth, leading him to commit suicide. Donna M. Corbett's discussion of Donald W. Nyrop (Northwest Airlines) provides a unique perspective of a man who was both a powerful government regulator and the chief executive of a highly profitable major airline at different stages of his career. The book, in short, provides a mixture of perspectives aimed at provoking fruitful discussion and debate.

It was not hard to match airlines and executives with authors. All of the persons who contributed to this volume are professional historians with outstanding scholarly credentials. In most cases they have devoted years of study to the executives they have written about and airlines they headed. Their credentials appear later in the book. I am deeply grateful to them for their unstinting cooperation throughout this project.

The contributors had complete freedom to develop their essays as they saw fit. I made no effort to assign specific analytical themes or to impose an interpretive framework on their efforts. My only requirement was that the essays be based at least in part on archival research or first-hand interviews, without neglect of the best secondary sources available. Otherwise, I was confident that eight leading scholars, all devoted to common professional goals, would produce a work of lasting value without undue direction on my part. Having given the authors free rein, it pleased me to see that a coherent product emerged from our individual labors, as my introductory essay indicates. In writing it, I drew upon my own understanding of what is significant about the development of the

American airline industry, based on my experience in coauthoring books about two enterprises, All American (a progenitor of USAir) and Delta. But I also tried to follow a path that seemed to emerge from the collective work of the contributors. I am highly pleased with the outcome.

I also asked the authors to aim at a diverse readership. I hope the resulting book proves useful in undergraduate and graduate courses in aviation and business history, but I will also be pleased if it receives attention from specialists in such disciplines as economics, law, and public policy. If it finds its way into the hands of elected and appointed officials who make decisions affecting the future of various modes of transportation, including commercial aviation, so much the better. I would also like it to find an appreciative audience among serious adult readers generally who travel in the air and wonder how this form of transportation evolved to its present state. Above all, I hope the book contributes to a more intelligent discussion of the merits or drawbacks of airline deregulation, a subject of vigorous policy debate ever since the Airline Deregulation Act was passed in 1978.

As the book's title indicates, it covers the period from the inception of the federal airmail system through the onset of deregulation, and concentrates mainly on the forty years following passage of the Civil Aeronautics Act of 1938. A later volume, to which some of the same authors are committed, will deal with the experience of selected airline executives with deregulation.

I wish to express my appreciation to professors Blackford and Kerr for their encouragement and advice. I am deeply grateful to staff members of Ohio State University Press, including Beth Ina, Charlotte Dihoff, Jean Matter, and Ruth Melville, who worked with me at various stages of the project. I thank William J. Hausman, editor of *Business and Economic History,* for permitting me to use a paper that I gave at an annual meeting of the Business History Conference as the basis for the essay I have contributed to this book. As always, I am indebted to colleagues at Auburn University, particularly David O. Whitten of the College of Business. Finally, I am most deeply obligated to my wife, Patricia, whose editorial skills and constant devotion to my personal and professional well-being are indispensable assets in everything I do. First and foremost, this book is for her.

Introduction

Ambivalent Relationship: Airline Executives and Federal Regulation

W. DAVID LEWIS

ISTRUST OF GOVERNMENT RUNS DEEP IN THE
business community. Rarely, however, do entrepre-
neurs turn down favors from public officials. American history abounds
in examples of largesse bestowed on private enterprise by elected lawmakers: protective tariffs, land grants, low-interest loans, tax exemptions,
and outright subsidies come immediately to mind. As a distinguished
historian once said, business people who preach the doctrine of laissez-
faire customarily do so in "a distorted fashion."[1] They have no desire for
government to take a hands-off attitude as long as it is favorable to their
own objectives. Things are different, however, when state or federal power
is exerted in the form of discipline or restraint, provoking anguished
protests about "big government," "bureaucratic red tape," and "irresponsible meddling." Market-oriented entrepreneurs necessarily look upon
government with what might best be described as "self-interested am-
bivalence." The result is a relationship filled with creative tension.

The shifting crosscurrents of business-government relationships are
nowhere more evident than in the history of the American airline industry, which would not have existed without federal help. One pioneering enterprise, the St. Petersburg–Tampa Airboat Line, conducted regularly scheduled flights across Tampa Bay in 1914, but swiftly collapsed,

never to be resumed, when the tourist season ended. Not until postal and military officials began experimental airmail operations linking Washington, Philadelphia, and New York City in May 1918 were the foundations laid for what ultimately became today's sprawling network of commercial air routes.

Except for a very few privately operated enterprises like Aeromarine Airways, which existed chiefly to take thirsty Americans out of the country to escape Prohibition, there was little air transport of anything but mail until 1925. Only small amounts of private capital were invested in a few scattered places to expedite shipments over short stretches of water, permitting late mail to reach vessels that had already left port. Ultimately, however, the expansion of federal airmail routes across the North American continent built up a backlog of operational experience, at great expense and loss of lives, that provided a firm basis for profit-seeking enterprise. The creation of a lighted transcontinental airway, permitting mail to be carried by night as well as by day, was one important part of this difficult and expensive process, which produced large deficits covered by the taxpayers. Flying almost 14 million miles and carrying over 300 million letters, the Post Office Department "demonstrated the practical value of air transportation and set the stage for the rapid development of the American airline industry."[2]

Federal officials had no intention of making airmail transport a permanent government activity; from the beginning, they aimed to surrender the system to private enterprise as soon as possible. In 1925 the Kelly Act began to take the Post Office Department out of the mail-carrying business by yielding all routes leading into the main New York–Chicago–San Francisco airway to private contractors. In 1927, that sole remaining artery was also turned over to profit-seeking entrepreneurs. When income was subtracted from appropriations, the creation of the system up to that point had cost the government about $14 million.

Government regulation of commercial aviation inevitably accompanied privatization. Indeed, businessmen clamored for regulation, recognizing in it an absolute prerequisite for orderly exploitation of the air. The Air Commerce Act, passed by Congress in 1926, "placed responsibility squarely on the federal government for establishing and maintaining airways and aids to navigation, licensing aircraft and airmen, and in general overseeing the development and safe operation of a national system of air transportation."[3] Under its first director, William P. Mac-Cracken Jr., the Commerce Department's Aeronautics Branch worked closely with private businessmen to promote their interests, avoiding coercion wherever possible and instead stressing voluntary cooperation through trade associations.[4]

The Hooverian Vision

The man mainly responsible for conceiving the system that evolved under the Kelly and Air Commerce acts was Herbert Hoover, America's foremost prophet of what one historian has called an "associative state." Hoover envisioned a commercial airway system in which businessmen, banded together in voluntary trade groups, would cooperate with government agencies to implement a "corporatist strategy." Under this approach, private capital would be blended with sympathetic federal assistance to promote the public welfare.[5]

Following the guidelines laid down by this benevolent paternalism, the American airline industry began to emerge in the late 1920s. It got a powerful boost from a wave of public air-mindedness created by Charles A. Lindbergh's dramatic nonstop flight from New York to Paris in 1927.[6] By the end of the decade, the roots of great enterprises like American, Eastern, TWA, and United—the future "Big Four" of American commercial aviation—had been planted.[7]

Despite these achievements, the fledgling industry was badly organized and uncoordinated. Furthermore, only a few companies were interested in carrying passengers, which was one of Hoover's basic objectives. Here, for the first time, the federal government began to impose a heavy hand. Walter Folger Brown, who became postmaster general after Hoover captured the White House in 1929, applied the pressure.

Brown belonged to the Progressive, or "Bull Moose," wing of the Republican Party. He subscribed to the views of Theodore Roosevelt, whose so-called New Nationalism was predicated on strong federal involvement in American economic life. More than any other person, Brown plotted the future course of American commercial aviation. His instrument, which he wielded like a bludgeon when necessary, was the Watres Act of 1930. This statute stipulated that henceforth airmail contractors would be rewarded not according to the number of pounds of mail they

1918   U.S. AERIAL MAIL PLANE DH 4 400 HP LIBERTY MOTOR
YEP. SHE is TAKING OFF

A British-designed, American-made de Havilland DH-4 aircraft takes to the sky in the early days of airmail operations in the United States. The hand-lettered caption suggests the sense of excitement attending the beginning of this experimental service. (Courtesy of the Auburn University Archives)

carried but according to the amount of space they provided for mail. The intent of the law was to stimulate the manufacture and use of large aircraft with ample room for passengers.

Brown construed the Watres Act as giving him sweeping powers to force reorganization on the airline industry. One of his primary aims was to put airmail operations in the hands of large, well-financed corporations and weed out small operators who lacked the means to carry out his ambitious plans. Summoning representatives of leading airmail carriers to Washington, he forced them to submit to mergers establishing three large transcontinental systems, American Airways, Transcontinental and Western Air (TWA), and United Air Transport. Another large enterprise, Eastern Air Transport, would operate along the heavily populated East Coast. Small businessmen were not invited to the meetings, and they had to sell out to the big combines.

The result was a highly consolidated industry in which three large holding companies—Aviation Corporation of America (AVCO), North American Aviation, and United Aircraft and Transport Corporation—not only owned airlines but also manufactured aircraft and aircraft components. Meanwhile, a large international flag carrier,[8] Pan American, emerged with a de facto monopoly on mail and passenger routes in Latin America. Being satisfied with its financially powerful leadership, Brown fostered its growth by paying it the maximum airmail subsidies permitted by law.

Although he was high-handed, Brown was impelled by the lofty vision of taking a fragile and chaotic industry and putting it on a sound, self-supporting basis. Furthermore, he did his best to insure that firms with a legitimate stake in certain routes that they were forced to surrender receive at least some compensation for their losses.[9] Nevertheless, businessmen who had poured much time, money, and effort into building pioneer airlines learned that federal intervention could be painful. Particularly notable among these entrepreneurs was Harris M. Hanshue, a former racing driver and automobile dealer who had created Western Air Express (WAE), which, at the time, was the largest and most successful airline in America. Its operations, however, did not come east of the Mississippi River and therefore failed to meet Brown's desires. To satisfy Brown's wish for a central transcontinental route from New York City to Los Angeles, an unwilling Hanshue was forced to merge most of WAE's system with two other enterprises. One of these, Transcontinental Air Transport (TAT), had organized a combined air (by day) and railroad (by night) route from New York to San Francisco. A smaller line, Pittsburgh Aviation Industries Corporation (PAIC), controlled a short but important segment that Brown wanted to graft onto his projected central route. The "shotgun wedding" that ensued produced a corporate entity originally known as Transcontinental and Western Air, or TWA.[10]

Hanshue was only one of several entrepreneurs hurt by Brown's reshuffling of the industry. Typical of those adversely affected was Collett Everman "C. E." Woolman, a former agricultural extension agent who had expanded a crop-dusting enterprise into a passenger line, Delta Air Service, flying between Texas and Atlanta. At most, Woolman and his financial partners got back only half of the money they had invested in the venture, which Brown obliged them to sell to American Airways. In 1934, the chairman of a congressional investigating committee asked Woolman, "You sold because you had to, did you not?" Woodman replied, "Well, it was that or else."[11]

For every businessman who was hurt by Brown's methods, however, someone else was helped. Among those benefiting was George R. Hann, a lawyer and financier from Pittsburgh with powerful friends on Wall Street. Hann's company, PAIC, came out of Brown's reorganization holding a balance of power in TWA. Indeed, PAIC's president, Richard Robbins, became TWA's chief executive. Besides profiting from the creation of TWA, Hann and his associates were also involved in another large holding company, the Aviation Corporation (AVCO), which had put together a sprawling network of individual carriers out of which came American Airways. Hann's career is a good example of how a well-connected entrepreneur could reap the rewards of federal intervention. It will be discussed in an informing essay contributed to this book by William F. Trimble.[12]

Although Brown's actions were peremptory, the Watres Act had its intended effect of stimulating airmail contractors to acquire larger planes and build passenger operations. Among the new airliners that began to be used were the Ford 4AT Tri-Motor, a rugged all-metal ship that could carry up to fourteen passengers; the Fokker Trimotor, a superficially similar plane whose wooden wing structure became a liability after a well-publicized crash in 1931; the Boeing 80A, a three-engine biplane that could hold eighteen travelers; and the Fokker F-32, a four-engine giant with luxurious accommodations for thirty-two people.[13] During Brown's tenure as postmaster general, passenger operations were expanded dramatically. United Air Transport alone carried 42,928 travelers in 1931, 89,933 in 1932, and 127,693 in 1933.[14]

Resentment and Reaction

Inevitably, resentment flared among businessmen whom Brown had not favored. In 1931, led by Thomas E. Braniff, who had created a passenger service between Tulsa and Oklahoma City, some small airlines formed the Independent Scheduled Air Transport Operators' Association and hired a lawyer to fight for their interests in Washington.[15] After Hoover was discredited by the Great Depression and turned out of the White House by Franklin D. Roosevelt, much more dramatic events took place. In 1934, Fulton Lewis Jr., an investigative journalist, found evidence that Brown had been flagrantly unfair in dispensing airmail routes under the Watres

Act. A sensational congressional investigation ensued, headed by Hugo Black, a Democratic senator from Alabama. Seizing information coming out of Black's inquest, and being well aware of an opportunity to damage Hoover's reputation further, Roosevelt canceled existing airmail contracts and ordered the army to fly the mail.

Despite collecting reams of testimony, Black's committee failed to prove that Brown had broken the law, however arbitrarily he may have acted. Meanwhile, ill-trained and badly equipped army pilots, carrying mail in an unusually severe winter, crashed in sufficient numbers to create a public uproar. Backtracking, Roosevelt and Postmaster General James A. Farley hastily restored regular airmail service under temporary contracts, at lower rates of compensation, to the previous operators while new regulatory legislation was prepared on Capitol Hill.[16]

Congress produced a new law, the Air Mail (Black-McKellar) Act of 1934, which imposed severe restrictions on carriers that had held airmail contracts under the Watres Act. In addition to cutting mail pay even more, the Black-McKellar Act prohibited interlocking connections between airline operators and aircraft manufacturers. Under such arrangements, financiers had produced and sold aircraft at high prices to airlines they controlled and passed the inflated cost on to travelers who paid excessive amounts for tickets. The new law also created an unwieldy regulatory structure in which responsibility for administering the airmail system was split between the Post Office Department, the Interstate Commerce Commission, and the Commerce Department. Firms that had previously held airmail contracts under the old system were disqualified from holding them under the new one. Executives who had attended Brown's infamous "spoils conferences" were barred from holding office in companies that received new airmail contracts.[17]

Realizing that only existing contractors had the equipment and experience necessary to carry airmail and that chaos would result from too literal an interpretation of the Black-McKellar Act, Farley adroitly circumvented the statute by permitting previous contractors to bid for new contracts merely by changing their names. American Airways became a new entity, American Airlines; Eastern Air Transport was now known as Eastern Air Lines; United Air Transport was henceforth United Air Lines; and TWA merely added "Inc." to its corporate title. The contractors thereupon won back most of their former airmail routes, albeit at significantly lower rates of compensation. They received some relief from an amendment to the Black-McKellar Act in 1935, but they still had to work hard to survive.

As usual, some businessmen benefited from what had happened. Several small companies against which Brown had discriminated, including Braniff and Delta, received airmail contracts and resumed operations, carrying both mail and passengers. Delta's new route, which became the foundation of a great airline, went from Dallas–Ft. Worth to Charleston, S.C., via cities like Birmingham and Atlanta.

On the other hand, the Black-McKellar Act inflicted irreparable hardship on some executives, many of whom had done nothing wrong but whose careers were ruined because they had attended Brown's "spoils conferences." Significantly, some of them had objected to Brown's maneuvering and suffered from his decisions. One person unjustly treated was Paul Henderson, who, as assistant postmaster general in the early 1920s, had rendered a distinct service to his country by spearheading the lighted transcontinental airway system. In 1925, Henderson left the government to become general manager of National Air Transport, a large corporation that soon became a component of an even bigger transcontinental airline, United Air Transport. As vice president of United, Henderson reluctantly participated in Brown's 1930 meetings, which he regarded as unlawful. Despite the fact that United's interests were adversely affected by Brown's awarding transcontinental routes to American and TWA, and that Henderson cooperated with the Black Committee by giving it valuable evidence, he was banished from the airline industry with a broken spirit and never recovered from his emotional devastation.[18]

Another businessman whose career was destroyed was Hanshue, who had attended the spoils conferences only to protect the legitimate interests of Western Air Express. After condemning the merger into which Brown forced him, Hanshue managed to save a small part of his once prosperous company from being absorbed into TWA. He was nursing this shrunken remnant back to health in 1934 when the Black-McKellar Act forced him to resign as its chief executive. Dispirited, Hanshue died in 1937 of what was officially diagnosed as a cerebral hemorrhage. As Robert Serling later stated, "There is no such official ailment as a broken heart."[19]

A Time of Troubles

Under the Black-McKellar Act, the Post Office Department awarded only semipermanent airmail contracts that were subject to the risks of periodic review. The Interstate Commerce Commission had authority to determine fair rates of compensation that were reevaluated annually. The Secretary of Commerce had broad power over all sorts of matters including "speed, load capacity, and safety features of equipment to be used on each air mail route, and to regulate hours and benefits of pilots and mechanics. Accounting practices of the carriers were . . . monitored by the Post Office and Interstate Commerce Commission."[20]

This regulatory hodgepodge did not provide a satisfactory basis for the stable development of the airline industry, which had a hard time surviving under the reduced postal rates now in effect. To repair the damage, Roosevelt appointed a five-member commission to recommend changes that would produce "a broad policy covering all phases of aviation and the relation of the United States thereto." The vice chairman was Edward P. Warner, an engineer with a long record of government service and a sympathetic attitude toward businessmen. Partly because of his influence, the committee proposed that a unified Air Commerce Commission be created to eliminate the unwieldy arrangement established in 1934, but the next few years were spent in wrangling and bickering over what precise form a permanent solution might take. For a time Roosevelt wanted to establish a broad national policy affecting all modes of transportation, something the United States continues to lack today. Eventually, however, he retreated from his position, and Congress considered various proposals, none of which commanded enough support to become law.

Meanwhile, the airline industry experienced chronic financial deficits under rates that were still much too low. Commercial operations were also hampered by austerity budgets that prevented badly needed improvements from being made on the country's airways. This lack of financial support was at least partly responsible for a spate of airline accidents, one of which claimed the life of Senator Bronson Cutting of New Mexico in 1935. Eight fatal crashes occurred in 1936. The pace quickened as five disasters took place between late December 1936 and late January 1937. Passenger revenue fell sharply after each of these tragedies as worried travelers chose trains, cars, and buses rather than planes. This reaction only compounded the financial problems of airlines and forced them to seek higher airmail subsidies.[21]

In 1936 the airline industry took a major step to put pressure on the federal government to relieve its problems. Nineteen airlines formed the Air Transport Association, a trade group "to promote and develop the business of transporting persons, goods and mail by aircraft between fixed termini, on regular schedules and through special service, to the end that the best interest of the public and the members of the Association be served." Edgar S. Gorrell, an aeronautical engineer and graduate of both West Point and MIT, became the first president of the ATA. A master organizer, he had coordinated the writing of a 280-volume history of American air combat in World War I before pursuing a postwar career in the automobile industry. After 1936 he fought tenaciously to promote the common interests of the airlines and helped draft legislation to solve their problems. Partly because of his efforts, the government appropriated $7 million in 1937 to improve air safety, especially by installing better radio systems.[22]

Nevertheless, debate dragged on between Congress and the White House about how to deal with the airline industry. Matters finally reached a climax because of technological developments that had taken place since the passage of the Watres Act. Brown's restructuring of the airline system had created competition between United and TWA for passengers on the central transcontinental route. Trying to move ahead of TWA, which used Fokker and Ford trimotors, United spearheaded the building of the first modern airliner, the Boeing 247, a streamlined plane that could carry ten passengers and cruise much faster than TWA's trimotors. To meet this threat, TWA contracted with the Douglas Aircraft Company to develop an even better ship, the DC-1, which was somewhat faster than the Boeing 247 and which had a superior cabin design. First flight-tested in 1933, the DC-1 was ready for a dramatic display of what competitive enterprise had accomplished by the time Roosevelt canceled mail contracts in 1934. On the last day of regular airmail delivery, before the army took charge of operations, a DC-1 piloted by TWA president Jack Frye and Edward V. "Eddie" Rickenbacker, soon to become general manager of Eastern Air Lines, established a speed record flying passengers and mail from San Francisco to Newark, New Jersey. The trip took approximately thirteen hours.

In May 1934, after regular airmail service was restored, TWA introduced an improved version of the DC-1, the fourteen-passenger DC-2, which could cruise at 170 MPH. It immediately proved superior to United's Boeing 247s, which carried four fewer travelers and cruised at only 155 MPH. Also left behind in the race for aerial supremacy was the Curtiss T-32 Condor, a twin-engine biplane used by both American and Eastern. It could carry up to fifteen passengers and provided bunks for sleeper service, but was slower than either the 247 or the DC-2. Further complicating the picture was the introduction of the sleek Lockheed 10-A Electra, which sold for the remarkably low price of $36,000, could exceed 200 MPH, and was particularly well suited for smaller airlines like Braniff, Delta, and Northwest.[23]

The obsolescence of the Boeing 247 and Curtiss Condor made it imperative for United, American, or Eastern, all of which used these planes, to respond to the crisis. American seized the challenge when its recently appointed chief executive, C. R. Smith, spearheaded a project resulting in the most revolutionary airliner ever built up to that time: the famed Douglas DC-3, which could carry twenty-one passengers and cruise at 180 MPH. Within a few years, virtually every airline in the country acquired DC-3s, investing large amounts of money at a time when funds were hard to come by.

The DC-3 finally broke the logjam in Washington. It was the first airliner ever built that could make money merely by transporting passengers. As such, it posed a serious threat to the struggling airline industry. Because no special permission was required from federal authorities to establish an all-passenger operation, any upstart with enough money could now enter commercial aviation without having to secure a contract from the Post Office Department. Suddenly an industry that had experienced a decade of hardship faced chaos.

Despite all the problems airline executives had experienced at the hands of powerful federal leaders like Brown and Roosevelt, they now had no alternative but to throw themselves at the mercy of the government. Never had the airline industry's need for stability been more acute. The heavy dose of regulation that the industry now swallowed showed how seriously it took the threat of losing its hard-earned passenger business to competitors who could buy DC-3s and fly anywhere they chose.

At this moment of crisis, political and economic circumstances played into the hands of airline executives and the government alike. Public concern about airline crashes had already created a groundswell of pressure for better airline regulation. Furthermore, 1938 was an election year in which the Roosevelt administration had suddenly become vulnerable because of the fiasco produced by FDR's recent attempt to pack the Supreme Court. Strikes and other labor problems became acute in the summer of 1937 as massive organizing drives spread throughout the steel, automobile, and other mass production industries following the passage of the Wagner Act. A sharp recession beginning late in 1937 further intensified Roosevelt's problems, forcing him to abandon budget cutting and revert to deficit spending.

Alarmed, but also heartened by these developments, conservative southern Democrats and northern Republicans began forming what turned into a long-enduring coalition, and Republicans anticipated substantial gains in the November 1938 elections. Under such circumstances, political leaders on both sides of the congressional aisle were motivated to show voters that they could take effective action to deal with important issues. With airline executives prepared to rush into the arms of the government for protection, politicians had a welcome opportunity to prove that they knew how to govern.

As evidenced by Brown's heavy-handed tactics, Roosevelt's abrupt cancellation of airmail contracts in 1934, and the passage of the punitive Black-McKellar Act, both parties had shown their willingness to impose federal power on the airline industry. However much many Republicans and Democrats differed on the details of regulatory policy, they could agree on the desirability of regulation itself. As the plight of the airlines became more and more acute, the necessary compromises were reached and a legislative landmark, the Civil Aeronautics Act, became law in June 1938.[24]

After nearly a decade of conflict, peace and stability finally came to the airline industry. Considering how difficult it had been for the airlines to win a settlement on which a majority of Democrats and Republicans could agree, it is not surprising that the New Order established by the Civil Aeronautics Act lasted for a long time. Ironically, the way the issues were resolved left the airline industry looking very much as it had after Brown restructured it. As one historian later said, "The Civil Aeronautics Act revived some basic principles of the Hoover era—government-industry linkages, limited competition, and restricted entry—and made them the core of national aviation policy for the next forty years."[25]

The New Order

The Civil Aeronautics Act became the cornerstone of American commercial aviation. It is hard to exaggerate its significance. For the first time, the airline industry was responsible to a single government agency, the Civil Aeronautics Authority. The agency's five-member board had the power to supervise all aspects of safety and economic development. A federal administrator was responsible for promoting air commerce, regulating air traffic, and establishing airways. An independent Air Safety Board was established to investigate accidents and set safety guidelines. To this degree, authority was still divided.

In 1940, acting under a governmental reorganization act passed in the preceding year, Roosevelt replaced the old CAA with an even stronger body, the Civil Aeronautics Board (CAB), which exercised both economic supervision of the airline industry and the functions previously vested in the Air Safety Board. An administrator of civil aeronautics, reporting to the secretary of commerce, was responsible for overseeing the federal airways system, developing airports, issuing airworthiness certificates for aircraft, and certifying airline pilots. As a quasi-legislative and judicial body, the CAB was based in the Commerce Department, but only for housekeeping purposes. The administrator reported to the president, but the CAB itself reported to Congress.

The CAB was one of the most powerful regulatory agencies in American history. Its control of the airline industry was virtually absolute. After 1938, no airline could perform airmail or scheduled passenger operations over any route without securing what was called a Certificate of Public Convenience and Necessity (CPCN) from the CAB or its earlier counterpart, the old CAA. Once service was established on a route, it could not be abandoned without formal permission. No new carrier could engage in commercial aviation without CAB sanction, and no merger between existing airlines could take place without the CAB's consent. All tariffs and charges for the transport of passengers and goods had to receive CAB approval. Certain questionable practices, including giving rebates, were prohibited. The business affairs of commercial carriers were open to federal inspection. Airlines could arrange schedules and select aircraft, but do little else without asking Uncle Sam's permission.

The fact that commercial airlines submitted to such sweeping supervision with little or no complaint says much about the demoralization of the industry in the 1930s, its fervent desire for protection against outside competition after the DC-3 was introduced, and its need for a stable system within which orderly growth could take place. From a business point of view, one of the greatest attractions of the New Order was that airlines could now be permanently certificated to operate on given routes, rather than have to submit to periodic review. Indeed, a route franchise became a form of property that one airline could sell to another, subject (of course) to CAB approval. Permanent certification greatly enhanced an airline's ability to secure long-term credit from major financial institutions. The right to continue operating routes flown before 1938 was virtually automatic; a carrier merely had to present evidence of giving satisfactory performance between May 14 and August 22, 1938, to be "grandfathered" on a pro forma basis.

But the airline industry had bought security at the price of surrendering control. One of the greatest powers of the CAB lay in the fact that its route awards, while permanent, were nonexclusive, giving the CAB the authority to ensure competition to promote the public interest. Thus no airline had a monopoly of the routes over which it flew; the CAB could admit other carriers to these airways at its discretion. Because the CAB controlled tariffs and fares, which were uniform throughout the industry, the only advantages one airline could secure over another in competing on such routes would lie in the speed and comfort of the aircraft it elected to acquire, the courtesy with which it treated passengers, and the convenience of the schedules it adopted. Service competition was in. Price competition was out.

The New Order and the Industrial-Military Complex

The emergence of the New Order was deeply related to fundamental trends emerging in the United States during the 1930s as international skies darkened and war loomed on the horizon. Many of the revolutionary features of the new airliners developed in that pivotal decade were spinoffs from advances in military technology. The Boeing 247, for example, was a spinoff of the B-9 bomber, which was developed for the Army Air Corps in 1931. The DC series evolved out of the expertise Douglas had gained by making military aircraft, which was originally its main stock-in-trade. The same phenomenon would continue after World War II, when the Boeing 707 would evolve from the KC-125 tanker, and jet engines for passenger liners would be developed from military power plants like the Pratt and Whitney J-57 and General Electric J-79.

Probably the most important result of the New Order created by the Civil Aeronautics Act was that it brought commercial aviation into a tightly knit family of mutually dependent government agencies, military contractors, and consumer-oriented industries. After years of turmoil, commercial aviation finally "belonged." It had become a valued member of a powerful combination of interests whose fundamental needs would remain the same throughout World War II and the cold war that soon followed.

Edgar S. Gorrell, a military man himself, was at home in the New Order. By the late 1930s, the domestically antagonistic phase of the New Deal was past and the energies of the nation were being devoted to something on which everyone could agree: the need to survive and prevail against common adversaries in a divided world. One of the most significant contributions Gorrell made to the Air Transport Association and the future development of the airline industry resulted from his awareness that the conflicts erupting in Europe and Asia would demand cooperation by the airline industry, the military establishment, and the federal government in the trials that lay ahead. Foreseeing that the government might nationalize air transport, just as it had nationalized the railroads in World War I, Gorrell worked out an alternative plan that permitted airlines to retain control of their own destinies while playing an indispensable role in the war effort that began even before the Japanese bombed Pearl Harbor. The result of Gorrell's cooperation with military leaders like Henry H. "Hap" Arnold was the Air Transport Command, created in June 1942. This commercial-military hybrid enlisted personnel and aircraft from privately owned companies to conduct massive airlift operations that kept huge quantities of people and materiel moving to and from far-off theaters of war. By fulfilling these responsibilities amid extremely adverse weather conditions and constant dangers, commercial carriers earned the gratitude of government and military leaders. This sense of obligation yielded great benefits after the war, when airlines previously limited to domestic travel were permitted to break the prewar stranglehold on international routes enjoyed by Pan American Airways, which had previously been the nation's "chosen instrument"[26] for commercial operations abroad.

Prosperous American airlines carrying American-made goods to all corners of the earth fitted smoothly into the nation's postwar hopes for a world in which the United States would be the dominant political and economic superpower. While World War II was still being waged, the Roosevelt administration was planning a future strategy that would permit American companies, including the country's airlines, to invade as many foreign markets as possible. In the words of Connecticut congresswoman Clair Booth Luce, "American postwar aviation policy is simple: We want to fly everywhere. Period!!!" The fact that Luce's husband, Henry R. Luce, owned the Time-Life-Fortune empire, which spoke for the internationalist wing of the Republican Party, indicated that the administration's strategy of aerial imperialism commanded wide bipartisan support.

This strategy menaced the interests of America's chief wartime ally, Great Britain, which was facing the end of its centuries-long dominance of world markets. At an International Civil Aviation Conference held at Chicago in 1944, a British-led coalition did its best to thwart American plans for global aeronautical supremacy but gained only a compromise framework for bilateral and multilateral agreements under which American commercial airlines would flourish. When the war ended, both the executive branch and Congress were poised to fight vigorously for the interests of American airlines abroad. Only recently battered and beleaguered, a well-protected but tightly controlled industry had forged strong bonds with a federal government and a huge military establishment firmly committed to its continuing prosperity.[27]

Masters of the Game

The New Order rewarded certain types of executive personalities better than others. Some people thrive in a bureaucratized environment. Others do not. Airline leaders who were by nature "insiders" received much more favorable attention from the CAB than extreme individualists who were temperamentally attuned to an earlier era and had difficulty with interpersonal relations in a strange new world of "organization men."

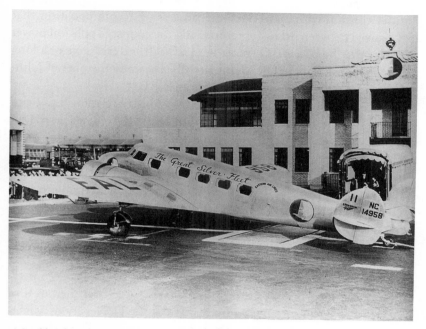

A Lockheed Model 10 Electra airliner acquired by Eastern Air Lines in the mid-1930s, in a photograph suggesting a dedication ceremony. Note the pristine condition of the plane and the markings indicating Eastern's corporate pride. (Courtesy of the Auburn University Archives)

The pathway to success in the New Order was exemplified by the burgeoning career of C. R. Smith, president of American Airlines, about whom Roger E. Bilstein has contributed an informative chapter to this book. Just before the war broke out, Smith joined forces with New York City's dynamic mayor, Fiorello LaGuardia, and a governmental agency, the Works Progress Administration (WPA), to build a big modern airport in Queens, near the recently completed Triborough Bridge. During the war Smith rose to the rank of major general as operational chief of the Air Transport Command, moving smoothly between New York City and Washington to organize and administer vast military supply lines. A Texas Democrat, Smith had close ties with a galaxy of powerful government leaders, including Jesse Jones, Sam Rayburn, and Lyndon B. Johnson, all of whom hailed from the Lone Star State. It was because of

Smith's consummate mastery of the process of accommodation that had evolved between private enterprise and the country's political power structure that he became the most successful airline executive of a long period spanning four decades. Ultimately he became a member of Johnson's cabinet, serving as secretary of commerce.

Smith's finesse in handling government-industry relationships helps explain his condescending attitude toward Eddie Rickenbacker, the ultraconservative chief executive of Eastern Air Lines. I will recount Rickenbacker's career in one of the chapters that follow. His personal and political roots were in the nineteenth century. An extreme individualist, he was uncomfortable with the New Order and bungled trying to steer his company through its regulatory intricacies. The art of compromise was foreign to his authoritarian nature, and his blunt, old-fashioned honesty, which led him to say exactly what he thought, was incompatible with the protocols and niceties of a new bureaucratic milieu.[28]

A good example of the success open to persons who were temperamentally and ideologically attuned to the New Order was the career of L. Welch Pogue, an Iowan who studied law at the University of Michigan and Harvard and became attracted to aviation law. The rapidity of Pogue's ascent in the political atmosphere created by the New Deal and World War II was breathtaking. He became assistant general counsel of the newly created Civil Aeronautics Authority in 1938, was promoted to general counsel of the reconstituted Civil Aeronautics Board in 1939, became CAB chairman in 1942, and played a leading role in working out the compromises that clinched America's victory at the International Civil Aviation Conference in 1944. After the war, Pogue left the government for the business world, becoming highly successful representing airlines in route cases and merger negotiations. He served on the board of directors of Western Air Lines and excelled as a lobbyist.[29]

Pogue never became chief executive of an airline, which is the reason there is no chapter about him in this book. One CAB chairman, however, did command an airline and is the subject of an authoritative essay by Donna M. Corbett. His name was Donald W. Nyrop.

Like Pogue, Nyrop was well attuned to the era in which he came of age. A banker's son from Nebraska, he studied at night for a law degree from George Washington University in the 1930s while working as an auditor in the U.S. General Accounting Office. Quickly becoming familiar with how bureaucracy worked, he advanced rapidly after Pogue hired him as a staff attorney for the CAA. There he became an expert on route proceedings and airline safety. When Pogue became chairman of the CAB, he made Nyrop his executive assistant. Shortly thereafter, Nyrop enlisted in the armed forces and became executive operations manager in the Air Transport Command. After the war he became an American delegate to assemblies of the International Civil Aviation Organization while working in the private sector monitoring the development of American overseas commercial operations for the Air Transport Association. In 1948 he returned to the federal hierarchy as executive assistant to Civil Aeronautics Administrator Delos W. Rentzel, whom he succeeded as CAA chief in 1950. Six months later, Harry Truman appointed him chairman of the CAB. Nyrop was less than forty years old at the time.

Expecting a Republican victory in the presidential election of 1952, Nyrop resigned from the CAB shortly before Eisenhower's landslide to join a Washington law firm that was heavily involved in airline route proceedings. His organizational skills resulted in his becoming director of the newly constituted Conference of Local Airlines, and he helped secure permanent route certification for small "feederlines" that were springing up around the nation. In 1954 he reached the pinnacle of his career when he became president of Northwest Airlines, a financially struggling but potentially lucrative carrier that had won a network of Great Circle routes to Asia and was better known as Northwest Orient. Nyrop's intense cost-consciousness and passion for standardization got Northwest quickly out of debt, and he transformed it into a highly profitable company. After he had spent twenty-three years at its helm, it was earning profits exceeding $50 million a year.

Nyrop's familiarity with the New Order enabled him to appreciate its flaws, particularly after he became head of an efficiently run airline and learned that the CAB rewarded competing firms that were not nearly as well managed as his own. Indeed, it seemed as if the CAB actually favored the weak instead of the strong. The reason why this was true was partly because of the dynamics of service competition.[30]

The Age of Service Competition

The New Order worked reasonably well until social, economic, and technological changes undermined the way it operated. Under the guidelines laid down in the late 1930s, American commercial aviation became an object of international envy. Looking back in 1972 at the achievements of the CAB, its chairman, Secor D. Brown, said, "A competitive system of privately owned airlines has created patterns of public service, systems of company organization and techniques of aircraft design and supply which have established the world model."[31] Whatever went wrong in the forty years that the CAB controlled the airline industry, there was much that went right. Nevertheless, it is a rare system that does not contain the seeds of its own destruction. The New Order proved no exception to this rule.

The basic problem facing the CAB throughout its history was to reconcile the financial interests of the airline industry with the convenience of the traveling public. There is no question that the CAB tried hard to accomplish this difficult feat. Its fundamental strategy was to promote service competition, which would benefit the public, while endeavoring to help airlines earn reasonable profits, which would benefit the industry. Unfortunately, these goals sometimes worked at cross purposes.

Being inherently committed to the idea that air travel was a good thing, the CAB wanted to extend its blessings to as many people as possible. One of the strategies it pursued was constantly expanding networks of air routes connecting as many places as political expediency dictated. Some of these routes were served by carriers already grandfathered in 1938. Others were awarded to new airlines that, at least theoretically, met stringent requirements designed to ensure that they were "ready, willing, and able" to serve the needs of the traveling public. The degree to which airlines met those needs was judged by the quality of service they rendered, measured in terms of such criteria as speed, comfort, and convenience.

This strategy was seemingly sound from a financial point of view. The more routes an airline was awarded, the more passengers it could serve, the more airplanes it could buy, and the more profits it could earn. But there was a basic flaw in such reasoning, because it assumed that the market for air travel would expand indefinitely and that increasing numbers of people would be willing to pay fares that would permit airlines to prosper. Unfortunately, these assumptions proved wrong, because markets were not as elastic as the CAB and the industry to which it was responsible assumed.

During World War II, large numbers of people, particularly members of the armed services, flew for the first time and became accustomed to that mode of travel. Partly for that reason, but also because of personal savings built up by civilians on the home front, both the CAB and the airline industry counted heavily on a vast expansion of markets after the war. Although more people did fly, however, they did not do so in the numbers anticipated. To some extent this lack of demand was caused by poor service rendered to the public during the immediate postwar years, when many people did take commercial flights for the first time and were repelled by dirty terminals, overcrowded airports, obsolescent planes, and other features of an industry caught in a transition for which it was unprepared. By 1947 the airline industry was reeling from deficits, the CAB had temporarily cut back on new route awards, and board members were recommending mergers to consolidate route systems that already seemed too large. A wave of labor problems related to the inflationary price trends of the postwar era did not help.

By 1948 the airlines were beginning to revive as carriers replaced old airplanes with more modern equipment and nagging labor problems were at least temporarily solved. The Korean War soon created some of the same type of demand that had benefited the industry in World War II by filling seats with passengers on military and war-related business. During this period the airlines learned that the best way to attract more passengers, aside from giving them better airport facilities, was to give them newer, faster, and larger planes and every imaginable amenity. Service competition paid off.

Emphasizing the quality of service rendered to the traveling public also made sense at a time when fear of flight was still keeping many people from venturing into the air. Giving them more speed, convenience, and comfort seemed the best way of overcoming their reluctance to fly.

Flying in an airliner was still a disagreeable experience. Only by giving passengers every possible comfort and convenience to divert their attention from the inevitable effects of frequent takeoffs and landings—bumping along at relatively low altitudes in noisy airplanes with cramped cabins—could the airlines win increased patronage from people accustomed to traveling on trains, automobiles, and ocean liners. Giving passengers no-frills service in such a period would have been self-defeating because it would have discouraged the public from using a relatively new form of transportation that already terrified many prospective customers. Instead, airlines did their best to advertise flying as a glamorous and romantic experience and made the most of what it unquestionably had to offer over other ways of getting places: speed and convenience. Competing airlines therefore came under great pressure to offer the most frequent connections possible to as many places as possible as fast and as comfortably as possible and, above all, as safely as possible. It was axiomatic that commercial aviation was a "service industry."

Meeting high service standards and making a profit at the same time was a demanding art. To be successful, airlines had to control costs without sacrificing comfort, convenience, and safety. But the costs that had to be incurred were quite formidable, especially when more and more convenient schedules were accompanied by offering people newer, faster, larger, and more luxurious airplanes, outdoing the competition in hiring attractive cabin attendants who gave unfailingly courteous attention to passenger needs, providing gourmet caliber meals with such accoutrements as fine flatware and glassware, china plates, and cloth napkins, and doing everything else that might make flight a romantic experience. Some airlines, like Delta, played this game well. Others, like Eastern, did not.

The CAB recognized that providing excellent service cost a great deal of money. Forcing airlines to reduce fares would have been a dubious way to discipline them, particularly in dealing with small, struggling airlines that were having difficulty competing with larger carriers capable of achieving at least some economies of scale. Instead, it made more sense to subsidize smaller airlines that were having financial trouble by giving them higher mail pay than larger carriers received. At the same time, the CAB awarded these struggling carriers long-haul routes to major cities to compensate for the inevitable losses they incurred providing short-haul service to smaller markets.

After World War II, the CAB regularly admitted small but aggressive airlines to long-haul routes that had previously been served by only one carrier. Usually the incumbent was one of the Big Four—American, Eastern, TWA, or United. In 1945, for example, the CAB gave a then-small enterprise, Delta, the right to fly nonstop between Chicago and Miami, a prime vacation route previously monopolized by Eastern. Responding to the challenge, Delta competed brilliantly with a strategy of excellent passenger service, shrewd aircraft selection, effective aircraft utilization, and consummation of a timely merger with a weaker airline, Chicago and Southern. Having nonunion employees, except for the pilots, helped Delta cut costs. In addition, Delta showed a great capacity for adroit political maneuvering in Washington at a time when the South was still solidly Democratic. The virtuosity with which Delta's amiable but extremely shrewd leader, C. E. Woolman, outgeneraled Eddie Rickenbacker, his crusty rival, became a textbook study in how to operate within the New Order.[32]

Another master of the game was Robert F. Six, about whom Michael Gorn has written an illuminating essay for this book. Six transformed Continental Airlines from a runt of an enterprise into a model carrier by closely monitoring costs, making wise choices in aircraft selection, buying as few airliners as he possibly could and utilizing them with maximum efficiency, securing routes that fitted his existing route system, rendering superior service, and playing by the rules. Flamboyant and profane, easily as much of a rugged individualist as Rickenbacker, he demonstrated far more skill in blending close cost control, in which Rickenbacker excelled, with outstanding customer relations, in which Eastern's chief executive was deficient. In Robert Serling's words, Continental was "an airline offering the service of an opulent Rome while being run like a Spartan army camp." Yet, however mercilessly Six drove his employees to be efficient, he was a master at sustaining high morale among them by communicating why he was asking for their best.

Six, a good organization man despite his rough edges, took care not to antagonize the CAB. Whereas Rickenbacker lost his temper when he needed to keep quiet, Six accepted regulatory defeats with good grace. "His acquiring support in high government circles," Serling stated, "was always done in a quiet, circumspect fashion." Six also ingratiated himself with the government by supporting the CIA and the Johnson administration in Laos and Vietnam.

Although Six lost many of his battles to secure new routes, he made the most of the struggles he won. One of his most crucial victories came in 1955 in the Denver Service Case, giving him the right to operate nonstop between four major cities with unlimited authority to pair them in any way he chose. This pivotal award transformed Continental overnight into a major airline. Six was particularly interested in building a coherent system with a strong western focus. In 1969, he achieved a lifetime dream by securing certification to provide service to Hawaii. Had Lyndon B. Johnson not been overruled by his successor, Richard M. Nixon, Six, who was a lifelong Democrat, would have received authority to fly all the way to Australia and New Zealand. Ultimately, Jimmy Carter gave him this prize in 1977. By that time, as deregulation loomed, Continental had for the first time become a transcontinental carrier by extending its western route system to Miami by way of Houston. Six, too, provides a textbook case in how to thrive under the New Order.[33]

The Dynamics of Indulgence

Unfortunately, not all of the companies upon which the CAB looked with favor were managed by Nyrops, Sixes, and Woolmans. One of the chief problems of the CAB was that it rewarded incompetence by granting favors to airlines whose managers did not deserve them. Instead of looking for the underlying causes of why certain companies did not succeed, it awarded them new routes so they could fail on an even grander scale. Certain heavily traveled commercial arteries thus became overloaded with more carriers than they could handle. Each of these carriers tried to compete by providing as many flights as possible, acquiring newer and faster planes, and thinking of better ways to please their patrons. The predictable result was half-empty planes competing for a market that turned out to be less elastic than expected.

The best—or worst—example of the CAB's overindulgence is the history of a regional carrier that was formed in 1936 in a merger combining two smaller entities into Pennsylvania-Central Airlines (PCA), whose routes fanned outward from Pittsburgh to such places as Baltimore, Washington, Buffalo, Chicago, and Birmingham. William F. Trimble has written perceptively about the history of PCA and one of its main financial supporters, George R. Hann, in his contribution to this volume.

During World War II, PCA performed outstanding service for the Air Transport Command in such inhospitable places as Alaska and Greenland, and maintained training schools for navigators and radio operators. As Robert Serling has stated, "No airline, large or small, served the armed forces with greater skill than Pennsylvania-Central."[34] Significantly, its military operations were much more extensive than its commercial activities had been before the war, which did not bode well for its prospects when it returned to normal domestic business in 1945. PCA desperately needed federal largesse if it was to survive, and it had no difficulty getting it from a grateful government.

Late in the war, the CAB granted PCA access to New York City. After 1945, the airline received more help in the form of new routes and authority to operate nonstop on some of the airways on which it already flew. Most of its routes, however, were too short to be remunerative and its losses mounted, forcing it to lay off 1,500 employees. In 1948 its leaders decided to move PCA's corporate headquarters from Pittsburgh to Washington and changed the carrier's name to Capital Airlines in an effort to emphasize its growing national status. The move made sense because Washington was a logical hub for Capital's expanded route system, but was particularly wise because the company's executives would be as close as possible to federal officials on whom the company's welfare depended. Had it not been for the mail subsidies it received, it could not have remained in business.

Capital's well-honed ties with politicians and government bureaucrats became the envy of the airline industry, but it also made a commendable effort to solve its fundamental problems. Its chief executive, James H. Carmichael, broke new ground in 1948 by gaining the CAB's permission to offer discounted service at night on aircraft that would otherwise have been idle. The CAB also awarded the company additional routes to Atlanta and New Orleans. Soon, however, other airlines began offering discounted fares, and Capital's woes continued. After failing to negotiate mergers that might have rescued the company, Carmichael took the daring step of acquiring a large fleet of British-made Vickers Viscount turboprops that delighted customers because of their smooth flying characteristics. Nevertheless, they were poorly suited to Capital's route structure, and the company suffered increasing financial hardships that the CAB tried to solve by granting the carrier yet more route awards. By this time, Capital's competitors were operating turbojet aircraft that were newer and faster than the Viscounts, and the airline was too deeply in debt on the British planes to follow suit. Maintenance costs mounted ruinously as Capital's pilots flew Viscounts at speeds they could not sustain without overheating.

At this point a merger was imperative or Capital would inevitably go bankrupt. The latter alternative was unacceptable to the CAB, which never let a line go under, however badly it was managed. After a scheme to split Capital's routes among five other airlines failed to materialize, the company pursued a merger with United, the only airline financially able to absorb Capital's debts. Because such an outcome might diminish competition by making one of the nation's largest airlines even bigger, the CAB dallied while Capital's hemorrhaging continued.

Having no other choice, the CAB finally consented to the merger between Capital and United, but held up formal approval for more than two months while Capital's situation grew steadily worse. When the merger finally went into effect on June 1, 1961, United, now the nation's largest airline, opened its jaws as wide as possible and swallowed Capital's assets, including the outmoded Viscounts, along with its manifold obligations. The result was a bad case of corporate indigestion. The first four weeks following the merger became legendary throughout the United system as "the month of torture."[35]

Among the owners involved in Capital's collapse was George R. Hann, whose career in American commercial aviation went back to the 1920s. Having been proscribed from active involvement in the industry because he had attended Brown's spoils conferences in 1930, he had ultimately returned to a formal role as Capital's board chairman. William F. Trimble has written that Hann "remained at arm's length on most management decisions" after Capital moved its headquarters from Pittsburgh to Washington, but did use his power in the company "to engineer the purchase of Vickers Viscount turboprops in 1955." When it became increasingly clear that acquiring the Viscounts had turned out badly, Hann "stepped down as chairman of the board as the company slid toward bankruptcy." He did, however, retain "major stock holdings in United." He also amassed "one of the world's most extensive collections of Russian icons" and lived for eighteen more years at his estate, "Treetops," at Sewickley Heights, near Pittsburgh. He died in 1979.[36]

Nonindulgence and Counterindulgence

If the CAB was overindulgent toward Capital, it pursued an opposite course in dealing with carriers whose leaders emphasized cost-cutting at the expense of giving passengers red-carpet treatment. The carrier that suffered most in this atmosphere was Eastern, whose chief executive, Eddie Rickenbacker, believed that an airline's responsibility to travelers was mainly to get them where they were going safely and dependably. Pampering them while they got there was another matter; giving the public too many frills would reduce profit margins. As L. Welch Pogue stated in an interview, Eastern's costs were "on a lower plateau" than those of any carrier in the industry. Simply put, Rickenbacker was a penny-pincher who calculated costs down to the lowest fraction of a cent. "If you watch your pennies," he liked to say, "the dollars will take care of themselves." Throughout most of the decade after World War II, therefore, Eastern's profits were extremely high; during the late 1940s, they were sometimes greater than those of the rest of the industry put together. Unfortunately for Rickenbacker, this Spartan image did not endear him to the CAB, whose staff was deluged with complaints about the allegedly poor quality of Eastern's service. This situation was ultimately disastrous for Eastern because, as Pogue said, there was nothing the CAB took more seriously than passenger complaints in determining route awards.[37]

It is conceivable that Eastern's service would not have been criticized so vehemently by passengers were it not for the fact that other airlines were trying so hard to please them. Perhaps Eastern's service was merely not as good as that of other airlines, though not necessarily bad. In any case, by wanting to maximize profits, even if such a policy resulted in below-average service, Rickenbacker was pursuing the wrong priorities at the wrong time. It was all too easy for the CAB to use Eastern's high profits as an excuse for increasing competition on its existing routes while refusing to award it new routes. After all, Eastern was financially strong, and Capital was financially weak. Why not, therefore, try to strengthen Capital at Eastern's expense by allowing it to compete with Rickenbacker's airline on heavily traveled routes? This policy was in fact practiced repeatedly by the CAB. Its result was to hurt Eastern, a financially healthy firm, while merely compounding the problems of Capital, a sick one, by permitting it to repeat the same mistakes on a grander scale. The CAB can hardly be blamed for admitting Delta, an extremely well managed carrier with excellent passenger service, to routes formerly monopolized by Eastern. Delta deserved such rewards and was prepared to make the most of them. To admit Capital to the same routes, however, was folly.

Delta and Capital were not the only carriers the CAB rewarded at Eastern's expense. National Airlines, which was based in Florida, was another. By favoring National over Eastern, the CAB showed that rendering acceptable passenger service covered a multitude of sins. Whatever else one could say about Rickenbacker, he was not unethical. The same, however, cannot be said with certainty about National's chief executive, George T. "Ted" Baker, whose career was shadowed by a reputation for shady dealings. George E. Hopkins has written a graceful and compelling chapter about Baker for this book.

In 1934, Baker bid successfully on a short airmail route in Florida and started National on its checkered history. Belying the grandiose name Baker gave it, National remained a small intrastate operation for ten years. Although it won a route to New Orleans in 1938, it had the lowest operating revenue in the industry by the time the United States entered World War II. Unlike Pennsylvania-Central, it flew mainly domestic cargo for the war effort and attracted adverse attention by helping young men from influential families evade military service by hiring them as "pilots" whose duties were less demanding than their local draft boards suspected. Nevertheless, National received authority from the CAB in 1944 to compete with Eastern between New York City and Florida. Despite National's already suspect reputation, it was prepared to provide Eastern with service competition on this lucrative vacation route.

During the immediate postwar period, Baker, who combined great personal charm with the instincts of a barracuda, alienated himself from the CAB because of his fierce opposition to unions, toward which the CAB was favorably disposed because of its Democratic leanings. After smashing his mechanic's union, Baker became involved in a bitter dispute with his pilots that led to the longest strike the airline industry had seen up to that time. Baker's open support of Republican presidential nominee Thomas E. Dewey, whom Baker thought would surely win the presidency in 1948, was another black mark against him among the Democratic majority on the CAB. During that year, when National suffered heavy financial losses because of the pilot's strike and the company's personnel was badly demoralized, the CAB launched an investigation looking toward dismembering its route system and parceling it out among other airlines.

After Truman defeated Dewey, however, Baker managed to get back in the CAB's good graces. Suddenly taking a conciliatory stance toward labor, Baker also underwent a well-publicized religious conversion. The basic reason the CAB tolerated and rewarded him, however, was because of the effective service competition he gave to Rickenbacker. Catering to celebrities and hiring the most attractive stewardesses in the industry, Baker advertised National as the "Airline of the Stars." He also catered to the traveling public's desire for speed; one of his greatest coups against Rickenbacker was becoming the first domestic jet operator by leasing two Boeing 707s from Pan American in 1958 to compete with slower Lockheed Electra turbojets Eastern had put in service between New York and Miami. Baker's greatest victory over Eastern in a route case came in 1961, when he won a transcontinental route to the West Coast that Eastern badly needed. One factor involved in the decision was the CAB's desire to punish Rickenbacker, who had unwisely offended incoming president John F. Kennedy by making intemperate speeches against him.

As Hopkins has indicated, National grew mainly because of Baker's fortunate choice of enemies. The hatred that existed between Baker and Rickenbacker was legendary throughout the industry, and the CAB disliked Rickenbacker more than it did Baker. Probably the only reason National became a trunkline at all was because it offered the CAB a convenient way to discipline Eastern. In 1962, having increased National's value by acquiring the new transcontinental route, Baker, who had heart trouble, decided to unload. After double-crossing Robert F. Six, with whom he made a verbal agreement that he ultimately refused to honor, Baker sold National to another bidder for $6.5 million and went to Europe, where he died in 1963.

Neither Capital nor National merited preferential treatment by the CAB at Eastern's expense. By being indulgent to Capital, nonindulgent to Eastern, and counterindulgent to National, the CAB contributed substantially to Eastern's decline, doing serious damage to a great carrier that had once been the most financially secure airline in the industry. As this process of reverse discrimination continued, Rickenbacker, who was incapable of hiding his feelings, said exactly what he thought and succeeded only in making things worse for himself. But he had much to be angry about. No airline executive was less prepared to survive in an age of service competition. Not until deregulation came to the industry in 1978 could a no-frills manager hope to succeed. By that time, Rickenbacker was dead.[38]

The Feederline Problem

In addition to showing the importance that the CAB attached to service competition, National's rise from the lowly status of a strictly intrastate carrier to that of a full-fledged trunkline provides a good example of another significant result of CAB policy: the gradual blurring of what started out as clear-cut distinctions between different classes of airlines. During World War II, because of its desire for as many Americans as possible to enjoy the advantages of air transport, the CAB decided to create "feederlines" that would connect relatively small cities with large nodal centers. Recognizing that feederlines would have a hard time making money operating short-haul routes, the CAB moved gingerly into authorizing their creation, specifying that they would receive only experimental certificates. Out of hundreds of applicants, the CAB selected a relatively few firms to receive feederline status. One of these companies was Robinson Airlines, a tiny carrier in upstate New York that would feed traffic into places like Buffalo, Albany, New York City, and Washington. William M. Leary has contributed an insightful chapter to this book about Robert E. Peach, who transformed Robinson into a much larger entity, Mohawk Airlines.

Like the history of Capital Airlines, Mohawk's history is a good example of how well-intentioned route awards from the CAB were ultimately counterproductive to the survival of companies that the CAB was trying to help. As Leary shows, Peach was an extremely aggressive entrepreneur who dreamed of transforming a minor carrier into a major one. Within only a few years, Mohawk developed from humble beginnings to a flourishing airline serving twenty-eight cities, with an operating revenue of $3 million and an annual profit of $160,000. Under Peach's driving leadership, Mohawk became the first feederline to fly pressurized aircraft and make the switch from piston-driven engines to jet propulsion.

Unfortunately for Peach, the CAB had not anticipated how rapidly feederlines would grow, and it was undecided about whether they should develop into full-fledged trunklines. Ultimately, however, the CAB acquiesced in promoting this type of change. It did so because it became caught between its desire to cut airmail subsidies and the inescapable fact that feederlines could not make money operating short-haul routes. Giving airlines like Mohawk the authority to serve larger cities, however, merely created the same problems on a larger scale. As Mohawk acquired larger and faster planes to provide the type of service its passengers desired, operating costs increased proportionately and things were soon back where they had started. Persistent labor problems occurred because Mohawk's pilots wanted the same wages paid by older and larger trunklines and demanded raises Mohawk could not afford. Such problems set off another round of route awards, followed by even larger losses and higher debts incurred in buying updated equipment.

Because the CAB pursued the same policy all over the country, the original distinction between feederlines and trunklines became hopelessly blurred as feederlines were permitted to serve larger and larger cities and started competing with older trunklines that already had too much competition to begin with. Trying to preserve some semblance of order, the CAB started calling carriers like Mohawk "regionals" instead of "feederlines." Soon, however, it was awarding the new "regionals" transcontinental routes. Meanwhile, the "regionals" began asking for permission to discontinue service to smaller communities on their original systems, and a new class of "local service" carriers was born, presumably to repeat the same process.

In one respect, this phenomenon was healthy, considering that growth and expansion are necessary features of a capitalist economy. But the process of change was disorderly, with a heavy fallout of impending bankruptcies that resulted in mergers in which stronger firms swallowed weaker ones. The consequences for individual entrepreneurs were severe. Peach committed suicide when Mohawk became part of a larger system.[39]

An Unanticipated Development: The Nonskeds

During the postwar period, a crisis came about in the airline industry because of something lawmakers had not anticipated when they established the New Order in 1938. Ironically, the situation was created by the growth of the military-industrial complex, of which the New Order was an integral part.

During World War II, pilots serving in the Air Transport Command glimpsed the possibility of making airlift operations private enterprises. When the war ended, large numbers of multiengine military transport planes could be acquired with very little capital. Showing the American

A photograph epitomizing the dramatic contrast between the new and the old. A newly acquired Douglas DC-8 B sits on a runway beside a Pitcairn Mailwing, used for airmail operations in the firm's early history. (Courtesy of the Auburn University Archives)

spirit of free enterprise, aggressive profit-seekers poured their energies into assembling fleets of secondhand planes, hiring pilots, contracting to transport people and cargo, and building a vast network of unscheduled charter operations.

This type of business developed in a regulatory limbo because the New Order had been established to serve the interests of airlines conducting scheduled flights. The appearance of nonscheduled airlines after the war worried established carriers whose leaders were naturally concerned that interlopers who had bought a motley assortment of aircraft at cheap prices would invade markets that existing airlines had worked hard to develop under stringent government regulation by acquiring the latest in fast, comfortable, up-to-date planes. The situation was very much like the one that had existed in the late 1930s when established carriers had become alarmed about the threat posed by the introduction of DC-3s. It was only natural that companies with strong vested interests in things as they were would try to make things as difficult as possible for the upstarts, which came to be called "nonskeds."

Roger D. Launius has written an informative chapter for this book about the most controversial nonscheduled operator, Orvis M. Nelson. A veteran of the Air Transport Command, Nelson built Transocean Air Lines into a thriving enterprise that came to be regarded as a major threat by entrenched interests who fought bitterly to block his progress. Announcing that he would "fly anything anywhere" and was "open to anything that would turn a profit," he conducted an amazing variety of operations ranging from carrying refugees to safety, transporting immigrants to new homes, providing badly needed humanitarian aid to far-flung corners of the earth, serving the armed forces as a military contractor, carrying cargo ranging from Afghanistan fishmeal to Swiss watches, and even supplying aircraft and personnel to the producers of films including *The High and the Mighty.*

Nelson's basic problem, familiar to any entrepreneur engaged in a start-up operation that rapidly reaches the takeoff stage, was a chronic shortage of operating capital. In order to raise the funding required for dependable long-term growth, he needed to receive certification from the CAB. After fighting with every resource at his command to get it, he failed because his efforts were blocked by the established airlines, which lobbied the CAB to reject his bid. Forced into bankruptcy, he never recovered from the collapse of the enterprise he had worked so hard to build.[40]

It is only natural to portray Nelson as a tragic hero, as R. E. G. Davies has done, and to see evil in the machinations that brought him down.[41] Launius, however, presents a different picture by discussing the threat that carriers like Transocean represented to firms already well entrenched in the airline industry. Considering the degree to which many airlines were already suffering from excessive competition, it is not surprising that they feared interlopers who would invade choice routes among large cities and ignore small short-haul markets that existing operators were obliged to serve at a loss. Such "cream-skimming," as Launius shows, was bound to arouse the type of resistance that Nelson encountered.

Cracks in the New Order

By the early 1960s, the system established in 1938 was threatened by internal problems and by external pressures. Without the advent of jet transportation, which brought unexpected economies of operation, the New Order might have collapsed sooner than it did. Commercial jets began to appear for the first time in the early 1950s when the British introduced the de Havilland Comet. Airline executives were naturally worried about the effect that jet propulsion would have on an established industry that was already insecure. Not knowing what impact a radically new type of aircraft would have, and realizing how expensive it would be to adopt the new technology, they went through a difficult transition in which mistakes in aircraft selection had tragic consequences for men like Rickenbacker, whose career was adversely affected by his decision to adopt the Lockheed Electra turboprop. Once the transition had been made, however, operators who made fortunate guesses were delighted by the operating characteristics of jet airliners that required far less maintenance than piston-driven types, burned cheap kerosene instead of high-octane gasoline, flew at high altitudes far above most turbulence, were quickly accepted by passengers because of the speed and convenience they afforded, and constituted a bonanza for most firms in the industry until the Arab oil embargo of 1972 produced a challenge from which some carriers never recovered.

Still, the transition to the jet era was turbulent, and it was accompanied by a steady crescendo of criticism directed at both the airline industry and the regulatory system under which it operated. A chain of events that would shake the New Order to its foundations and ultimately abolish it altogether had already begun.

By the early 1960s, 70 percent of Americans had still never taken a commercial flight. It was increasingly clear that the advent of jet transportation, bringing with it larger and more powerful aircraft that cost extremely large amounts of money, demanded a new approach to attracting potential customers into the air. To a considerable extent, competition between airlines under the old rules merely led the same passengers to switch from one carrier to another and failed to develop the tantalizing mass market that seemed to be lurking if only the right strategy could be found to develop it. Service competition was already giving way to price competition as airlines established two or even three different classes of fares and set aside large numbers of seats for passengers who received lower standards of service in exchange for paying a lower fare. Long accustomed to promoting aviation as a service industry, executives debated the implications of a fundamental shift in marketing strategy that was already under way.

Predictably, Robert F. Six was in the vanguard. No person in the industry had done more to combine fine service with cost-cutting economies. Some of Continental's flights could make money with a 37 percent load factor. Yet Six, a maverick who somehow worked effectively within the bureaucratic maze of the New Order, had sensed that the established system under which he had thrived for so long was basically flawed. "There are millions of Americans," he declared, "who desire basic 'no-frills' jet transportation at more economical rates. . . . Broadening markets by using mass production long has been the cornerstone of the American free enterprise system. There is no reason to believe that this time-tested principle will not work just as well in air transportation as it has in other industries."[42]

As Michael Gorn shows, Six wanted to enhance competition in an industry that would remain closely regulated. Some people, however, did not agree. George Johnson, a newspaperman who became an Air Corps navigator in World War II and a biographer after that conflict, picked up on Six's theme in a passionate attack on the airline industry. Johnson's 1964 book, *The Abominable Airlines,* was comparable to a shotgun blast, scattering pellets in all directions. Some of his evidence was self-contradictory, but most of it pointed to one conclusion: that price competition should replace service competition on the nation's airways. Judging the CAB from this point of view, Johnson found it hopelessly obtuse. "Although the board is charged by law with promoting airline service 'at reasonable charges,' it had conducted exactly one general passenger fare investigation in its history—in 1969 after sharp prodding from Congress," Johnson declared. "Having dutifully genuflected to Capitol Hill, the board then gave the airlines what they had been getting without investigation—another raise."[43]

Under the New Order, Johnson said, the CAB had coddled airlines at the same time it had encouraged them to coddle passengers. Such policy was misguided, he argued. If poorly managed airlines went bankrupt, let them go bankrupt. If they could not make profits at existing fares, cut high fares and the amenities that went with them, and learn how to make profits as the Nyrops, Sixes, and Woolmans did: by increasing efficiency and productivity. Such arguments have become familiar today; indeed, they are now orthodox. They represent the common language of a deregulated airline industry that has long since abandoned the ideal of service competition. They conjure up an image of jet airplanes as flying buses, with passengers packed into as many seats as the cabins will hold, eating peanuts and crackers instead of cooked meals, being served by flight attendants who are no longer selected primarily for their good looks, and having no concept of aviation as an activity invested with overtones of glamour and romance. Except for a few fastidious passengers who sit in the first-class section, flight has become a standardized commodity.

The time was ripe for such a momentous switch, because airline flight, however uncomfortable it might sometimes be, was not nearly as disagreeable by the dawning of the jet age as it had once been. Thanks to the vigilance of regulatory agencies like the Federal Aviation Agency, which in 1958 replaced the CAA, commercial aviation was much safer; occasionally tragedies did occur, but certainly not with anything like the frequency that they had in the mid-1930s. Perhaps because jet flight was more comfortable and less dangerous, few persons considered flying a romantic activity. "While the airlines, by the fifties, had succeeded in taking much of the fear out of flying, they also succeeded in making it almost banal," states a historian of changing American styles. "The airliner . . . was as unextraordinary to the passenger as a Pullman car."[44]

According to the same author, the last "romantic airliner" had been the Lockheed Constellation. Part of the romance these aesthetically pleasing planes offered, however, was the discomfort of flying in them. "The Super Connies," writes a seasoned British traveler, Alexander Frater, "had triple-finned tails and bodies lean as a greyhound's, but were so noisy that conversing passengers often had to lip-read." Frater remembered sitting beside a singer who was returning to the United States from Australia. Her tour had been a disaster; three days after arriving in Sydney, she was "still deafened by the racket of the four 2,200 h.p. conventional Wright radials," and could barely hear the musicians who were accompanying her.[45]

By the early 1960s, passengers no longer needed to be coddled. Airsickness became less common; jet aircraft flew well above the level at which bumpiness is normally experienced. Only when taking off and descending for a landing did passengers feel turbulence, which was formerly chronic throughout a flight. Most of the time it was as if one were in a cocoon. Such conditions did not provide the stuff of which legends are made.

Except for variations in size, jet airliners were pretty much alike. Except for the number of engines with which they were equipped, it was hard to tell them apart. Because of the scientific principles on which they were designed, their aerodynamic features were increasingly uniform. For that reason, airlines began painting their fuselages in striking, even garish, ways. Inside, however, they were all the same. A traveler could predict how their cabins would look before entering them.

Deregulation: The Collapse of the New Order

It was a new era, demanding an entirely new outlook based on faith in market-driven capitalism. At about the same time Robinson was writing *The Abominable Airlines,* Alfred E. Kahn, an economics professor at Cornell University, was preaching what became the credo of the future: "that market forces should be allowed to control economic enterprise and that government regulation was counterproductive." Within less than two decades, Kahn would be chairman of the CAB. Within four years, the CAB would be dead. The rebels would have not only captured the fort but demolished it.[46]

Whither the Airline Industry?

During the historical epoch in which the Civil Aeronautics Act was passed, few people would have believed that the twentieth century would end with every major nation in the world committed in one way or another to a free market economy. Deregulation reigns. Does that necessarily represent progress? Such questions are outside the purview of this book, which deals only with the American airline industry from its beginnings to the dawn of the jet age. Another volume will follow, consisting of case studies drawn from the experiences of executives like Robert L. Crandall,

Carl C. Icahn, Frank Lorenzo, and Frederick W. Smith. For the present, the essays in this book provide what historians are best prepared to supply: a perspective against which to examine the present and imagine the future.

Clearly, deregulation has been no panacea. It has merely created new problems with which executives and federal officials alike must cope. Significantly, when deregulation did come, it came largely from outside. With few exceptions, leaders within the airline industry itself dreaded it. If reregulation should come, as many people think it inevitably will, it will be partly because the industry wants it, just as it wanted it in the late 1930s when a New Order was established that ultimately died four decades later. The business community is still as it always has been. Entrepreneurs may distrust government, but they will court its intervention if it suits their purposes to do so.

One thing, however, is predictable. If a reregulated airline industry lurks in the future, it will not be exactly like the New Order established in the late 1930s. Nor should it be, because experience gained from the past should help lawmakers avoid making the same mistakes that their predecessors did. The CAB and the regulatory ethos it represented were products of a time when statism was in style, even in those few nations that clung precariously to a democratic form of government in a world dominated by various forms of totalitarianism. Hopefully, that era died in the 1980s amid the self-evident failure of command economies and the demolition of the Berlin Wall.

Meanwhile, we should consider a question asked by R. E. G. Davies in 1988 as he completed the second edition of the most sweeping history of American commercial aviation written to date: "Is air transport simply a means of making money, or is it a public service, in the conduct of which the public must be protected?"[47]

Notes

1. Fred Albert Shannon, *America's Economic Growth* (New York: Macmillan, 1951), 421.

2. William M. Leary, "U.S. Air Mail Service," in Leary, ed., *The Airline Industry* (New York: Facts on File, 1992), 484–86. For a detailed scholarly account of these developments, see Leary's *Aerial Pioneers: The U.S. Air Mail Service, 1918–1927* (Washington, D.C.: Smithsonian Institution Press, 1985).

3. William M. Leary, "Air Commerce Act of 1926," in Leary, ed., *Airline Industry*, 13. For an authoritative scholarly overview of the developments covered in the following paragraphs, see Nick A. Komons, *Bonfires to Beacons: Federal Civil Aviation Policy under the Air Commerce Act, 1926–1938* (1978; reprint, Washington, D.C.: Smithsonian Institution Press, 1989).

4. David D. Lee, "William P. MacCracken Jr.," in Leary, *Airline Industry*, 285–89.

5. David D. Lee, "Herbert Hoover and the Golden Age of Aviation," in William M. Leary, ed., *Aviation's Golden Age: Portraits from the 1920s and 1930s* (Iowa City: University of Iowa Press, 1989), 127–47.

6. For provocative interpretations of Lindbergh's achievement and its significance, see Roger E. Bilstein, *Flight Patterns: Trends of Aeronautical Development in the United States, 1918–1929* (Athens: University of Georgia Press, 1983), 131–32, 162–66, and John William Ward, "Charles A. Lindbergh: His Flight and the American Ideal," in Carroll W. Pursell, ed., *Technology in America: A History of Individuals and Ideas*, 2d ed. (Cambridge: MIT Press, 1990), 211–26.

7. For overviews of this process, see esp. Henry Ladd Smith, *Airways* (New York: Alfred A. Knopf, 1942), and R. E. G. Davies, *Airlines of the United States to 1914*, 2d ed. (Washington, D.C.: Smithsonian Institution Press, 1988), 31–108.

8. A flag carrier or flag line is an airline designated as the principal carrier for its country of origin. It receives financial subsidies from the national government.

9. For careful assessments of Brown and his work, see David D. Lee, "Walter Folger Brown," in Leary, *Airline Industry*, 82–89, and F. Robert Van der Linden, "Progressives and the Post Office: Walter Folger Brown and the Creation of United States Air Transportation," in William F. Trimble, ed., *Pioneers and Operations*, vol. 2 of William M. Leary and William F. Trimble, eds., *From Airships to Airbus: The History of Civil and Commercial Aviation* (Washington, D.C.: Smithsonian Institution Press, 1995), 245–60.

10. In addition to the accounts of this episode in Davies, *Airlines of the United States*, 89–93, and Smith, *Airways*, see Robert J. Serling, *The Only Way to Fly: The Story of Western Airlines* (Garden City, N.Y.: Doubleday, 1976), 109–27.

11. W. David Lewis and Wesley Phillips Newton, *Delta: The History of an Airline* (Athens: University of Georgia Press, 1979), 28.

12. See also Trimble's essay, "George R. Hann," in Leary, *Airline Industry*, 203–4.

13. Enzo Angelucci and Paolo Matricardi, *World Aircraft, 1918–1935* (Chicago: Rand McNally, 1976), 222–23, 234–37.

14. Frank H. Taylor, *High Horizons*, rev. ed. (New York: McGraw-Hill, 1962), 58.

15. Davies, *Airlines of the United States*, 134.

16. David D. Lee, "Airmail Episode of 1934," in Leary, *Airline Industry*, 23–26.

17. David D. Lee, "Airmail Act of 1934," in ibid., 22–23.

18. W. David Lewis and Wesley Phillips Newton, "Paul Henderson," in ibid., 212–14.

19. Serling, *The Only Way to Fly,* 142–43.

20. Davies, *Airlines of the United States,* 194.

21. For a detailed summary of the state of the nation's airlines in 1937, emphasizing their chronic safety problems and the perilous financial condition of the industry, see Robert J. Serling, *Maverick: The Story of Robert Six and Continental Airlines* (Garden City, N.Y.: Doubleday, 1974), 4–7.

22. Dominick A. Pisano, "Edgar S. Gorrell," in Leary, *Airline Industry,* 189–91. See also Robert Burkhardt, "Air Transport Association," in ibid., 28–29.

23. Angelucci and Matricardi, *World Aircraft,* 250–57, 261–62. For up-to-date accounts of the technological trends that occurred in commercial aviation during the 1930s, see Roger E. Bilstein, *Flight in America: From the Wrights to the Astronauts,* 2d ed. (Baltimore: Johns Hopkins University Press, 1994), 83–123, and T. A. Heppenheimer, *Turbulent Skies: The History of Commercial Aviation* (New York: Wiley, 1995), 46–74.

24. On the background and provisions of the Civil Aeronautics Act, see esp. Arnold E. Bridden, Ellmore A. Champie, and Peter A. Morrane, *FAA Historical Fact Book: A Chronology, 1926–1971* Washington, D.C.: Department of Transportation, Federal Aviation Administration, 1974), 34–35; Davies, *Airlines of the United States,* 200–203; John H. Frederick, *Commercial Air Transportation,* rev. ed. (Chicago: Richard D. Irwin, 1946), 15–20; Robert M. Kane and Allan D. Vose, *Air Transportation* (Dubuque, Iowa: Kendall/Hunt, 1969), 31–32; Komons, *Bonfires to Beacons,* 366–79; and Smith, *Airways,* 288, 357–62.

25. David D. Lee, "Herbert Hoover," in Leary, *Aviation's Golden Age,* 127–47.

26. A chosen instrument is an airline designated as a country's principal carrier for certain destinations or geographic regions. The airline may receive special consideration from its government in the allocation of mail contracts, passenger routes, and so on.

27. On these developments and their implications for the postwar world, see Roger E. Bilstein, "International Civil Aviation Congress" and "International Civil Aviation Organization," in Leary, *Aviation Industry,* 245–48; and Eugene Sochor, *The Politics of International Aviation* (Iowa City: University of Iowa Press, 1991), 1–21. On the Luces' postwar visions, see Robert E. Herzstein, *Henry R. Luce: A Political Portrait of the Man Who Created the American Century* (New York: Scribner, 1994), 266–80 and W. A. Swanberg, *Luce and His Empire* (New York: Scribner, 1972), 180–13.

28. On the contrasting careers of these two key figures, see W. David Lewis, "Edward V. Rickenbacker" and Roger E. Bilstein, "C. R. Smith," in Leary, *Airline Industry,* 398–415, 435–46.

29. Paul A. Cleveland, "L. Welch Pogue," in Leary, *Airline Industry,* 371–73.

30. For a perceptive summary of Nyrop's career, see Donna M. Corbett, "Donald W. Nyrop," in Leary, *Airline Industry,* 322–30.

31. Secor D. Browne, foreword to Davies, *Airlines of the United States,* xi.

32. Lewis and Newton, *Delta.*

33. William M. Leary, "Robert F. Six," in Leary, *Airline Industry,* 428–33; Robert J. Serling, *Maverick: The Story of Continental Airlines* (Garden City. N.Y.: Doubleday, 1974), esp. 171.

34. Robert J. Serling, *When the Airlines Went to War* (New York: Kensington, 1997), 99.

35. Myron J. Smith Jr., "Capital Airlines," and Lloyd H. Cornett Jr., "James H. Carmichael," in Leary, *Airline Industry,* 94–95, 95–99; Taylor, *High Horizons,* 213–24.

36. Trimble, "George R. Hann," in Leary, *Airline Industry,* 204.

37. Interviews of L. Welch Pogue and V. E. Gouldener by author. Gouldener, the source of the Rickenbacker quotation, worked for Rickenbacker for many years.

38. George E. Hopkins, "George T. Baker" and "National Airlines," in Leary, *Airline Industry,* 47–51, 302–4.

39. William M. Leary, "Robert E. Peach," in Leary, *Airline Industry,* 363–66.

40. Roger D. Launius, "Orvis M. Nelson" and "Transocean Air Lines," in Leary, *Airline Industry,* 309–13, 459–63.

41. For an account of Nelson's career written from this perspective, see R. E. G. Davies, *Rebels and Reformers of the Airways* (Washington, D.C.: Smithsonian Institution Press, 1987), 101–18.

42. Quoted in George Johnson, *The Abominable Airlines* (New York: Macmillan, 1964), 64.

43. Ibid., 65.

44. Phil Patton, *Made in USA: The Secret Histories of the Things That Made America* (New York: Grove Weidenfeld, 1992), 222.

45. Ibid., 223; Alexander Frater, *Beyond the Blue Horizon: On the Track of Imperial Airways* (New York: Scribner, 1986), xiv–xv.

46. Robin Higham, "Alfred E. Kahn," in Leary, *Airline Industry,* 248–49.

47. Davies, *Airlines of the United States,* 678.

Bibliographical Essay

Until recently, works dealing with federal regulation of American commercial aviation were written mostly by economists, resulting in a bountiful harvest of books and articles that are frequently cited in the essays in this volume. Because such works are often intended as textbooks for courses in transportation and management in business and economics curricula, they rapidly go out of print or are updated in new editions. In either case, there is no need to mention them at this point because readers of this book will encounter them in the endnotes that follow. Valuable as such works are, they characteristically do not give a human face to the developments with which they deal. The present volume is predicated on the belief that historians have a unique function to perform in discussing the economic regulation of airlines by presenting richly textured accounts of interactions between people without neglecting the underlying business and financial context within which executives and regulators alike must work. The case study method is particularly valuable for this purpose.

The publication of William M. Leary's *The Airline Industry,* (New York: Facts on File, 1992), as part of the multivolume Bruccoli Clark Layman *Encyclopedia of American Business History and Biography,* was a landmark in the historiography of American commercial aviation. Thirty-eight professional historians contributed essays on individual airline executives, the enterprises they headed, labor leaders, and federal regulators, making available for the first time conveniently accessible accounts of the major persons involved in creating a great industry. Without this pioneering work, the present book could scarcely have been created.

Although the authors who contributed to *The Airline Industry* are research scholars with deep knowledge of archival sources, the case studies in the book are usually based on secondary sources. Except for those essays dealing with a relative handful of the most important persons who shaped the airline industry, most of the accounts presented in the book are relatively brief, being of the variety one would find in standard reference works like the *Dictionary of American Biography.* The present volume is predicated on a desire to provide extended essays on selected individuals based on archival research as well as the most pertinent secondary studies. Because the volume ends with passage of the Airline Deregulation Act of 1978, a sequel is planned that will contain comparable essays dealing with airline executives in the deregulation era.

In concept and layout, *Airline Executives and Federal Regulation* is modeled on *Aviation's Golden Age: Portraits from the 1920s and 1930s,* edited by William M. Leary (Iowa City: University of Iowa Press, 1989). That volume, consisting of case studies of persons who played prominent roles in the development of American aviation, contains four essays bearing significantly on the economic regulation of commercial airlines: Richard P. Hallion, "Daniel and Harry Guggenheim and the Philanthropy of Flight" (18–34); Nick A. Komons, "William P. MacCracken Jr. and the Regulation of Civil Aviation" (35–59); Roger E. Bilstein, "Edward Pearson Warner and the New Air Age" (113–26); and David D. Lee, "Herbert Hoover and the Golden Age of Aviation" (127–47).

A brief discussion of existing works dealing with the history of American commercial aviation will help put the present volume in perspective. Paradoxically, there is widespread agreement among historians that the best general study of the subject is also the oldest and was written not by a professional historian but by a lecturer in journalism at the University of Wisconsin. Henry Ladd Smith's *Airways: The History of Commercial Aviation in the United States* (New York: Alfred A. Knopf, 1942) is particularly remarkable for the compelling insights it gives into the character and personalities of the pioneers who created the American airline industry. Its chief limitation lies in its being restricted to the industry's seedtime, but it has otherwise never been surpassed. For this reason, it was a real service to the scholarly community when Smithsonian Institution Press reprinted it in 1991, making it more readily available to a new generation of historians, aviation enthusiasts, and the general reading public. Smith also wrote *Airways Abroad: The Story of American World Air Routes* (Madison: University of Wisconsin Press, 1950), which was reprinted by Smithsonian Institution Press in 1991.

Since the publication of Smith's pioneering works, several books have appeared dealing in general with the history of American commercial aviation. The most significant of these, containing an extraordinary amount of information, is R. E. G. Davies, *Airlines of the United States since 1914* (London: Putnam, 1972), now available in a revised edition (Washington, D.C.: Smithsonian Institution Press, 1982). This monumental study, written by an eminent authority who has for many years been Curator of Air Transport at the National Air and Space Museum, is an indispensable guide to any person who wishes to study any aspect of the American airline industry. Davies has also presented valuable perspectives on ten significant commercial airline pioneers (Walter T. Varney, Ralph O'Neill, Robert Six, Howard Hughes, James H. Carmichael, Stanley D. Weiss, Orvis Nelson, Edward Daly, Frank Lorenzo, and Donald C. Burr) in *Rebels and Reformers of the Airways* (Washington, D.C.: Smithsonian Institution Press, 1987). Other general histories of American commercial aviation include Oliver E. Allen, *The Airline Builders* (Alexandria, Va.: Time-Life Books, 1981), containing elaborate illustrations, and Carl Solberg, *Conquest of the Skies* (Boston: Little, Brown, 1979). Anthony Sampson, *Empires of the Sky* (New York: Random House, 1984), and T. A. Heppenheimer, *Turbulent Skies: The History of Commercial Aviation* (New York: Wiley, 1995) discuss American developments in a broader international context. All four of these books were written for nonscholarly readers but offer valuable insights.

No well-documented scholarly monograph exists on the history of the American airline industry from its beginnings to the present day, but there is an increasingly rich literature pertaining to individual airlines or specialized topics. William M. Leary has written an authoritative work on the genesis of American commercial aviation, *Aerial Pioneers: The U.S. Air Mail Service, 1918–1927* (Washington, D.C.: Smithsonian Institution Press, 1985). Works dealing with specific airlines include R. E. G. Davies, *Delta: An Airline and Its Aircraft* (Miami: Paladwr Press, 1990); R. E. G. Davies, *Pan Am: An Airline and Its Aircraft* (New York: Orion Books, 1987); W. David Lewis and Wesley Phillips Newton, *Delta: The History of an Airline* (Athens: University of Georgia Press, 1979), and W. David Lewis and William F. Trimble, *The Airway to Everywhere: A History of All-American Aviation, 1937–1951* (Pittsburgh: University of Pittsburgh Press, 1988), dealing with the early history of an enterprise that went through various name changes and is now known as U.S. Airways. Richard Hallion has made a significant contribution to the early history of American commercial aviation in *Legacy of Flight: The Guggenheim Contribution to American Aviation* (Seattle: University of Washington Press, 1977). George E. Hopkins has written two scholarly studies of the development of airline pilot unionization: *The Air Line Pilots: A Study in Elite Unionization* (Cambridge: Harvard University Press, 1971) and *Flying the Line: The First Half Century of the Air Line Pilots Association* (Washington, D.C.: Air Line Pilots Association, 1982). Hopkins has also sensitively edited the recollections of a Pan American executive, Sanford B. Kauffman, as *Pan Am Pioneer: A Manager's Memoir, from Seaplane Clippers to Jumbo Jets* (Lubbock: Texas Tech University Press, 1995), with copious annotations that are easily as valuable as the text of the book itself.

Several works by nonacademic historians dealing with the history of specific airlines or airline executives are based on extensive research and have contributed significantly to the essays contained in the present volume. Marylin Bender and Selig Altschul, *The Chosen Instrument* (New York: Simon and Schuster, 1982), is an authoritative, well-written account of Juan Trippe and Pan American Airways, based on extensive research in a wide variety of primary and secondary sources. Robert J. Serling has placed all students of American commercial aviation in his debt with well-researched and entertainingly written "informal histories" of airlines and airline leaders that show an admirable grasp of human character. Books by Serling that have been extremely helpful to authors of the essays that follow include *Eagle: The Story of American Airlines* (New York: St. Martin's/Marek, 1985); *From the Captain to the Colonel: An Informal History of Eastern Airlines* (New York: Dial Press, 1988); *Howard Hughes' Airline: An Informal History of TWA* (New York: St. Martin's/Marek, 1983); *Maverick: The Story of Robert Six and Continental Airlines* (Garden City, N.Y.: Doubleday, 1974); and *The Only Way to Fly: The Story of Western Airlines, America's Senior Air Carrier* (Garden City, N.Y.: Doubleday, 1976). Frank J. Taylor, *High Horizons: Daredevil Flying Postmen to Modern Magic Carpet—The United Air Lines Story,* rev. ed. (New York: McGraw-Hill, 1962), is a useful work that should be superseded by a more up-to-date synthesis.

John J. Nance, *Splash of Colors: The Self-Destruction of Braniff International* (New York: William Morrow, 1984), deals principally with events that transpired after deregulation but contains an introductory chapter on the earlier history of Braniff Airways. George W. Cearley Jr., *Eastern Air Lines: An Illustrated History* (Dallas: privately printed, 1983, 1985), is chiefly valuable for its maps, illustrations, and detailed descriptions of airliners utilized by Eastern.

A significant contribution to aviation history resulted from a Conference on the History of Civil and Commercial Aviation (ICCA92), held at the Swiss Transport Museum at Lucerne, Switzerland, in 1992. The proceedings of that conference were edited by William M. Leary and William F. Trimble in *From Airships to Airbus,* a two-volume work published by Smithsonian Institution Press in 1994. Particularly significant regarding the economic regulation of commercial aviation is an essay by F. Robert van der Linden, "Progressives and the Post Office: Walter Folger Brown and the Creation of United States Air Transportation," in the second volume, *Pioneers and Operations,* edited by Trimble, 245–60, based on a doctoral dissertation that van der Linden later completed at George Washington University. The publication of that dissertation, now in prospect, will provide much fresh information about Brown's key role in shaping the American airline industry.

The best study of the history of economic regulation of commercial aviation is Nick A. Komons, *Bonfires to Beacons: Federal Civil Aviation under the Air Commerce Act, 1926–1938* (Washington, D.C.: U.S. Department of Transportation, 1978; Washington, D.C.: Smithsonian Institution Press, 1989). This book is part of a series of well-documented works on the history of the Civil Aviation Administration and its successor, the Federal Aviation Administration. Later volumes in the DOT series include John R. M. Wilson, *Turbulence Aloft: The Civil Aeronautics Administration amid Wars and Rumors of Wars, 1938–1953;* Stuart R. Rochester, *Takeoff at Mid-Century: Federal Civil Aviation Policy in the Eisenhower Years, 1953–1961;* Richard J. Kent Jr., *Safe, Separated, and Soaring: A History of Federal Aviation Policy, 1961–1972;* and Edmund Preston, *Troubled Passage: The Federal Aviation Administration in the Nixon-Ford Term, 1973–1977.* The only extended history of the Civil Aeronautics Board itself is Robert Burkhardt, *CAB—The Civil Aeronautics Board* (Dulles International Airport, Va.: Green Hills, 1974); see also William A. Jordan, *Airline Regulation in America: Effects and Imperfections* (Baltimore: Johns Hopkins University Press, 1970), and Jordan's essay, "Civil Aeronautics Board," in Donald R. Whitnah, ed., *Government Agencies* (Westport, Conn.: Greenwood Press, 1983), 61–68. A stellar work providing insight into the place of commercial airline regulation in the overall development of American regulatory policy is Thomas K. McCraw, *Prophets of Regulation* (Cambridge: Belknap Press of Harvard University Press, 1984), which contains a chapter (see

222–99) on Alfred E. Kahn. Safety regulation of aviation is well covered in Donald R. Whitnah, *Safer Skyways: Federal Control of Aviation, 1926–1966* (Ames: Iowa State University Press, 1966).

Roger E. Bilstein has written extensively on the way the economic regulation of commercial aviation fits into a broader context of American aviation. See especially Bilstein's *Flight Patterns: Trends of Aeronautical Development in the United States, 1918–1929* (Athens: University of Georgia Press, 1983).

Many trade books that need not be cited here have been written about the development of American commercial aircraft, often with lavish illustrations. Two recent scholarly works that deal with historically significant commercial aircraft within the broader perspective of the aircraft manufacturing industry are Roger E. Bilstein, *The American Aerospace Industry: From Workshop to Global Enterprise* (New York: Twayne/Macmillan, 1996) and Donald M. Pattillo, *Pushing the Envelope: The American Aircraft Industry* (Ann Arbor: University of Michigan Press, 1998).

George R. Hann, Pittsburgh Aviation Industries Corporation, and Pennsylvania Air Lines

WILLIAM F. TRIMBLE

ON MARCH 28, 1934, GEORGE R. HANN, PRES-ident of Pittsburgh Aviation Industries Corporation (PAIC), the parent of Pennsylvania Air Lines, one of the nation's largest regional carriers, submitted his letter of resignation to George S. Davison, the chairman of PAIC's board of directors. "I deem it quite essential," Hann wrote, to resign "in view of the controversy which has arisen with the United States Government."

Hann's resignation came at a climactic moment, following years of turbulence in American commercial aviation. From little more than a loose collection of small companies run by ex–World War I aviators and barnstormers in the mid-1920s, the industry had quickly matured into a multimillion-dollar business funded by major investors and operated by experienced managers determined to make air travel a part of the American transportation system. Government regulation played a key role in this transformation. Through the Department of Commerce and the Post Office, Washington exercised increasing control over air transport, licensing operators and pilots, setting safety standards, establishing air-mail routes, and choosing contractors to fly those routes. Hann's PAIC had been one of the blessed few in the early 1930s to benefit from the government's largesse, only to fall out of favor when the new administration

*George R. Hann in a portrait painted in
the 1950s. (Courtesy of Stephen P. Nash)*

of Franklin D. Roosevelt and a reform-minded Congress sought to restructure the airlines and institute new airmail contract bidding procedures. Hann's position as president of PAIC was no longer tenable in the
new milieu, making his resignation inevitable.

Hann neither forgot nor forgave. To the end of his long life, he believed that he and other executives had been forced out of the business in
1934 as a result of sheer political vindictiveness and that the fledgling airline industry did not recover from this blow until World War II.[1]

George Hann and PAIC illustrate the complexities of big business and
airline regulation in the late 1920s and early 1930s. Hann saw aviation as
an attractive investment opportunity, provided the industry underwent
a managerial reorganization and rationalization to place it on what he
considered a firm, businesslike footing. In many ways his ideas about the
aviation industry followed the pattern of the managerial revolution identified by Alfred D. Chandler Jr. Steeped in the prevailing atmosphere of
industrial Pittsburgh, Hann saw all around him the success of professional management and high throughput in large-scale multiunit enterprises. He believed the same model could be made to fit aviation. If that
meant pushing aside some of the pioneers who had created the first airlines, so be it.

Hann's vision of the future of the industry coincided with that of
major New York investors, among them Clement M. Keys and Lehman
Brothers, who saw immense profit potential in both air transportation
and aircraft and engine manufacturing, but only if there were consoli-

dations to bring the industry under closer financial and managerial control. In Washington at the same time, those responsible for regulatory policies and implementation wanted to create favorable conditions for business growth and to guarantee the public interest through the creation of a safe and efficient airline network. Wall Street and Washington briefly worked together in an uneasy partnership, only to have it end abruptly amid a public uproar and congressional investigations of collusion and corruption in the aviation industry.[2]

Hann's Path to Airline Leadership

George Rice Hann was born in Birmingham, Alabama, on November 7, 1891, the son of Charles and Annie Sykes Hann. His father was a well-known and prosperous shoe retailer with stores in Birmingham and Montgomery, but when George was still a small boy, the family moved to Brookline, Massachusetts, outside Boston. After graduating from the exclusive Phillips Andover Academy in 1909, Hann went off to Yale, where he received his bachelor's degree in economics in 1913. He then made his way to Pittsburgh, where Henry R. Rea, a director of the Union Trust Company, persuaded him in 1914 to join what at that time was one of the city's leading banking and investment firms. Up to that point, Hann had not seriously considered working in Pittsburgh, believing that New York or Boston was more attractive. But Rea was persuasive, convincing Hann that he could carve out a niche for himself and the company if he specialized in new federal income tax laws. On his own initiative, Hann took evening courses at the law school of the University of Pittsburgh, eventually earning his degree in 1919. Meanwhile, he worked his way up through the Union Trust Company, becoming one of its most valued young financial counselors and an expert in tax law.

World War I interrupted Hann's career, as it did for so many young men of his generation, but following a stint as an officer in the navy he was back in Pittsburgh in 1919. He quickly resumed his work with Union Trust, taking responsibility for the huge estate of Henry W. Oliver, an iron magnate and former associate of Andrew Carnegie. Hann's adroit management of that complex and lucrative account was nearly a career in itself. More important, it placed the young and ambitious man in contact with some of the wealthiest and most influential people in the city.[3]

Aviation at the time was of only peripheral interest to the movers and shakers of Pittsburgh, a city that had been built on steel and heavy manufacturing enterprises. Nor did Hann himself have much interest in flying and the aviation industry, although he recalled the thrill he had experienced in 1914 when he went up for the first time in an airplane. Visiting friends in London, he went out to Croydon, where Claude Grahame-White, one of the most notable of the aviators of the pioneering "Birdman Era," offered to take paying customers up for a brief whirl around the field. Hann vividly recalled the flight, during which the airplane reached an altitude of no more than 200 feet, as "a novel and delightful adventure," but he saw nothing at the time to make him think that aviation was then or would ever be much of a business.[4]

Fully occupied making money for himself and the Union Trust Company while expanding his connections in the Pittsburgh business world, Hann gave little thought to the investment potential of aviation until 1926. That fall, through an acquaintance, Hann met Robert Law, a Pittsburgher who had married the daughter of the founder and owner of the Barnsdall Oil Company. On one of his frequent visits to New York, Hann met a friend of Law's, Toby Freeman, who at the time was in the middle of a financial survey of the Fairchild Aviation Company. Freeman, in turn, introduced Hann to Sherman Fairchild, who had built his reputation in the aviation industry with a brilliantly innovative aerial camera and wanted to expand into aircraft manufacturing and other activities. Impressed with Fairchild's intelligence and youthful enthusiasm, Hann and Law undertook a highly successful underwriting program that generated sufficient capital to allow Fairchild to expand his company and its operations in Farmingdale, New York. As a member of the Fairchild board of directors, Hann took a direct interest in the company's affairs, helping to bring onto the board Graham B. Grosvenor, formerly of the Otis Elevator Company, and Robert Lehman, a Yale classmate and associate of the investment house of Lehman Brothers. Through Grosvenor and Lehman, Hann met others in New York who had taken an interest in aviation—among them Richard F. Hoyt, Paul Henderson, Juan Trippe, John F. O'Ryan, and Lamotte T. Cohu.[5]

Already involved in what he hoped would be a lucrative new enterprise and investment opportunity, Hann remained unsure about the future of aviation as a business until the spring of 1927. On May 21, Charles

A. Lindbergh eased his Ryan monoplane onto the turf at Le Bourget Field outside Paris, successfully completing a nonstop solo flight across the Atlantic. After a tumultuous welcome in New York, Lindbergh took the *Spirit of St. Louis* on a three-month cross-country odyssey that amounted to a hero's grand tour. The event energized a business community that was ripe to put its money into something new and exciting. As Hann recalled years later, the Lindbergh flight generated "real enthusiasm" among investors. "Without his memorable and well-publicized flight, it would have required years and years" to build up the capital needed for the major expansion of the industry. Moreover, Hann thought Lindbergh himself projected just the sort of All-American image that businessmen wanted to see. "How fortunate," Hann emphasized, "that the hero was such a splendid, unassuming character. . . . That he was such a quiet, serious young aviator gave his ocean conquest the additional lift that so benefited aviation in all categories."[6] The so-called Lindbergh boom is largely a myth, for business interest in aviation had already manifested itself well before 1927. As Hann's recollections demonstrate, however, the transatlantic flight made his job easier when he sought additional investors in what many had previously considered an overly risky undertaking.

As the nation basked in the glow of the Lindbergh flight, Hann and Sherman Fairchild got together in 1928 to discuss the possibilities of a major aviation business venture. Fairchild was already negotiating to acquire the Embry-Riddle Company, which had a contract to fly the mail between Cincinnati and Chicago, and he was interested in buying other operators with airmail routes. Hann, Fairchild, and Grosvenor took Bob Lehman aside one day and sounded him out on whether his father and Lehman Brothers might be interested in expanding his firm's interest in Fairchild into underwriting a larger and potentially even more lucrative company with nationwide operations. Lehman arranged a meeting between Hann and his father, who expressed some reservations about the idea, but thought that if it were not too expensive and Hann could attract another firm, Lehman Brothers might be willing to go along. Hann therefore approached another of his Yale classmates, W. Averell Harriman, who himself ran a big investment house in New York, to see if he was interested. He was. The result was a joint venture announced by Lehman Brothers and the Harriman interests on March 5, 1929, to underwrite a

$40 million, two-million-share offering in what became known as the Aviation Corporation, or AVCO. Graham Grosvenor was president. Harriman was chairman of the board, Lehman was chairman of the executive committee, and Hann served as vice chairman of both.[7]

AVCO and PAIC

Its coffers brimming, AVCO immediately went on a major buying spree, scooping up Colonial Airways Corporation in New England, Universal Aviation Corporation in Chicago, Embry-Riddle in Cincinnati, Interstate Airlines running from Chicago to Atlanta, and Southern Air Transport in Fort Worth. Some of these enterprises themselves were holding companies: Colonial, for instance, owned Colonial Air Transport, Colonial Western Airways, and Canadian Colonial Airways. Universal had absorbed Continental Airlines, Braniff Air Lines, and Central Airlines, although the latter two did not have airmail contracts. Along with the airlines came a variety of aerial photography operations, flight schools, and airports. AVCO was an unwieldy hodgepodge of disconnected lines. As Hann recalled, "It turned out to be a tough job putting all of these operations together into a coordinated system," but the experience showed him that there was money to be made in organizing and financing large aviation companies with numerous subsidiaries.[8]

While he was negotiating the financing of AVCO, Hann began to wonder if what he had been able to accomplish in New York might not also work on a smaller scale in Pittsburgh, where he knew that there was plenty of investment capital ripe for the taking if the right situation presented itself. The city, he thought, had been something of an aviation backwater, off the main transcontinental route and unable to match its archrival, Cleveland, in airport development and aircraft manufacturing. Back in Pittsburgh in May 1928, following one of his many trips to New York, Hann decided to test the waters. He first talked to A. L. Humphrey, president of Westinghouse Air Brake, who thought the Steel City had missed a great opportunity when the automobile industry had located in Detroit. Humphrey, whose company had a major contract during World War I to manufacture Le Rhone rotary engines for the United States Air Service, thought Hann might be on to something. He put Hann in touch with William L. Monro, president of the American Window Glass

Company, whose son, C. Bedell Monro, had a strong interest in flying and aviation. A Harvard graduate, the younger Monro had coauthored a boy's adventure book, *The Quest of the Moonfish*. In 1928 he was teaching English at the University of Pittsburgh, but he was restless in the academic world and saw opportunities in the airline business. When Hann met him, Monro and his brother-in-law, Frederick R. Crawford, were trying to raise the capital to operate a passenger airline between Pittsburgh and New York.[9]

Hann decided that the best way to demonstrate to the Pittsburgh people what investment potentials there were in aviation was to take them to New York and show them around. He invited more than two hundred local businessmen, bankers, and civic leaders to go to New York on a private train provided by the Pennsylvania Railroad, which itself was taking an interest in aviation. Hann, Humphrey, W. L. Monro, and Taylor Allderdice, another leading businessman, joined with the industrial committee of the chamber of commerce to pick up the expenses. The group, eventually numbering more than one hundred people, left Pittsburgh on July 12 for the overnight trip, then took a Long Island Railroad train out to Garden City for a tour of the Curtiss factory. From there the party continued on to Farmingdale to see the Fairchild operation, with some of the guests taking a ride in one of Fairchild's new FC-2 cabin planes. Dinner that evening was at Montauk Point, where Hann had arranged for the Pittsburghers to meet with Richard E. Byrd, Clarence Chamberlin, John F. O'Ryan, A. C. "Dutch" Goebel, and other aviation luminaries. After spending the night at the Montauk Inn, the group enjoyed a leisurely day before returning to Pittsburgh on the evening train. Hann, Taylor Allderdice's son Norman, and Graham Grosvenor flew to Cape Cod for a few days before Hann went back to Pittsburgh.[10]

Now confident that he would be able to get the financial support needed for a local aviation company, Hann conferred with Bedell Monro, Norman Allderdice, and another young and respected Pittsburgh businessman, Richard W. Robbins. They drew up a prospectus for a holding company, Pittsburgh Aviation Industries Corporation (PAIC), and agreed to divide up the responsibilities for the planned sale of stock, with the understanding that no single investor could hold more than 1,000 shares at $25 per share. Hann waited until near the end of the solicitation campaign before contacting one of the most influential businessmen in the

An advertisement for Pittsburgh Aviation Industries Corporation, which sought to develop aircraft manufacturing in the city in 1929–30. (Author's collection)

city, Richard B. Mellon, who was happy to buy shares in the new company and who suggested that his son, Richard King Mellon, might also want to come in. His brother, W. L. Mellon, was another early investor in PAIC. The Mellon family, with major holdings in Gulf Oil and Alcoa, saw PAIC as an ideal complement to their companies' already well established aviation interests. Altogether, by the fall of 1928, the subscription effort had netted $1,150,000.[11]

Incorporated on November 15, 1928, PAIC included in its leadership Gulf Oil executive George S. Davison as chairman of the board, Humphrey as chairman of the executive committee, Hann as president, Robbins as executive vice president, Norman Allderdice as vice president, and Monro as secretary-treasurer. Retired army colonel Thurman H. Bane, an aeronautical engineer and former commanding officer at McCook Field in Dayton, headed the company's technical staff, which included Harold S. Martin, another former Army Air Service officer. On the board were W. L. Monro, Taylor Allderdice, and many of the city's leading businessmen, among them Arthur E. Braun, John F. Casey, J. H. Hillman Jr., Roy Hunt, W. L. McCune, Maurice Falk, H. H. Robertson, and H. B. Rust. After several organizational meetings, the board met for the first time on December 13 in a small suite of offices in the Henry W. Oliver Building in Pittsburgh. The company initially had five subsidiaries: Pittsburgh Air Transport Corporation, which was to engage in charter flying; Pittsburgh Aviation Securities Corporation, an investment and financial advisory company; Pittsburgh Aviation Management Corporation, which was to provide marketing and managerial assistance to other aviation firms; Pittsburgh Aerial Survey Corporation, which was to explore ways of using aerial photography; and Pittsburgh Aircraft Agency Corporation, an aircraft and engine sales and service company. Within six months, PAIC added the Penn School of Aviation to its already diverse holdings and made an unsuccessful foray into aircraft manufacturing with the Pittsburgh Metal Airplane Company.[12]

Developmental Strategy

Like many other businessmen in the 1920s, Hann self-consciously downgraded the profit motive and emphasized the establishment of PAIC as both a civic and community enterprise and a means of bringing order to the chaos of the aviation industry. When he approached people during the subscription campaign, Hann emphasized that PAIC was a "civic community enterprise" and that an investment in the company was an indication of one's "concern for the growth of [the] city and its place in the Nation." Throughout PAIC's formative stages, Hann tirelessly boomed aviation in the city and region, never missing an opportunity to emphasize that the company and its planned activities were in the best interests of Pittsburgh and its people. In an article in the local chamber of commerce publication in early 1929, Hann pointed out that PAIC had been formed "for the purpose of developing aviation, in all of its phases, along broad and constructive lines." PAIC planned to work closely with the chamber of commerce and the Aero Club of Pittsburgh to enhance

Pittsburgh's national standing and to encourage the growth of a new in-dustry, which Hann was confident would bring "inestimable benefits" to the city. Hann and other businessmen in the twenties also saw their involvement in aviation as a way of rationalizing an unruly and anarchic industry. A large and well-funded company, Hann said, could "cover the same operations as would a dozen smaller companies" and do so "in a businesslike, progressive, and co-operative manner."[13]

From the start, Hann and others with PAIC recognized that the air-line business offered the most profit potential for the company, but there was one major proviso: The company had to have an airmail contract. PAIC's technical staff began with a thorough survey of possible air routes in and out of Pittsburgh, spending months and flying thousands of miles. The routes that seemed most promising were between Pittsburgh and Washington, and between New York and Columbus, Ohio, via Phila-delphia, Harrisburg, and Pittsburgh. In the interim, Hann did not hes-itate to use the Mellons' influence in the Republican administration in Washington to alert the Department of Commerce and the Post Office to PAIC's efforts to expand aviation in the area, fully expecting favorable treatment if and when the company began airline operations. He wrote to Postmaster General Walter Folger Brown in March 1929 to notify him of the company's plans, stressing its professional and businesslike ap-proach to the development of aviation in the Pittsburgh area. Mean-while, Robbins concentrated his efforts in Harrisburg, lobbying for and eventually securing a $200,000 appropriation for the construction of a lighted airway between Pittsburgh and Philadelphia. PAIC also became the major player in the site selection and construction of the Harrisburg Airport at New Cumberland. After the airport's completion in August 1930, PAIC took over as operator of the field, seeing it as an impor-tant intermediate stop on what the company hoped would be a regular Philadelphia-Pittsburgh passenger line.[14]

But Hann knew that the easiest way for the company to break into the airline business was to acquire an existing airline, preferably one with an airmail contract. The only operator in Pittsburgh that qualified was Clifford Ball, Inc. Following passage of the 1925 Kelly Air Mail Act, which authorized the postmaster general to contract with private aviation companies for carrying the mail, Ball was among the first to submit a bid. A reasonably well-to-do automobile dealer who ran a modest fixed-base operation at Pittsburgh-McKeesport Airport (renamed Bettis Field in late 1926), Ball and several partners put together a package for flying the mail between Pittsburgh and Cleveland, with a stop in Youngstown, Ohio. On March 27, 1926, the Post Office awarded Ball Contract Air Mail (CAM) 11, the last of the routes selected in the first round of bidding. Problems lining up investors and raising capital forced Ball to delay the start of operations until April 21, 1927, when the first Waco 9 mail plane took off from Bettis Field bound for Cleveland, only 121 air miles distant. A short but profitable route, CAM 11 earned money for Ball, allowing him to upgrade equipment and offer passenger service in 1928. Receiving the full $3-per-pound rate allowed by the Kelly Act, Ball took in more than $160,000 in federal compensation in 1928 alone, making his company particularly attractive as a takeover target for the aggressive PAIC.[15]

Hann saw that the acquisition of an airport could be used to leverage Ball into selling his company, but knew that PAIC had to do its homework first. After a survey of the existing flying fields in the Pittsburgh area, the company found that none fully suited its needs. Of the airports studied, forty-acre Bettis Field was the most attractive, despite its small size, limited area for expansion, and the occasional visibility problems caused by smoke from the steel mills in the Monongahela River valley, only a few miles away. Hann later recalled that during the first six months of 1929 Ball approached PAIC with at least two offers to sell Bettis, only to have PAIC reject them because its technical staff was convinced that the airport was not adequate for its needs. But, considering how important Ball and Bettis were to the company's long-term plans for the development of air transportation, the more likely scenario is that PAIC was the suitor, backing off when Ball held out for more money than PAIC was willing to pay when he threatened to pull out of Bettis and relocate his airmail operation at Rodgers Field northeast of the city.[16]

Frustrated at being unable to buy Bettis Field, PAIC decided to pursue the next best alternative and develop its own airport. Following surveys, the company found a 640-acre site on relatively level land just south of the city of Butler, about twenty-five miles north of Pittsburgh. PAIC quietly bought the land through the Philadelphia Company, one of its stockholders, and after negotiations with Ball fell through, began building the airport in the spring of 1929. When it opened on September

27, 1929, during a two-day air show, Pittsburgh-Butler had cost PAIC $500,000. But it was an impressive facility, featuring a pair of 6,000-foot runways, two commodious brick hangars, and a large administration building, providing more than enough space for all of PAIC's flying operations. Few could dispute Hann's boast that the field was "the largest and probably the best equipped airport in the state of Pennsylvania." At one point, though, Ball remarked to Hann that the new airport site seemed too far from the city. Hann acknowledged that the distance from Pittsburgh was a problem, but argued that it did not matter, because once the airport was in operation PAIC was in a position to decide where the airline industry would locate.[17] Pittsburgh-Butler Airport, then, was an outflanking maneuver used more as a means of pressuring Ball into selling his airline (and its valuable airmail contract) to PAIC than it was a serious attempt at providing an alternative landing facility for new airlines eager to compete for passengers in the Pittsburgh market.

Ball continued to expand his own operations in 1929 and 1930, in the process ironically becoming less willing to go along with PAIC while simultaneously making his company more attractive to the big holding company. With new equipment, more frequent operations, and added personnel, Ball's line carried nearly 100,000 pounds of mail in 1929 and brought in $291,000 in federal subsidy. The next year, the mail poundage fell off, with a corresponding decrease in revenue to $172,000. Ball did sell Bettis Field, but not to PAIC. Instead, Aircraft and Airways of America, Inc., bought the airport, which became part of the huge Curtiss-Wright conglomerate when Aircraft and Airways sold out to the Curtiss group in April 1929. Ball used the profits from the airmail and the sale of Bettis to pay for new airplanes equipped for night service on the Pittsburgh-Cleveland route and to buy passenger aircraft for an extension of his line from Pittsburgh to Washington in August 1929. In 1930, Ball added a big twelve-passenger Ford Tri-Motor to his fleet and reorganized his company into Pennsylvania Airlines (PAL).[18] He had every reason to think that he was in a strong position in 1930 and that in a new round of airmail contracts he might do even better.

Realizing that Ball could attain an unassailable position in Pittsburgh's air transportation market, especially if he received an extension to his airmail contract, Hann acted quickly. In July 1929, he wrote to W. Irving Glover, the assistant postmaster general, to alert him to some of the deficiencies of Bettis Field as the terminal for Ball's planned passenger service from Pittsburgh to Washington. Too small, surrounded by hills and ravines, and plagued by visibility problems, Bettis was inadequate and unsafe. A month later, Hann conveyed the same message to his friend Hainer Hinshaw of AVCO. He thought Ball was "making a mistake in hopping full loads of passengers out of Bettis Field," and considered that it was time for the Department of Commerce to get more "hard-boiled" about permitting such passenger lines to be formed. PAIC also kept track of Ball's Pittsburgh-Washington service during 1929 and 1930, finding that, although it was supposed to be a scheduled service, in fact many, if not most, of the flights wound up being canceled due to bad weather or the lack of passengers.[19]

Hann's anti-Ball campaign was not the deciding factor leading to Walter Folger Brown's decision that Ball's operation was inadequate for the level of airmail and passenger service he anticipated, but it helped influence Brown's thinking. In September 1929, Brown informed Ball that he would not receive a new route certificate, charging that he had mailed heavy objects back and forth over his line to increase the amount of airmail pay. Ball believed that Hann had supplied Brown with false information, and he vehemently denied the accusation, but the damage had been done. Regardless of the specific nature of the alleged wrongdoing or Hann's role in the issue, it was apparent by the end of the year that Ball had lost Brown's confidence and that the postmaster general did not see his airline as a major player in the nation's new air transportation network. In April 1930, Brown stipulated that Ball could continue to operate the airline for only six more months, recommending that he use the time to seek out a buyer who could bring a greater degree of stability and financial security to the company.[20]

Hann's ideas about bringing order to the aviation industry in Pittsburgh coincided with those of Postmaster General Brown about a rationalized nationwide airmail system. On January 14, 1930, Brown made a speech in Cleveland in which he outlined some of the changes he planned to make in airmail operations. Worried that many of the airlines were losing money, Brown suggested abandoning the variable per-pound rate of airmail pay and replacing it with one based on a weight-space percentage that would encourage companies to use larger aircraft and transport mail on regular passenger flights. Augmented passenger revenue, coupled with federal assistance to those airlines flying "essential" routes, Brown believed, would reduce the government's overall costs and guarantee prosperity for the nation's air transport industry. An activist and progressive believer in the power of the federal government to effect reform and foster economic development, Brown took over the Post Office in 1929 committed to using his authority to restructure the nation's airlines into a consolidated and well-financed transportation system. Hann was delighted by the speech, praising Brown for his commitment to aviation and remarking that the industry was lucky to have such a good "friend at court." He reminded Brown of the money PAIC had spent on developing aviation in the Pittsburgh area and the efforts that it had made in the state to build the infrastructure needed for safe and reliable air travel.[21]

Throughout the early months of 1930, Brown worked with congressmen and a committee of aviation consultants to draft new airmail legislation intended to limit competition and promote greater efficiency among the airlines. Passed on April 29, the McNary-Watres Act, named for its principal backers, Senator Charles D. McNary, a Republican from Oregon, and Congressman Laurence H. Watres, a Republican from Pennsylvania, eliminated the old per-pound method of payment and instituted a new rate based on space available. In addition, the act granted the postmaster general broad authority to award new contracts to the lowest responsible bidder and in the public interest to "make any extensions or consolidations" of existing airmail routes without opening them to competitive bidding. Finally, the law stipulated that existing airmail contractors who had held contracts for at least two years could exchange them for route contracts valid for ten years.[22]

Here at last was PAIC's long-awaited opportunity. The company had spent more than a year establishing its position, spending money on a variety of aviation projects, and intensely lobbying in Harrisburg and Washington. Clifford Ball had fallen out of favor with the Post Office and was under pressure from Brown to sell his company to a larger and more financially stable firm. On May 19, Brown brought all the major airline executives to Washington and sat down with them to work out agreements to divide up their business in keeping with his grand rationalization schemes. Hann and Robbins attended the meetings for PAIC, and Ball represented Pennsylvania Airlines. Wanting to be sure that Ball's operation would "pass into the hands of people who were responsible," Brown preferred a PAIC-PAL merger, but Ball, determined to drive the hardest bargain possible, insisted on his right to talk with other potential buyers. During the meetings in Washington, Ball entertained offers from Daniel Sheaffer of Transcontinental Air Transport (TAT) and from Graham Grosvenor of AVCO, but Brown disapproved of both deals. When the conferences ended on June 4, Brown secured an understanding from Ball and PAIC that they would try to negotiate a settlement.[23]

All that was left, then, for Cliff Ball was PAIC. During the summer of 1930, Ball met with Richard Robbins and other PAIC officials, receiving assurances from them that they would give him a "square deal" if he went along with them. Negotiations went on into the early fall until finally, under pressure from Brown, Ball's attorney, John H. Orgill, and William P. MacCracken, representing PAIC, hammered out an agreement on October 24. The deal permitted PAIC to buy 8,000 shares of Pennsylvania Airlines stock at $10 per share, with Ball retaining 5,750 shares, to be held in escrow until called in by Ball on thirty days' notice. PAIC would buy an additional 6,250 shares at $10 per share to augment the airline's operating capital and reimburse Ball for a $5,000 fine and $22,000 in mail pay that Brown had withheld from the year before for alleged postal violations. Ball would stay with the company as vice president and general manager with a salary of $12,000 per year. Some of the members of PAIC's executive committee objected that the amount paid to Ball was too high considering PAL's assets and the length of its route, but others pointed out that with the buyout came such valuable equities as the pioneering route from Pittsburgh to Washington, which under the terms of the McNary-Watres Act would likely form the basis for a valuable airmail route extension. Brown quickly approved the arrangement, thinking that it would bring stability to the airline while still allowing Ball to remain actively involved in its operation. With the PAIC-PAL deal wrapped up, the Post Office issued its coveted route certificate, guaranteeing the airline exclusive operating privileges between Pittsburgh and Cleveland until May 1936.[24]

Pennsylvania Airlines underwent a transformation, infused with PAIC money and committed to performing up to Brown's high expectations. Harold Martin took over the day-to-day running of the airline, nominally working for Ball, but in reality reporting to Hann and others in the

PAIC hierarchy. Martin instituted standardized accounting procedures and streamlined maintenance, but the biggest change he accomplished was acquiring multiengined equipment in an effort to lure more passengers to the Pittsburgh-Cleveland and Pittsburgh-Washington routes. Not long after the acquisition, PAIC reported a fivefold increase in the miles flown with mail over the CAM 11 route, a doubling of the monthly average mail poundage, and, most significant considering Brown's objectives in reorganizing the airmail system, a reduction in the cost per pound of mail from $3.00 to $1.75. Although plagued by unusually bad weather during the first three months of 1930, the airline accumulated 207,000 passenger miles during the year, nearly all of them on the Pittsburgh-Washington route. Martin reported that PAIC lost more than $134,000 during 1930, considerably more than it had lost in 1929, but most of the losses came from the aerial survey and airport operations. Despite all of Hann's objections to Bettis Field, it remained PAL's Pittsburgh terminal, benefiting from its proximity to the city and major upgrades paid for by the Curtiss-Wright interests.[25]

A major priority for Pennsylvania Airlines in 1931 was securing an airmail contract between Pittsburgh and Washington. Brown saw the connection primarily as a way to improve links between Washington and Chicago; previously, airmail for the Windy City had to be routed through New York and Cleveland. But he also wanted the airmail route out of the city to be "the finest operation in the whole country," expecting it to showcase his accomplishments in reforming air transportation. Having flown the passenger route between Pittsburgh and Washington for more than a year and now established as one of Brown's favored few airlines, PAL was the logical candidate for such distinction.

Hann again took the lead in contacting people in Washington about PAL's interest in the new route and the pioneering equity it enjoyed, while Robbins handled most of the negotiations with the Post Office. At the end of February, Robbins learned that PAL would receive the contract under the provisions of the McNary-Watres Act, which gave the postmaster general the power to extend routes without opening them to competitive bidding. Service was first scheduled to begin on April 1, when the Department of Commerce completed the lighted airway between the two cities, but Brown delayed the beginning of service until PAL received three new Stinson trimotors, which were more suitable for

One of the Fairchild cabin monoplanes used by Clifford Ball to carry passengers and mail between Pittsburgh and Washington in 1929. (Library and Archives Division, Historical Society of Western Pennsylvania, Pittsburgh, Pa.)

passenger flying than the single-engine Fairchilds the airline initially wanted to use. Not until June 8 did PAL begin daily airmail flights over the new route, with Brown and other officials taking the first flight from Washington and participating in the inaugural ceremonies that evening in Pittsburgh.[26]

Pennsylvania Airlines expanded its operations in 1931, flying nearly 450,000 scheduled miles and more than 6,000 passengers, nearly all of them in multiengined aircraft. The company fitted radios to all of its passenger airplanes and leased a network of weather reporting stations and a teletype system for ground communications and dispatching. PAL also benefited from the completion of a big new air terminal in Pittsburgh. Opened on September 11, 1931, at a cost of $3.5 million, Allegheny County Airport was larger, better equipped, and more conveniently located than Bettis Field. The new airport was a boon to PAL, as the airline increased its operations to three round-trip flights a day from Pittsburgh.[27]

Bettis Field was the terminal for Pennsylvania Airlines until Allegheny County Airport opened in 1931. (Library and Archives Division, Historical Society of Western Pennsylvania, Pittsburgh, Pa.)

At the end of 1931, Hann reflected on the year's achievements. Emphasizing the importance of passengers and the public acceptance of air travel, he stressed how "responsible air transport companies," working with federal regulatory agencies, had generated what he considered a "banner year" for aviation. Air travel, Hann maintained, was safe and dependable, and considering the time savings involved, not expensive in comparison with the alternatives. Hann had high praise for Brown and the part he had played in ensuring the success of the airlines. To those who questioned the expense to the taxpayer, Hann countered that the total annual expenditure for the airmail was only $20 million, an "infinitesimal premium" to pay for one of the world's best air transport systems. Moreover, he said, the federal role in aviation was in keeping with the government's traditional support for other forms of transportation, asking, "Is there anyone who will question the wisdom of the Federal land grants to the railroads, or of Federal aid in the building of national roadways, or in fostering our merchant marine?"[28]

Hann and the Origins of TWA

In addition to the Pennsylvania Airlines takeover, Hann and PAIC played major roles in creating Transcontinental and Western Air in 1930. If anything, the tale is even more convoluted than the story of the maneuvering that led to PAIC's acquisition of Cliff Ball's operation, but it had similar origins in PAIC's determination to be a factor in the emerging national airmail system. PAIC's considerable investment in aviation in the region, highlighted by ownership of Pittsburgh-Butler Airport, lobbying for a quarter-million-dollar lighted airway between Pittsburgh and Philadelphia, and a share in the new Harrisburg airport, placed the company in a strong position to claim priority rights if and when Transcontinental Air Transport (TAT) decided to begin flying across the state.

Formed in May 1928 as a joint venture of the Pennsylvania Railroad and Clement Keys's North American Aviation, TAT was an odd creation from the start. Concerned about the safety of flying over the mountainous eastern and western segments of the transcontinental route, the airline carried passengers by overnight train to Columbus, Ohio, from which point they flew to Waynoka, Oklahoma, boarded another overnight train to Clovis, New Mexico, and finally picked up a flight to Los Angeles, completing the journey in two days. Without an airmail contract, the company piled up major losses, despite the quality and efficiency of its air-rail service.

On "frequent visits" to Washington in 1929, Hann made a point of informing the Post Office that TAT had done nothing to develop passenger flying east of Columbus and that PAIC deserved something in return for the "hundreds of thousands of dollars" it had put into aviation in Pennsylvania. In early 1930, at about the time when TAT was getting ready to initiate passenger flights on the eastern leg of the route, Hann, Robbins, and Humphrey began talks with Daniel Sheaffer of the Pennsylvania Railroad to determine what PAIC would get for its pioneering equity on the route through the state. In June, PAIC and TAT agreed to join forces. The two companies would bid on an airmail contract between New York and Kansas City, while PAIC would take over principal responsibility for flying passengers on the New York to Columbus leg of the transcontinental route. But events soon overtook the company, as Postmaster General Brown moved ahead with his plans to revamp the national airmail network.[29]

When Brown issued his invitations to the major airline operators to attend the Washington conferences in the spring of 1930, he had in mind the formation of three major transcontinental routes. At the time, there was only one such airway—the northern route from New York to San Francisco via Chicago, jointly run by National Air Transport and Boeing Air Transport. Brown wanted two additional routes. One would run through the center of the nation from New York to Los Angeles via Pittsburgh, St. Louis, and Kansas City. The other would go across the southern tier of states from Atlanta through Dallas–Fort Worth and El Paso to Los Angeles.

While Brown had all the major players in Washington, he determined that TAT and Western Air Express were the two companies best suited to operate the central line, and he pressured them to reach an agreement. Neither party was especially excited about the prospects of a merger, least of all Harris Hanshue, Western's president. Hann, on the other hand, looked forward to bringing the two together. He made a point of reminding both parties, as well as the Post Office, of PAIC's interest in the transcontinental route and said that any agreement between TAT and WAE must in some way involve his company. On July 15, in New York, Hann, Sheaffer, and Hanshue reached a tentative agreement. The two companies would each subscribe to 237,500 shares of stock of the 500,000 available in a new company to be known as Transcontinental and Western Air, Inc. (TWA). PAIC would acquire the remaining 25,000 shares through payment in cash, while the new company would take over a half-interest in Pittsburgh-Butler Airport and assume PAIC's "commitment" at Harrisburg Airport, payable over three years. Hann doubted that the document would be acceptable to some of the key members of PAIC's executive committee, who insisted that the company receive at least a 10 percent interest in TWA and that TWA take over full control of Pittsburgh-Butler Airport, which members of the committee valued at $500,000. Hann met with Hanshue and Sheaffer at "Treetops," his new home in the Pittsburgh suburb of Sewickley Heights, but the pair refused to recognize a greater role for PAIC and balked at paying a half-million dollars for an airport soon to be worth much less once the new Allegheny County facility opened. Seeing that no compromise was possible, Hann told Sheaffer that he wanted him "to appreciate that I have made every effort . . . to settle this controversy as partners dealing with partners," but failing that he saw no alternative other than going to Washington and leaving it up to the postmaster general to arbitrate a settlement.[30]

Through July and into August the negotiations continued, with Brown casting a watchful eye over the proceedings. Finally, Hann and PAIC conceded the company's 5 percent interest in TWA and the half-interest in Pittsburgh-Butler, provided TWA more realistically valued its equipment and cut expenses in every way possible to increase the efficiency of its operations. Years later, Hann recalled that "whether we received 15, 10, or 5 percent" did not matter as much as securing a midcontinent route passing through Pittsburgh. But he might have added that in the final compromise, concluded on August 22, all three parties agreed that Robbins would serve as PAIC's representative on TWA's board. When Hanshue resigned as president the following year, Robbins replaced him, placing PAIC in an even stronger position to influence the airline's direction.[31] While not all that Hann wanted, the TWA settlement demonstrated his persistence, the high level of his bargaining skills, and his manipulation of the regulatory system to gain for PAIC a foothold in what promised to be a lucrative new enterprise of far more than local and regional significance.

Conflict Renewed

Everything seemed in place for the Post Office in the late summer of 1930 to award a certificate to the new TWA to operate over the midtranscontinental line. Unfortunately, another competitor emerged to upset Brown's carefully laid plans. An upstart carrier named Pittsburgh Airways had been created in 1929 by James G. Condon and Theodore Taney, with backing from Pittsburgh department store magnate Oliver M. Kaufmann. Starting on November 1, Pittsburgh Airways Travel Airs offered twice weekly passenger service between Bettis Field and New York, with a stop in Philadelphia. On April 15, 1930, the airline introduced daily service to New York.

Brown, however, did not consider Pittsburgh Airways to be part of his grand scheme for the nation's airlines, and so he did not invite Condon and Taney to the Washington conferences held later that spring. Nevertheless, the operation had gained a good deal of attention with

its scheduled passenger service, and for a time it looked like a more viable prospect for takeover than a recalcitrant Cliff Ball. Hann vigorously
denied it, but PAIC at one point, when it was casting about for an airline
partner, talked to the Pittsburgh Airways people about a possible buyout,
if only to let Ball know that he was not the only alternative. But Condon and Taney wanted more than even cash-rich PAIC was willing to
pay, making any deal between the two firms impossible.[32]

Pittsburgh Airways determined to make its voice heard before Brown
made a decision on the midtranscontinental line. Not invited to the
Washington meetings, Condon and Taney reached an understanding
with United States Airways, a subsidiary of Denver and Ohio Transport,
which ran a passenger line between Dayton and Youngstown, to make a
joint bid on the central airmail route. The agreement stipulated that if
the bid were successful, the three firms would merge to form a new company, United Aviation Company, underwritten by Oliver Kaufmann and
two other financiers for at least $1 million in operating capital. Aviation
bid 64 percent of the maximum 40 cents a mile on the route, only to see
Brown award the contract on September 30 to TWA, the company he
favored from the start, at 97.5 percent of the maximum. Brown justified
his choice by emphasizing that TWA was the lowest "responsible" bidder and pointing out that the contract advertisement stipulated that the
company must have at least 250 miles of its route flown at night. Despite
loud protests from Pittsburgh Airways that the night flying clause had
been illegally inserted into the advertisement, Brown refused to budge
on his decision. In the end, United States Airways received its own mail
contract, and United Aviation ceased to exist—even on paper. Amid a
great deal of hoopla, TWA inaugurated service on October 25. Brown
came to Pittsburgh for the ceremonies welcoming the first flight from
Newark, after which he boarded a new TWA Ford Tri-Motor at Bettis
Field for the Pittsburgh to Columbus leg of the thirty-six-hour transcontinental service. Pittsburgh Airways, meanwhile, had little choice but to
soldier on in direct competition with TWA over the Pittsburgh–New
York route, accumulating mountains of debt in the absence of a mail
contract before finally dissolving into bankruptcy in November 1931.[33]

Despite Brown's support and Post Office favoritism, PAIC and Pennsylvania Airlines continued to lose money in 1933, causing Hann and
others to consider various cost-cutting measures. Among the victims of

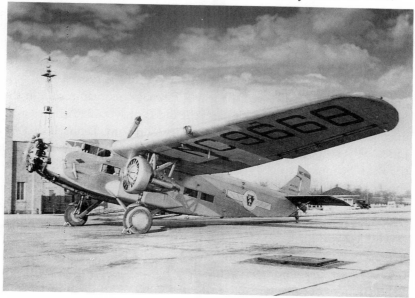

A Pennsylvania Airlines Ford Tri-Motor at Bettis Field in 1930. (Library and Archives Division, Historical Society of Western Pennsylvania, Pittsburgh, Pa.)

Hann's and PAIC's economies in 1933 was Cliff Ball. Despite appearances of amity, Ball had never been comfortable with his position as vice president and found himself routinely bypassed by Harold Martin on important operations decisions. Ball protested some of the airline's reductions in personnel and argued against the decision to terminate the carrier's station-to-station teletype system, leading to friction with Martin and other company officers. Hann eventually concluded that Ball was "not in a position to pull a heavy oar" with the company.

When Martin reported to the board in 1933 that it was hard to justify both his and Ball's $12,000 salaries, Ball's days with the company were numbered. After buying 750 of Ball's shares in 1932, PAIC acquired the remaining 5,000 on October 1, 1933, for a total of $50,000, taking over sole ownership of Pennsylvania Airlines. Ball submitted his letter of resignation the same day, but remained on the payroll until the end of the month. He harbored bitterness toward Hann and PAIC for years afterward. For his part, Hann thought that PAIC had treated Ball fairly and expressed surprise that Ball thought differently; throughout their three-year professional association he had no indications from Ball that there had been any problems. Nevertheless, Ball felt that he had been treated shabbily and that PAIC had never accorded him the recognition he deserved for the risks he had taken in getting the airline started.[34]

The buyout of Ball paved the way for a major reorganization in the fall of 1933, whereby both PAIC and the old Pennsylvania Airlines were dissolved and their assets acquired by a new company, Pennsylvania Air Lines. This corporation had two components: an Airline Division and the Penn School Division, which operated flight schools at Pittsburgh-Butler and Allegheny County airports. PAL continued to acquire new equipment, until by the middle of 1933 its fleet consisted entirely of twelve-passenger Ford Tri-Motors, flying five round-trips daily. Scheduled miles flown increased from 654,187 in 1932 to 851,265 in 1933, and the number of passengers went up from 7,791 in 1932 to 12,265 in 1933. In addition, the airline set up a new maintenance base in Cleveland and upgraded its radio equipment to handle the additional traffic from the discontinued teletype system. Although the company was still not yet profitable, Hann remained convinced that cost-cutting and attention to efficiency would soon turn things around.[35]

Problems under a Democratic Administration

Ultimately, Brown's heavy-handedness in restructuring the nation's airmail system had major consequences when the Democrats secured control of Congress and the White House in 1933. Complaints from operators who were excluded from the 1930 conferences and did not secure contracts under the McNary-Watres legislation led to a series of muckraking articles by columnist Fulton Lewis Jr., charging collusion between the Post Office and airlines, the illegal awarding of airmail contracts and contract extensions, and other wrongdoing by the Republicans in Washington. In September 1933, Senator Hugo L. Black of Alabama began conducting hearings into the matter, relying on information from Lewis and airline executives whom Brown had spurned to generate an atmosphere generally hostile to the former postmaster general and the companies thought to have benefited from his favoritism.[36]

Black subpoenaed information from the airlines, calling for testimony and written statements from the aggrieved parties about what were now usually referred to as the "spoils conferences" that Brown had called in Washington in the spring of 1930. Cliff Ball was one of those who responded. Vacationing in Florida in the winter of 1934, Ball provided Black with detailed answers to specific questions about the PAIC–Pennsylvania Air Lines merger and the roles played by Hann and Brown. Ball categorically denied that he had ever mailed heavy objects over the Pittsburgh-Cleveland route in order to boost his airmail pay, and charged that Hann had threatened to put him out of business if he did not go along with what PAIC was doing in Pittsburgh. When he refused, he said, Hann had conspired with Brown and others in the Post Office to remove him from the airline business in 1930.[37]

Hann voluntarily supplied Black and Post Office officials with information relating to PAIC and the Pennsylvania Air Lines takeover. Hann said that representatives of PAIC had met with Ball on a number of occasions in 1929 and had offered to buy his company, only to have him refuse to sell. Ball's operation at the time, Hann stated, "was neither adequately financed nor was it properly equipped for any such major operations as the Post Office required," particularly for passenger and mail flights to and from Washington. Under those circumstances, and not through coercion or collusion, Ball ultimately agreed to sell to PAIC, receiving in return a generous settlement that allowed him to remain with the airline. "At no time," Hann said, did PAIC "use political pressure, either through the efforts of its officers or any of its directors or stockholders" to secure favorable treatment in Washington. Hann and Robbins requested an opportunity to appear before Black's committee to state their case, but Black did not call any PAIC people to testify.[38]

By the end of January, the Black Committee had not turned up anything illegal but had enough evidence of shady deals and general malfeasance to warrant a recommendation to President Roosevelt that all airmail contracts be canceled pending completion of new reform legislation. Roosevelt issued the cancellation order on February 9, 1934. Ten days later, the Army Air Corps began flying the mails, only to suffer a disastrous series of accidents and fatalities that turned the exercise into a public relations nightmare for the early New Deal.[39]

The army did its best under trying conditions, but it was soon apparent that the only recourse would be to restore the airmail routes to the airlines. Before the Post Office opened bids for new, temporary airmail contracts, however, Farley inserted the proviso that no airlines which had been involved in the "spoils conferences" were eligible to bid. Hann was appalled. He prepared a detailed brief on PAIC's activities in which he justified the company's activities up to and through the "spoils conferences." PAIC, he insisted, had not been formed to create a monopoly on the aviation business in western Pennsylvania, and none of its executives had made any money from the enterprise. Hann denied that there had been any collusion with Brown. He maintained that he and the company had had no "promise, direct, indirect, or by inference, of a contract from the Post Office Department," and that he and other PAIC officials would have been "most derelict in their obligation to their community, their employees and their stockholders had they not attended" the Washington conferences. As for Ball, he had not in any way been coerced into selling out to PAIC. In fact, he had chosen PAIC because it had made him a fair offer—better by far than some of the other ones he had entertained in the summer and early fall of 1930. "The deal met with the approval of Mr. Brown, not for the reason of granting PAIC a favor or forcing out Clifford Ball," said Hann, who continued to believe that what PAIC had paid for Ball's operation was "disproportionate" to the miles flown or the physical assets of his company.[40]

Hann pled his case to the best of his abilities, but could do little to alter the course of events. Like other companies, Pennsylvania Air Lines had to change its name to qualify for bidding on the temporary routes. So it became Pennsylvania Air Lines and Transport Company. More significant, for Hann especially, was the stipulation that the renamed companies could not retain executives who had attended the "spoils conferences." Reluctantly, Hann had to step down as president of PAL, and his place was taken by his trusted colleague, Bedell Munro. Embittered by the "ruthless" airmail cancellation, Hann wrote that Farley and Roosevelt had "plunged backwards seven centuries to the Dark Ages before Magna Carta and Runnymede [sic]." Renamed, and under leadership untainted by the "spoils conferences," PAL bid successfully on the Cleveland-Washington route on April 20, and within a few days resumed operations under the provisions of the temporary legislation.[41]

In the interval, the congressional mill ground out a new airmail law. Despite all their protestations that neither the airlines nor Brown had done anything wrong, the renamed carriers recognized it was inevitable that Congress would in some way punish them for their alleged transgressions and that they would not be able to operate in the same way they had done under the previous regime. Passed on June 12 and quickly signed into law by Roosevelt, the Black-McKellar Act, cosponsored by Black and Senator Kenneth McKellar, Democrat from Tennessee, was a compromise between those who wanted a complete overhaul of the system and others who thought that only modest reforms were needed. The law made permanent the temporary airmail contracts awarded in April and gave the postmaster general authority to extend them "for an indefinite period." Rates would be strictly controlled, not by the Post Office but by the Interstate Commerce Commission. At the same time, the law embraced the principle of competitive bidding, satisfying those who had complained so loudly about Brown's actions in 1930. Other provisions of the act broke up big aviation holding companies (it would have forced a breakup of PAIC had the company not already been reorganized), permanently banned all those who had attended the "spoils conferences" from positions of leadership in the industry, and placed limits on the salaries of airline executives. A bitter pill for the airlines to swallow, Black-McKellar did not begin to solve all of the problems of a regulatory system that had grown up on an ad hoc basis and badly needed rethinking. But it did highlight the major issues involving commercial aviation and got both the government and the industry thinking about what else needed to be done to bring order out of chaos.[42]

At every opportunity Hann defended Brown for his vision of aviation's future and condemned the short-sightedness of those involved in the cancellation controversy. In a letter to W. Irving Glover in June 1942, Hann said that "this Country of ours is greatly indebted to Mr. Brown for the constructive air transport accomplishments brought about during his Administration, and for the basic foundation upon which the present air transport system has developed." Black and Roosevelt, on the other hand, were the villains in the saga, being responsible for acting "so dictatorially" in "slamming the door" on the airlines in 1934. For Hann, the result of the cancellation was a "calamity" that set American aviation back five years and contributed to the nation's lack of preparedness in the early years of World War II.[43]

Hann and the Emergence of Capital Airlines

PAL soon won an airmail contract for the route from Cleveland to Milwaukee, a logical extension of the Washington-Cleveland line, but faced renewed competition in 1934 from Central Airlines. Begun by James Condon with major financial backing from John D. and Richard W. Coulter, the sons of a wealthy Greensburg, Pennsylvania, coal operator, Central bid on the Cleveland-Pittsburgh-Washington route, winning it with an offer more than four cents per mile lower than PAL's. PAL kept the Cleveland-Milwaukee airmail route, but had to be content with a passenger-only operation between Cleveland and Washington. Both companies, PAL and Central, had a hard time stemming the flow of red ink. Central had the more attractive airmail route, but was hampered by the relatively low rate of pay it received from the federal government, and its aging Stinson trimotors were unattractive to passengers. PAL, boasting a fleet of speedy and comfortable Boeing 247Ds acquired from United, succeeded in boosting its passenger volume. Without an airmail contract on the Cleveland-Washington connection, however, it, too, lost money. As Hann recalled, "The resulting competition was a losing battle for each of the two struggling companies." Eventually, Sigmund Janas of American Airways precipitated an internecine battle with Condon and the Coulters for control of Central, opening up the possibility of a merger with PAL.[44]

No longer directly involved in PAL's day-to-day management, Hann nevertheless remained one of the company's principal stockholders and continued to exercise influence in its direction. With Central in turmoil, he and Munro saw an opportunity to take over that airline and end the costly competition between it and PAL. While expressing support for Condon and the Coulters, Hann quietly began negotiations with Janas through friends in New York. A deal was soon struck, and PAL bought Janas's controlling stock in Central for what was later estimated to be $600,000. The new company, renamed Pennsylvania-Central Airlines (PCA), expanded its operations but continued to lose money. Not until the passage of the Civil Aeronautics Act of 1938 did PCA and other airlines begin to enjoy prosperity in a new regulatory environment. Under the Civil Aeronautics Authority and, after 1940, the Civil Aeronautics Board, PCA gained route extensions and increases in airmail pay that helped bring it closer to profitability.[45]

In the late 1930s, Boeing 247Ds acquired from United Airlines were the mainstay of Pennsylvania-Central Airlines, the predecessor of Capital Airlines. (Library and Archives Division, Historical Society of Western Pennsylvania, Pittsburgh, Pa.)

After World War II, PCA challenged the major carriers on longer routes, breaking out of its regional cocoon and renaming itself Capital Airlines in 1948, in part to reflect a more aggressive national strategy. Hann remained on the sidelines until that year, when he returned to the company as chairman of the board. Back in a familiar position after having "cooled his heels" since the 1930s, Hann wasted little time before he began agitating for more federal assistance to the airline industry, reminding everyone about the "catastrophe" caused by the 1934 airmail cancellation. Given the centrality of commercial aviation to the nation's transportation system and its importance to the country's defense, he urged federal regulators to increase airline subsidies in order to insure against repeating past mistakes. In the late 1940s and early 1950s, Hann lobbied the CAB—in particular board member and fellow Pittsburgher Harmar Denny—to give Capital more long-haul routes, and he used his influence to press for an end to Eastern's "virtual monopoly" on routes from the Northeast to Florida. With retroactive mail pay, an innovative coach service on the heavily traveled New York–Pittsburgh–Chicago route, a fleet of four-engine Lockheed 049 Constellations, and new connections to the South, Capital achieved relative prosperity by the mid-1950s, becoming the nation's fifth largest airline.[46]

Encouraged by the company's financial turnaround, Hann and Capital's president, James H. Carmichael, decided to move out of the piston era by purchasing forty Vickers Viscount turboprops in 1954. Although the acquisition of the sleek British aircraft was a dramatic and risky venture, the move gave Capital a competitive edge on many of its routes, including its nonstop New York to Chicago service and its popular connections to Florida. But declining revenues, labor troubles, and the increased debt load imposed by the Viscount acquisition eventually proved to be more than Capital could bear. A shakeup at the top level of the company in 1957 saw retired Air Force general David H. Baker, formerly of the Air Material Command, replace Carmichael as president and chief executive officer, while Carmichael moved over to take Hann's position as chairman of the board. Hann, meanwhile, became chairman of the airline's executive committee. Ambitious plans to add Convair 880 jets to the Capital fleet came to nothing as the company fell behind on payments to Vickers and slid toward bankruptcy in late 1959. Finally, in the spring of 1960, under pressure from stockholders claiming mismanagement and with Vickers unwilling to renegotiate the Viscount debt, Hann had to step down as chairman of the executive committee. The end came only a few months later when United Air Lines announced the purchase of Capital. The merger, formalized in 1961, made United the nation's largest air carrier.

Conclusion

Vigorous well into his ninth decade, Hann remained active in Pittsburgh and New York financial circles until he died at his beloved "Treetops" on June 5, 1979.[47] He left a varied legacy to the airline industry. His leadership of Pennsylvania Air Lines demonstrates the close links between entrepreneurship and federal regulation in the late 1920s. Hann represented a commonly held belief among businessmen in the late 1920s that organization and efficiency were critical for success and that the federal government had a responsibility to create an environment friendly to those companies that best demonstrated the characteristics needed to compete at that level. In the absence of an independent regulatory agency, responsibility for oversight of the nation's airlines fell de facto to the Post Office Department, which had the power to determine which companies received mail contracts and which ones did not. So it was that Hann's progressive business philosophy meshed with that of Walter Folger Brown, whose purposefulness led him to the conviction that the government had a primary role in encouraging the development of air transportation through the active promotion and support of an oligopoly made up of those businesses Brown thought best suited to function in the new and uncertain world of commercial aviation. For a time, the business-government symbiosis worked well, as a favored few companies like PAL prospered under Brown's firm hand. But with a change in the political scene in 1933–34, bringing with it a desire in both the White House and Congress to reform airmail legislation, Brown's elaborate edifice came crashing down, taking with it entrepreneurs like Hann who had been enthusiastic participants in Brown's grand scheme. To the end of his days, and despite experiencing considerable success as an airline financier in the 1950s and 1960s, Hann always considered the airmail cancellation and its aftermath one of the great injustices of the Roosevelt administration and the early New Deal.

Notes

1. George R. Hann to George S. Davison, March 28, 1934, files of George R. Hann, in possession of Stephen E. Nash, Sewickley, Penn. (hereafter cited as Hann files); interview with George R. Hann, Sewickley, Penn., Dec. 2, 1976, pp. 13–16. Copies of this and other interviews of Hann by the author are in the archives of the Historical Society of Western Pennsylvania, Pittsburgh (hereafter cited as HSWP). For a sketch of Hann's career, see William F. Trimble, "George Rice Hann," in William M. Leary, ed., *Encyclopedia of American Business History and Biography: The Airline Industry* (New York: Facts on File, 1992), 203–4.

2. Nick A. Komons, *Bonfires to Beacons: Federal Civil Aviation Policy under the Air Commerce Act, 1926–1938* (Washington, D.C.: Department of Transportation, Federal Aviation Administration, 1978), 195–98; Alfred D. Chandler Jr., *The Visible Hand: The Managerial Revolution in American Business* (Cambridge: Harvard University Press, 1977), 3–4, 10–11, 372–73, 494.

3. Frank C. Harper, *Pittsburgh of Today: Its Resources and People*, vol. 3 (New York: American Historical Society, 1931), 81–82; Hann interview, Nov. 1, 1976, pp. 1–2, HSWP.

4. Hann interview, Nov. 1, 1976, p. 1, HSWP.

5. Ibid., pp. 2–4.

6. Ibid., p. 6.

7. *New York Times*, March 6, 1929; R. E. G. Davies, *Airlines of the United States since 1914* (London: Putnam, 1972), 99–100; Hann interview, Nov. 1, 1976, pp. 11–12, HSWP.

8. Davies, *Airlines of the United States since 1914*, 100–106; Hann interview, Nov. 1, 1976, pp. 12–15, HSWP.

9. William F. Trimble, "George R. Hann on the Early Aviation Industry in Pittsburgh," *Western Pennsylvania Historical Magazine* 61 (July 1978): 233–34; William F. Trimble, "C. Bedell Monro," in Leary, ed., *Encyclopedia of American Business History*, 294–95.

10. *New York Times*, July 14, 1928; Trimble, "Hann on the Early Aviation Industry," 234–37.

11. Trimble, "Hann on the Early Aviation Industry," 237–38.

12. Ibid., 238–39; "The Pittsburgh Aviation Industries Corporation," Hann files; "Pittsburgh Aviation Industries Corporation, Pennsylvania Air Lines, Inc.," Apr. 17, 1934 (brief prepared by Hann for the Senate airmail investigations in 1934), p. 11, Hann files (hereafter cited as PAIC Brief, Apr. 17, 1934).

13. Trimble, "Hann on the Early Aviation Industry," 238; George R. Hann, "The Purpose of Pittsburgh's Big New Aviation Industries Corporation," *Greater Pittsburgh*, Jan. 12, 1929, pp. 11–12.

14. Hann to Walter Folger Brown, March 22, 1929, Hann files; William F. Trimble, *High Frontier: A History of Aeronautics in Pennsylvania* (Pittsburgh: University of Pittsburgh Press, 1982), 156–57.

15. William F. Trimble, "Remembrances of Bettis Field: An Interview with Kenneth W. Scholter," *Pittsburgh History* 76 (winter 1993–94): 171–72; Trimble, *High Frontier*, 129–30.

16. PAIC Brief, Apr. 17, 1934, p. 8, Hann files; Clifford Ball, summary statement for Black Committee, n.d., pp. 4–5, Clifford Ball Papers, Historical Society of Western Pennsylvania (hereafter cited as Ball Papers, HSWP).

17. Trimble, "Hann on the Early Aviation Industry," pp. 240–41; H. E. Marsden to Hann, Apr. 1, 1929, Hann files; George R. Hann, "Address at the Dedication of Pittsburgh-Butler Airport," Sept. 28, 1929, Hann files; Ball, summary statement for Black Committee, n.d., p. 5, Ball Papers, HSWP.

18. *Aviation* 26 (Apr. 20, 1929): 1335; Trimble, *High Frontier*, 158.

19. Hann to Irving Glover, July 13, 1929, Hann files; Hann to Hainer Hinshaw, Aug. 13, 1929, Hann files; Hann interview, Dec. 2, 1976, Sewickley, Pa., pp. 23–24, HSWP.

20. Ball, summary statement for Black Committee, n.d., pp. 1–2, Ball Papers, HSWP; Senate, *Hearings before a Special Committee on Investigation of Air Mail and Ocean Mail Contracts,* 73d Cong., 2d sess. (Washington, D.C.: Government Printing Office, 1934), pt. 6, pp. 2598–99; pt. 7, p. 2748.

21. *New York Times,* Jan. 15, 1930; F. Robert van der Linden, "Progressives and the Post Office: Walter Folger Brown and the Creation of United States Air Transportation," in William F. Trimble, ed., *From Airships to Airbus: The History of Civil and Commercial Aviation,* vol. 2, *Pioneers and Operations* (Washington, D.C.: Smithsonian Institution Press, 1995), 245–50; PAIC Brief, Apr. 17, 1934, Hann files; Hann to Brown, n.d., Hann files; Hann to Harper W. Spong, Harrisburg Chamber of Commerce, Jan. 20, 1930, Hann files.

22. Van der Linden, "Progressives and the Post Office," 250–51; Komons, *Bonfires to Beacons,* 200–201.

23. Komons, *Bonfires to Beacons,* 202–4; PAIC Brief, Apr. 17, 1934, pp. 24, 32, Hann files; Ball, summary statement for Black Committee, n.d., pp. 12–13, Ball Papers, HSWP.

24. Ball, summary statement for Black Committee, n.d., pp. 14–16, Ball Papers, HSWP; PAIC Minute Book, excerpts, Aug. 28, 1929, Oct. 24, 1930, Hann files; PAIC Brief, Apr. 17, 1934, pp. 32–33, Hann files.

25. PAIC Brief, Apr. 17, 1934, pp. 33–35, Hann files; *1929 Annual Report of the Pittsburgh Aviation Industries Corporation and Subsidiary Companies,* p. 1, Hann files; H. S. Martin, statement at directors' meeting, Jan. 19, 1931, Hann files; *Aviation* 31 (Aug. 1932): 346; Hann interview, Dec. 2, 1976, pp. 33–34, HSWP.

26. PAIC Brief, Apr. 17, 1934, pp. 32, 34, Hann files; Sen. David A. Reed to Hann, Dec. 4, 1930, Hann files; Hann to Brown, Jan. 4, 1931, Hann files; memo, Richard Robbins re Washington and Norfolk visit, Feb. 28, 1931, Hann files; Robbins to Brown, Apr. 1, 1931, Hann files; *Pittsburgh Post-Gazette,* June 8, 1931.

27. George R. Hann, "To the Employees of Pennsylvania Air Lines—A History" (Dec. 1933), p. 5, Hann files; *Greater Pittsburgh* 12 (Sept. 1931): 13–14; *The Aircraft Year Book for 1932* (New York: Aeronautical Chamber of Commerce of America, 1932), 43–44.

28. George R. Hann, "Aviation Progress in 1931," Hann files.

29. PAIC Brief, Apr. 17, 1934, pp. 20, 24–25, Hann files.

30. Hann to D. M. Sheaffer, July 5, 1930, Hann files; Hann to Sheaffer, July 15, 1930, Hann files; memorandum of agreement between Transcontinental Air Transport, Inc., and Western Air Express, Inc., July 15, 1930, Hann files; Hann to Sheaffer, July 19, 1930, Hann files.

31. Richard Robbins to Executive Committee, TWA, Feb. 24, 1931, Hann files; Hann interview, Dec. 2, 1976, pp. 17–18, HSWP.

32. Henry Ladd Smith, *Airways: The History of Commercial Aviation in the*

United States (New York: Alfred A. Knopf, 1942), 178; Ball, summary statement before Black Committee, n.d., p. 14, Ball Papers, HSWP; Hann memo in response to Taney testimony before Black Committee, 1934, Hann files.

33. Smith, *Airways*, 178–83, is still the best account of United Aviation. See also Trimble, *High Frontier*, 163. For additional material on TWA, see Senate, *Hearings on Air Mail Contracts*, 73d Cong., 2d sess., pt. 4, pp. 1635–41; for the inaugural TWA flights, see *Pittsburgh Post-Gazette*, Oct. 25, 1930.

34. Hann interview, Dec. 2, 1976, pp. 32–33, HSWP; Ball, summary statement before Black Committee, n.d., p. 16, Ball Papers, HSWP; PAIC Brief, Apr. 17, 1934, p. 32, Hann files; Martin to Ball, Oct. 2, 1933, Hann files; Hann memo in response to Taney testimony before Black Committee, 1934, Hann files; Johnny Evans to editor, *Pittsburgh Press*, March 1, 1989, author's collection.

35. George R. Hann, "1928—Pittsburgh and Aviation—1933," *Greater Pittsburgh* 15 (Jan. 1934): 28, 44–45; George R. Hann, "To Employees of Pennsylvania Air Lines: History," Dec. 1933, 3–5, Hann files; "Pittsburgh Aviation Industries Corp.," *Aero Digest* 24 (March 1934): 23–28, 64.

36. Komons, *Bonfires to Beacons*, 249–51.

37. Ball to Sen. Hugo Black, Jan. 29, 1934, Ball Papers, HSWP; Ball, summary statement before Black Committee, n.d., pp. 1–2, 4, 7–8, Ball Papers, HSWP.

38. Memo, George R. Hann, Jan. 11, 1934, Hann files.

39. Van der Linden, "Progressives and the Post Office," pp. 254–56.

40. Komons, *Bonfires to Beacons*, pp. 264–65; Hann to Farley, Apr. 17, 1934, Hann files; PAIC Brief, Apr. 17, 1934, pp. 6, 19, 24, 30–33, 37, 41–43, Hann files.

41. "Statement of George R. Hann, Chairman of the Executive Committee, Pennsylvania Air Lines, Inc.," Apr. 20, 1934, Hann files.

42. Komons, *Bonfires to Beacons*, 266–69.

43. Hann to W. Irving Glover, June 11, 1942, Hann files; George R. Hann, "The Air Mail Cancellation and Its Cost to the Nation," undated ms., probably 1941, Hann files.

44. "Report, PAIC," Nov. 1, 1934, p. 2, Hann files; *Aviation* 35 (Apr. 1936): 68; *Aviation* 33 (Nov. 1934): 340, 347; Hann interview, Dec. 2, 1976, pp. 25–26, HSWP.

45. *Pittsburgh Bulletin Index* 109 (Oct. 29, 1936): 21–22; Hann interview, Dec. 2, 1976, pp. 25–26, HSWP; Komons, *Bonfires to Beacons*, 347–79; Trimble, *High Frontier*, 200–201, 213–14.

46. Trimble, *High Frontier*, 236–37, 251–52; Hann, speech, "Are We Going to Be So Dumb as to Make the Same Mistake Twice?" Sept. 15, 1948, Hann files; Hann to Clarence W. Young, Department of Commerce, Jan. 10, 1947, Hann files; *Aviation Week* 60 (Feb. 22, 1954): 101–2.

47. Trimble, *High Frontier*, 251–52; Lloyd H. Cornett Jr., "James H. Carmichael," in Leary, ed., *Encyclopedia of American Business History*, 98; *Aviation*

Week 60 (June 14, 1954): 16–18; *Aviation Week* 67 (July 29, 1957): 39; Lawrence I. Peak to chairman, Civil Aeronautics Board, Record Group 197, National Archives; Capital Airlines, Inc., Exhibit UC-717, CAB Docket no. 11699, vol. 6, Records of the Civil Aeronautics Board, Record Group 197, National Archives; *Pittsburgh Post-Gazette,* June 6, 1979.

Bibliographical Essay

I found most of the information on Hann and his career in his personal files, which are now in the possession of Stephen E. Nash of Sewickley, Pennsylvania. Additional information comes from three interviews I had with Hann at his home in November and December 1976. Transcripts of these interviews are located in the archives of the Historical Society of Western Pennsylvania, Pittsburgh. One of the interviews was excerpted and published as "George R. Hann on the Early Aviation Industry in Pittsburgh," *Western Pennsylvania Historical Magazine* 61 (July 1978): 233–45. Another valuable primary source on Pennsylvania Air Lines and its takeover by PAIC are the Clifford Ball Papers, also in the archives of the Historical Society of Western Pennsylvania. Biographical sketches of Hann and Ball are in Frank C. Harper, *Pittsburgh of Today: Its Resources and People,* vol. 3 (New York: American Historical Society, 1931), 81–82, 104–5. An obituary of Hann appears in *Pittsburgh Post-Gazette,* June 6, 1979. For early Bettis Field, see William F. Trimble, "Remembrances of Bettis Field: An Interview with Kenneth W. Scholter," *Pittsburgh History* 76 (winter 1993–94): 170–12.

For background on Capital Airlines and its financial problems in the late 1950s, see Capital Airlines, Inc., Exhibit UC-717, CAB Docket no. 11699, vol. 6, Records of the Civil Aeronautics Board, Record Group 197, National Archives.

Of considerable value to researchers of the early contract airmail routes and the controversy over their consolidation by the Post Office in 1930 is the extensive testimony recorded in Senate, *Hearings before a Special Committee on Investigation of Air Mail and Ocean Mail Contracts,* 73d Cong., 2d sess. (Washington, D.C.: Government Printing Office, 1934).

Contemporary periodicals are also useful in piecing together the story of PAIC, Pennsylvania Air Lines, and their successors. In particular see *New York Times,* July 14, 1928, March 6, 1929, Jan. 15, 1930; *Pittsburgh Post-Gazette,* Oct. 25, 1930, June 8, 1931; *Aviation* 26 (Apr. 20, 1929), 31 (Aug. 1932), 33 (Nov. 1934), 35 (Apr. 1936); *Aviation Week* 60 (Feb. 22, 1954), 60 (June 14, 1954), 67 (July 29, 1957); *Greater Pittsburgh* 12 (Sept. 1931), 15 (Jan. 1934); *Aero Digest* 24 (March 1934); *Pittsburgh Bulletin Index* 109 (Oct. 29, 1936). *The Aircraft Year Book for 1932* (New York: Aeronautical Chamber of Commerce of America, 1932) is a valuable source for information not only on Pennsylvania Air Lines but on other early carriers as well.

A landmark in business history with important perspectives on attitudes toward efficiency and scale is Alfred D. Chandler Jr., *The Visible Hand: The Managerial Revolution in American Business* (Cambridge, Mass.: Harvard University Press, 1977).

There is a growing literature on the airline industry and key people involved in its formative years. For general overviews and interpretations, readers should consult R. E. G. Davies, *Airlines of the United States since 1914* (London: Putnam, 1972) and Nick A. Komons, *Bonfires to Beacons: Federal Civil Aviation Policy under the Air Commerce Act, 1926–1938* (Washington, D.C.: Department of Transportation, Federal Aviation Administration, 1978). Dated, but still useful, is Henry Ladd Smith, *Airways: The History of Commercial Aviation in the United States* (New York: Alfred A. Knopf, 1942).

For more specific information on the companies and personalities covered in this chapter, see William F. Trimble, *High Frontier: A History of Aeronautics in Pennsylvania* (Pittsburgh: University of Pittsburgh Press, 1982); William F. Trimble, "George Rice Hann," "C. Bedell Monro," and Lloyd H. Cornett Jr., "James H. Carmichael," in William M. Leary, ed., *Encyclopedia of American Business History and Biography: The Airline Industry* (New York: Facts on File, 1992), 95–99, 203–4, 294–95; and F. Robert van der Linden, "Progressives and the Post Office: Walter Folger Brown and the Creation of United States Air Transportation," in William F. Trimble, ed., *From Airships to Airbus: The History of Civil and Commercial Aviation*, vol. 2, *Pioneers and Operations* (Washington, D.C.: Smithsonian Institution Press, 1995), 245–60.

C. R. Smith: An American Original

ROGER E. BILSTEIN

IN 1958, *TIME* MAGAZINE PORTRAYED CYRUS Rowlett Smith, president of American Airlines, on its cover and defined him as "a living legend in aviation." Over six feet tall and weighing 192 pounds, C. R. Smith was undeniably an imposing figure. "A rough and tough man's man, he often peppers his speech with four-letter words, [and] can shoot out orders like a gangster on the loose," wrote an admiring reporter from *Time*. "With the shrewd calculation of a gambler, the financial sagacity of a banker, and the dedication of a monk, he has propelled American Airlines into first place in the industry and in the process has done more than any other man to improve the service and standards of U.S. airlines."[1]

As one of the largest and most complex air transportation companies in the country, American Airlines found the Civil Aeronautics Board (CAB) to be a buffer against interlopers as well as a hindrance to some of its own expansionist moves. In a different context, because Smith often followed a strategy of acquiring new equipment ahead of the competition, operational and technological problems sometimes engaged his airline in critical safety issues with federal entities like the Civil Aeronautics Administration (CAA) and its successor in 1958, the Federal Aviation Agency (FAA). There were other issues involving labor organizations such as the Air Line Pilots Association and government guidelines regarding work hours for active flying duty. Other relationships between American Airlines and government entities were somewhat subtle but nonetheless substantive. For example, Smith and federal regulators clearly differed on questions of excess capacity and the industry's financial health—issues that often impinged on Smith's plans for route expansion and/or debt load in the acquisition of newer, larger passenger transports. Through it all, American Airlines forged ahead, maintaining a premier position in the industry through a combination of shrewd marketing, outstanding service, astute financing, and savvy public relations that sustained its growth amid the crosscurrents of a regulatory environment.

Unlike many of his contemporaries in the airline business, particularly in the case of highly individualistic and opinionated executives like Eddie Rickenbacker of Eastern Air Lines, Smith did not have an aversion to collaboration with the federal government and its agencies, especially when he perceived benefits as a result. Early on, during the 1930s, he turned to the government for favorable loans in the acquisition of improved equipment. With the establishment of an American Airlines executive office in Washington during the 1950s, its role was not to conduct guerrilla warfare with the government but to keep abreast of bureaucratic trends and adjust to bureaucratic realities. In many ways, Smith's later appointment to a cabinet post in the Johnson administration reflected his catholic view of the airline industry as a business in concert with a federal presence as it evolved within national and international environments. To paraphrase Melvin Kranzberg's famous dictum about the impact of technology, one might say that from C. R. Smith's point of view, federal regulation was neither good nor bad—nor was it neutral.

C. R. Smith and the Emergence of American Airlines

Born in 1899 in the sleepy west Texas hamlet of Minerva, Smith rose steadily to success from hardscrabble origins, holding a series of jobs as cottonpicker, office boy, and bookkeeper in a bank. After taking courses at the University of Texas, he became an accountant for Peat, Marwick and Company, and then joined the Texas-Louisiana Power Company, which also operated a small airline, Southern Air Transport. Smith became vice president and general manager of Southern Air Transport in 1930, setting the stage for his role in what came to be known as American Airlines.[2]

Like most air operations in the United States that developed between the two world wars, American Airlines emerged as an amalgam of various smaller companies. One example was Robertson Aircraft Corporation, set up to take advantage of the Air Mail Act of 1925 and carry mail under government contract. Robertson began in 1926 with the St. Louis–Chicago route, with Charles A. Lindbergh as one of its fledgling pilots. During the late 1920s and early 1930s, an aggressive holding company, the Aviation Corporation, acquired some two dozen smaller mail and passenger lines, which gave it considerable geographic coverage. For example, Colonial operated along the eastern seaboard and into Canada; Universal (an evolution of Robertson) was a midwestern line. Interstate linked Chicago to Atlanta, and Southern Air Transport not only covered the South but also flew from Atlanta all the way to Los Angeles. There were other operations as well, resulting in a kaleidoscopic conglomerate, a grab bag "fleet" of aircraft, and parochial managers who fiercely protected their local fiefdoms. But the various units also represented an invaluable legacy of authorized routes stretching from New England to the Pacific coast. These airways formed the basis for longer flights between city pairs—an operational benefit that proved to be profitably effective for subsequent schedules.

Errett Lobban Cord, a major investor of the era, began to impose some order, with American Airlines finally emerging as a rationalized entity in 1934. As a promising young executive with Southern Air Transport, C. R. Smith was named president of the reorganized air carrier. At about the same time, congressional investigations resulted in a major shakeup of the airline industry, leading to federally mandated changes in route structures and mail contracts. Smith quickly recognized the significant role of government authority in airline operations. In the meantime, he continued to standardize equipment, develop passenger business, and buy modern airliners like the Curtiss Condor (the country's first "sleeper" design) and the Douglas DC-2. Smith's drive to attract and hold more passengers meant hiring the company's first stewardesses in 1933 and advocating a bigger and better successor for the fourteen-passenger DC-2. Smith harried Douglas to build the redoubtable DC-3, which entered service with American Airlines in 1936. In many ways, this acquisition represented American's biggest step forward in the 1930s and rested squarely on Smith's inclination to take advantage of direct federal assistance.

American needed improved airliners to offer sleeper service and compete with TWA and United on coast-to-coast schedules. During a legendary long-distance phone call to Donald Douglas in California, Smith persuaded the manufacturer to take his order for twenty new planes to be called the Douglas Sleeper Transport (DST). With improved performance and capacity in comparison with its immediate predecessor, the DC-2, the day-flight version of the DST, designated the DC-3, featured twenty-one passenger seats. During the debate with Douglas over the new transport, Smith promised that he could pay for his new planes with a $4.5 million loan from the government. Smith soon departed for Washington, D.C. To fund his Douglas contract, Smith intended to use a line of credit from the Reconstruction Finance Corporation (RFC), an agency established by the Hoover administration and continued by Roosevelt's New Deal Democrats.

Smith clearly felt confident that he could rely on the RFC's tough boss, Jesse Jones, an old Texas acquaintance. After years in the rough-and-tumble arena of Texas commerce, Smith felt at home with the business philosophy of the New Deal Democrat and the way in which Jones approached such multimillion dollar deals. Something of the fraternal business world of Jones and his cronies can be gleaned from stories about them as they functioned in Texas during the 1950s. Returning from Washington to live in Houston, Jones gravitated to the Lamar Hotel, where old friend George Brown maintained a private suite—number 8F—populated by a clubby group known as the "8F crowd" that indulged in loosely ritual pursuits of dominoes, cards, yarns, politics, drinks, and deals. Even in the 1930s, Jones adhered to a concept of a wide-ranging, extended "family" of Democratic friends, cohorts, and financiers, bound together in a shared network of tradition and acquaintances. Although the RFC's program obliged him to consort with the eastern money crowd, Jones still entertained an emotional sense of anticolonialism in regard to eastern banking. He entertained an equally strong loyalty to Houston and to Texas. He believed in extending credit and stimulating the economy, and he expected the RFC to yield a long-term profit. With his brawny frame, easygoing personality, Democratic political affiliation, business reputation, West Coast manufacturing contracts, and impeccable native-Texan credentials, Smith easily fit into the orbit of Jesse Jones.

With its twenty-one-passenger capacity, the DC-3 helped end the airlines' reliance on mail subsidies, permitting American as well as its competitors to make money on passenger traffic alone. American Airlines also became a leader in responsible, persuasive sales campaigns that attracted a broader cross-section of the public to air travel, benefiting the industry as well as itself. By 1938, American Airlines operated from a busy headquarters in Chicago, with flights to major cities in the Northeast as well as throughout the Midwest. From its earlier legacy of patchwork routes, additional schedules out of Chicago stretched through the Southwest to destinations in California. Consequently, Smith's company flourished as a major national air service that also possessed an enviable series of connections, making it a powerful transcontinental airline system.[3]

Broadened Horizons

Shortly after the United States entered World War II in 1941, American and other airlines surrendered half their fleets to the U.S. Army Air Force's newly constituted Air Transport Command (ATC). Thousands of airline workers under contract joined military personnel in developing the ATC into an efficient global airway with 200,000 personnel who not only flew planes but serviced and modified them and built airfields in every corner of the world. Well known by now in Democratic circles and respected in Washington, Smith surfaced as one who could effectively assist the organization and operation of this new intercontinental air transport system. The final imprimatur came from General Henry H. "Hap" Arnold, commander of the U.S. Army Air Force. Commissioned as a colonel in 1942, Smith took a leave of absence from American to serve as chief of operations for the ATC. By the time Smith departed military service with the rank of brigadier general, he possessed unique experience in managing international air routes.[4] On his return to American Airlines, Smith aggressively pursued options to enable foreign passenger schedules, but the chief obstacle to expanded global service seemed to be the Civil Aeronautics Board.

From the company's start, the directors of American Airlines displayed

C. R. Smith served during World War II as a senior officer in the Air Transport Command. Posed under the wing of a C-54, he is seen here with Franklin D. Roosevelt during the president's visit to Hawaii in the summer of 1944. Smith maintained close ties with Texas Democrats and with the national party. (Courtesy of American Airlines)

an obvious interest in foreign passenger operations. During the late 1930s, the company offered a combination airliner and steamship travel package to Bermuda. In 1936, American began a two-year agreement with Deutsche Zeppelin-Reederei, advertising designated routes to New York by air with connections to Lakehurst, New Jersey, to board the dirigible *Hindenburg* for a two-day crossing of the Atlantic. These arrangements ended with the dirigible's fiery destruction the following year and the increasingly bellicose attitudes of the Nazi regime in Germany. In 1941, on the eve of the war, American Airlines offered a few flights to Toronto, and it began service to Mexico in 1942. Initially, a majority of the CAB panel had opposed the route authority from both Dallas and San Antonio to Monterey and on to Mexico City. But in the interests of national security, President Roosevelt opted for additional air service and overrode the CAB decision, awarding American a temporary certificate for the duration of the war. In the spring of 1946, American won a permanent certificate, but the company's Mexican ventures waxed and waned over succeeding decades due to shifting equipment and operational priorities as well as continuing stiff challenges from companies like Pan Am and Braniff, which already had a considerable presence in Central and Latin American air transport. American's principal foreign interest involved routes over the North Atlantic, where corporate storms with the CAB were already in full fury.

Controversies over the award of international routes swirled around the CAB from its earliest years of existence in the 1940s. One of the first major issues involved a petition from American Export Airlines (Amex) when its organizers filed an application with the original Civil Aeronautics Authority in the spring of 1939. The application, for a North Atlantic route, represented a clear challenge to Pan Am's jealously guarded international prerogatives. This was especially true over the prestigious North Atlantic airway to Britain and the Continent. In the words of historian Donald Whitnah, Amex's challenge touched off a "monumental political battle," one that unfolded even as the fledgling CAB was trying to find its wings. The CAB became an official entity on July 1, 1940; later that month, the board evaded Pan Am's legal fusillades and held that Pan Am's monopoly over the North Atlantic violated the public interest. Trippe fiercely contested this continuing threat to his airline's hegemony over the Atlantic, and Pan Am kept filing legal objections through 1941. Trippe was only partially successful in crippling potential competition; Amex finally received a temporary passenger certificate, although it failed to win a mail contract.

All of this became a moot issue during World War II. Amex, Pan Am, TWA, American, and others all became contractors to the military services for international and intercontinental air transport operations. The route certification process was suspended for the duration. Debate erupted again during the summer of 1945, when the CAB considered the North Atlantic Route Case in the context of postwar airline expansion. Although Pan Am strenuously argued its case for a single designated U.S. flag line (providing Pan Am with its famous "chosen instrument" status)[5] to compete effectively with national flag lines from individual European countries, the CAB opted for more competition among U.S. flag carriers. Along with Amex, the board also granted authority to Trans World Airlines to operate across the North Atlantic. The CAB clearly wanted to increase the options available for U.S. travelers on international routes and consequently gave Braniff Airways new destinations in Latin America. Northwest Airlines received authority to expand across the Pacific.[6]

The Amex controversy first erupted in 1936, when a shipping company called the American Export Line decided to give its Atlantic Ocean rivals some real competition by establishing a transoceanic air service. The company's aviation subsidiary became American Export Airlines, acquired a Consolidated PBY-4 flying boat to begin survey flights, and in 1939 applied for certification to operate a route across the Atlantic to Britain and France. The outbreak of war delayed commercial service, although Amex took delivery of a trio of big Vought-Sikorsky flying boats with four engines. During the war, Amex flew these planes under contract to the U.S. navy. One of them, a VS44A, made the first nonstop crossing of the Atlantic by an airliner, crossing from Newfoundland to Foynes, Ireland, in 1942. The Amex Sikorsky flying boats made some four hundred wartime crossings, and Amex crews also flew Douglas C-54 transports for the Air Transport Command on various routes to North Africa.

As chief of the ATC, Smith apparently considered Amex's operations as an expedient opening to expand American Airlines in the postwar era. During 1944, even before Smith stepped back into civilian life, American's wartime executive team made a bid for ownership of Amex. On July 5, 1945, the CAB issued a judgment that approved the merger of Amex and American. At the same time, the board took a momentous step forward by awarding American Airlines route authority to Europe in the North Atlantic Route Case. American Export Airlines, American's subsidiary, now entered the field of transoceanic U.S. carriers to compete with haughty Pan Am, long recognized as the sacrosanct "chosen instrument" of U.S. international airlines. This was a serious challenge to Pan Am, in that the CAB clearly accepted an inherent advantage for American Airlines, since its large, mature network in the United States would feed into the newly acquired overseas routes to Europe. Although TWA received transoceanic permissions at the same time, its smaller domestic network was seen to be at a disadvantage in comparison with the American Airlines System, as American's combined domestic and foreign services were known. Pan Am, still in possession of a much more intricate overseas network across the Atlantic, the Pacific, the Caribbean, and into Latin America, was blocked by the CAB from acquiring a U.S. domestic route system, which would have created a far too powerful global operator. At the same time, the CAB appeared to hedge its beneficence in new routes to Amex by withholding mail contracts, a form of subsidy that provided Pan Am with a solid support for its far-flung operations. During the CAB hearings in 1945, Pan Am's political allies in Congress made sure that the "chosen instrument" retained this invaluable advantage over its U.S. rivals.[7]

For all that, the CAB presented Amex with permanent route authority to a series of highly desirable European destinations, giving the challenger a fighting chance to develop a good passenger base for financial viability. From several major eastern cities, along with Chicago and Detroit, Amex listed flights to both Glasgow and London's Hurn Airport. The original CAB charter also gave Amex the right to launch subsequent services from Iceland into the Baltic regions to cities such as Stavanger, Stockholm, Helsinki, and Leningrad as well as Moscow. A third permission involved New York departures to Europe via Ireland, London, and Amsterdam.

With a promising lineup of European destinations, American's postwar venture into intercontinental service represented a sudden leap ahead. At first glance, Smith's airline may have seemed to have overreached itself, since the history of American had been so tightly bound to U.S. domestic routes. At the same time, Smith's tenure with the Air Transport Command had given him several years of firsthand experience in air transport operations on a global scale. The corporate offices of American also had a number of Smith's former ATC cohorts to bring international air transport experience into the parent organization. Moreover, Amex itself carried the benefit of its own wartime operations into the postwar environment. There were some inevitable organizational changes. In the autumn of 1945, American Export Airlines became American Overseas Airways (AOA), operating as the Trans-Atlantic Division of the American Airlines System. Smith sat as president of the System and ran its domestic services; Harold R. Harris, a senior vice president, directed AOA.

Harris had to move fast in establishing his division's postwar services. Obtaining CAB route authority was one thing; meeting the stiff competition from TWA and a feisty Pan Am was another. In addition, competition was rapidly taking shape from aggressive European flag carriers like British Overseas Airways Corporation (BOAC), Swissair, Dutch KLM, and Air France. Different equipment added another dimension of change. Flying boats such as the venerable Sikorskys had enabled first-generation intercontinental routes to get under way quickly by flying between major coastal seaports. Due to wartime technological advances, land planes represented the next generation, with schedules that linked national capitals and major inland cities. Flying boats gave way to four-engine air transports like the Douglas DC-4. Parlaying its wartime experience with the C-54 military version of the DC-4, management at AOA adroitly conducted survey flights and dispatched its first passenger plane on October 23, 1945.[8]

The plane, a DC-4, carried a traditional American Airlines "Flagship" sobriquet, the *Flagship London,* and departed from New York's LaGuardia Field at 3:30 p.m., followed by a stop at Boston. The plane refueled at Gander, Newfoundland, and headed across the Atlantic, touching down at Ireland's Shannon Airport early in the afternoon of October 24, 1945. American Airlines/AOA had completed the first passenger flight in a land-based airliner across the North Atlantic.

During November, AOA made the most of its CAB charter by announcing weekly round-trip service between Washington, D.C., and London, with daily flights offered by the end of the year. Regular service to Stockholm and Copenhagen began early in 1946. The inaugural flights for all of these services were invariably accompanied by heavily publicized ceremonies, with champagne bottles to christen the nose of the airliner. These elaborate occasions became something of an American Airlines hallmark; Smith also liked to invite public figures to gain extra news coverage. Among the bottlewielders on such occasions were Margaret Truman, daughter of the president, and Swedish film star Signe Hasso, who shattered the champagne bottle over the nose of *Flagship Scandinavia* on its maiden flight to Stockholm.

But the DC-4, which performed yeoman service on innumerable overseas and long-distance domestic routes, was soon outclassed by more advanced airliners. AOA's rivals equipped their services with faster pressurized transports like the Lockheed Constellation. AOA followed suit, acquiring Lockheed Model 049 Constellations, which offered meals actually cooked aloft, and pampered passengers on these "Mercury Service" flights, which became a byword for high-class standards on the North Atlantic routes. The CAB granted additional route authorization to Frankfurt and Berlin. In the spring of 1949, AOA began acceptance of eight new Boeing Model Stratocruisers. With their spacious cabins and sophisticated lower-deck cocktail lounges, the Stratocruiser service kept AOA in the vanguard of premium service on routes between the United States and Europe. Additionally, AOA conducted contract operations, using its older DC-4s, in support of airfield construction in Iceland. The company also contracted its DC-4 equipment to the U.S. Air Force during the Berlin blockade of 1948–49. From its base in Frankfurt, AOA flew up to forty flights per week into the Berlin area.[9]

Strategic Retreat

By this time, AOA had even won a CAB decision to receive a mail subsidy. But C. R. Smith decided to sell American's overseas division. Several factors carried weight in the decision. For one thing, the overseas division rarely operated at a profit. As AOA, the division had a reputation for superior service in comparison with TWA and Pan Am, but it remained too small to mount a truly effective alternative to its larger competitors. Further competition from European flag lines seemed to make the situation even more problematic. The AOA division depended heavily on the parent company's resources for domestic marketing and for financial advice and funding as well. Some of Smith's own officers began to grumble that they spent more time on AOA's problems than on domestic operations, which clearly carried the transatlantic division. Smith agreed. "Every time I look around for one of my key officers to get something done around here, I find he's off somewhere in Europe working on some AOA problem. Management is spending 90 percent of its time on an operation that's producing only 10 percent of our revenues."[10]

A special planning committee reminded Smith about the nagging problem of AOA's finances. The CAB had finally given AOA some overseas mail subsidy relief, set at 42 cents per mile. By comparison, TWA received 56 cents and Pan Am got 72 cents per mile. The committee validated the growing concern that AOA diverted much of American's management assets, noted accelerating foreign (and subsidized) competition from additional North Atlantic entries like SAS, the Scandinavian consortium of Norway, Denmark, and Sweden, and concluded that AOA would probably never generate more than 20 percent of American's overall revenues. Given the high costs of maintaining transatlantic services, the report buttressed Smith's inclination to divest.

Confidential feelers had already gone out to Pan Am late in 1948, and the two parties signed an agreement on December 13, 1948. Working out final details and a final sales price of $17,450,000 took an additional seventeen months. But in May 1950, the CAB rejected the sale of AOA to Pan Am because it was not in the public interest. The board felt that Pan Am would gain too much dominance in the international market and severely compromise the operations of TWA. However, CAB decisions dealing with international routes needed presidential approval, and the case went forward to the White House and President Harry Truman.

After Truman affirmed the CAB decision in June 1950, he suddenly dropped a bombshell by reversing himself, overruling the CAB and authorizing the merger of AOA with Pan Am. Controversy still swirls around Truman's change of heart, a move that prompted CAB chairman Joseph J. O'Connell to resign in protest. There was plenty of heartburn as well within the executive ranks at American Airlines, where Ralph Damon, corporate president, abruptly resigned and just as abruptly popped up as president of TWA.

Late in the war, Damon had been named executive vice president of American. Philosophically committed to international expansion, Damon had acted as American's spark plug in the acquisition of American Export Airlines. After Smith's return to American in 1945, Damon became president of the airline system when Smith was elevated to an elite post as chairman of the board. It was Damon who most frequently found himself at odds with Pan Am's Juan Trippe, who vigorously pushed the concept of a single international airline as the chosen instrument of the United States to compete against the heavily subsidized national airlines based in Europe. Among Trippe's proposals was one to organize a single U.S. flag carrier in which the major U.S. airlines held stock. Damon viewed this as just another of Trippe's schemes to continue Pan Am's dominance on the world's major airline routes. Damon, in fact, had argued in congressional hearings that wartime experiences through the Army's ATC and the Navy's Air Transport Service had prepared America's domestic airlines for successful participation in postwar international air travel. He advocated allocation of such routes in a process similar to the CAB's practices in awarding domestic routes. With congressional support for such initiatives, the CAB had awarded its early postwar Atlantic route certificates to TWA and to American Airlines.

When Smith decided to shed AOA, he conducted negotiations in secret, bypassing Damon. Some sources suggest that Howard Hughes had already approached Damon to take over TWA; in any case, Damon soon resigned in the wake of the AOA/Pan Am merger announcement and within a few days became president of TWA. He then spent the next two years opposing the merger and battling Pan Am's continuing campaign to succeed as the nation's "chosen instrument."[11]

Damon must have felt some vindication when the CAB first rejected the merger, and satisfaction at Truman's initial response, followed by considerable frustration with the president's reversal on the issue. Debate continues over the reasons for Truman's action. His first response, to oppose the CAB and block the merger at Pan Am's expense, made sense. TWA, based in St. Louis, was a strong political force in Missouri, where Truman had built his political base. But the native Texan C. R. Smith, the argument goes, retained potent political and economic ties in Texas, especially through Speaker of the House Sam Rayburn. Carlene Roberts, American's regulatory expert in Washington, D.C., appears to have found a solution to the imbroglio by brokering a clause allowing TWA to compete with Pan Am on certain routes. As one of Washington's premier lobbyists, Roberts maintained influential lines to the White House via one of Truman's presidential aides as well as through presidential secretary Matt Connelly. TWA's new president, Ralph Damon, later remarked that Roberts was perhaps the most influential lobbyist in Washington.

At the same time, TWA's legal counsel was debating details of the sale in litigation that went all the way to the Supreme Court, which upheld the legality of the contract. In the end, the CAB agreed to cut a deal. TWA got access to Frankfurt and London (keenly desired by Damon), Pan Am received a CAB concession to fly into Paris and Rome, AOA officially went to Pan Am, and the deed was done. Truman gave approval in July 1950; Pan Am took over in September.

Years later, Smith seemed less sure about the wisdom of selling off

American's position over the North Atlantic. "On the basis of the situation at the time of the decision, we did right, I believe," he mused. "On the basis of the situation many years later, the decision is debatable."[12]

Postwar Domestic Operations

In addition to bureaucratic turbulence over the North Atlantic, there were clashes involving choice routes across the United States. For the most part, the CAB supported trunk carriers on major routes, including the coast-to-coast flights. The domestic "Big Four" (American, United, TWA, and Eastern) continued their dominance of these choice operations between major regional cities as well as transcontinental service. Nonetheless, smaller trunk carriers like Braniff, Continental, Delta, National, and Western fought tenaciously to extend their operations, often at the expense of the major airlines. The Big Four's share of revenue-passenger miles declined from 82 percent in 1938 to 71 percent in 1954. At the same time, the industry's total revenue-passenger miles rose from about 480 million before the war to 16.7 billion after the war, providing ample opportunities to pursue profits.[13] The pursuit often involved choosing the right kind of aircraft, effectively folding them into the carrier's route pattern, developing an optimum pattern, and making the right decisions for expanded service. Working with the CAB did not always result in trouble-free route development decisions.

In the spring of 1945, anticipating the growth and complexity of postwar airlines, Smith moved into a newly created position as chairman of the board. Ralph Damon had served as vice president and now moved up to president. *Time*'s business section thought that all of these developments boded well for the future: "C. R. and Damon work together as smoothly as the motors on one of their DC-3s." The company operated over 9,457 miles of routes and applied to the CAB for nearly twice as much. With a roster of 86 planes in 1945, Smith talked of a much larger fleet. "Any employee who can't see the day when we will have 1,000 planes had better look for a job somewhere else," he declared.[14]

The airline had already taken important steps to achieve postwar dreams. One move had been to strengthen its presence in Washington, D.C., in order to track changes in congressional politics, lobby the right people, and keep a close eye on shifting bureaucratic horizons at the CAB.

American Airlines set a precedent not only in establishing a permanent office in 1942 but also in naming a woman to play a key role there—Carlene Roberts. She graduated from the University of Oklahoma and became a social worker before joining the staff of the Oklahoma Chamber of Commerce as a secretary. Her efficiency and ability to interact effectively with people impressed O. M. Mosier of Braniff Airways, who went on to American Airlines as a vice president and offered Roberts a job. She excelled in personnel work.

When American shifted its headquarters from Chicago to New York's LaGuardia Airport in 1939, Roberts brilliantly orchestrated the entire move of some 700 employees, from technicians and tools to anxious parents and their children's first day of kindergarten. When American's Washington, D.C., administrative office opened in 1942, Roberts, age twenty-nine, was put in charge. "She dealt expertly with government agencies, [and] got to know important people in and out of Congress," wrote *Time,* and in the process she "became an accomplished lobbyist for the airline's projects." In July 1951, she received a salary of $25,000 per year and won promotion to vice president of American Airlines, the first woman in the airline industry to hold such an elevated position. Given the rapid change of the industry, Roberts had more than enough to do.[15]

After the war, American quickly introduced large four-engine airliners like the 300 MPH DC-6, which also featured pressurization. Additionally, the airline bought the pressurized Convair CV-240 twin-engine transport as a DC-3 replacement. Pressurized equipment like these postwar planes enabled more flights to cruise above threatening weather, take advantage of better high-altitude flying conditions, maintain schedules, and introduce a major improvement in passenger comfort.

Acquisition of new aircraft sometimes brought serious technical problems. In the case of the DC-6, both United and American airliners experienced in-flight fires in 1947; United's plane crashed, but American's crew managed a dramatic emergency landing in New Mexico. In concert with the CAA, Douglas Aircraft counseled operators to ground their DC-6 fleet until a special investigative team could find answers. After reviewing the available information, American's representatives and Douglas engineers suspected leakage of volatile, high-octane aviation gas from an overflow valve during the transfer of fuel between tanks. This was a standard procedure, to maintain proper trim of the aircraft in flight and to practice efficient fuel management. Some preliminary flight tests seemed even more compromising, suggesting that errant fuel ran back under the fuselage, where an air scoop—linked to the plane's heating system—sucked the fuel into heating elements and erupted. Conclusive tests with telltale dye (and a shutdown heater) followed at the CAA's Technical Development and Evaluation Center in Indianapolis. Cooperating with the CAA's Center and American Airlines personnel, Douglas redesigned and relocated the fuel vent, thereby eliminating the hazard.

Reentering service with the CAA's blessing, the DC-6 compiled an enviable record for safety and reliability. Its immediate successor, the DC-6B (also flown by American) became known as the most economical piston-engine airliner ever built. In the process of this evolution, Smith's airline owed much to its own technicians and the manufacturer's engineers. Also, Smith clearly reaped the benefits of the CAA's verification of the problem and the agency's subsequent endorsement of the DC-6 as a safe airliner.[16]

By 1951, American counted 145 planes in its fleet and over 14,000 employees. With revenues of $118.7 million, the airline collected more cash from travelers than the New York Central Railroad. The company listed $140 million in total assets. Financially, American had emerged as the soundest airline in the United States. An admiring assessment of the airline came from a detailed article in *Fortune* magazine, which described C. R. Smith as "a big, pleasantly profane Texan." The magazine applauded Smith's shrewd standardization of equipment, so that the company basically had to maintain and overhaul only two types of planes: sixty-six DC-6 and DC-6Bs, plus seventy-nine Convair 240s. Although the company retained fourteen DC-4s, which shared many components with the newer Douglas transports, they were being phased out. The DC-6 models used common versions of the Pratt and Whitney R-2800 engines, the same powerplant used by the Convairs, and the DC-4 transports used R-2000 engines from the same engine manufacturer. The company also succeeded by planning big and by paying close attention to customer satisfaction. Under C. R. Smith, the airline always seemed adventurous. "Historically, American has always preferred to pioneer rather than to play financially safe and let the competition take the risks," *Fortune* noted approvingly. "C. R. Smith, as a matter of fact, has come to be known as a man who is always ready to take the calculated risk and do his calculating in a spacious way. Right now, his daring is paying off."[17]

Some imaginative steps did not always have satisfactory results, however. By the time American completed its sale of American Overseas Airlines, including a final settlement with American Export Lines, which still owned some 20 percent of the stock, American Airlines Incorporated had lost about $900,000. From the vantage point of 1951, Smith still felt he had made the right move by selling the intercontinental operation. "The smartest thing we ever did," he insisted, "was to get the hell out."[18]

Other calculated gambles worked out more favorably. In 1945–46, when American committed itself to dozens of new DC-6 and Convair 240 transports, the company knew this meant wholesale replacement of its entire existing fleet, with attendant costs and delays in terms of training, maintenance, inventory, and integrating the new generation planes into scheduled operations. No other airlines at the time appeared willing to commit to such a dramatic conversion. To help finance his "spectacular gamble," as *Fortune* put it, the company sold $40 million in preferred stock. Including loans and credit, American's executive team knew that it was mortgaging the company's future by a total of $80 million and made an assumption that the inevitable dislocation during the equipment changeover could be artfully managed. With some perturbations, the gamble worked. American's last DC-4 retired from passenger service in 1948 (the remainder were used in cargo and contract operations), and the final DC-3 bowed out on March 31, 1949. Much to the annoyance of competitors still using the plane as primary equipment, American turned over its last DC-3 to a museum.

Considering its huge investment in modern aircraft, American clearly intended that its new vice president, Roberts, would play a key role in keeping track of developments at the CAB's office. Early in its career, the board sometimes seemed to follow the dictum that everybody needed a chance, and it handed out routes with only cursory assessment of economic realities for the competitors. In the postwar era American and its cohorts spent much time and money in Washington trying to protect their networks from occasional poachers and a politically susceptible CAB.[19]

Competitive Strategies and Tactics

Meanwhile, American competed vigorously for available passengers on routes also served by rival airlines. The CAB frowned on cut-rate fares, concerned by potentially ruinous fare wars. American, however, came up

with one low-fare plan that not only satisfied the CAB but also represented a shrewd marketing strategy that often worked effectively for other
airlines.

The idea appeared in 1948, when Smith badgered a study group to
consider some sort of incentive plan to attract enough traffic to recover
a reduced tariff. The study group carefully followed daily load factors
over six months and uncovered a distinctive pattern. The favorite travel
days were Sunday and Friday afternoons, as business travelers either departed on business trips or returned home. After juggling potential schedules and operating costs, the group came up with a scheme that pleased
Smith and kept the CAB placated. For wives who flew with husbands at
full fare, American Airlines offered a 50 percent discount during the lowest passenger-load periods Saturday noon to Sunday noon and Tuesday
through Thursday, the latter weekdays comprising the lowest load factor
days. The so-called Family Fare Plan became popular with many travelers
and generated additional revenues for American. Before long, other competitors advertised similar options, still with the CAB's blessing.[20]

Nonetheless, such family fare programs were not at all comparable to
the idea of an entire plane full of budget-priced seats offered as "coach
fares," in contrast to the customary planeload of passengers who all paid
first-class prices, since the airlines still offered what amounted to one-
class service. For the most part, travel for the masses in the postwar years
owed its origins to the impact of nonscheduled airlines, known in the industry as "nonskeds," who packed air transports with economically priced
seats. This upstart group bought cheap, war-surplus transports, hired pilots from the ranks of thousands of ex-military officers, kept operational
costs under tight control, and became aggressive renegades. Their biggest
appeal came on long-haul routes, where established scheduled airlines had
reigned supreme. The bumptious nonskeds came up with the idea of
group travel, advertised bargain-basement fares to tantalizing vacation
spots, and attracted many people who had never flown before. The major airlines tried to control them by relying on regulatory strictures applied through the CAB.

Stanley Weiss, a veteran of the Air Transport Command, operated one
of the most nettlesome nonskeds, known as the North American Airlines
Agency. Weiss and a partner began just after the war, running a lone war-
surplus DC-3 as a cargo line dubbed Fireball Air Express (FAE), with

nonscheduled service between California and New York. After carrying a few adventurous passengers, the CAB granted Weiss an operational passenger certificate as a "large irregular carrier," to differentiate FAE and other companies like it from intrastate carriers who flew much shorter routes, usually in small general aviation aircraft. In 1948, reacting to an increasing tempo of operations like those of Weiss, the CAB announced a limit of eight round-trip flights per month for the "large irregular carriers." Over the next two years, Weiss ingeniously created a North American Airlines Agency, purchasing a collection of six similar large irregular carriers. Operating as a ticketing organization that sold transcontinental seats on each of the individual companies, North American Airlines combined the CAB certificates of all the operators. In this way, Weiss could patch together a coordinated schedule of transcontinental flights priced at $99 one way and $160 round-trip. The scheduled transcontinentals charged $159 for a first-class one-way fare; $110 for one-way night coach. The bargain flights eschewed amenities dispensed by the regular carriers and always flew at 85 percent capacity, all of which kept operating costs under control. Sometimes flight departures were delayed a day or two until the requisite number of seats were sold, but the cheap fares kept passengers coming. If irregular schedules brought low prices, many travelers clearly didn't mind.

During the early 1950s, complaints to the CAB from the scheduled carriers grew in volume and indignation, especially after 1951, when North American Airlines (NAA) began operating DC-4 transports, which not only appealed to passengers but also made NAA look like a big, regular airline. By the mid 1950s, NAA introduced fast, pressurized DC-6B transports, making it a thoroughly modern operation. Publicity brochures and other marketing literature (produced in cooperation with Douglas Aircraft) pitched NAA as one of the accepted air transport companies that offered several long-distance city connections as well as coast-to-coast flights at bargain prices. Other renegades, following the example of NAA, not only competed on United States domestic routes but also won military contracts for overseas flights. In Europe, during the Berlin Airlift, the nonskeds carried 25 percent of the passengers and 57 percent of the cargo tonnage. During the Korean War, 50 percent of commercial air tonnage flown into the zone of warfare arrived aboard aircraft of nonsked contractors.

Confronted by the continuing success of NAA on the choice transcontinental runs, Smith and American Airlines were especially blunt in presentations to the CAB. They argued that an airline named North American, for instance, should not be allowed to operate in view of the confusion created by the similarity to American Airlines' own name. In any case, in July 1955 the CAB took steps to revoke North American Airline Agency's collection of operating certificates due to "serious and willful violations" of the CAB's economic regulations. The CAB's case notes stressed that the North American Airline group had been denied its routes due to the "unwillingness of the North American Airlines group to comply with the Act and the board's regulations." Clearly, NAA had been making passenger flights in a manner that was neither intended nor countenanced by the original CAB certificates. Despite months of determined legal maneuvering, NAA's authority to operate expired early in 1957, and the Supreme Court upheld the CAB's position.

Still, the legacy of Weiss and his cohorts changed the nature of operations for American, its companions in the Big Four, and other airlines. They had used the CAB as a buffer to fend off the nonskeds, but consequently found it prudent to emulate them. Forced to offer coach fares on major routes in order to be competitive, American began some coast-to-coast coach fares in 1949, and about 7 percent of the airline's patrons flew coach class by 1951. Three years later, nearly a quarter of American's passengers bought coach tickets, and the number kept rising. Thanks to the CAB, Weiss attracted an untapped clientele of families and non-business travelers who had never flown. With the CAB's change of heart, American and others took advantage of this legacy and expanded it many times over.[21]

Stimulating Technological Change

Smith always wanted to equal or exceed the competition in speed over American's domestic routes. The DC-6B continued to be an efficient transport, but TWA acquired an improved Lockheed airliner in 1951, the L-1049 Super Constellation, which raised Smith's blood pressure. The new series of Constellations not only beat the DC-6B in speed but could also offer nonstop service on east-bound transcontinental trips, taking advantage of the prevailing winds. Characteristically, Smith wanted a better airplane—one that could outspeed the Super Constellation and fly nonstop coast-to-coast in either direction. Moreover, the management at American now accepted the idea of coach travel as a solid source of revenue. Acquisition of a newer and faster transport would permit the transfer of older DC-6 models to serve this promising new market. Accordingly, Smith sent a terse memo to American's engineers, directing them to develop specifications for a coast-to-coast airliner.

At about the same time, the airline industry began to pick up rumors about an improved version of the Curtiss-Wright R-3350 radial engine. The engine manufacturer proposed to uprate this proven engine in a conversion arrangement, using exhaust gases fed through a turbine system to increase available horsepower. Called a turbo-compound engine, it could raise the horsepower, speed, and range of the new transport for American Airlines. The company's engineering department argued that the new power plant could be mated to a lengthened DC-6B; the plane's efficient seating, clean design, and higher horsepower would give it the advantage over TWA's Super Constellations.

At this point, the only problems appeared to be convincing the conservative Douglas Aircraft Company to proceed with such a design and to consider whether or not the plane had a useful life before the new generation of jet transports displaced it. Truculently, Smith leaned on Douglas until they finally agreed to forge ahead with the new DC-7, but only after Smith threatened to take his business to a different manufacturer. Even though American eventually operated a fleet of 58 models of the DC-7, and a DC-7C version flew on some of Pan Am's transoceanic routes, the plane seemed to be only a qualified success. Part of the difficulties stemmed from the powerplant, and part stemmed from operating characteristics that embroiled the Civil Aeronautics Authority in a controversial ruling that subsequently led to conflict with the pilot's union and a strike that nobody really wanted. In attempting to respond to technical operating factors that had been unanticipated, the federal regulatory agency actually wound up supporting C. R. Smith, but some related labor-management perceptions created a nasty problem for Smith and his airline.

The production version of the DC-7 delivered to American came with four Curtiss-Wright Turbo-Compound R-3350 engines, each rated at 3,250 horsepower. The new engines also mounted more efficient four-bladed propellers, and the fuselage included a forty-inch stretch to accommodate added passenger seats. Typical cruising speed went up to 360 MPH, compared with 311 MPH for the DC-6B and 327 MPH for the Super Constellations. For the inauguration of commercial service from New York to Los Angeles on November 29, 1953, American pulled out all the stops, with a special plastic model of the plane in American's livery produced by the Revell Company, a lavish reception scheduled in Hollywood, the presence of sundry movie stars, and the nonstop flight itself, with seats filled mainly by the press. The plane got as far as Colorado Springs, where a balky engine required a forced landing. The complex turbo-compound system proved troublesome during the plane's entire operational career. Even when all four engines worked, there were often other predicaments.[22]

During 1954, American's eastward service began to set records for commercial flights. One DC-7, pushed by tailwinds, roared from Los Angeles to New York's Idlewild Airport in six hours and ten minutes. A day later, American set an unofficial record over the same route with a flight that took only five hours and fifty-one minutes. The difficulties occurred on westbound flights, when strong headwinds proved to be more of a hindrance than planned. The Civil Aeronautics Administration had a rule that limited airline pilots to no more than eight hours of flying time on a scheduled run. Prior to the era of nonstop transcontinental schedules, crew changes en route were simply part of the routine. With the advent of the DC-7, eastbound trips normally took less than eight hours. No problem. Some westbound nonstop flights landed within the eight hour envelope; with headwinds, many did not. American's engineers worked overtime to squeeze more power from the engines and try other aerodynamic tricks to meet the CAA limitations. The airline's management finally accepted the inevitable, realizing that miscalculations about western headwinds at the DC-7's best operational altitudes were going to result in consistent flights over the eight-hour limit. This admission produced a scheduling problem that dropped into the lap of the CAB.

Both pilots and CAB officials had held off taking action, hoping for a technological fix, until the pilots formally requested a break in westbound flights to land at a designated airport and take on a fresh crew. American and other carriers wanted a CAB waiver, arguing the peculiarities of the case. During subsequent hearings, the airlines convinced the board that such a waiver would not endanger passengers on delayed nonstop flights of over eight hours. The board accepted arguments from airline management that the total "duty time" of pilots (time included on the ground in multistop operations) would actually be somewhat less, on the average. The Airline Pilots Association protested vehemently, and pilots at American went on strike, even though only 5 percent of American's pilots would be affected by the rule. Most of these airmen were senior pilots who actually preferred the coast-to-coast nonstop duty as a less demanding operational assignment. But the ALPA leadership was angry about American's reluctance to renegotiate the technical aspects of the issue. On American's side, Smith had long mistrusted ALPA leadership. The strike lasted from July 31 until August 24, 1954, a time of heavy travel that clearly hurt American's revenues. In the end, American won its point in obtaining a waiver of the eight-hour rule as it applied to DC-7 coast-to-coast schedules. The ALPA won concessions in terms of overtime benefits and certain other work rules. The CAB action favored American and its Big Four cohorts, but it came with some added expenses.[23]

Seeking New Routes

Even though the Big Four criss-crossed the United States on assigned routes, parceled out and presided over by the CAB, each airline evolved a philosophy and style of operations that became something of a signature. Eastern Air Lines possessed a high proportion of short-haul routes, and many longer ones involved a series of stops. Because of this segmentation, Eastern's managers concluded that the wisest operational strategy depended on keeping its fleet in the air as much as possible. In short, Eastern aimed for the greatest utilization of its equipment. American's longer route and coast-to-coast schedules led to a somewhat different style of utilization during the late 1940s and early 1950s. "American Airlines . . . finds no virtue for its own purposes in flying an airplane whenever it becomes available," noted the editors of *Fortune* magazine, "which may be at some ungodly hour of the night." American chose to put its planes in the air when it most suited the convenience of customers. Instead of flying a nearly empty transport in the middle of the night, American's dispatchers absorbed the cost of an empty airliner sitting on the tarmac until a full load materialized in the morning. "In trade language," *Fortune* explained, "American prefers a high load factor to high utilization."[24]

Nevertheless, American consistently tried to add new destinations. Beginning in 1953, the CAB opened a series of hearings. In November 1955, the CAB rendered its decision in the Denver Service Route Case. Within its provisions, American won authority to fly nonstop service between Chicago and San Francisco, using Chicago as an interim stop between San Francisco and New York. During the fall, the CAB also handed down its judgment on the Southwest/Northeast Service Case, giving American a new route, Houston–New York via Nashville and Pittsburgh. But the new authority also awarded to Braniff in this case erased American's monopoly elsewhere, including the route between Dallas and the lucrative New York market.

For many years, American tried to acquire routes in the South and Southeast that would feed into existing service between Dallas and the West Coast, thus creating a strong transcontinental network through the southern tier of states. Rival airlines in the South eyed American's western market with equal acquisitive passion. The CAB's interest in sustaining smaller operations often frustrated American Airlines' petitions for new routes. Shrewdly, Smith garnered cooperation from others of the "Big Four" (and sometimes regional airlines) and forged other sorts of route extensions to tap new market centers. As a means of building traffic across the southern tier, American cooperated in selected interchange routes from 1949 to 1961. Passengers in Miami, for example, bought a single ticket to the West Coast and made the trip in the same airplane; at intermediate stops, crews from National, Delta, and American boarded the plane and piloted the flight over appropriate segments along the way. Understandably, American wanted to win authority to fly into the Southeast region and accrue ticket payments for the whole journey.

Because American was already a major carrier, it usually faced problems in implementing this approach. Under the prevailing law, whenever the CAB considered one new request, it also had to weigh additional applications from rival airlines as alternative ways to achieve the same additional service. Invariably, such alternative considerations affected schedules other than the original application. Each round of deliberations by the CAB could result in both "wins" and "losses," as in Braniff's clearance for Dallas–New York trips. A somewhat similar conundrum happened to American in the Southern Transcontinental Route Case, debated in 1960–61. American hoped for a solid, coast-to-coast award and came out of the proceedings with two additional western routes, Houston–Los Angeles and Houston–San Francisco, with several intermediate stops. But American did not receive the authority it desired for flights from California through Dallas and on into the southern and southeastern markets. Instead, Delta and National won major transcontinental routes from Florida to West Coast cities such as San Diego, Los Angeles, and San Francisco. Consequently, potential traffic carried by American from Texas to western destinations now shifted to Delta and National. Continental also received a certificate for Houston–San Antonio–El Paso–Tucson–Phoenix–Los Angeles, adding to American's problems.[25]

Attempting Expansion through Mergers

For American, the CAB seemed to serve best as a buffer against all-out predators that wanted to gain pieces of American's longer routes between major cities and along its transcontinental network. At the same time, Smith's own hunting expeditions for major trophies were often constrained by the same CAB. In contrast to its major competitors, Smith's airline actually acquired relatively few new destinations. The CAB's tilt in support of the smaller trunklines substantially checked American's frequent efforts to expand. In the "Southwest/Northeast Service Case," the CAB's findings specifically acknowledged that "the Board's objective is to so strengthen the smaller trunks . . . to continue to compete effectively with the larger carriers." According to the company's own annual report of 1968, less than 20 percent of American's passenger miles came from routes awarded since 1938. The average for major U.S. domestic carriers, on the other hand, came to 40 percent or more. American's few additional routes came slowly, one at a time, carefully argued and won during CAB hearings over several decades after the war. There were some exceptions, as when the company attempted a substantial expansion through direct takeover of another airline. Such moves were bound to be controversial, because acquisition of an entire system would inevitably trigger alarm in the boardrooms of other immediate competitors.

Consequently, Smith moved boldly but carefully in these matters. One such move occurred just after the war; the second transpired in the early 1960s.

Smith's role in the ATC made him well acquainted with the political scene in Washington, D.C. During the first several years after the end of the war, American operated a bifurcated headquarters, with Smith often spending more time in Washington than he did in New York City. Ambitious airlines bombarded the CAB's staff with postwar route applications; Smith wanted to be in the middle of the action in order to advance American's own aspirations and to fend off zealous new competitors as well as chesslike moves of old guard carriers like United, TWA, and Eastern. American submitted a number of its own individual route requests to the CAB, but its key strategy involved a bid to acquire Mid-Continent Airlines.

After close analysis, Smith and his planning staff concluded that at least 60 percent of Mid-Continent's destinations represented new cities for American Airlines, ranging from Minneapolis/St. Paul in the upper Midwest, to Des Moines, Omaha, and Kansas City in the Midwest, to New Orleans on the Gulf Coast. Smith's team had the merger papers filed with the CAB before the end of 1945, but legal tangles and counter-applications from agitated rivals delayed the proceedings until 1952, when the CAB denied American's move. Instead, the regional carrier, Braniff, took over Mid-Continent, consolidating the former's routes through the Midwest and eliminating the latter as something that the CAB perceived to be a comparatively anemic transportation system.[26]

The turbulence occasioned by American's gesture toward Mid-Continent subsided soon enough. Smith's next significant merger campaign generated so much heartburn in the industry that he eventually found it more prudent to retreat. In 1962, Smith announced a move to take over none other than one of his cohorts in the Big Four: Eastern Air Lines.

The proposed marriage of American and Eastern involved several diverse events. Looming in the background was the fact that American no longer reigned as the country's biggest air transport organization. During the spring of 1961, United Air Lines completed its acquisition of Capital Airlines. American had also taken a look at ailing Capital before United successfully argued its case before the CAB. But American's offi-

Smith took over Southern Air Transport and its biplanes in 1930. By 1973, the date of this photograph, Smith had become an elder statesman of the airline industry. The decorative motif in his tie represents the silhouette of a jet airliner. In later years he spent nearly as much time with industry affairs as with his own airline. (Photo by Fabian Bachrach. Courtesy of American Airlines)

cers balked at Capital's debt structure; moreover, Capital's route network in the Northeast basically duplicated that of American. Smith understood that Capital had to find a merger partner and simply made a better fit with United. Consequently, he realistically stepped aside to let Pat Patterson of United become a successful suitor. But the resulting United-Capital merger meant that American's main rival in the airline community now had bragging rights in terms of size.

As it turned out, American was already in the process of discussions that promised an even more dramatic merger. At Eastern, board chairman Laurance Rockefeller had become increasingly skeptical of Eddie Rickenbacker's stewardship. Consequently, in 1959, Eastern brought in a new president and CEO, Malcolm A. MacIntyre, who had just finished a one-year tour as the undersecretary of the United States Air Force. Before that, MacIntyre had been one of C. R. Smith's trusted lawyers at American Airlines. Early in his tenure at Eastern, MacIntyre launched the pioneering Air Shuttle service between New York City and Washington, but even the success of this innovative operation had not staved off mounting troubles for Eastern, which lost nearly $10 million in 1961. From his position on Eastern's board, Rockefeller continued to wield considerable influence. Unknown to Eastern's management, Rockefeller and C. R. Smith began discussing a merger during the year. American filed a merger application with the CAB in January 1962.[27]

By the time the deadline arrived for filing statements with the CAB, the board had twenty-six lengthy briefs to consider. Only one of the briefs supported the American and Eastern merger: the Chamber of Commerce of Corpus Christi, Texas, somewhat plaintively argued that the state would benefit from additional schedules over Eastern's existing connections. All the other depositions, especially those from the airline community, remained adamantly opposed. Smaller airlines, like Continental, Delta, and Piedmont, heatedly argued that a combination of the country's second and fourth largest airlines would quite simply put them at an insurmountable disadvantage. For the first time in the memory of the CAB staff, even the Justice Department weighed in with a negative opinion, noting that the postmerger airline would account for 85 percent of the intercity traffic in seven key market regions. Consequently, the Justice Department ominously concluded that the wedding of American and Eastern "would adversely affect transportation in the U.S." The CAB's own Bureau of Economic Regulation issued an equally discouraging set of preliminary remarks, with phrases such as "would create a monopoly . . . competitive imbalance . . . the public interest in the long run would be disadvantaged." More trouble seemed to be brewing on Capitol Hill, where A. S. "Mike" Monroney, chair of the Senate Aviation Subcommittee, and Emmanuel Celler, head of the House Antitrust Subcommittee, voiced opposition to the whole idea.[28]

How had American and its management appeared to have so badly miscalculated their CAB proposal? For one thing, Smith apparently believed that his benign acquiescence during United's takeover of Capital would be reciprocated by Patterson and other carriers. There was also the fact that American would have emerged as the incontestably biggest airline in the nation, an accolade that Smith had temporarily ceded to United but did not wish to surrender permanently.[29] Moreover, from American's point of view, there were worthwhile business reasons for the merger that Smith believed should also make sense to the CAB and to the airline industry as a whole. Despite the potential for the merged airline to dominate certain market areas, the deal would still leave some 70 percent of the nation's air transport business to other carriers. The merger represented a good fit, since Eastern's network covered territory in the mid-Atlantic coastal region and throughout the Southeast, where American was less of a presence. Eastern's peak seasons of winter and spring would balance American's heavy traffic in summer and fall.

Moreover, Alan Boyd, President Kennedy's own appointee as CAB chair in 1961, had said that he was in favor of mergers to create financially stronger companies, especially when the costs of big, new jet airliners came to $5 million or $6 million each. Eastern, in its CAB presentations, noted that its route system of short hops, service to many smaller cities, marginal load factors, and skyrocketing costs necessitated a merger with a partner such as American, whose traffic patterns included many long-haul routes and major cities, yielding strong income. Jointly, American and Eastern declared that their union would represent a means of "correcting the costly duplications of routes and facilities which are crippling air transportation."[30]

A fascinated national press followed the progress of the proposed merger of two airline kingpins through a series of intense CAB hearings that ensued during the summer and fall of 1962. United Air Lines became the principal antagonist, supported by seriously affected regionals, principally Delta and Continental, that served the Southeast, Gulf Coast, and Southwest. Even though the board's economic regulation bureau clearly questioned the merger, the CAB often overruled the board in its final report. "Despite the turbulence," *Newsweek* reported in August, "American and Eastern remained hopeful of a successful, if not entirely smooth, flight." American's own public releases remained aggressively upbeat: "In its starkest terms, the issue in the American-Eastern merger is: Is there going to be an efficient and dynamic air transportation system capable of meeting the vital future requirements of our national economy, or will the industry be allowed to decay?" Eastern, for its part, insisted that its merger with American would save $150 million per year in terms of capital and related expenses for Eastern alone.[31]

By December, the merger turbulence reported by *Newsweek* had become a dark storm. In a 119-page report, CAB examiner Ralph L. Wiser recommended that the board not approve the union of American and Eastern, and the national press carefully dissected the issues. Basically, news stories repeated Wiser's argument that the merger would disrupt the competitive balance of the industry. In the Northeast particularly, American would have new routes so as to create a monopoly. Also, the merger would lead to additional and unjustified competition on the southern transcontinental route, to the sharp disadvantage of carriers like Delta. Reporters picked up on the Examiner's sharpest barbs, which were aimed at Eastern, run by the increasingly conservative and outspoken Eddie Rickenbacker. That airline's problems were not caused primarily by an unfavorable route structure and unwarranted competition; rather, as news magazines recounted the gist of Weiser's report, Eastern suffered from competition because the airline had dithered too long in acquiring jets and had also done a poor job of scheduling. Many problems were the result of strikes at Eastern and the company's poor public relations. Further, Wiser declared that declining profits in the industry stemmed not from excess competition but from excess capacity. Additionally, news writers repeated the CAB examiner's argument that future board policy should buttress smaller carriers rather than permit members of the Big Four to get bigger.

For a short time, Smith remained hopeful that the board would disavow the examiner's truculent report. Since the merger also involved international routes (Mexico, Bermuda, and Puerto Rico), the last word in such cases still rested with the White House. Perhaps President Kennedy would decide to adopt American's arguments to sustain a healthy solvency over excessive competition. Smith also hoped that his long friendship with a fellow Texan, Vice President Lyndon Baines Johnson, might also win a favorable opinion from Kennedy. From the beginning, American's legal strategy rested on an interpretation that the Federal Regulation Act of 1958 exempted regulated airlines from antitrust laws. This was an optimistic reading of the law that simply didn't find any sympathy in the Kennedy administration. Early in 1963, Smith made his own decision about the merger after he picked up consistent reports about the mood among the board members to vote no. Before the board met, Smith called Eastern's management to advise canceling the deal. By this time, Eastern wanted to avoid any more negative publicity. Smith then authorized a news release from American that announced the cancellation of merger discussions, avoiding the discomfiture of an adverse finding from the CAB.[32]

Into the Jet Era

In the hearings regarding the American-Eastern merger, the issue of ragged finances simply as a function of excess capacity underscored a debate that had already engaged Smith, the airlines, the CAB, and the press. In the decade after 1945, there had been a series of roller-coaster thrills as the airline industry sorted out its traffic patterns, new equipment, and finances. Having arrived at some semblance of stability by the mid-1950s, analysts looking into the future were both optimistic and cautious about the next decade. "Once again," Forbes reported in 1956, "glowing predictions about the future of air transportation are pouring out of every airline office in the land." Some airline operators predicted a doubling of air traffic by 1960; even the cautious CAA projected the number of passengers to double, hedging its bet by putting the threshold at 1965, when domestic airlines would carry 70 million passengers.

For many observers, the most pressing issue concerned the impending arrival of expensive jets and whether or not Smith was justified in gambling that rising numbers of passengers would fill jet airliner seats. As *Forbes* summed it up, "If the expected traffic doesn't materialize by the time the big jets begin rolling off the lines at Douglas and Boeing, every airline, including American, may be in for some woeful lumps."[33]

Smith, for his part, was ready to move into the new environment of jet transports. The management team at American remained confident that their aggressive techniques of finance, strategic planning, and market development would be more than adequate to cope with the imminent challenge of the jet generation. Some people in the regulatory agencies continued to express concerns about funding for the costly new jets and worried that excess capacity might erode load factors. All of these problems could lead to financially weakened carriers whose eventual collapse would degrade the nation's air services. Smith bowled ahead, full of confidence for his industry and his own airline and ready to confront skeptics and the CAB in print.

Smith always liked to best his competition by purchasing bigger, faster planes and buying them ahead of other operators. He argued that such aircraft invariably outperformed their predecessors and made more money. Jets would do the same thing. To this end, American planned to have a $75 million fleet of Lockheed Electra turboprops in service by 1958. The following year, American also scheduled the inauguration of Boeing 707 transcontinental operations, a jet fleet represented by an order of $165 million. American's strategy of buying quantities of new planes ahead of everybody else gave its accountants the advantage of writing off the costs of these new aircraft before the next generation of fleet replacement orders went out to manufacturers. In 1956, American's fleet was 67 percent depreciated, compared with TWA, which reported 46 percent, and United, which reported 58 percent. With annual depreciation charges for American at a much lower rate, the return on investment worked out much higher.[34]

Not every business pundit who looked at the CAA's budget figures and traffic statistics felt the same robust confidence as Smith. A *Fortune* piece in February 1956 criticized the industry, chiding them in the article's title, "The Airlines' Flight from Reality." In particular, the article predicted that all the indicators pointed toward excess capacity by the early 1960s, when new turboprops and jet airliners would begin to arrive on top of the existing piston engine fleet of aircraft. Smith bluntly reminded readers that the CAA had underestimated passenger-miles in the past and appeared to be making the same mistake in its predictions for the early 1960s. More to the point, argued Smith, airlines would proceed to retire large components of their piston fleet in favor of the more productive turboprops and jets; the overcapacity implied by the CAA and *Fortune* simply would not materialize. He stressed the gas turbine's cheap fuel, lighter weight, and smaller frontal area, which decisively reduced parasitic drag. In retiring older equipment in favor of better, more productive planes, Smith acknowledged the CAB's favorable practice of "permitting depreciation rates and charge-offs in keeping with the technical advances of the airplane."

Finally, Smith admitted that the rising costs of planes might seem daunting but would be overcome by better utilization rates, aggressive merchandising especially to fill out seasonal and weekly fluctuations, and continuing increase in traffic volume. Smith closed on a cautionary note. If the CAB continued to expand the routes of some carriers, sometimes pitting five or more airlines against each other along some networks, disaster could follow. "This could result in thinning out of the traffic potential," Smith argued, "making it more difficult to obtain load factors essential to economical operation." This aspect "could conflict with the airlines' program for 1961."[35]

By 1958, with jets due for introduction the next year, the news media ran optimistic stories, often focusing on C. R. Smith, since American planned to inaugurate domestic service with the Boeing 707 in January of the following year. *Time* reported that any spot on earth could be

Rising Airplane Costs (excluding spare parts)	
Douglas DC-6	
1946	$588,000
1949	$751,000
1951	$874,000
Douglas DC-6B	
1951	$941,000
1953	$1,023,000
1955	$1,494,000

Source: Fortune, July 1956, 12.

reached in a day's flight by jetliner, shrinking the world by 40 percent. "Weekend flights to London and Paris will be as easy," *Time* promised, "perhaps easier than weekend drives to the country in jampacked Sunday traffic." In this heady environment, American and other airlines optimistically eyed the 70 percent of adult citizens who had never flown and expected a highly enthusiastic response to jet airliners. American reported that its first eight weeks of transcontinental jet flights were already booked solid. The only major problem seemed to be a lag in airport modernization and airway traffic control upgrades to handle faster jets.[36]

Subsequent events proved unsettling for Smith, the CAB, and the airlines. In early 1962, despite crowded air terminals, the carriers seemed to be in financial straits. *U.S. News and World Report* printed an interview with C. R. Smith, "Why Airlines Are in Trouble," to try to sort out answers. Basically, Smith reiterated his position that the CAB permitted too many carriers on productive routes. There was too much duplication of some network segments. That was an important reason why American argued for its merger with Eastern.[37] But with the collapse of the Eastern merger option, American had to face other realities.

For all of Smith's optimism, the early transition to jet aircraft did not occur smoothly, especially for American. The Lockheed Electra, powered by a quartet of Allison turboprops, turned out to have excellent performance, entering service first with Eastern in January 1959, followed by

American a few days later. But in September 1959, one of Braniff's Electras crashed, followed by an accident with Northwest in March of the following year. The FAA imposed speed restrictions while federal, airline, and manufacturers' investigators looked for answers. Their combined analysis finally identified and explained the problem as a severe vibration phenomenon leading to structural weakness of the wing. The speed restrictions lasted until January 1961, when final modifications to production and service aircraft were completed. With a fleet of thirty-five Electra transports assigned to key routes, Smith remained grateful to the FAA for not imposing a ban on all flights. Such a grounding would have constituted a major problem for American; the compromise with the FAA to follow strict speed restrictions represented a successful balance between safety and financial exigency. Even so, load factors suffered as did American's balance sheets throughout the Electra's market network.[38]

American experienced additional market problems and budget setbacks with the Convair 990A, a somewhat larger and presumably faster version of the high-performance Convair 880 ordered in 1956 by TWA and Delta. Predictably, Smith wanted a faster jet to outrun TWA, but the vaunted 990A never met its promised speed, despite some innovative aerodynamic fixes in terms of airfoil sections and unusual "antishock fairings" at the wing's trailing edge to enhance high-speed cruise capability. American put the type into service in March 1962, but Smith grumpily began to phase the disappointing jetliner out of service within a matter of months. Clearly, the higher speeds and aerodynamic quirks of the new jet airliners brought additional potential for operational conundrums, even for as shrewd a figure as C. R. Smith.[39]

There were other decisions inflicted by the CAB that created frustrations. During the Southern Transcontinental Route Hearings, in the spring of 1961, American hoped to obtain nonstop authority from Atlanta and Miami to the West Coast. But the results dashed Smith's hopes, as National and Delta suddenly emerged as transcontinental carriers and Braniff won authority to fly into New York. In the end, American not only came away with nothing, but also had to accept a new ruling that left its last pair of unduplicated routes (Dallas–New York and Dallas–Los Angeles) open for competition from other airlines.[40]

Nonetheless, Smith's airline continued to flourish, occasionally adding an additional scheduled flight, reflecting the general effects of prosperity in the United States. During the 1960s, all airlines, including American, benefited from the nation's economic growth. By 1970, per capita disposable income had doubled from the level of 1940; the national GNP rose from $355 billion to $727 billion. All of this fueled airline travel during the 1960s, when the number of annual airline passengers on scheduled carriers soared from 56 million to 158 million.[41] Smith and his cohorts decisively tapped that 70 percent of potential airline passengers who had not flown during the previous decade.

Conclusion

The career of C. R. Smith represented an on-again, off-again relationship with the government's air service regulators—a "civilized" marriage of bureaucratic propriety. The CAB's position materially aided American's aspirations for transatlantic operations, and the government's eventual decision to bless the purchase of American Overseas Airlines by Pan Am formalized Smith's change of heart. American Airlines made its point during the DC-7 crew controversy, and the CAA eventually acceded. The CAB served as an effective cohort in skirmishes with the nonskeds; government research assistance helped solve the DC-6 in-flight fires; the FAA's forbearance during the Lockheed Electra hiatus saved American from severe hardship on many of its routes. On the other hand, the CAB clearly frustrated American's drives for dramatic expansion by acquiring Mid-Continent in 1952 and merging with Eastern a decade later. Smith and the CAB each entertained quite opposite views on the issue of excess capacity.

Meanwhile, American picked up a domestic route here and there, continually consolidating its domestic market and its firm position as a major coast-to-coast airline system. The company still cast glances at the prospects of routes abroad. During the 1940s and 1950s, American essayed occasional forays into the Latin American arena, using connections to Mexico City as a beachhead. These sorties were often troublesome, involving only a handful of weekly runs and intermittently cut off by CAB rulings. Beginning in 1966, American fared better in the Transpacific Route Cases, with periodic flights to destinations in the Southeast Pacific, including New Zealand and Australia. These represented a growing degree of flexibility by the CAB in expanding competition on international routes. American's broad domestic network, feeding into expanding patterns of overseas travel, made it a powerful contender. Pacific flights were followed by Caribbean destinations; by the time deregulation became a reality in 1978, American's experience on foreign routes facilitated successful expansion. During the early 1990s, American had become one of the principal operators across the Atlantic.[42]

By this time, Smith had long since retired, surrendering control of American Airlines in 1968. Smith's continuing association with the inner circles of the Democratic Party, along with his Texan connections, kept him near the top of various lists for political assignments. He accepted a request from President Johnson and served nine months as secretary of commerce in 1968. Following his stint as federal bureaucrat and later as an investment banker, he returned to American as president for several months in 1973–74 during a time of administrative turmoil in the boardroom. On his second departure, in 1974, Smith announced his intention to stay retired. He explained that he had a DC-6 mind; the new jet-age industry moved too fast and involved too many changes.

Nonetheless, he continued to keep an eye on his airline and on the industry he had helped shape. Late in 1977, on the eve of deregulation, he exchanged correspondence with Albert Casey, who had taken over as head of American. They discussed the possibility of united action by the major airlines to alert the public about the potential pitfalls of an unregulated airline industry. As he looked at the situation, Smith worried about the future and confessed that he "would not give very good odds about the future of the airlines."[43] In retrospect, Smith's worries seemed premature. American not only survived in the crosscurrents of the new competitive environment but seemed to flourish. Its success was a fitting legacy.

Notes

1. "Jets across the U.S.," *Time,* 17 November 1958, 87.

2. Aspects of Smith's background come from miscellaneous public relations releases in the files of the C. R. Smith Aviation Museum Archives, cited hereafter as SAMA. The author wishes to thank Jay Miller, museum director, and Shannon Risk, archivist, for access to these files and for continued assistance on this project. Thanks also to Bret Nelson, M.A., J.D., who helped me negotiate the thicket of legal sources. I also wish to acknowledge Carlene Roberts Lawrence, one of the

first women to hold a major executive position in the airline industry, who reviewed the manuscript covering her years at American Airlines and supplied additional information. For a review of Smith's career and leadership at American Airlines, see Roger Bilstein, "C. R. Smith," in William M. Leary, ed., *Encyclopedia of American Business History and Biography: The Airline Industry* (New York: Facts on File, 1992), 435–46, cited hereafter as Leary, *Airline Industry*.

3. Details of American's genesis are recounted in R. E. G. Davies, *Airlines of the United States since 1914*, rev. ed. (Washington, D.C.: Smithsonian Institution, 1982). See also Henry Ladd Smith, *Airways: The History of Commercial Aviation in the United States* (New York: Knopf, 1942). For a colorful summary of the RFC connection and the DC-3's origins, see Frederick Allen, "The Letter That Changed the Way We Fly," *American Heritage of Invention and Technology* 4 (fall 1988): 713. For the Lamar Hotel's "8F" crowd, see Barry J. Kaplan, "Houston: The Golden Buckle of the Sunbelt," in Richard M. Bernard and Bradley R. Rice, *Sunbelt Cities* (Austin: University of Texas Press, 1983), 203–4; on the attitudes of Jesse Jones and the ideology of anticolonialism he shared with many Texans, see Walter Buenger, "Jesse Jones," in Kenneth Hendrickson and Michael Collins, eds., *Profiles in Power: Twentieth-Century Texans in Washington* (Arlington, Tex.: Harlan Davidson, 1993), 71, 78–80.

4. Bilstein, "Smith," in Leary, *Airline Industry*, 438; author's correspondence with Carlene Roberts Lawrence. There is much anecdotal material and detail on Smith's career in Robert J. Serling, *Eagle: The History of American Airlines* (New York: St. Martin's Press, 1985). Smith and the ATC are discussed on pp. 160–64, 167–80.

5. A flag line is an airline designated as the principal carrier for its country of origin. It receives financial subsidies from the national government.

A chosen instrument is an airline designated as a country's principal carrier for certain destinations or geographic regions. The airline may receive special consideration from its government in the allocation of mail contracts, passenger routes, and so on.

6. On Smith's early adventurous forays into international connections and dirigible travel, I have relied on file materials from the Smith Aviation Museum, along with relevant brochures, photos, and scripting from museum exhibits about American Airlines in the 1930s. See also Henry Ladd Smith, *Airways Abroad: The Story of American World Air Routes* (Madison: University of Wisconsin Press, 1950), 273, 340, which comments on the Mexican forays. On the early CAB imbroglios over North Atlantic routes and the Amex affair, see Donald Whitnah, "Civil Aeronautics Board," in Leary, *Airline Industry*, 105–7; and *Pan American Airways Co. vs. CAB and American Export Lines, Inc.*, U.S. Circuit Court of Appeals, 2d Cir., July 16, 1941, 121 F. 2d *810 United States Aviation Reports* (1941), 138–50.

7. James M. Mangan and Michael W. Carnegie, "American Export Airlines, American Overseas Airlines: A Short History" (August 1978), typescript report; *American Airlines Department of Economic Planning*, "Foreign Policy May Come Fast," memo (March 28, 1944). Copies in SAMA, Foreign Policy Files; Smith, *Airways Abroad*, 54–61.

8. Serling, *Eagle*, 186–89; Smith, *Airways Abroad*, 226–44; Mangan and Carnegie, "American Export," 1–7.

9. Mangan and Carnegie, "American Export," 7–12.

10. C. R. Smith, undated memo, "To the Employers of American Airlines, Inc. and of American Overseas Airlines, Inc.," in SAMA, Foreign Policy Files; Serling, *Eagle*, 225–26. Smith quotation is from the latter.

11. Mangan and Carnegie, "American Export," 7–13; Smith, *Airways Abroad*, 317–19; North Atlantic Route Transfer Case, CAB Docket No. 3589 et al., July 10, 1950, *United States Aviation Reports* (September 1950), 335–45.

12. "Merger Agreement in Final Stages: Sale of American Overseas Airlines to Pan Am Airways," *Aviation Week*, 13 February 1950, 44; Carl Solberg, *Conquest of the Skies: A History of Commercial Aviation in America* (Boston: Little, Brown, 1979), 306–9; "Riding High in a New Era: A Conversation with C. R. Smith," *Nation's Business* 54 (March 1966): 47. Smith quotation is from the latter. Wesley Phillips Newton gives a somewhat different version of the final CAB decision, writing that "Trippe approached Secretary of State George C. Marshall, who persuaded President Truman to reverse the CAB decision against Pan American." Newton, "Juan T. Trippe," in Leary, *Airline Industry*, 475.

13. Whitnah, "Civil Aeronautics Board," in Leary, *Airline Industry*, 106. Between 1942 and 1958, American maintained a periodic presence in Mexico through a wholly owned subsidiary, American Airlines de Mexico, flying mainly Mexico to Dallas and San Antonio. Nonetheless, Smith failed to win a direct Chicago-Mexico nonstop flight until 1957; American essentially remained a continental U.S. operation.

14. "A General's Return," *Time*, 25 June 1945, 76. No U.S. airline ever achieved 1,000 planes. During the 1990s, American deployed 630–40 aircraft (excluding American Eagle commuter planes); United displayed 560–70 in the same period.

15. "Who Said, It Can't Be Done!" *Airplanes*, May 1942, 14, 20 (an American Airlines corporate publication); press release, American Airlines, 18 July 1951; both in SAMA, in folder marked Files/People; "First Woman," *Time*, 30 July 1951, 79.

16. For a cogent summary of the stalwart DC-6 and DC-6B transports, see Arthur Pearcy, *Douglas Propliners: DC-1 to DC-7* (Shrewsbury, U.K.: Airlife, 1995), 137–46. On the fuel vent issue, see Solberg, *Conquest of the Skies*, 314–15; John R. M. Wilson, *Turbulence Aloft: The Civil Aeronautics Administration amid Wars and Rumors of Wars, 1938–53* (Washington, D.C.: Government Printing Office, 1979), 243–47.

17. "Big Money Airline," *Fortune*, December 1951, 87–88, 154.

18. Ibid., 90.

19. Ibid., 90–92; Office of Corporate Affairs, "History of American Airlines, Inc., with Emphasis on Its Corporate Developments," 1966, 20–22, SAMA files; C. R. Smith, "Why Airlines Are in Trouble," *U.S. News and World Report*, 19 February 1962, 74–75.

20. "Big Money Airline," 158; Serling, *Eagle*, 235–36; Civil Aeronautics Board, *Handbook of Airline Statistics* (Washington, D.C.: Government Printing Office, 1963), 452.

21. Davies, *Airlines*, 447–53; Joseph E. Libby, "North American Airlines," in Leary, *Airline Industry*, 315; Libby, "Stanley D. Weiss," ibid., 496–97; North American Airlines brochures and marketing items from the author's collection; "Denver Service Case," *Civil Aeronautics Board Reports*, 22 CAB, Docket 1841 et al. (14 November 1955), 1179. However, in the process, the nonskeds also brought air cargo to the fore. Even though American became an early postwar pioneer in air freight as a service offered by scheduled airlines, Smith eventually looked askance at this venture. "The airfreight business," he growled in 1956, "has had more false prophets than any business in the world except uranium. It's no bonanza." Quoted in "The Cautious Pioneer," *Forbes*, 1 June 1956, 6.

22. Davies, *Airlines*, 333–34; Solberg, *Conquest of the Skies*, 353–54; Kenneth Munson, *Airliners since 1946*, 2d rev. ed.(New York: Macmillan, 1975), 31, 53, 125; "Bigger, Faster, More Powerful," press release, n.d., American Airlines, SAMA Aircraft Files/DC-7; "DC-7 Nonstop Mercury Service," ibid.

23. "Board Hearings End on 8Hr. Crew Rule," *Aviation Week*, 31 May 1954, 16; "Non-Stop Strike?" *Fortune*, August 1954, 35; Serling, *Eagle*, 272–73; Stuart Rochester, *Takeoff at Mid-Century: Federal Aviation Policy in the Eisenhower Years, 1953–1961* (Washington, D.C.: Government Printing Office, 1976), 47–48.

24. "Big Money Airline," 92.

25. George W. Cearley Jr., *American Airlines: An Illustrated History* (Dallas: George W. Cearley, 1981), 59; "Big 4 Route Outlook: More Competition," *Aviation Week*, 30 March 1953, 79–80; "Aviation: Regulatory Statesmanship," *Life*, 4 July 1960, 75; "Denver Service Case," 22 CAB, Docket 1841 et al. (14 November 1955), 1178–1315; "Southwest/Northeast Service Case," *Civil Aeronautics Board Reports*, 22 CAB, Docket 2355 (21 November 1955), 522–52; "Route Development: Southern Transcontinental Service Case," *Annual Report of the Civil Aeronautics Board, 1961* (Washington, D.C.: Government Printing Office, 1961), 15; "Southern Transcontinental Service Case," *Civil Aeronautics Board Reports*, 33 CAB, Docket 7984 et al. (14 November 1961), 701–969. American's selected interchange routes in force at times between 1949 and 1961 from the Southeast to California are tabulated in Davies, *Airlines*, 613, table 18.

26. American Airlines, *American Airlines Annual Report* (New York: American

Airlines, 1965), 5, copy in SAMA Files; Serling, *Eagle*, 192; Davies, *Airlines*, 341; "United Capital Merger Case," *Civil Aeronautics Board Reports*, 33 CAB, Docket 11699 (April 3, 1961), 307–416; CAB quote from "Southwest/Northeast Service Case," *Civil Aeronautics Board Reports*, 22 CAB, Docket 2355 (21 November 1955), 52.

27. Serling, *Eagle*, 335, 348; W. David Lewis, "Eastern Air Lines," in Leary, *Airline Industry*, 164; "Setback for Airline Mergers," *Business Week*, 1 December 1962, 31.

28. "Turbulence Ahead," *Newsweek*, 13 August 1962, 62, 66.

29. Serling, *Eagle*, 348–49.

30. "Competition v. Solvency," *Life*, 7 December 1962, 83; "Setback," *Business Week*, 31; "Turbulence," *Newsweek*, 66; "Why Airlines Are in Trouble: Interview with C. R. Smith," *U.S. News and World Report*, 19 February 1962, 76.

31. "Turbulence Ahead," *Newsweek*, 66. Later in the proceedings, Delta, the leading carrier in the South and Southeast, became a major factor in opposing the American-Eastern merger.

32. For characteristic examples of press coverage on the American-Eastern merger and the CAB's position, see "Setback," *Business Week*, 31; "Competition," *Time*, 83–84. For other details, see Serling, *Eagle*, 349, 352; "Mergers and Intercarrier Relations," *Annual Report of the Civil Aeronautics Board, 1963* (Washington, D.C.: Government Printing Office, 1963), 14.

33. "Cautious Pioneer," *Forbes*, 25.

34. Ibid., 56; Smith, "What the Airlines Expect from the Jet Fleet," *Fortune*, July 1956, 112.

35. Ibid., 112–13, 122, 126; D. A. Saunders, "The Airlines' Flight from Reality," *Fortune*, February 1956, 90–95.

36. "Jets across the U.S.," *Time*, 82, 87, 89.

37. "Why Airlines Are in Trouble," *U.S. News and World Report*, 74, 76–77.

38. Robert J. Serling, *The Electra Story: The Dramatic History of Aviation's Most Controversial Airliner* (Garden City, N.Y.: Doubleday, 1963).

39. Munson, *Airliners since 1946*, 163–64, 167; David Mondey, ed., *Encyclopedia of the World's Commercial and Private Aircraft* (New York: Crescent Books, 1981), 14.

40. Serling, *Eagle*, 336; Department of Transportation, *FAA Historical Fact Book: A Chronology, 1926–1971* (Washington, D.C.: 1974), 107.

41. Leary, introduction to *Airline Industry*, xxiv.

42. Lloyd H. Cornett Jr., "American Airlines," in Leary, *The Airline Industry*, 40–43.

43. Letter, "confidential," Smith to Albert Casey, 5 November 1977; Casey to Smith, 15 November 1977, copies in SAMA files, "Correspondence: C. R. Smith." Smith died April 4, 1990.

Bibliographical Essay

There is a large collection of archival materials dealing with American Airlines in the C. R. Smith Aviation Museum located at Dallas–Fort Worth Airport in Grapevine, Texas. The museum and its archival collection is supported by American Airlines. The archives are comparatively recent, rapidly growing, and subject to reorganization. The collection includes correspondence and memoranda under C. R. Smith's name, as well as a pertinent collection of letters and news articles about Carlene Roberts Lawrence, a corporate executive with American. Additional subject collections in the Smith Aviation Museum archives include Foreign Policy Files, Aircraft Files, Airline Route Files, and the chronologically arranged Press Release files. There is also a collection of corporate annual reports. The museum exhibits themselves are efficiently organized and include a number of artifacts that convey information useful to historical researchers. One example is the exhibit of tickets and travel brochures that describe America's travel connections with Germany's transatlantic Zeppelin dirigibles in the late 1930s.

For aspects of legal issues and debates over America's domestic and postwar overseas routes, researchers can begin by consulting various serial publications that are standard references in law library collections. These include *United States Aviation Reports* and *Civil Aeronautics Board Reports*. Other federal sources include yearly agency summaries, such as *Annual Report of the Civil Aeronautics Board*. The CAB has also published an invaluable compendium of chronological data and a broad range of airline information under the title *Civil Aeronautics Board, Handbook of Airline Statistics* (Washington, D.C.: 1963).

Because C. R. Smith became such a recognized spokesman for the airline industry, a number of magazines either solicited articles under his name or ran articles submitted by him. Various pieces attributed to Smith appeared in such magazines as *U.S. News and World Report* as well as *Fortune* and other business magazines. In addition, his role in promoting air travel, plus the reputation of American Airlines as a leader in the industry, meant that Smith and his company both received considerable press coverage. Contemporaneous news stories about Smith and American Airlines in major periodicals, often written as in-depth reports, represent a highly useful source of information. Representative articles on Smith and American Airlines appeared in *Newsweek, Time, Nation's Business, Business Week,* and elsewhere, including the aviation media.

For a comprehensive overview of airlines that puts the story of American in proper context, the starting point is R. E. G. Davies, *Airlines of the United States since 1914* (Washington, D.C.: Smithsonian Institution Press, 1982). An older, but invaluable, work is Henry Ladd Smith, *Airways: The History of Commercial Aviation in the United States* (New York: A. A. Knopf, 1942), as well as his *Airways*

Abroad: The Story of American World Air Routes (Madison: University of Wisconsin Press, 1950). Both are based on extensive use of federal hearings, congressional debates, and correspondence with significant figures in the aviation community. William Leary, ed., *Encyclopedia of American Business History and Biography: The Airline Industry* (New York: Facts on File, 1992), is an unusually informative collection of essays on specific airlines as well as biographies of leading figures in the industry. Robert Serling, an experienced aviation journalist, has published a highly readable book, *Eagle: The History of American Airlines* (New York: St. Martins, 1985), with many lively vignettes and discussions of corporate milestones. There is also a wealth of details about American Airlines as a company in George W. Cearley Jr., *American Airlines: An Illustrated History* (Dallas: G. W. Cearley Jr., 1981). Written for airline enthusiasts, its attention to illustrations of airline transports, advertisements, route information, and ephemera make it useful for scholars as well. For specifics about American's airline equivalent, see Kenneth Munson, *Airlines since 1946*, 2d rev. ed. (New York: Macmillan, 1975), which continues to be a convenient and informative reference.

Donald W. Nyrop: Airline Regulator, Airline Executive

DONNA M. CORBETT

IN 1954, AT THE AGE OF FORTY-TWO, DONALD W. Nyrop was at the peak of his profession. A Washington lawyer specializing in aviation, he maintained a busy private practice. At the same time, as director of the Conference of Local Airlines, he was leading a crucial lobbying campaign for favorable legislation. As former chairman of the Civil Aeronautics Board (CAB) and former head of the Civil Aeronautics Administration, Nyrop knew his way around federal agencies as well as anyone, and he always received a warm welcome on Capitol Hill.

But in 1954 Nyrop left Washington for Saint Paul, Minnesota, and embarked on a new career, one with broader challenges but greater risks. After a two-year, off-and-on courtship from the company's board of directors, Nyrop finally agreed to become president of Northwest Airlines. It proved a match made in airline heaven; over the next twenty-four years, Nyrop and Northwest became nearly synonymous. Nyrop's emphasis on efficiency, economy, and safety, familiar to any of his former government colleagues in Washington, became Northwest Airlines' new hallmark. But even as president of a major airline, Nyrop could never truly leave Washington behind. As long as the airline industry remained under federal

The Civil Aeronautics Board in 1951: (clockwise from top) Josh Lee of Oklahoma, Oswald Ryan of Indiana, Donald W. Nyrop of Nebraska (chairman), Chan Gurney of South Dakota, and Joseph P. Adams of Washington State. (Courtesy of Donald W. Nyrop)

regulation, Northwest's fortunes were inextricably tied to government decisions that were reached nine hundred miles away from the airline's Minnesota headquarters.

Nyrop's Background and Rise to Leadership

Donald William Nyrop was born in 1912 in the small town of Elgin, Nebraska. With two college-educated parents, he grew up in a house filled with good books and stimulating conversation. According to one of Nyrop's sisters, their father, a banker in the tiny community, detested wastefulness (he was known within the family, for example, for insisting that the children turn off electric lights not in use) but appreciated quality. As befitted the son of a small-town banker, Nyrop learned the value of a hard-earned dollar and a reputation for fair-dealing.[1]

After completing a bachelor's degree at Doane College in Crete, Nebraska, Don Nyrop spent a year teaching history and coaching basketball at a small Nebraska high school; during the summer he traveled across the state as advance man for the Democratic candidate for U.S. Senate. Nyrop had no intention of making either teaching or elective politics his career, however, and he soon moved to Washington, D.C., and continued his studies. He entered the George Washington School of Law, studying and attending classes at night, while by day he worked as an auditor in the U.S. General Accounting Office.

Nyrop quickly learned that in Washington, especially among government attorneys, personal relationships counted for a great deal, and so, upon completing his law degree in 1939, he sought the advice and friendship of L. Welch Pogue, general counsel of the Civil Aeronautics Authority. The "old CAA," as it eventually became known, combined the safety and economic regulatory responsibilities of both the later Civil Aeronautics Board and the Federal Aviation Administration. Pogue was delighted to become acquainted with the young Nebraskan (although an Iowa native, Pogue had attended the University of Nebraska), and he immediately offered Nyrop an opportunity to interview for an opening in the new route proceedings section of the General Counsel's office.

Nyrop's adept performance in an interview with one of the old CAA's most irascible attorneys led to his first employment in the aviation field. After a few months' immersion in the regulatory tangle of route proceedings, Nyrop began work on the legal aspects of aircraft accident investigation. He found this assignment especially interesting, particularly when he worked with Frank Caldwell, an old aviation hand who had started as an operations manager for Boeing Air Transport in the mid-1920s. From Caldwell, a colorful, tobacco-chewing westerner, Nyrop learned "the difference between a good safe operation and just another average one," an insight that would serve him well in years ahead.[2]

In the field of aviation law, Nyrop's career quickly gained breadth. In addition to route proceedings and safety issues, he acquired experience in airport matters when Pogue assigned him to handle problems arising during the building of Washington National Airport. With his growing legal expertise, Nyrop was kept quite busy. Years later, an American Airlines stewardess, Grace Cary, remembered her annoyance when one of her Washington to New York flights was delayed to accommodate a government official on urgent business. The government official, as it turned out, grew up not far from her hometown in Nebraska. She and Nyrop were married the next year.

In 1940, L. Welch Pogue became chairman of the Civil Aeronautics Board, the new entity established by President Roosevelt's government reorganization to replace the five-member board of the old Civil Aeronautics Authority. Pogue invited Nyrop to become his executive assistant. But the Second World War ended Nyrop's new assignment after less than a year.

During the war, Nyrop literally circled the globe for the Air Transport Command. Although assigned to ATC's Washington headquarters as executive operations officer, Lieutenant Colonel Nyrop flew frequently to Europe and traveled across Asia. Among his varied wartime experiences he could recall a tense night in Shanghai, sleeping fitfully under the wing of a C-54 soon after Japanese troops evacuated the region.

Decorated with the Legion of Merit and released from the military in January 1946, Nyrop joined the Air Transport Association, the industry organization of United States airlines. With war's end, airlines were beginning to prepare for new overseas routes, and at ATA Nyrop handled matters relating to the establishment of airways and airports, meteorology, and communications. In 1946 and 1947, he was a member of the official U.S. delegations to the International Civil Aviation Organization (ICAO) assemblies. Soon government service beckoned again. In August 1948, he became executive assistant to Civil Aeronautics Administrator Delos W. Rentzel. Less than a year later, Rentzel appointed him deputy administrator, placing him in charge of operations for the entire Civil Aeronautics Administration.[3]

The Central Aeronautics Administration, precursor to the later Federal Aviation Administration, was an arm of the Department of Commerce. It was the federal agency charged with oversight of aviation's technical aspects, such as airways, airports, and air traffic control. While the Civil Aeronautics Board concerned itself with economic regulation, licensing, and accident investigation, the CAA (successor to the original 1926 Commerce Department Aeronautics Branch) issued regulations and operated the aviation infrastructure used by private pilots, airlines, and—although this was a thorny issue in the 1940s and 1950s—domestic military flights.[4]

As deputy administrator, Nyrop was clearly second-in-command at the CAA, with responsibility for budgets, personnel, and management. Administrator Rentzel, a charming, personable Texan with good technical knowledge of aviation, was happy to leave administrative matters to others. Rentzel, Nyrop recalled, "painted with a broad brush and needed someone to fill in the details," and command of details was a Nyrop specialty. Nyrop told one audience that he intended to apply "business principles" to CAA operations "to increase efficiency and effect economies."[5]

Efficiency and economy were desperately needed at the CAA, at least according to one legislator. As deputy administrator, Nyrop learned to face repeated grilling by Congressman John J. Rooney, the New York Democrat who headed the House Appropriations Committee. (A typical Rooney question, in a hearing on Alaskan airport funding, was "What is the population of Alaska?") Rooney forever sought to stamp out "incompetence and poor administration," typified by such wasteful practices as private use of agency automobiles. Nyrop learned to prepare carefully for budget hearings, and ultimately he gained an important ally in Rooney, who recognized their shared commitment to cutting waste. In six months, Nyrop was able to identify six principal areas for budget cutting, resulting in a savings of $2,458,000 to taxpayers. "You know, that is one thing I always liked about Mr. Nyrop," said Appropriations Committee member Cliff Clevenger in one hearing. "He was frank with us. If we cut him he would not bellyache or sulk. He went out and did a better job than he was going to do if we had not cut him."[6]

In the summer of 1950, President Truman, preoccupied with the outbreak of war in Korea, needed to find a quick replacement for CAB chairman Joseph O'Connell, who had just resigned to protest the White House's clumsy mishandling of the American Overseas–Pan American merger case. (The president had at first disapproved, then approved the merger, by all appearances wholly ignoring the CAB's judgment.) Juggling appointments, Truman moved Nyrop's boss, CAA Administrator Rentzel, to the Civil Aeronautics Board to serve as its chairman. Nyrop was the natural candidate to succeed Rentzel, and Truman sent his nomination to the Senate on September 19. With praise from members of Congress and the industry trade press ("A better choice could not have been made," wrote influential editor Wayne Parrish) and after a Senate confirmation hearing filled with praise for Nyrop's abilities, his commitment to government economy, and his Nebraska roots, Donald W. Nyrop's appointment as Administrator of Civil Aeronautics was confirmed on September 20, 1950.[7]

At the age of thirty-eight, Nyrop became head of a federal agency with more than 18,000 employees and an annual budget of $187 million. With his experience as deputy administrator, Nyrop needed no time to learn his way around the agency. He immediately took a keen interest in aviation safety issues. He oversaw the development and testing of runway approach lighting, then selected the parallel banks of lights that became the international standard. He increased CAA oversight of airline operations. As the Korean War progressed, he negotiated the competing demands of civilian and military aviation for aircraft and spare parts. A move to place the CAA under military control for the duration of the "limited mobilization," as Nyrop called the Korean crisis, met his firm opposition, thereby saving civil aviation from an unfortunate precedent.[8]

Six months into his CAA tenure, Nyrop was called to the White House. President Truman explained that he was preparing to appoint Delos Rentzel to an undersecretary post in the Department of Commerce. Would Nyrop accept appointment as chairman of the Civil Aeronautics Board? Nyrop was reluctant to leave the CAA, where he felt he was making genuine progress in improving aviation safety. But he also felt that he couldn't say no to the president. Nyrop's nomination was sent to the Senate on March 19, 1951, and confirmed the following month.[9]

Nyrop's Policies as an Airline Regulator

In selecting Nyrop as chairman of the Civil Aeronautics Board, Truman seemed to have made an easy decision. Nyrop was, after all, following in Rentzel's footsteps. But Nyrop was not interested in merely following someone; industry gossip reported his "determination to be known as an independent thinker, rather than a rider of Rentzel's coat tails up the promotion ladder."[10] Nyrop was also well aware of the CAB's tradition of internal squabbling, and he little relished the thought of guiding a government agency run by committee.

Fortunately for Nyrop, however, Truman was committed to the recommendations of the Hoover Commission, which suggested that regulatory commissions be headed by a single strong administrator. "Administration by a plural executive is universally regarded as inefficient," the Commission reported, and it urged that the CAB and similar boards vest all administrative responsibility in the chairman. Truman issued a government reorganization plan to implement the Commission's proposal.

Nyrop, a proven strong administrator, therefore happened to become chairman of the Civil Aeronautics Board just as the chairman's office itself was gaining additional authority.[11] He wasted no opportunity to take advantage of this centralization, readily applying to the CAB the cost-cutting principles he had practiced at the CAA. The number of CAB automobiles decreased from 23 to 17, and its fleet of aircraft was reduced from ten to seven. The CAB closed two regional offices and four field hearing examiner offices. The staff was reorganized, and housekeeping functions, such as accounting, were taken over from the Department of Commerce. New Rules of Practice were issued, and the backlog of pending cases began to be reduced.[12]

The postwar years had brought a heavy workload to the CAB, as demand for air travel increased and the aviation industry struggled to meet it. As Nyrop stepped into the CAB chairmanship, a noisy debate over the future of irregular air carriers was erupting. Irregular or nonscheduled airlines were a postwar phenomenon, the combined product of readily available war-surplus aircraft, a large number of unemployed military-trained pilots, and easily available government-sponsored financing. Granted an exemption from the CAB's usual strict determination of carrier fitness, small "airlines" sprang up across the country. One 1946 estimate claimed there were 2,400 "airlines" in the United States, all but 17 of them nonscheduled. By the early 1950s, approximately 63 so-called large irregulars routinely transported passengers, some of them duplicating regular airline routes at drastically reduced fares.[13]

At the Senate hearing to confirm Nyrop's CAB appointment, he and Rentzel were branded as potential tools of the scheduled airlines because they both had worked within the airline industry. Amos E. Heacock, president of the Aircoach Transport Association, an organization of unscheduled carriers, testified that while Nyrop and Rentzel were "capable administrators, and I would not want for any better people to call friends," he was opposed to their nominations on the basis of their industry backgrounds. Heacock detected hostility to nonscheduled airlines everywhere; even the director of the Civil Service Commission, former congressman Robert Ramspeck, received his condemnation because he too had worked for the Air Transport Association.[14]

Heacock and other nonscheduled airline lobbyists voiced no objections to Nyrop's handling of the Civil Aeronautics Administration. As administrator, Nyrop had devoted special attention to the safety problems of irregular carriers. In fact, some of his reluctance to leave the CAA stemmed from his sense that the agency was making great progress toward improving the irregulars' safety records.[15] But at the Civil Aeronautics Board, Nyrop would face more complex and fundamental issues, including questions of how, where, and even whether the nonscheduled airlines should be permitted to operate.

On the question of irregular air carriers, as in all other matters, the Civil Aeronautics Board was required to act in accordance with the Civil Aeronautics Act of 1938. This landmark legislation, which served as the underpinning of all government regulation of aviation, demanded that the broad national interest, and not parochial demands (including calls for unsustainably cheap air transportation), would dictate the development of air routes. The Act proscribed "destructive competition."[16] Federal regulators were required to sustain a rational, orderly airline system, not a wildly competitive, *caveat emptor* free-for-all.

But rational discussion of a nationwide airline system seemed sorely lacking in 1951. It was, the board said, "a time when the air is charged with controversial bitterness, widely circulated propaganda, and misinformation touching the broader issues of low-fare transportation." Popular magazines found wide readership by featuring stories and pictures of air crashes; many of these stories were directed specifically against the irregular carriers. "DEATH Rides the Bargain Airlines," shouted one magazine headline. "Don't Fly the Unscheduled Air Lines!" warned another, promising "the shocking facts about murder in the air." Meanwhile, "the scheduled airlines of the United States" placed full-page advertisements in many newspapers, directly challenging readers to consider their safety in selecting a nonscheduled or scheduled airline for their next flight.[17]

Irregular airline operators liked to portray themselves as archetypical small businessmen, fighting valiantly against their large competitors' attempts to drive them out of business. The irregulars' campaign received a small boost when the Senate Select Committee on Small Business agreed to look into their complaints. But the committee's brief report, which rather naively portrayed the "nonskeds" as daring entrepreneurs boldly attempting to introduce new ideas to a coddled industry, was largely ignored.[18]

Irregular airlines were not without their problems. Amos Heacock's own airline, Air Transport Associates, eventually lost its operating authority for flagrantly violating CAB regulations. Some irregulars, operating on a shoestring, were so cash-strapped that passengers had to "pass the hat" to pay for aircraft refueling at intermediate stops. One irregular flight from Burbank, California, to Newark never arrived, despite three days en route. The aircraft was delayed eleven hours at Burbank, seven hours at Hutchinson, Kansas, and fifteen hours at Kansas City, before the flight finally terminated in Philadelphia, stranding its passengers there.[19] In the meantime, the regular certificated airlines, which had strict schedules to maintain, could not simply wait to take off, as irregulars did, until every seat was sold.

Even the president of the United States wondered about the irregulars. In a memorandum to Nyrop, Truman wrote, "I've been very much worried about the nonscheduled airlines situation." Truman had asked one of his White House aides to take a closer look at the irregulars and prepare a report on them. "We are faced with a serious situation," Truman told Nyrop, "and I'd like very much to have some concrete action on it more for the safety and saving of lives than for any other reason."[20]

Truman's concern for safety meshed with Nyrop's. Continuing the program Nyrop began at CAA, the CAB conducted special safety investigations of irregulars and promulgated new safety regulations. Each irregular carrier was required, for the first time, to designate a chief pilot and check pilots, and flight training standards were upgraded. The board's enforcement division went to work on violations of economic regulations, and in September 1951 Nyrop announced a major investigation "to determine whether the air transportation needs of the United States require the services of the large irregular air carriers, and, if so, to determine the appropriate number" and route structure.[21]

Some of the large "nonskeds" gained a following by providing coach-type service on heavily traveled routes. Coach service, which combined high-density seating, off-peak schedules, and no-frills flights, was hardly a new idea; scheduled airlines had experimented with coach services since 1948. But the "nonskeds" only aimed to operate in the most profitable markets. The CAB, faced with an application for transcontinental coach service by four irregulars, concluded that if nonscheduled airlines were routinely permitted to skim off the cream of scheduled routes—without the scheduled airlines' "traditional public service obligation" of also serving unprofitable routes—destructive competition would result.[22]

Even before joining the CAB, Nyrop felt that one of the airline industry's "shortcomings" was its failure to lower fares. In a 1950 speech delivered as Administrator of Civil Aeronautics, Nyrop noted that only one-third of scheduled airline passengers were flying on pleasure trips. "Coach service," he noted approvingly, "is an effort to increase public acceptance of air travel."[23]

Before World War II, air transportation had always been a first-class form of travel. Airlines, with their advantage of speed and their limited capacity, felt no need to compete directly with railroads' day coaches. Early air fares were often described as equaling the cost of "rail plus Pullman," an attainable sum for a middle-class traveler, but not inexpensive. While the air traveler did have the further advantage of free meals and refreshments provided en route, one early 1929 analysis suggested that long-distance air travel would prove more economical than rail travel only for persons with yearly incomes of $10,000 or more.[24]

In a 1951 decision, the CAB stated: "In the opinion of this board, progressively lower fares must be a major objective and natural incident of any new transportation development. Unless air transportation can be brought within the reach of many people of limited means, it will not be able to fulfill its obligation to the American people." Referring to federal airline subsidies with language Andrew Jackson would have approved, the board continued, "Indeed, there could be no justification for a national policy which has poured millions of dollars of the people's money into the building up of a vast air transportation system if that system were to be permanently restricted to persons of means and denied to the masses of the people."[25]

In a speech before an airport operators' conference, CAB chairman Nyrop predicted, "In time, coach travel may well be the predominant form of air travel within the United States," and he acted to fulfill this prophecy. In late 1951, the CAB announced in a policy statement that certificated airlines would be expected to expand their coach services. Nyrop met privately with every airline president, explaining the importance the board attached to coach service expansion. Some airline executives accepted the CAB's initiative; others, like United's William A. "Pat" Patterson, came to Washington prepared to fight it. But face-to-face conferences persuaded even the most reluctant that the board seriously intended to pursue its policy. Coach passenger mileage soon accounted for 16 percent of domestic air traffic, and fares were reduced by 11 percent within one year. For the first time, a $99 transcontinental airline fare became a reality.[26]

Coach services lowered the price of air travel for passengers; Nyrop also aimed to lower the cost for taxpayers. Since the birth of American commercial aviation in the mid-1920s, airlines received federal assistance in the form of airmail payments. These government payments deliberately exceeded the airlines' actual costs of carrying the mail, and thereby indirectly subsidized the emerging industry. In his 1950 budget message to Congress, and in subsequent budget messages, President Truman urged the enactment of legislation that would separate subsidy payments from the actual compensation for carrying mail. Under Truman's plan, the Post Office Department would continue to pay airlines for providing airmail service, while the Civil Aeronautics Board would subsidize airlines from its own appropriated funds. Subsidies would come clearly and directly from the taxpayers, not from Post Office revenues.

Truman was not against subsidizing airlines. "Federal financial assistance has been a major factor in the industry's rapid growth," he told Congress, "and should be continued to the extent necessary for the sound development of civil aviation." But "in the light of the industry's present stage of development," Truman declared, it was time to "evaluate the cost of this aid in relation to its benefits."[27]

Shortly after Nyrop's confirmation as CAB chairman, Senator Edwin C. Johnson, chairman of the Interstate and Foreign Commerce Committee, invited Nyrop to his office. Johnson, an enthusiastic advocate of subsidy separation, urged Nyrop to focus particularly on this issue. The senator had been angered by former CAB chairman Joseph O'Connell's refusal to act on subsidy separation without specific congressional authorization.[28] But Nyrop had no such qualms; as his tenure at the CAA had already shown, any proposal that promised more careful accounting of government expenses and a reduction in costs to taxpayers was certain to meet his approval.

Over hours of congressional testimony, Nyrop evaluated various Senate and House bills to achieve subsidy separation. On the Senate side, six bills vied for the Commerce Committee's attention. Senator Johnson favored the establishment of statutory mail rates, actual mail rates specified in the legislation itself. He suggested that this policy would save both airlines and the government the time and expense of administrative procedures to determine rates. Nyrop and the other Civil Aeronautics Board members, however, favored retaining the hearing process, by which the CAB would determine a fair service rate, one "based upon the cost of carrying the mail which includes a fair return on investment."[29]

While waiting for Congress to act, Nyrop and the board moved ahead with plans to remove the Big Four airlines (American, Eastern, TWA, and United) from subsidy altogether. Nyrop warned the Senate Commerce Committee that the CAB's objective was to place as many air carriers as possible on a final, or nonsubsidy, mail rate "as soon as possible irrespective of any legislation that may be passed by Congress." Nyrop also promised that the board would move ahead with its "administrative subsidy separation" program, in which funds for subsidy and funds for mail pay would be clearly designated.[30] With or without Congressional action, the CAB now was determined to disclose to the public exactly how much subsidy each airline was receiving from the federal government.

On July 9, 1951, the CAB announced action on both fronts. No longer would subsidy be "hidden" in airline mail pay; both amounts would be disclosed publicly. In addition, the board announced that the Big Four airlines would agree with the CAB's determination, in the pending mail rate case, to reduce their mail pay rates to a purely compensatory, nonsubsidy level. In conferences with the four airlines, they also agreed to return nearly $5 million in excess mail payments to the federal treasury.

In agreeing to these terms, the Big Four avoided lengthy hearings; they also avoided publicly airing their complaints about the new subsidy separation program. Nyrop had warned Senator Johnson's committee that subsidy separation's progress would "depend largely upon the degree of acceptance by the industry" of the principles enunciated in the CAB's Big Four mail rate decision. Nyrop conferred personally with airline presidents, persuading them of the board's determination to carry out its program. Although most airline executives detested subsidy separation (American's C. R. Smith was a notable exception), they reserved their private expressions of displeasure for Nyrop and other CAB members. Public opinion, after all, could hardly be counted on to support "hidden" gifts to an industry annually accepting $130 million from the government.[31]

Within the next seventeen months, the Civil Aeronautics Board placed ten domestic airlines on subsidy-free mail rates. By October 1952, more than 90 percent of domestic airmail was carried by subsidy-free carriers. The combination of administrative subsidy separation and the CAB's accelerated decision making in mail rate cases resulted in an estimated annual savings of $13 million to the government. In addition, as the board recalculated mail rates, it ordered airlines to refund more than $15 million to the federal treasury.

Nyrop described the CAB's administrative subsidy separation as "one of the most important actions of the Board in its thirteen years of existence."[32] The Civil Aeronautics Board had acted without waiting for Congress; it had demonstrated exceptional independence by implementing a major program without the passage of authorizing legislation. Although bills requiring subsidy separation continued to be introduced in Congress, Nyrop's "administrative" separation rendered them less critical.[33] In removing airlines from subsidy—and by publicly disclosing the amount of subsidy granted to airlines that still required it—the CAB's actions signaled the increasing maturity of the airline industry. In a sense, subsidy separation, by laying open to public view the precise cost of federal assistance to airlines, set the stage for future debates about the value and cost of government support and regulation of the airline industry.

But in the early 1950s the American public may have wished for more government regulation of air travel, not less. On August 27, 1951, the minutes of the Civil Aeronautics Board recorded, "The Chairman [Nyrop] expressed his concern over the high number of fatalities incurred in aircraft accidents this year." Air safety remained among Nyrop's primary concerns, as it had been when he headed the CAA, and he proposed to "present an affirmative program" for the board's consideration.[34] Sensitive to public perceptions on aviation safety, he wanted to halt a trend that, if continued, could seriously damage the industry's reputation and hinder its progress.

But within the next few months, the safety of air travel would become a topic of mass public concern. In late December 1951, Nyrop told reporters he was "greatly concerned about the recent series of C-46 accidents." War-surplus Curtiss C-46 aircraft were in widespread use, especially among irregular air carriers. Pointing out that there had been "three C-46 accidents in the last fifteen days," Nyrop and the board's executive director, James M. Verner, joined accident investigators and climbed aboard the CAB's DC-3. They flew to upstate New York, site of a C-46 crash, where Nyrop became the first CAB chairman to visit an accident scene. Shortly thereafter, not waiting for the lengthy investigation to be completed, the CAB issued an emergency temporary regulation reducing the maximum take-off and landing weights of C-46 aircraft in passenger service.[35]

As the winter of 1951–52 continued, however, newspaper headlines were filled with more news of dramatic air crashes. Heaping extra notoriety upon aviation's already blackened reputation, the most spectacular accidents occurred near New York City, the center of the American news media industry.

On December 16, 1951, less than two weeks before President Truman reappointed Nyrop for another term as CAB chairman, a C-46 operated by Miami Airlines, an irregular carrier, crashed shortly after taking off from Newark Airport. Circling to return to the airport with an engine fire, the aircraft struck buildings in the surrounding community of Elizabeth, New Jersey, before crashing on a riverbank, killing all 46 aboard. Less than a month later, an airliner undershot its approach to LaGuardia Airport, landing in water. On January 22, an American Airlines Convair 240 on approach to Newark struck a six-story building, destroying it and several others, killing all 23 aboard and 6 persons on the ground. On February 11, a National Airlines DC-6 taking off from Newark struck an apartment house. This time 29 aboard the airplane and four apartment occupants were killed. In all, five accidents occurred in Elizabeth, New Jersey, alone, leaving the community in an uproar and gripping the entire New York area with a newfound fear of airplanes.[36]

Less than four hours after the National DC-6 accident, Newark Airport was closed. Nyrop, who had been up all night, telephoned the White House early the next morning and requested an appointment to see the president. Less than a month had passed since Truman's memorandum expressing his concern over the safety of irregular air carriers.

The president responded with alacrity when Nyrop suggested the appointment of a special presidential commission to study the safety of the nation's airports. The question of the commission's membership arose. When Nyrop suggested that the commission should be headed by well-known civilian and military pilot James Doolittle, Truman responded, "That's just the man!" and ordered his staff to find the famed aviator immediately.[37]

The White House announced the creation of the President's Airport Commission just as the Senate Commerce Committee held a closed hearing to discuss the Newark accidents with Nyrop and CAA administrator Charles Horne.[38] Another committee, composed of airline executives, Nyrop, and other government officials, met in New York and struggled to deal with the nationwide airline scheduling and traffic problems caused by the Newark Airport closure. As a result of their deliberations, LaGuardia Airport was permanently closed to international flights. Meanwhile, the citizens of Elizabeth, New Jersey, were so "crash-jittery" that when a pile of old tires caught fire a mile from the closed airport, many called police to report an airplane accident.[39]

Nyrop recognized that one way to restore public confidence in airport safety was to acknowledge that complaints about airport noise were "a reasonable and just criticism." For more than two years, residents surrounding Newark Airport had complained of the nuisance of sharply increased aircraft noise. Construction was continuing on a new runway that would alleviate some of the noise problem, and along with preferential runway use (which would direct the noise away from populated areas), Nyrop suggested continuing public education on the airport's value to the local economy. A few months later, the Doolittle Commission issued its report, "The Airport and Its Neighbors," which also suggested a renewed emphasis on reducing airplane noise, as well as improving runways, airport planning, pilot training, and cockpit standardization.[40]

But the Doolittle report offered little comfort to farsighted airline and airport executives who already were bracing for the arrival of jet transports. American Airlines president C. R. Smith and the director of the New York Port Authority wrote to Nyrop, pleading with the CAB to begin to address the operational problems inherent in aircraft "that cannot land and take off at our metropolitan airports without the roar of a banshee."[41] But jet aircraft were already among Nyrop's concerns. In 1950, while CAA administrator, he warned a Massachusetts Institute of Technology conference about the variety of airport problems soon to be posed by jets, from hot exhaust blasts to air traffic delays.[42] In 1952 he proposed legislation to offer loans and funding to defray development costs of passenger jet prototypes. In doing so he faced opposition from the U.S. Air Force, which feared that any civilian jet development would hinder military aircraft production. Problems posed by the development of jets also figured prominently in other roles Nyrop played in Washington; in addition to his CAB chairmanship, President Truman appointed him as chairman of the interdepartmental Air Coordinating Committee and as a member of the National Advisory Committee for Aeronautics.[43]

One day, while meeting with President Truman on other matters, Nyrop was astonished to discover that the president, despite having so many other problems demanding his attention, was concerned about the effect of foreign-made jet aircraft on the future of the American aviation industry. Nyrop was fortunate to serve as Civil Aeronautics Administrator and CAB chairman under a president who demonstrated genuine interest in aviation matters. As a senator, Truman had taken great pride in his role in the passage of the Civil Aeronautics Act of 1938.[44] As president, Truman decorated the Oval Office with models and prints of airplanes. He seemed to enjoy making final decisions on international air routes, a role which the Act vested in the president for foreign policy and national security reasons. Nyrop truly respected Truman, with whom he shared midwestern roots and an appreciation for plainspokenness. The president and Mrs. Truman returned Nyrop's genuine regard with tellingly gracious gestures, such as an impromptu tour of the newly renovated White House private quarters and flowers sent to Mrs. Nyrop upon the birth of one of her children.[45]

In late August 1952, Nyrop told President Truman that he was thinking of leaving the Civil Aeronautics Board. In September he submitted his resignation. At his last official meeting in the Oval Office, Nyrop presented President Truman with a bound volume containing all international route decisions Truman had approved. While Nyrop was chairman, the first postwar transatlantic route awards were due for renewal, and Truman (despite opposition within his own administration) encouraged him to begin proceedings for the issuance of permanent certificates to Pan American and TWA. This complex and politically charged route proceeding was completed in just nine months.[46] As chairman, Nyrop always strived to provide Truman with the board's best advice on international cases, presented in a well-organized and timely fashion. In doing so, he helped the administration recover from its 1950 political gaffe, when CAB chairman Joseph O'Connell resigned in protest. While Truman clearly prized the finely bound volume Nyrop handed him, the departing CAB chairman had already given the president a more valuable gift: establishing an orderly process for White House review of international route decisions.[47]

From Federal Regulator to Airline Executive

Nyrop's resignation was effective November 1, 1952. With Truman's impending retirement and with the Democratic candidate, Adlai Stevenson, given little chance of election, Nyrop's reappointment as CAB chairman would have been unlikely. "It is regretted," wrote *American Aviation* editor Wayne Parrish, "that the CAB will be without the services of Mr. Nyrop who proved not only to be fair-minded to an extreme, but an excellent administrator and organizer. We trust he will find an important spot in industry where he can put his many talents to good use." Nyrop was still young, just forty years old, but the strenuous pace of the last few years encouraged him to seek a change. Meanwhile, the remaining board members, still smarting from their loss of administrative control after Truman's reorganization, decided to curb the next chairman's power. "Mr. Nyrop proved to be an eminently able chairman, certainly one of the very best," Parrish explained, "but by the same token his devotion to getting things done rubbed several of his colleagues the wrong way."[48]

After a brief vacation, his first in several years, Nyrop returned to Washington ready to enter private law practice. He joined the firm of Klagsbrunn, Hanes and Irwin, "a young law firm and a very good one," and began representing cities seeking direct or additional service in government route proceedings. In March 1953, Nyrop also became Washington director of the newly formed Conference of Local Airlines, representing the fourteen local service airlines.[49] Through congressional testimony and personal meetings with senators and representatives, he led the local service carriers' fight for legislation authorizing permanent certificates. Nyrop also demonstrated an unforeseen talent for grassroots lobbying when he marshaled a campaign to flood the office of Commerce Secretary Sinclair Weeks (an opponent of local service certification) with telegrams from communities benefiting from local airline service.[50]

In the summer of 1954, three members of the board of directors of Northwest Airlines visited Nyrop's Washington law office. Expecting that they had come to ask him to do legal work for the airline, Nyrop was surprised when they offered him the airline's presidency. Perhaps he should not have been surprised; he had been offered Northwest's presidency once before, soon after he had announced his resignation from the CAB. But in 1952 Nyrop had already committed to joining the law firm, and, characteristically sensitive to potential conflicts of interest, he felt it would be inappropriate to move directly from a government post to the industry he had just helped to regulate.

Nyrop responded to Northwest's latest offer by asking for sixty days in which to study the airline and weigh his decision. Given the perplexity of Northwest's problems, sixty days must have seemed very short.

Northwest's most recent president, Harold R. Harris, a veteran of Pan American and Panagra, had been forced out after only one year. Harris antagonized the airline's local Minnesota directors with plans to move the company to New York and to split it into separate operating divisions after the Pan American model. Northwest's precarious financial condition required weekly meetings to count the cash on hand, which rarely revealed enough to meet payroll beyond the next thirty-five or forty days. New airplanes were desperately needed but required financing that seemed impossible to obtain. Aircraft which Northwest did own were heavily mortgaged.[51]

As Civil Aeronautics Administrator and as CAB chairman, Nyrop was well aware of Northwest Airlines' problems; in fact, those problems had reached a peak in 1950–51, when Northwest's astonishingly poor luck with Martin 2-0-2 aircraft included some type of accident, on average, every forty-five days. In February 1951, Administrator Nyrop led a team of top safety investigators on a special inspection of Northwest and ordered two weeks of Washington conferences with the airline's top officials. Nyrop ordered Northwest to retrain pilots, to upgrade maintenance, and to establish tighter restrictions on poor-weather operations.[52]

On August 30, 1954, Nyrop announced his acceptance of Northwest Airlines' presidency at a press conference in St. Paul. "I believe in the future of this carrier," he confidently declared. At the age of forty-two, he became the youngest president of a major airline. His decision to join Northwest was based on both professional and personal reasons; while an opportunity to run the world's eighth largest airline "doesn't come along very often," Nyrop noted, he and his wife, Grace, also looked forward to raising their children in their native Midwest.[53] But for the next

Northwest Airlines president Donald W. Nyrop. (Courtesy of Donald W. Nyrop)

ten months, the Nyrops, well ahead of their time, would endure a commuter marriage, as Mrs. Nyrop, with two small children and expecting twins, temporarily stayed behind in their Virginia home.

Fortunately for the Nyrop family, route case business often sent the new airline president back to Washington. Three crucial cases were pending before the CAB, involving Northwest's Hawaiian, Alaskan, and Asian routes. Of these, permanent certification of Northwest's transpacific routes was most critical, for without permanent certification the airline could not obtain its desperately needed long-term financing for equipment and other investments.[54]

The transpacific route was the jewel of Northwest Airlines' system. Although its international route authority, like most other airlines', dated only from the postwar awards of 1946, it bore a significance transcending even its economic value to the Minnesota airline. For a century, the Twin Cities of Minneapolis and St. Paul, located at the navigational head of the Mississippi River, aspired to connect the interior of the North American continent with the trade of the Orient. In the nineteenth century, Saint Paul's legendary railroad magnate, James J. Hill, "the Empire Builder," gradually extended his Great Northern Railway from the Mississippi to the Pacific, and further planned to capture Asian trade with a fleet of transpacific steamships. In the early 1930s, Northwest's founder, Colonel

L. H. Brittin, a keen student of transportation, paralleled the Empire Builder's route as his fledgling airline expanded westward. Croil Hunter, Brittin's successor, who still served as chairman of Northwest's board when Nyrop arrived, began planning air routes to Asia even before the Second World War. Nowhere was the airline's pride in its transpacific service more evident than in its name: after 1946 it chose to call itself "Northwest Orient," a name which resonated with distant, exotic flair, even when applied to a short hop between Minneapolis and Fargo.[55]

In 1946 the CAB granted Northwest a Great Circle route across the northern Pacific, from Seattle to Tokyo and beyond to China, Korea, and the Philippines. The new route authority was temporary, only to last seven years. The CAB expressly reasoned that the airline's wartime experience, in which the Northwest flew more than 17 million miles between the U.S. and Alaska (including along the Aleutian Islands, the necessary transpacific refueling point in the days of DC-4s), had familiarized Northwest with the problems of far-north operations.[56]

Juan Trippe, president of Pan American, had had his eye on the Great Circle route across the Pacific at least since 1931, when Charles and Anne Morrow Lindbergh flew their well-publicized "North to the Orient" survey flight. Before the war, Pan American opened the longer route across the central Pacific (via Hawaii and Midway) and gained permanent operating authority. But these gains did not keep ever-ambitious Pan American from grasping for more. In 1947, before Northwest could begin its Orient service, Congress again considered "chosen instrument" legislation, through which Pan American would be designated the sole United States flag carrier. For years, Trippe lost no opportunity to point out that Pan American would be "compromised" by competing with domestic rivals.[57] Having failed in its legislative attempt at sole dominance of international flying, Pan American would spend the next decade challenging the CAB to discontinue or to duplicate Northwest's route authority. Meanwhile, Northwest Orient, operating sparsely loaded 44-passenger DC-4s across vast ocean distances, pioneered Great Circle route service alone.

At about the same time that Nyrop was considering the offer to join Northwest Airlines, the Civil Aeronautics Board voted on its decision in the Transpacific Certificate Renewal Case. A rumor around Northwest, which Nyrop later dismissed, suggested that his hesitation in accepting the airline presidency stemmed from a desire to know the CAB's decision before committing himself. Even though the rumor was untrue, it pointed to the importance of the transpacific routes to the airline's future. Without the Pacific, Northwest would be among the weakest domestic carriers: a transcontinental carrier, but one whose route across the northern tier of states served the smallest population and suffered the greatest seasonal traffic imbalance.

Despite these weaknesses, Northwest's domestic system had already been weaned from government subsidy under CAB chairman Nyrop. As Northwest president, Nyrop was determined that the airline's international routes should also be free from dependence on taxpayers. "Subsidy," he often said, "is like a cost-plus contract. It undermines efficiency." By January 1955, Nyrop was convinced that Northwest could operate entirely self-sufficiently.[58] Northwest subsequently filed a formal request that the Civil Aeronautics Board discontinue its transpacific subsidy payments. This bold step, which other carriers chose not to imitate, received little embellishment from Northwest's president: "That's the responsibility of all airlines," Nyrop noted simply. But the unprecedented move sent strong signals to the banking community, whose help Northwest needed to finance fleet improvements, and to CAB members, who now had an additional reason to choose Northwest for route awards.[59]

The CAB would soon have a chance to test Northwest's theory that a subsidy-free airline should have an advantage in route contests. The CAB's first vote in the Transpacific Renewal Case, which leaked to the aviation trade press in August 1954, was three-to-two in favor of Northwest's renewal of Great Circle authority and against Pan American's duplication of the route. The two votes cast against Northwest were based on the belief that eliminating Northwest would reduce the government's Pacific area subsidy bill. But for the next three months, as Nyrop prepared to assume Northwest's presidency, the CAB continued to debate its transpacific decision. During these debates, Commerce Secretary Sinclair Weeks and Undersecretary Robert B. Murray Jr. (author of an influential Air Coordinating Committee report favoring the "chosen instrument"), lobbied the board to decide against Northwest, using subsidy reduction as their argument. The board, which was supposed to render an independent judgment, faced unprecedented Commerce Department involvement in its decision.[60]

Cartoon about President Eisenhower's changed decision on Northwest Airlines' Hawaii route in 1955. (Courtesy of Donald W. Nyrop)

The CAB finally submitted its long-awaited decisions on the Transpacific and West Coast–Hawaii cases to President Eisenhower late in 1954. For Northwest Airlines, the news was nearly all good. The CAB unanimously recommended that Northwest be given sole permanent authority to fly the Great Circle route to Tokyo. It also recommended that Northwest remain the sole carrier between the Pacific Northwest and Hawaii. Pan American lost its bid to duplicate or replace Northwest on both routes.[61]

For weeks, the decisions remained at the White House awaiting presidential approval. Then on February 1, without consulting anyone at the Civil Aeronautics Board, the White House issued a press release containing Eisenhower's letter to the CAB giving his instructions for final orders on both cases. (Normally, only the final signed orders were released to the press—by the CAB itself.) In publishing this correspondence before the final orders had been prepared or signed, Eisenhower, in an unfortunate precedent, further opened the air route approval process to external political pressure. Every dissatisfied party in international air route cases could now be expected to appear on the White House doorstep.[62] The orderly, consultative handling of international cases established for the Truman administration under CAB chairman Nyrop was now only a memory.

Eisenhower ordered the CAB to reverse Northwest's permanent transpacific certification in favor of a temporary, seven-year renewal. He denied outright Northwest's authority to serve Hawaii. His stated reason was to reduce the government's subsidy bill. Eisenhower seemed blithely unaware that Northwest's rapidly dwindling subsidy requirements were well below Pan American's; Northwest even had pledged publicly, in oral argument before the board, to serve Hawaii without any subsidy.[63] But Pan American's massive Washington lobbying machinery operated in high gear; having lost in the CAB, it now succeeded in persuading the Eisenhower administration to expand Pan American's Hawaii rights and to keep open the future possibility of replacing or duplicating Northwest on the Great Circle route. Commerce Secretary Weeks, a laissez-faire industrialist who was reportedly dissatisfied with the CAB's decision, was Eisenhower's primary adviser.[64]

Unlike Pan American, Northwest had no large permanent lobbying staff in Washington, so Nyrop lost no time after Eisenhower's decision was announced.[65] He was aboard the next flight to Washington, where meetings were arranged with the Minnesota congressional delegation. As Nyrop stepped off the airplane at National Airport, the first of thousands of telegrams were beginning to arrive at the Capitol and White House, and newspaper editorialists across the upper Midwest had begun to sharpen their barbs.

Nyrop spent an entire afternoon with Minnesota Congressman Walter Judd, briefing him on every aspect of the case. Judd and Republican Senator Edward J. Thye prepared to lead a delegation to a rare Saturday morning meeting at the White House.

Entering the Oval Office, Senator Thye, Representative Judd, and acting CAB chairman Gurney reportedly were greeted dryly by the president: "Welcome to counsel for Northwest Airlines." With Sherman Adams and other top advisers present, he led a "table-pounding" meeting, with Eisenhower, one observer noted, "doing the pounding." Gurney informed the president that Northwest had, in fact, gone off subsidy. The former general, accustomed to relying upon a chain-of-command to provide objective facts, was furious at his advisers for providing incomplete and erroneous information. Learning, apparently for the first time, that his order had overturned a unanimous CAB vote, Eisenhower agreed to change his decision.[66]

Eisenhower wrote to acting CAB chairman Gurney on February 7. "I desire to amend my letter of February first with reference to the West Coast–Hawaii case," he stated. "Since my original action in this case I have received from you information . . . that within two years all air line subsidies in the Pacific area will probably have been eliminated." Eisenhower asked for temporary certificates for both Northwest and Pan American to serve the Seattle/Portland–Hawaii run. In a press conference two days later, Eisenhower vaguely explained: "Information came to my attention that convinced me I had made an error."[67] Editorial cartoonists had a field day lampooning the commander-in-chief's vacillations.

But the restoration of Northwest's temporary authority to serve Hawaii provided the airline little respite from Pan American's continuing challenges to its transpacific system. Despite the negative publicity, the Eisenhower administration continued to intervene in the CAB's transpacific route cases. Within three years, Eisenhower overturned four more CAB rulings, each time to the benefit of Pan American.

Eisenhower's heavy-handedness provoked controversy again in 1957, when Northwest finally won its permanent transpacific authority. A month later, however, Eisenhower, dissatisfied that Pan American had been excluded from competing on the Great Circle route, asked the CAB to reopen the interminable Transpacific Case once again. In response Nyrop took the extraordinary step of publicly charging the White House with favoritism, petitioning the CAB to "aggressively assume its full responsibilities" by keeping the president informed in route matters. In hangars and cockpits at Northwest Airlines, fingers pointed to an Eisenhower family member employed by Pan American as the reason for White House partiality. In Washington, the House voted to establish a special subcommittee to investigate White House intervention in the decisions of "quasi-judicial" regulatory agencies, while the Senate voted to limit presidential authority in international air route matters.[68]

The Transpacific Route Case continued to be reincarnated, in one form or another, for the next decade. Competition on the Great Circle route had once been economically unfeasible. But as Japanese and other Asian economies boomed during decades of postwar growth, Pan American and other airlines sought to capture as much of the lucrative traffic as they could.

But to Northwest Orient, a smaller carrier with a limited domestic system, threats to its Great Circle hegemony struck at its very ability to survive. Northwest desperately needed to correct the deficiencies of its domestic system. It had become the fourth transcontinental carrier in 1945, when it obtained authority to serve New York from Minneapolis, Milwaukee, and Detroit. In September 1955, after sixteen years of seeking New York–Chicago rights, this essential gap in Northwest's northern transcontinental route was finally closed.[69] But Northwest still faced a major problem in the seasonality of its "northern 'cold weather' route system." Without north-south traffic flows, the airline flew proportionally much more traffic during spring and summer months, and less during winter, than any other carrier. Before 1954, Northwest employees learned to expect annual wintertime furloughs; in Minnesota, highly skilled pilots, accustomed to navigating the vast expanse of the North Pacific, could be found operating St. Paul streetcars until they were called back to the airline in the spring.[70]

In November 1954, just after Nyrop's arrival at Northwest, the CAB, acknowledging Northwest's seasonality problem, approved an interchange agreement between Northwest and Eastern, providing through-plane service between Minneapolis–St. Paul and Miami via Chicago.[71] Finally in April 1958, the CAB added Miami, Tampa, and Atlanta to Northwest's route system, its first domestic warm-weather routes and first new domestic cities since 1947.[72]

In this and other domestic route decisions, Northwest benefited from the CAB's wish to bolster a smaller, presumably weaker, trunkline. "The development of a sound air route structure for the Nation," the board stated, "requires in the selection of a carrier a consideration, among other things, of the applicants' competitive positions and their relative need for strengthening."[73] In coming years, as Northwest gained in financial stature, it would find itself less a beneficiary and more an opponent of such reasoning.

As a CAB chairman who had assumed all the board's administrative responsibilities, Nyrop proved himself a great believer in centralization. As president of Northwest Airlines, Nyrop plunged into every aspect of airline management. He spent early morning hours at the airport, traveled to every station, and could be found sharing lunch with mechanics at their workbenches. He was even seen trimming the hedge at Northwest's St. Paul headquarters building. Nowhere was his eye for detail more apparent than in the realm of cost cutting. Years of testifying in Congressman Rooney's Appropriations Committee hearings had strengthened Nyrop's keen eye for finding waste in budgets, and Northwest executives soon learned that they would have to justify every cent their departments requested. Nyrop insisted that invoices should remain attached to packages containing spare parts so mechanics could see their prices.[74] Cost consciousness quickly became the Northwest way of life.

But cost consciousness came naturally to Northwest's midwestern workforce. As Nyrop and Northwest treasurer Donald Hardesty once explained to Wall Street analysts, "We're just a couple of country boys from the middle west trying to apply the basic philosophy of running a good farm to running an airline." Simple, direct solutions were sought for every problem. When Nyrop commissioned a new headquarters for Northwest, for example, he located it right at the airport, where it could combine maintenance base and executive offices under one roof. Midwestern appreciation for thrift and simplicity dictated everything at Northwest Orient, from the spartan design of its windowless offices to its lean organization chart. Despite (or perhaps because of) his government experience, Nyrop abhorred committees, and Northwest had none. Nyrop ran the airline with precision and by the force of his own personality.[75]

When it came to spending airline funds, Nyrop acquired an industry-wide reputation for frugality. But despite his affinity for tight budgets, he thought nothing of spending money "where it really counted," in expenditures related to safety. Nyrop devoted many dollars of funding and hours of staff time to basic research in meteorology and aircraft safety. When the airline industry was plagued by a series of "jet upset" accidents in the early 1960s, Northwest's chief pilot, Paul Soderlind, devoted himself to uncovering the cause. With Nyrop's blessing, he then embarked on an FAA-sponsored tour, lecturing on his findings at other airlines. Soderlind and Northwest's chief meteorologist, Daniel F. Sowa, also collaborated on pioneering studies of dangerous turbulence and began issuing wind shear warnings to Northwest pilots as early as 1962. Nyrop's carrier management was, in itself, a safety enhancement; decades before the industry focus on "aging aircraft," he contended that newer, well-maintained aircraft provided the best, safest service. Such aircraft, not incidentally, carried the highest resale value.[76]

Northwest's enviable safety record and financial strength were inter-twined. According to *Flight International,* Northwest was "known world-wide not only for its belt-tightening and profits but also for its technical and operational wizardry." When a British aviation writer, J. M. Rams-den, published a book on *The Safe Airline,* he chose Northwest Orient as his model.[77]

Nyrop's keen interest in aviation safety dated from his days as a young government attorney, when his mentor Frank Caldwell took him along to accident sites. At Northwest, Nyrop's devotion to safety demonstrated a continuation of his sense of public service. As an airline executive, Ny-rop held to certain tenets unchanged since his CAB days. Although he reported to stockholders and not to a president and Congress, Nyrop maintained that airlines were a "quasi-public" service, and he felt this view was shared by others in the industry, most notably by American's C. R. Smith. As Northwest president, Nyrop devoted many days to vis-iting cities, large and small, on Northwest's route system. Community leaders often sought schedule adjustments or additional service, and Ny-rop was frequently able to oblige, thanks to Northwest's efficiency and low debt load. By the 1970s, even the smallest cities on the airline's system were served with newer jet aircraft.

Over two decades, Nyrop gradually rebuilt Northwest Airlines. Ear-lier, Northwest had benefited from its relatively weak position among airlines. When the CAB awarded Northwest new turnaround service to Pittsburgh, Cleveland, and Detroit in 1955, it acknowledged Northwest's "need for strengthening." Eastern, then an airline citadel, argued that its "equipment purchase program" exceeded that of any other airline and therefore guaranteed more and better service. The CAB responded: "If this were the test in selection of carriers, we would always be forced to choose the strongest and richest carrier."[78] Two decades later, the airline world had changed. Eastern was weakening, beginning its inexorable slide toward bankruptcy, and Northwest was a favorite of investors for its steady profitability.

Northwest's high profitability relative to other airlines attracted wide attention. Although it remained among the smaller trunklines, airline economists scrutinized its route characteristics and "the caliber of the carrier's management" to explain its superiority over larger airline peers.[79] In a 1969 brief to the CAB, Northwest pointed out that it had "sometimes been praised—but more often assailed" for its profitability. "The reason for Northwest's outstanding financial success," its attorneys contended, "lies not in any inherent route advantages, but in its management efficiency." Such efficiency would permit Northwest "to offer a superior pattern of service" when awarded routes.[80]

But leading the industry in efficiency had its disadvantages. Other airlines argued that, with its "deep pockets," Northwest would not be hurt by diversion of traffic as other airlines might. If the CAB accepted this argument, Northwest insisted, "Carriers would be put on notice that the price of efficiency is denial of route awards." The board should reward efficiency, not penalize it.

Anticipating Deregulation

As chairman of the Civil Aeronautics Board, Donald Nyrop had encouraged airlines to become more efficient in order to reduce taxpayers' subsidy burden. Years later, his lieutenants went before the board to argue repeatedly that "if efficiency becomes known as a board criterion for carrier selection, there will be a greater emphasis on efficiency by all carriers."[81] But the CAB ultimately rejected Northwest's argument. In coming years, the Civil Aeronautics Board would repeatedly point to Northwest's "steadily profitable" record as a reason for rejecting its route applications.[82]

As a result, by the mid-1970s, frustration with the regulatory process was a repeated theme heard at Northwest Airlines. In efficiency and economy of operation, the airline far surpassed its industry peers. It had invested in safety research to the benefit of the entire aviation community. The airline had not required a dollar of government subsidy in two decades. In short, Northwest Airlines met all the criteria that would have drawn the CAB's approval under chairman Donald Nyrop. Yet the CAB continued to deny Northwest's applications for new routes.

In some ways, Nyrop behaved as though the Civil Aeronautics Board did not matter. Unlike other airline presidents, he steadfastly refused to woo CAB members. When the CAB held route hearings in vacation destinations like Hawaii or Florida, other airlines routinely sponsored receptions and cocktail hours for the CAB staff and participants. Northwest did not. Nyrop, when asked, would state that such frills were pointless and not cost-effective. His answer reveals as much about his own refusal, as CAB chairman, to be swayed by external pressures as it does about his legendary frugality. Nyrop was acutely sensitive to potential conflicts of interest, and he detested impropriety. Executives at other airlines sometimes flagrantly attempted to influence CAB examiners, but Nyrop would have none of it. One of his officers explained, "If anyone had been tempted to talk [illegally] to another airline, Nyrop would have told him, 'Get your own attorney.'" He absolutely insisted that his airline and its executives "stay clean."[83]

But Northwest's appetite for new routes, especially those which would provide domestic feed into its international system, continued unabated. Craving a Miami–Los Angeles route, which would link Northwest's transpacific system with the airline gateway to South America, Nyrop tried a different tactic. As CAB chairman, Nyrop advocated airline mergers "as a method of correcting existing unbalance in economic opportunities between air carriers."[84] In 1969, he proposed to merge Northwest with Northeast Airlines. The CAB was willing to allow the merger, but only without the prized route. Two years later, Nyrop tried again, this time proposing a merger with National Airlines. But the merger failed to meet the approval of National's board. Northwest continued to apply for the Miami–Los Angeles route, and in 1975, when a CAB examiner recommended Pan American for the award, Nyrop (who rarely granted interviews) complained to the press. The CAB "passes out routes to the poorest airlines. We have been penalized over the last several years because of our success."[85]

But in one area, Northwest experienced less than unqualified success. Labor relations throughout the airline industry reached a contentious nadir in the 1970s, and as a consistently profitable airline with high labor productivity, Northwest was a ready target for labor unrest. Although Eastern and TWA had more strikes from the 1950s to the 1970s, Northwest's seemed to make a stronger public impression.[86] Particularly lengthy strikes, including a 160-day walkout by the Brotherhood of Railway and Airline Clerks in 1970 and a 109-day strike by the Air Line Pilots Association (ALPA) in 1978, led wags to christen Northwest "Cobra Airlines" for its employees' willingness to "strike at anything."

But even strikes failed to hinder Northwest's profitability, which only fueled the unions' and public's frustration. Eastern Air Lines chairman

Floyd Hall observed of Nyrop, "Don's always been pretty tough on labor, in that he just won't take any nonsense." Nyrop simply refused to let any strike completely shut down the airline, and he attributed Northwest's uninterrupted profitability to this firm policy. Flights were curtailed, but operations continued. Management pilots kept planes in the air, and management employees regained valuable frontline experience on the ramp and behind ticket counters.[87]

Labor unions, however, detected another reason for Northwest's continued profits. In 1958, the CAB approved a novel pooling arrangement among airlines, the Mutual Aid Pact. The signatory airlines (there were fifteen by 1978) agreed that when one of their members faced a labor strike, the unstruck carriers would fund up to half of the struck carrier's operating expenses. Presumably the funds would come from windfall profits earned by unstruck competitors.[88]

By 1978, two airlines, National and Northwest, had earned more in MAP payments than the other airlines combined. In the 1970s, over several strikes, Northwest collected an estimated $182 million from the MAP fund. Meanwhile, striking ALPA pilots were paid $450 to $750 in monthly strike benefits, assessed from other airlines' union members. To observers outside the airline, neither side appeared motivated to end strikes quickly.[89]

The 1978 ALPA strike came at a crucial moment. With his accustomed focus on controlling costs, Nyrop was, according to one observer, "trying to position Northwest to compete in what [he] expects will soon become a deregulated industry." At the same time, with deregulation legislation pending, the attention of Congress and the Carter administration was focused on the airline industry. The Northwest pilots' strike added another ingredient to an already bubbling political cauldron. With labor unions pointing to the MAP as the cause of prolonged strikes, public officials in Northwest's upper Midwest region began a campaign against the Pact. Fifty congressmen cosponsored a resolution demanding that the CAB outlaw it. Although the CAB authorized additional temporary air service, it received stacks of letters from Montana, the Dakotas, Minnesota, and Washington state complaining that the strike had left travelers stranded.[90]

Because advocates of airline deregulation were selling their bill as "pro-consumer" legislation, such consumer complaints carried unusually great weight in Washington. At the same time, airline labor unions so detested the Mutual Aid Pact that they were able to put aside their misgivings about deregulation in order to see the MAP outlawed. For the unions, it was a Faustian bargain. The MAP was outlawed, but deregulation brought greater labor upheavals in the form of airline bankruptcies and failures. Airline unions, wrote one observer, "might as well have sold Manhattan for $24."[91]

But the move toward airline deregulation did not unduly concern Donald Nyrop. When the earliest murmurs of deregulation began to be whispered about the capital, Nyrop privately told Northwest's top Washington executive not to worry. Whatever happens, he assured her, "We'll still be in business." Northwest's financial strength would be its great bulwark against any sudden competitive assault. In public, however, Nyrop spoke disparagingly of deregulation's prospects. Citing the example of Sidney, Nebraska, a community of 6,000 served by four unprofitable airline flights per day, he pointed out that whenever an application for discontinuation of service was filed, Nebraska's two "free market" Republican senators urged the CAB to deny the application.[92]

As political pressure for deregulation mounted, airline executives trooped to Washington to share their laments on the CAB's failings. Nyrop grasped a perfect opportunity to return to some of his favorite themes. As the third week of Senate hearings on deregulation began in April 1977, Nyrop testified that "Northwest Airlines is in favor of 'real deregulation,'" which he defined as reductions in CAB administrative expenses and CAB-required airline paperwork, as well as a reduction in airline subsidies. Pointing out that local service subsidy had reached $80 million per year, he suggested that the time had come to legislate an absolute limit on subsidy payments.

Nyrop contended that there was no need to disassemble the Civil Aeronautics Act of 1938. "Really the problem is not the Act," he told senators. "It may well be the actors." He complained about the CAB's route case decisions in which Northwest's well-known efficiency argument was ignored or disparaged by the CAB. "The CAB, after operating for 40 years, now says they can't determine which carriers are the most efficient. But they can determine which are the least efficient and then pass out route awards."

"The proponents of deregulation in 1974 and again in 1975 really only wanted one thing," he continued. "They wanted lower passenger fares."

Donald W. Nyrop with Northwest Airlines route map in December 1958. (Courtesy of Northwest Orient Airlines)

But "coach fares have risen substantially less than the general price index," and he detailed how airlines had been affected by the exorbitant fuel prices of the 1970s energy crisis and by increases in labor and aircraft costs. Nyrop nevertheless opposed a legislative provision allowing airlines to increase fare levels 10 percent per year. He believed airlines should be permitted to raise fares no more than 5 percent annually. But "the way you stabilize the price of air transportation," he reminded, is by "awarding routes to the most efficient carriers."[93]

By November 1977, Nyrop had concluded that the pending deregulation bills could only result in more, not less, airline regulation. "It will require more taxpayer money to be spent by the CAB," Nyrop told the Harvard Business School Club of Minnesota, and the board "will need more people to handle the paperwork created." "If they had true deregulation in mind—to abolish the CAB—then we'd be all for it," he told his audience.[94]

But a year later, in October 1978, Nyrop could barely contain his glee as Northwest Airlines benefited from the CAB's first tentative steps toward deregulation. Joining the crowd of airline representatives lined up outside the CAB's Washington headquarters ravenous for new "first come, first served" route awards, Northwest strolled away with a handful of carefully chosen, critical new routes. Avoiding the sudden euphoric voraciousness of other airlines, like Braniff, which then could not digest their newly acquired routes, Northwest asked only for additions that complemented its system. "Now we've got the box clean around the United States," Nyrop said as he reviewed the awards, which included northeast-Florida and southern transcontinental routes. Better still, as the airline with the lowest airplane utilization rate, Northwest was more prepared than any of its competitors to meet the CAB's 45-day deadline for starting service. With the first European cities soon to be added to Northwest's route map, Nyrop had built a formidable three-continent airline system that no one could have imagined when he joined Northwest in 1954.[95]

Retirement

As 1978 drew to a close, Nyrop was already past Northwest's usual retirement age. Still it came as a shock to many employees when he announced he was retiring. To the popular press, which liked to portray Northwest's labor relations as a "battle of wills" between Nyrop and employees, he seemed a divisive figure, too controversial for a conservative midwestern airline. But to many Northwest employees, Don Nyrop was synonymous with Northwest Airlines. After twenty-four years, he was the only airline chief executive many of them had ever known, and his retirement marked the end of an era. Longtime employees knew him "as a warm, considerate man who goes out of his way to perform acts of kindness," and they regarded him with genuine affection.[96] In years ahead, Nyrop would be an honored guest at reunions of retired Northwest employees, feted by the same pilots who once fought him across the bargaining table, characterized always as the man who built Northwest Orient.

Nyrop remained on Northwest's board of directors for five more years. By 1989 Nyrop could only watch as his once unassailable airline, freed from CAB supervision, succumbed to the 1980s takeover frenzy. CAB

chairman Nyrop once had fretted over the financial fitness of certain airlines; now a "leveraged buyout" burdened his beloved Northwest with
more than $3 billion of debt. Fallen to the control of a group of Cali-
fornia investors led by a disaffected former director, Gary Wilson, and
Alfred Checchi, an aspiring politician, Northwest soon began to lose
money. Orders for new aircraft had to be canceled, and Northwest (which
under Nyrop had bought or sold an aircraft, on average, every twenty-two
days) labored on with one of the oldest aircraft fleets in the nation.

But that was still in the future when, at the end of 1984, in accordance
with the provisions of the Airline Deregulation Act, the Civil Aeronautics
Board prepared to disband. Donald W. Nyrop, like other former CAB
members, was invited to Washington to attend ceremonies marking the
end of the CAB's half century of service. But Nyrop, despite his earlier
fervent wish for regulatory reform, could already see that airline deregulation would fail to live up to its promise. Ever vigilant for signs of
government waste, his long-standing concern for efficient use of the
taxpayers' money unchanged, Nyrop could only shake his head in dis-
may. Federal subsidies to ensure "essential air service" to small communities, promised by congressional advocates of the Deregulation Act, were
growing. They would soon exceed the airline subsidies paid annually under the now-discarded system of federal regulation.[97]

Notes

1. *Minneapolis Tribune,* Oct. 22, 1972. Unless otherwise noted, information on
Nyrop's early career comes from personal interviews. Many Northwest Airlines
employees recall Nyrop walking the halls of the airline's headquarters, turning off
lights in unoccupied offices.

2. Quotation from Nyrop interview, Dec. 12, 1989; L. Welch Pogue interview,
May 13, 1992.

3. "Donald W. Nyrop," *Current Biography Yearbook for 1952* (New York: H. W.
Wilson, 1952), 451–53; *Aviation Week,* June 13, 1949.

4. Arnold E. Briddon and Ellmore A. Champie, *Federal Aviation Agency His-
torical Fact Book* (Washington, D.C.: GPO, 1966), 14–15, 17; John R. M. Wilson,
*Turbulence Aloft: The Civil Aeronautics Administration amid Wars and Rumors of
Wars, 1938–1958* (Washington, D.C.: GPO, 1979).

5. *Aviation Week,* June 13, 1949; Nyrop quoted in Wilson, *Turbulence Aloft,*

272, and in "Business Flying Gains Show Utility of Plane, Forum Told by Nyrop," *CAA Journal,* June 15, 1950; "Biography of Delos Wilson Rentzel," Official File, Truman Papers, Harry S Truman Library, Independence, Mo.; Aeronautical Radio, Inc., *The ARINC Story* (Annapolis, Md.: ARINC, 1987), 41–58.

6. House Committee on Appropriations, *Second Supplemental Appropriation Bill for 1950,* 81st Cong., 1st sess., 1949, 557, 559; House Committee on Appropriations, *Department of Commerce Appropriations for 1952,* 82d Cong., 1st sess., 1951, 117–31, 165; House Subcommittee on Dept. of Commerce Appropriations, *Department of Commerce Appropriations for 1951,* 81st Cong., 2d sess., 1950, 1487; Wilson, *Turbulence Aloft,* 278.

7. "Nominations Sent to the Senate on September 19, 1950," Official File, Truman Papers; "Nyrop of CAA," editorial, *American Aviation,* Nov. 13, 1950; Rep. Carl Albert to Truman, Aug. 18, 1950, Rep. Tom Steed to Truman, Aug. 22, 1950, Rep. W. G. Stigler to Truman, Aug. 26, 1950, and L. Welch Pogue to Truman, Sept. 27, 1950, Official File, Truman Papers; Senate Committee on Interstate and Foreign Commerce, *Nominations to CAB and CAA,* 81st Cong., 2d sess., 1950, 19; *CAA Journal,* Oct. 15, 1950; *New York Times,* Sept. 21, 1950.

8. "Administrator Explains Procedures for Obtaining Civil Planes and Parts," *CAA Journal,* Jan. 20, 1951; Nyrop, "Civil Air and National Defense," *Skyways* 10 (March 1951): 10–11, 48–49, 54; "Civil Aviation Reassured by Nyrop on Role in National Defense Plans," *CAA Journal,* Nov. 15, 1950; "Will the CAA Be Militarized?" *Flying* 48 (Jan. 1951): 15, 61; *New York Times,* Feb. 26, 1951; Wilson, *Turbulence Aloft,* 283.

9. Nyrop interviews, May 1, 1990, June 9, 1997; *New York Times,* Apr. 18, 1951.

10. "Washington Talk," *Aviation Week,* July 9, 1951.

11. Truman, "Special Message to the Congress Summarizing the New Reorganization Plans," and "Special Message to Congress Transmitting Reorganization Plan 13 of 1950," *Public Papers of the Presidents . . . 1950* (Washington, D.C.: GPO, 1965), 201–2, 209. The CAB's reorganization became effective May 24, 1950. See also Nyrop to Truman, Oct. 22, 1952, Official File, Truman Papers.

12. Nyrop, "Report on Civil Aviation, June 1951 through October 1952," *Journal of Air Law and Commerce* 19 (1952): 462–69. (This is the published version of a report Nyrop submitted to President Truman upon his resignation from the CAB. See Nyrop to Truman, Oct. 31, 1952, Official File, Truman Papers); Senate Committee on Appropriations, "Departments of State, Justice, Commerce, and the Judiciary Appropriations for 1953," 82d Cong., 2d sess., 1507.

13. Geoffrey Perrett, *A Dream of Greatness: The American People, 1945–1963* (New York: Coward, McCann, and Geoghegan, 1979), 49; *CAA Journal,* Oct. 20, 1951.

14. Senate Committee on Interstate and Foreign Commerce, "Nomination of

Delos W. Rentzel of Texas to Be Under Secretary of Commerce for Transportation, Nomination of Donald W. Nyrop of Nebraska to Be a Member of the Civil Aeronautics Board," unpublished hearing transcript, 82d Cong., 1st sess., 1951; *New York Times,* Apr. 7, 1951. Rentzel had worked for American Airlines.

15. Nyrop interviews; Nyrop's reluctance to leave CAA (although perhaps not his reasoning) was well known; see Senate Commerce Committee, "Nomination of Delos W. Rentzel," 107.

16. Civil Aeronautics Act of 1938, Title I, section 2. This interpretation of the Act appears in the CAB's opinion in *Transcontinental Coach-Type Service Case,* 14 CAB 722–23 (1951).

17. *Transcontinental Coach-Type Service Case,* 14 CAB 721 (1951); Amos Heacock testimony in Senate Commerce Committee, "Nomination of Delos W. Rentzel," 147–49. The headlines appeared in *Coronet* and *Cosmopolitan* magazines.

18. Senate Select Committee on Small Business, *Report on Role of Irregular Airlines in United States Air Transportation Industry,* 82d Cong., 1st sess., 1951; *New York Times,* Apr. 5, 1951.

19. *Annual Report of the Civil Aeronautics Board,* 1951, 66–70; House Subcommittee on Departments of State, Justice, Commerce, and the Judiciary Appropriations, *Departments of State, Justice, Commerce, and the Judiciary Appropriations for 1953. Department of Commerce,* 82d Cong., 2d sess., 1952, 261–62; *CAA Journal,* Dec. 20, 1951. Tales of astonishingly inconvenient nonsked flights abound. Congressman Carl Hinshaw telephoned Nyrop to report the details of his secretary's nightmarish nonscheduled flight from Burbank, California, to Washington: scheduled to leave on Sunday evening, her flight finally arrived in Washington on Tuesday afternoon. Nyrop to Board Members, Jan. 5, 1952, Box 11, General Records, Office of Chairman, Records of the Civil Aeronautics Board, National Archives, Washington, D.C.

20. Truman to Nyrop, Jan. 15, 1952, President's Secretary's Files, Truman Papers.

21. Nyrop, "Report," 466; *CAA Journal,* Oct. 20, 1951.

22. *Transcontinental Coach-Type Service Case,* 14 CAB 721 (1951).

23. Nyrop speech on "The CAA and the Airlines," quoted in *CAA Journal,* Nov. 15, 1950.

24. James G. Woolley and Earl W. Hill, *Airplane Transportation* (Hollywood, Calif.: Hartwell, 1929).

25. *Transcontinental Coach-Type Service Case,* 14 CAB 721 (1951).

26. Nyrop interview, June 9, 1997; Nyrop, "Report," 464–65.

27. Truman, "Annual Budget Message to the Congress: Fiscal Year 1951," *Public Papers . . . 1950,* 94; "Special Message to the Congress on Increasing the Postal Rates," *Public Papers . . . 1951,* 168; "Annual Budget Message to the Congress: Fiscal Year 1952," *Public Papers . . . 1952–53,* 83. Subsidy separation had been advocated in the Hoover Commission's report on the Post Office.

28. Nyrop interview, May 3, 1997; O'Connell to Johnson, Oct. 27, 1949; Johnson to O'Connell, Oct. 31, 1949, Box 12, General Records, Office of Chairman, CAB Records.

29. Senate Committee on Interstate and Foreign Commerce, *Separation of Air Mail Pay from Subsidy,* 82d Cong., 1st sess., 1951, 60–100; see also House Committee on Interstate and Foreign Commerce, *Air Mail Subsidies,* 82d Cong., 2d sess., 1952, 79–126.

30. Senate Commerce Committee, *Separation of Air Mail Pay from Subsidy,* 60–100; Nyrop, "Report," 462.

31. *New York Times,* July 10, 1951; *CAA Journal,* Sept. 20, 1951; Nyrop, "Report," 462–63; Senate Commerce Committee, *Separation of Mail Pay from Subsidy,* 100; Nyrop interview, May 3, 1997; *American Airlines, Inc., et al., Mail Rates,* 14 CAB 558 (1951).

32. Nyrop quoted in *CAA Journal,* Nov. 20, 1951; Nyrop, "Report," 462–63.

33. Basil J. F. Mott Jr., "The Effect of Political Interest Groups on CAB Policies," *Journal of Air Law and Commerce* 19 (1952): 379–410, provides details of the subsidy separation issue up to 1951; Nyrop interviews. The biographer of former CAB chairman James M. Landis erroneously credits Congressman John F. Kennedy, with Landis as his legislative aide, for subsidy separation. In fact, Kennedy's bill was one of eleven introduced in the House that never attained passage. See Donald A. Ritchie, *James M. Landis: Dean of the Regulators* (Cambridge, Mass.: Harvard, 1980), 169; *Congressional Quarterly Almanac, 1952* (Washington, D.C.: Congressional Quarterly, 1952), 341. Interestingly, Landis had been an opponent of subsidy separation while CAB chairman (Mott, 397).

34. Minutes of CAB board meeting no. 767 (unpublished typescript provided by Donald W. Nyrop).

35. *New York Times,* Jan. 1, 2, 1952; Wilson, *Turbulence Aloft,* 285; James M. Verner interview, June 20, 1997; *CAA Journal,* Feb. 20, 1952.

36. *New York Times,* Dec. 27, 1951; CAB accident reports, summarized in *CAA Journal,* June 20, 1952; Wilson, *Turbulence Aloft,* 259–61.

37. Nyrop interview, May 3, 1997. Other members of the Doolittle Commission were CAA administrator Charles Horne and MIT professor Jerome C. Hunsaker. Truman to Doolittle, Feb. 20, 1952, in Truman, *Public Papers . . . 1952–53* (Washington, D.C.: GPO, 1966), 161–62.

38. *New York Times,* Feb. 21, 1952; Senate Committee on Interstate and Foreign Commerce, "Executive Session. Investigation of Airplane Accident at Elizabeth, New Jersey, and Matters Relating to Newark Airport," confidential unpublished hearing, 82d Cong., 2d sess., 1952.

39. *New York Times,* Feb. 13, 16, 17, 1952. Nyrop also testified before a grand jury impaneled in Union County, N.J., to determine criminal responsibility for the Elizabeth accidents. Grand Jury Presentment, Jan. 2, 1952, Truman Papers.

40. Senate Commerce Committee, "Matters Relating to Newark Airport," 50–51; President's Airport Commission, *The Airport and Its Neighbors* (Washington, D.C.: GPO, 1952); *CAA Journal,* June 20, 1952, 53, 56. An Elizabeth resident who lost his wife and children in one of the Newark accidents touchingly wrote to Truman to express his appreciation for the work of Doolittle and the CAB. Albert Ragone to Truman, Sept. 4, 1952, Truman Papers.

41. Austin J. Tobin to Nyrop, Sept. 6, 1952; C. R. Smith to Nyrop, Sept. 5, 1952. Box 27, General Records, Office of Chairman, CAB Records.

42. "Rapid Development of Jet Aircraft Presents Airport Planning Problem," *CAA Journal,* Oct. 15, 1950; "Administrator Sets Up Advisory Committee for Prototype Aircraft," *CAA Journal,* Jan. 20, 1951; "Nyrop Cites Steps Taken to Assist Civil Aviation," *CAA Journal,* Feb. 20, 1951.

43. Senate Committee on Interstate and Foreign Commerce, *Prototype Aircraft Development—Construction Differential,* 82d Cong., 2d sess., 1952, 45–65; *New York Times,* May 13, 1952; Secretary of Commerce Charles Sawyer to Truman, Mar. 28, 1951, Truman Papers.

44. Nyrop interview, June 9, 1997; Margaret Truman, *Harry S Truman* (New York: William Morrow, 1973), 103–4; Pogue interview. Aviation writer Wayne Parrish also noted Truman's legislative role and his continued "keen interest in air transportation." See Parrish to Matthew J. Connelly, Nov. 29, 1950, Official File, Truman Papers.

45. Nyrop interview, May 3, 1997. Nyrop's respectful relationship with Truman contrasted with that of fired CAB chairman James M. Landis, who patronizingly considered Truman a "small, small man" and derided his preference for maps and charts in understanding route matters. See Ritchie, *James M. Landis,* 143.

46. Nyrop interviews; Nyrop, "Report," 466; *North Atlantic Certificate Renewal Case,* 15 CAB 1053 (1952).

47. Nyrop to Truman, Sept. 29, 1952, Truman to Nyrop, Oct. 15, 1952, Official File, Truman Papers; Nyrop interview, June 9, 1997. Truman proudly mentioned the volume (now in the Truman Library) in an aviation speech in December 1952; see Truman, *Public Papers . . . 1952–53,* 1085–86. For accounts of the North Atlantic Route Transfer case and O'Connell resignation, see O'Connell to Truman, July 3, July 6, 1950, and Truman to O'Connell, July 5, 1950, Truman Papers; *Washington Post* and *Washington Star,* July 9, 1950; *Air Traffic Digest* 3 (July 13, 1950); Carl Solberg, *Conquest of the Skies: The History of Commercial Aviation in America* (Boston: Little, Brown, 1979), 307–9.

48. "Nyrop and the CAB," editorial, *American Aviation,* Nov. 10, 1952; *Aviation Week,* Oct. 27, 1952; Nyrop interview, Dec. 12, 1989.

49. Nyrop quoted in *Minneapolis Star,* Jan. 7, 1955; Nyrop interviews; *Aviation Week,* Mar. 30, 1953.

50. Senate Committee on Interstate and Foreign Commerce, *Revision of Civil Aeronautics Act,* 83d Cong., 2d sess., 1952, 461–69; Senate Committee on Interstate and Foreign Commerce, *To Provide Permanent Certificates for Local Service Air Carriers,* 83d Cong., 2d sess., 1954, 5–15, 117–31; Senate Committee on Appropriations, *Departments of State, Justice, and Commerce and the U.S. Information Agency Appropriations, 1955,* 83d Cong., 2d sess., 1954, 1756–67; House Committee on Interstate and Foreign Commerce, *Permanent Certificates for Local Service Air Carriers,* 83d Cong., 2d sess., 1954, 1–57; *American Aviation,* Aug. 30, 1954; Nyrop interviews.

51. *Minneapolis Tribune,* Feb. 16, Mar. 5, 1954; Kenneth D. Ruble, *Flight to the Top* (Eden Prairie, Minn.: privately printed, 1986), 125; Nyrop interviews, Dec. 12, 1989, May 1, 1990.

52. In late 1951, Northwest's president, Croil Hunter, detailed some of the airline's problems in "A Confidential Report Regarding the Inability of Northwest Airlines, Inc. in Domestic Operations to Be Permanently Self-Sustaining at Service Mail Rates," which he addressed to CAB chairman Nyrop. A later report to the CAB, "History of the Martin 2-0-2 Aircraft in Northwest Airlines, Inc. Domestic Operations," details the airline's safety problems and the government and public response. Northwest Airlines, Inc. Records, Minnesota Historical Society, St. Paul, Minn.; Nyrop interview, Dec. 12, 1989.

53. "New NWA President Isn't Jumping to Any 'Solutions,'" *Minneapolis Tribune,* Aug. 31, 1954; *NWA News,* October 1954; *Minneapolis Star,* Jan. 7, 1955; Nyrop interview, Dec. 12, 1989; *Aviation Week,* Sept. 6, 1954.

54. *Minneapolis Star,* Jan. 7, 1955; *Minneapolis Tribune,* Oct. 18, 1954.

55. Albro Martin, *James J. Hill and the Opening of the Northwest* (St. Paul: Minnesota Historical Society Press, 1991), 471–74; "The Jim Hill of Aviation! Who Will He Be?" *St. Paul Pioneer Press,* Oct. 17, 1926, clipping in L. H. Brittin Papers, Minnesota Historical Society; general discussion of Northwest's route development can be found in Stephen E. Mills, *More Than Meets the Sky* (Seattle: Superior, 1972) and Ruble, *Flight to the Top.*

56. *Northwest Airlines, Inc., et al., Pacific Case,* 7 CAB 209 (1946).

57. Senate Committee on Interstate and Foreign Commerce, *Consolidation of International Air Carriers (Chosen Instrument),* 80th Cong., 1st sess., 1947; for Pan American's earlier attempt, see Senate Committee on Commerce, *To Create the All-American Flag Line, Inc.,* 79th Cong., 1st sess., 1945. Noel F. Busch, "Juan Trippe," *Life,* Oct. 20, 1941, 124.

58. Ruble, "Northwest's Nyrop, Master of Control," *Corporate Report* 6 (1975): 17–19, 74–79; Nyrop interviews; *Minneapolis Tribune,* Jan. 8, 1955.

59. Nyrop quoted in *Minneapolis Star,* Jan. 7, 1955; Nyrop interviews; Ruble, *Flight to the Top,* 136–37.

60. *American Aviation,* Aug. 16, 1954, Feb. 14, 1955.

61. *Transpacific Certificate Renewal Case,* 20 CAB 47 (1954); *West Coast Hawaii Case,* 20 CAB 7 (1954); *Aviation Week,* Feb. 14, 1955.

62. *Aviation Week,* Feb. 14, 1955.

63. Oral argument transcript, May 28, 1954, 127–28, CAB Docket 5589 et al., CAB Records; "NWA Sees Subsidy-Free Pacific Operations," *American Aviation,* June 7, 1954.

64. *American Aviation,* Feb. 14, 1955. For Weeks's pro-business viewpoint, see Eric F. Goldman, *The Crucial Decade—and After: America, 1945–1960* (New York: Vintage Books, 1960), 241–42.

65. Nyrop felt a large Washington lobbying staff was not cost-effective; Nyrop interviews. A Northwest flight engineer, writing to acting CAB chairman Gurney, stated, "All of us are aware of Pan American's huge lobby in Washington, D.C., and certainly hope that it isn't necessary for each company to have that kind of pressure to get equality." Wayne Hokenson to Gurney, Feb. 4, 1955, in Docket 5589 et al., CAB Records.

66. Nyrop interview, June 9, 1997; *American Aviation,* Feb. 14, 1955.

67. Eisenhower, *Public Papers of the Presidents . . . 1955* (Washington, D.C.: GPO, 1959), 242–43, 260–61.

68. *Aviation Week,* Aug. 12, Sept. 16, Oct. 14, 1957. A common rumor at Northwest (detailed in Paul Prestegaard to Eisenhower, Mar. 10, 1956, Docket 5589 et al., CAB Records) had Eisenhower's "son-in-law" as a Pan American executive, but the Eisenhowers' only surviving child was a son. Another rumor, repeated by newspaper columnist Drew Pearson, described an Eisenhower nephew as a Pan Am manager. Pearson, "The Washington Merry-Go-Round" in *Washington Post,* May 30, 1957; Nyrop interviews; John W. Campion interview, May 4, 1997.

69. *New York–Chicago Service Case,* 22 CAB 973 (1955); *Northwest Airlines News,* Oct. 1955; *Minneapolis Star,* Oct. 31, 1955; *Aviation Week,* Feb. 9, 1959; Ruble, 99.

70. Nyrop quoted in *Northwest Orient Airlines News,* Apr.-May 1958; Northwest Airlines, Inc. to CAB, "A Confidential Report Regarding . . . Service Mail Rates," 14–16; Vincent A. Doyle interviews.

71. *Northwest-Eastern, Equipment Interchange,* 19 CAB 351, 355 (1954).

72. *Great Lakes–Southeast Service Case,* 27 CAB 843 (1958); *Northwest Orient Airlines News,* Apr.-May 1958, Jan.-Feb. 1959.

73. *Northwest Airlines, Pittsburgh-Cleveland and Detroit Restriction Case, and New York–Chicago Service Case,* 23 CAB 945 (1955). See also *New York–Chicago Service Case,* 22 CAB 973 (1955).

74. Nyrop and Norman Midthun interviews; Ruble, *Flight to the Top,* 133–34.

75. Ruble, 133–34, 201; Nyrop interview, Dec. 12, 1989; Donald Hardesty and Norman Midthun interviews; Hugh D. Menzies, "Don Nyrop Keeps a Tight

Rein on Northwest," *Fortune,* Aug. 14, 1978, 142–46; "Fiscal Management Plus Cost Control Make Northwest Great," *Air Transport World,* Sept. 1976 (reprint in Northwest Airlines Records).

76. Nyrop interview, Dec. 12, 1989; Soderlind and Sowa interviews; Ruble, *Flight to the Top;* Robert J. Serling, *Loud and Clear* (Garden City, N.Y.: Doubleday, 1969), 84–87, 100–101.

77. *Flight International,* Feb. 23, 1978; Ramsden, *The Safe Airline* (London: Macdonald and Jane's, 1976).

78. *New York–Chicago Service (Northwest Restriction),* 23 CAB 945–46 (1955).

79. William E. Fruhan Jr., *The Fight for Competitive Advantage: A Study of the United States Domestic Trunk Air Carriers* (Boston: Harvard Business School, 1972), 52.

80. Brief of Northwest Airlines, Inc. to the Civil Aeronautics Board, *Twin Cities–Milwaukee Long-Haul Investigation,* Sept. 10, 1969, 9, 12 (copy located in Minnesota Department of Aeronautics Records, Minnesota State Archives).

81. Northwest argument summarized by Administrative Law Judge William A. Kane Jr. in Recommended Decision, *Chicago-Vancouver Route Proceeding,* 75 CAB 543–44 (1977).

82. *Chicago-Montreal Route Proceeding,* 71 CAB 1122 (1976), 1134n; *Fort Myers-Atlanta Case,* 68 CAB 1213 (1975); *Service to Omaha and Des Moines, Reopened,* 69 CAB 366–68, 417–18 (1975); Campion interview, May 4, 1997; Steven G. Rothmeier interviews, Jan. 20, Apr. 30, 1997.

83. Nyrop interview, June 9, 1997; Campion interview, May 2, 1997; Rothmeier interview, Jan. 20, 1997. In its 1976 *Service to Saipan* opinion (70 CAB 1287), the CAB, citing Rules of Procedure violations by Pan American and Continental, stated: "If conduct violations were the determinative criterion, Northwest, whose prosecution of its application discloses no misconduct, would merit the award." Continental obtained the route.

84. Nyrop, "Report on Civil Aviation," 465.

85. *Northwest-Northeast Merger Case,* 55 CAB 942 (1970), 56 CAB 103 (1971); *Wall Street Journal,* Nov. 12, 1969, Mar. 2, Mar. 11, 1971; *New York Times,* Mar. 11, Sept. 4, 1971, *Minneapolis Star,* May 28, 1975; Nyrop quoted in *Minneapolis Star,* Nov. 5, 1975.

86. *Wall Street Journal,* Apr. 12, 1977.

87. Hall quoted in *Minneapolis Star,* May 28, 1975. Hall's successor at Eastern, Frank Borman, praised Nyrop as ultimately "pro-labor" for providing his employees with job security by running a lean, efficient airline. Borman, *Countdown* (New York: William Morrow, 1988), 324–25.

88. *Six-Carrier Mutual Aid Pact,* 29 CAB 168 (1959); *Mutual Aid Pact Investigation,* 40 CAB 559 (1964); and *Airlines Mutual Aid Pact,* 54 CAB 481 (1970). Northwest was not among the original signatories of the pact, joining in 1960.

89. *Aviation Week and Space Technology,* Aug. 21, 1978; *Newsweek,* July 24, 1978; *Business Week,* Sept. 4, 1978; *U.S. News and World Report,* July 31, 1978.

90. *Business Week,* Sept. 4, 1978; *Airline Executive,* July 1978; *U.S. News and World Report,* July 31, 1978; *Aviation Week,* Aug. 21, 1978.

91. Thomas Petzinger Jr., *Hard Landing: The Epic Contest for Power and Profits That Plunged the Airlines into Chaos* (New York: Times Business, 1995), 89.

92. Yoshie Ogawa interview, June 19, 1997; *Minneapolis Star* editorial, Nov. 8, 1975.

93. Senate Committee on Commerce, Science, and Transportation, *Regulatory Reform in Air Transportation, Part 3,* 95th Cong., 1st sess., 1977, 1464–84. Some economists (unlike consumer advocates) cited the discretionary authority to raise fare levels without regulatory review as an argument in favor of the 1978 Deregulation Act. This would enable airlines, in a notoriously capital-intensive industry, to meet their expected needs for equipment replacement. See Paul W. MacAvoy, *The Regulated Industries and the Economy* (New York: Norton, 1979), 76–77.

94. Nyrop quoted in *St. Paul Dispatch,* Nov. 18, 1977, and in *Minneapolis Star,* Nov. 18, 1977.

95. *St. Paul Pioneer Press-Dispatch,* Oct. 28, 1978; Campion interviews. Northwest's new European routes were approved by President Carter on January 26, 1978. See *Transatlantic Route Proceeding,* 75 CAB 616 (1977).

96. *Minneapolis Tribune,* Oct. 22, 1972.

97. Nyrop interview, Dec. 12, 1989.

Bibliographic Essay

Few secondary sources exist on the airline regulatory world of the early 1950s. General histories of the Truman administration tend to ignore aviation, and aviation histories tend to ignore public policy. One exception, Carl Solberg's *Conquest of the Skies: A History of Commercial Aviation in America* (Boston: Little, Brown, 1979), remains the most sophisticated history of the United States airline industry; the author, a former *Time* editor, well understood the interrelations of politics, economics, and airlines. John R. M. Wilson's *Turbulence Aloft: The Civil Aeronautics Administration amid Wars and Rumors of Wars, 1938–1953* (Washington, D.C.: GPO, 1979), is the official FAA history volume which includes Donald W. Nyrop's tenure as administrator. It scrupulously avoids discussion of the CAB or of the close interactions between the two agencies. The contemporary *CAA Journal,* published by the agency, held no such qualms and discussed both CAA and CAB developments with equal detail. Unfortunately, it ceased publication in 1952.

Donald W. Nyrop's history as a public servant is best told in government documents. He regularly testified in congressional hearings, and the transcripts make palpable the growing respect he received from members of Congress. The *Annual Reports of the Civil Aeronautics Board* detail Nyrop's administrative achievements as chairman. *CAB Reports* contain cases decided during his chairmanship. Nyrop's own comprehensive report to President Truman on his CAB tenure was published in *The Journal of Air Law and Commerce* 19 (autumn 1952).

The National Archives holds the surviving records of the CAA and CAB. The Harry S Truman Presidential Library, Independence, Missouri, contains many interesting documents related to Nyrop's government posts. Nyrop himself kept typescript copies of the official CAB minutes from his chairmanship.

Nyrop's twenty-four-year tenure as president of Northwest Airlines was the longest in the airline's history and encompassed many crucial events. No history of Northwest Airlines could be complete without a full acknowledgment of his unique imprint. Kenneth D. Ruble, a former Northwest advertising manager, published *Flight to the Top* (privately printed in Eden Prairie, Minn., 1986). Subtitled "How a Home Town Airline Made History . . . and Keeps on Making It," it reads exactly as one would expect. To his everlasting credit, however, Ruble managed to interview many figures important in the airline's development before their contributions could be lost or forgotten.

Stephen E. Mills, *More Than Meets the Sky* (Seattle: Superior, 1972), is a wide-ranging photo album with limited text, later republished as *A Pictorial History of Northwest Airlines* (New York: Bonanza Books, 1980). *Northwest Orient,* an album of airplane photographs with text by Bill Yenne (New York: Gallery Books, 1986), unfortunately contains historical inaccuracies too numerous to mention.

The best published descriptions of Nyrop and Northwest Airlines come from business and industry insiders. Articles in *American Aviation, Aviation Week, Air Transport World, Fortune,* and the *Wall Street Journal* capture events and Nyrop's unique style as an industry leader. The flight operations side of Northwest Airlines is explored in J. M. Ramsden, *The Safe Airline* (London: Macdonald and Jane's, 1976), and in Robert J. Serling, *Loud and Clear* (Garden City, N.Y.: Doubleday, 1969).

Among original sources, a small collection of Northwest Airlines records is housed at the Minnesota Historical Society in St. Paul. Despite abortive attempts to establish a corporate archives in the 1970s and 1980s, Northwest Airlines has destroyed much of its own history; most surviving archival materials are in private hands. The Northwest Airlines employee publication, variously incarnated as *The Beam, NWA News, Northwest Airlines News,* and *Passages,* is invaluable for understanding management priorities.

To interview participants is both an essential duty and a great joy for the student of recent history. Dozens of Northwest Airlines employees and retirees have volunteered their thoughts on Nyrop and his leadership of their airline. Among Northwest alumni, Nyrop's regulatory staff, including Yoshie Ogawa, Steven G. Rothmeier, Allan K. Pray, and especially John W. Campion, provided essential information. Pilots Norman Midthun and Vincent A. Doyle ably described the atmosphere at Northwest Airlines before and during the Nyrop presidency. Mr. and Mrs. James M. Verner uniquely offered valuable perspective on both Nyrop's government and airline careers. Former CAB chairman L. Welch Pogue, known throughout Washington for his ability to spot legal talent, recalled with great alacrity his hiring of the young government attorney. Most importantly, of course, the author owes a special debt to Donald W. Nyrop, who has provided many hours of airline education with great generosity and patience.

Robert F. Six: Continental Giant

MICHAEL H. GORN

CONTINENTAL AIRLINES FOUNDER ROBERT F. Six possessed big appetites. As a young man he earned a reputation as a free-spirited playboy and aviator. In middle age he married two of the reigning queens of the entertainment industry. In later years he ran his airline with an unquenchable thirst for expansion. He swore like a sailor and made no apologies for his love of the hunt. Yet, paradoxically, Six operated Continental with an exquisite attention to minutiae, belying his flamboyant public persona. He developed a legendary knowledge of the smallest details of the business; he set high standards and insisted his employees measure up to them. Six's attitude toward federal regulation bore the same paradoxical quality. For a man who lived exactly by his own lights, he operated with astonishing ease, dexterity, and success in the tightly corseted world of the Civil Aeronautics Board (CAB).

Early Life

The surname of this pivotal airline executive appeared in the records of northern California at the turn of the twentieth century. After training as a physician, Clarence Logan Six migrated from Indiana to the Golden

State and settled in Stockton. Like his sixteenth-century Dutch ancestors, who had been linen merchants and pawnbrokers, Six proved to be ambitious. He courted and married Genevieve Peters, the daughter of Major J. D. Peters, a Genoese mariner, river boat operator, and developer of the deep-water canal linking San Francisco, Sacramento, and Stockton. Clarence Six not only married well but improved his professional standing by specializing in plastic surgery, a new medical art developed during World War I. The family enjoyed solid comfort.

Early in their marriage, Genevieve Six gave birth to the first of three children. Robert Forman Six, born June 25, 1907, once described his childhood with the equivocal expression "not unhappy." While the family lived in comparative affluence and while father and son shared a love of hunting, fishing, and the wilderness, the younger Six failed to satisfy his parents' expectations. Clarence Six wanted him to be a doctor; young Robert dismissed the idea without a further thought. The boy considered a nautical career and dreamed of the U.S. Naval Academy, but his grades—especially in mathematics—doomed his chances. He graduated from Weber Grammar School in Stockton "by working," as he admitted, "just hard enough to skin through." His father tried to rescue his slumping academic career by enrolling him in St. Mary's Catholic High School in Oakland, but even the Christian Brothers could not coax him over the obstacle of algebra. At seventeen, the headstrong young Six decided to drop out of school. Clearly, he left not for the lack of intellectual ability; in later life he would become famous for his sparkling analytical powers, as well as for his capacity to understand a balance sheet. Rather, Six fell under an impulse too strong to deny—an instinct to live firsthand, rather than acquire experiences vicariously.[1]

For the next ten years, Robert Six tasted life with abandon. Divorcing himself completely from the genteel aspirations of his family, he worked first in a factory. Then he shipped out aboard tankers in the Standard Oil fleet, eventually achieving the rank of able-bodied seaman. The time on the high seas toughened him, exposing him to some hard characters and teaching him to live rough. His legendary temper and his profane tongue both stemmed from this period. But Six needed steadier employment. He found it in Stockton as a bill collector for the Pacific Gas and Electric Company's credit department. Although very young, his imposing height of six feet four inches and weight of over 200 pounds imparted confidence to his employers. "Every [Monday] morning," he recalled, "I would leave in my Model A with a stack of bills and a set of tools. If a farmer couldn't pay his bill, I'd just climb the nearest pole and literally cut off his power." The rugged rookie became practiced at terminating unpaid rural accounts. But he also did more.

Inspired by the bravery of Charles Lindbergh's unaccompanied flight across the Atlantic in May 1927, the twenty-year-old decided like so many of his generation to become an aviator. The only problem with his resolution: he tried to fulfill his ambition on PG&E's time clock. Rather than shimmying up power poles, he spent part of his days strapped in the cockpit of a little OX-5 Alexander Eagle Rock biplane taking pilot's training at Stockton Airport. Miraculously, he continued the ruse for two years before his bosses at the utility company discovered his activities and fired him. "But that's what aviation does to you," he once told an audience. "I've never known an industry that can get into people's blood the way aviation does." By then, however, he had earned his wings with license number 5772 and found a job more suited to his boisterous temperament, flying the public as a dollar-a-ride stunt pilot.[2]

At the tender age of twenty-two, Six tried his first business venture. With money from his mother's estate (she died suddenly from pneumonia) he purchased an old three-seat Travel Air biplane. The only pilot flying the company's only plane, he brashly called his operation the Valley Flying Service, offering scenic and charter flights in the skies over the Bay area. On the weekends he raced his airplane, performed in aerial shows, and took lessons from no less than Ray Hunt, the famous aerobatics daredevil. But the weekdays brought little business, and to find a more secure career in the cockpit he moved to San Francisco and applied to Boeing Air Transport's first flight school. The enrollment fee of $5,000 was high, but it opened the possibility of instrument training and of becoming a commercial airline pilot. He lost the opportunity in typical Six fashion: he persuaded students attending Boeing's mechanics classes to spend their nights coaxing more speed from his Travel Air. When his flight instructor heard rumors, he laid into him: "Six, you're nothing but a bad influence. I'm expelling you from this school." Then the young miscreant found himself in even worse trouble. In quick succession he undershot a runway in a Pitcairn borrowed from a United test pilot and almost destroyed it, ran out of fuel in a Jenny and crash-landed it, and made an emergency touchdown in a Salinas bean field when his Travel Air's crankshaft failed. The farmer chained his plane to a fence until Six paid for the beanstalks ruined on impact. As a result of these mishaps, Boeing refused his application for readmittance to its school.[3]

Catastrophe followed catastrophe. Squeezed by the Great Depression, Valley Flying Service ceased operations. With nothing more to lose than the remnants of his inheritance, Six embarked on the ship *Tatsaru Maru* for Shanghai, where he hoped to fly for the China National Aviation Company, a carrier running amphibious aircraft over the Yangtze River to the eastern city of Chongqing and operating Stinsons north along the East China Sea to Beijing. He only found part-time work as a copilot on the firm's test flights and resided the entire time at the Metropole Hotel in Shanghai. Nonetheless, China made a lasting impression on Six, one which he would redeem many decades later. He left after only eighteen months, returned to the United States briefly, then journeyed to France and Spain where he spent a year and the last of his mother's legacy. Broke and unemployed, he returned to San Francisco.

While overseas, Six acquired a degree of sophistication and worldly knowledge, and he came across as a dashing figure with indifferent morals. Women found his tales of foreign adventure and his tall, energetic presence irresistible. Men identified with his flying exploits, his ready resort to fists, and his elaborately obscene vocabulary. Yet, at twenty-seven, he had reached a crossroads: he would either fulfill his inner promise or spend his days at manual labor and his nights on barstools. For a while it seemed almost certain he would take the low road. By now his father had died, and after the exhilaration of travel he felt "at loose ends, cast adrift." For a time Six plunged into the earthier side of San Francisco life. He took a job as a laborer in a cement plant, then drove a delivery truck for the *San Francisco Chronicle*. A friend described him as a "tough, crude roustabout who just threw bundles of newspapers off to delivery boys at various distribution centers." Until his 2:30 a.m. shift, he devoted his evenings to playing cards at the local police station. His pay evaporated, and his only distinction resulted from crossing a picket line during a longshoremen's strike called by the powerful union chief Harry Bridges; the newspaper awarded Six a gold medal for heroism.

What transformed Robert Six? He discovered himself through a woman's love and through his passion for aviation. Among his many fe-

Workhorse of the Shanghai to Beijing corridor during Six's test pilot interlude with the China National Aviation Company, this particular Stinson Reliant served as a flight research vehicle for the National Advisory Committee for Aeronautics. (Courtesy of the National Aeronautics and Space Administration, Washington, D.C.)

male admirers, a striking divorcée named Henriette Erhart Ruggles, the daughter of Pfizer Pharmaceutical chairman William H. Erhart, attracted his attention. The consequences of their meeting reversed Six's life. Suddenly, he found himself in the best San Francisco society. He started to save his earnings and think about his future. After the horrible death of Henriette's two children in a house fire, she and Six found themselves drawn together. Despite her father's misgivings, they began married life in August 1934. Aviation, likewise, proved to be Six's salvation. In 1935 he teamed with his friend Monty Mouton to form Mouton and Six, the first Pacific Northwest distributor of aircraft produced by Walter Beech. They sold both new and used Beechcraft with some success.[4]

Delighted to be back in the business he loved, Six harbored an even greater aspiration than his present partnership. This desire reflected an awakening self-knowledge. Almost thirty, he realized he possessed the wherewithal to act on a bigger stage. He had experience in business, the advantages of travel, a roughhewn charisma, and steadily improving social connections. Mixing with the better sort proved instrumental at a party attended by Six and Thomas F. Ryan III, recent purchaser of Hanford Airlines. When Six told Ryan he longed to operate an air carrier, Ryan promised to introduce him to a San Francisco entrepreneur named Louis Mueller. A hard-nosed businessman and World War I flight instructor, Mueller and his partner, Walter T. Varney, owned a small company called Varney Air Lines. Varney had been one of Mueller's trainees in flight school. They opened their company in 1925 as a ferry service across San Francisco Bay and expanded in April 1926 with the award of minor airmail routes between Elko, Nevada, and Pasco, Washington, via Boise, Idaho. After they added service to Salt Lake City, United Airlines bought them out for $2 million.

But Varney, a tireless promoter, could not stay out of the air. He made several abortive attempts to start anew, only to try a fourth time in 1934 with Varney Speed Lines, Southwest Division. Between February and June of that year, the administration of Franklin D. Roosevelt, charging fraud and collusion among the private airmail carriers, stripped them of their routes and turned over the nation's aerial delivery of letters and packages to the Army Air Corps. Sixty-six accidents resulted, twelve pilots died, and the whole system lay in wreckage. When the president allowed the Post Office to resume bids from the airlines, Varney and Mueller captured an obscure north-south link between Pueblo, Colorado, and El Paso, Texas, via Albuquerque, New Mexico. The major airlines showed no interest because they preferred the east-west lines, which generated the richer coast-to-coast mail contracts. At this point, beset by debt and failure, Varney decided to abandon the business, leaving the wily Mueller to salvage what he could. From his office in San Francisco he pared down staff, sold one of the firm's four Lockheed Vegas, and fought for months to find a fresh infusion of capital to serve the Pueblo to El Paso corridor.

The answer to Mueller's dilemma appeared in the big shape of Robert Six. After Tom Ryan's introduction, the two men met to negotiate. The diminutive Mueller proposed selling Six 40 percent of Varney's stock for $90,000. He also demanded a $20,000 personal bonus. Shocked by the cost but convinced that Mueller would not compromise, Six assented. He conveniently forgot to inform his partner-to-be that he had no money, only the vague hope that his father-in-law would act as his banker. William Erhart pronounced it a bad bargain, but family harmony prevailed and he agreed to supply the $90,000. He also ceded the all-important stock voting rights to his son-in-law. Six presented Mueller a note for the additional $20,000 and reported for work on July 5, 1936. He started with three contradictory roles: as Mueller's major stockholder, as Mueller's partner, and as Mueller's operations manager (for which he received $400 per month).[5]

A Young Executive

In short order Six found himself commuting between the refined pleasures of San Francisco and the rowdy setting of El Paso, Texas, at the southern extreme of Varney's route system. Mueller realized early that he had chosen a formidable partner, "very aggressive and ambitious, with a great desire to learn." From his vista on the Mexican border, Six had to learn fast. Varney offered but one round-trip a day on its 520-mile route between El Paso and Pueblo, attracting only nine paying customers in its first two weeks of service. Without the airmail subsidy of 17 cents per plane mile, it was doomed; with it, Varney barely survived. Six devised a daring plan, based on a bluff, to save the company. He flew to Washington, D.C., to meet with postal officials, demanding that his airline should be paid not 17 cents per mile but the maximum 33.3 cent rate awarded carriers that flew fielded two-engine aircraft. Six informed them that Varney would shortly modernize and supplement its "fleet" of three single-engine Vegas with an equal number of eight-passenger Lockheed Model 12s, a cousin of the bigger Electra and capable of speeds of 213 miles per hour. He won the higher subsidy.

But this victory hinged, in turn, on the success of the two other high-risk events. To make good on his pledge to the Post Office, Varney would have to purchase the expensive new Model 12s, but the company had no money. Six and Mueller exercised their persuasive powers on Lockheed, which agreed to sell them all three L-12s at the discounted price of $118,500, with just $15,000 down payment. They raised the money by offering their homes and other personal property as security to the Bank of El Paso, which wrote the loan. The Model 12s entered service in July 1937. But one more high hurdle remained. Government regulations now required two-way radios in all twin-engine aircraft. Unfortunately, the L-12s did not come so equipped, and Varney had no means to buy them. This fact sent Six back to the air. This time he traveled to Chicago to visit United Airlines president W. A. Patterson, whom Mueller had recently introduced to Six over drinks in Oakland. Patterson remembered Six as something of an upstart at their initial encounter. But the young executive made his plea for the loan of a few radios so convincingly that Patterson—who happened to believe that all airlines benefited from mutual cooperation— changed his mind about his junior colleague. "I'll lend you whatever equipment you need," said the United chief. "Give it back when you can afford to buy your own." A few weeks after Patterson came to the rescue with the radios, he gave Six yet another boost. Having bought the new aircraft, Varney needed more destinations in order to fill its cabins. Patterson agreed to split with Six the routes resulting from the purchase of Wyoming Air Services' mail authority—routes the smaller carrier never could have purchased on its own. United agreed to buy Denver-Cheyenne; Varney received Denver-Pueblo, for the first time linking the tiny carrier to a major city. Robert Six never forgot Patterson's generosity.

After such audacity, trial by fire, and success, it became clear that Six should run the company, as he began to do already. He even renamed it. Showing characteristic bravado and optimism, as well as a stubborn defiance of its present size, he pulled down the Varney signs and replaced them with ones proclaiming Continental Airlines. He also scrapped the ponderous old advertising slogan, "The Route of the Conquistadors" in favor of the evocative and picturesque phrase, "Fly the Old Santa Fe Trail." Then he transferred headquarters and all fifteen employees from El Paso to Denver, the new hub of operations. Finally, on February 3, 1938, the Continental board of directors, acting on Louis Mueller's suggestion, elected the thirty-year-old Six president. Just like Patterson, the hard-boiled Mueller had become a zealous supporter of Six, acknowledging that he "picked up the responsibilities of being an executive very rapidly. He had a lot of imagination."[6]

Once installed as Continental's leader, Six relied again and again on these same attributes. The times demanded no less. During the period in which Six joined Varney and became an airline executive, forces gathered in the nation's capital to transform the industry, resulting in the Civil Aeronautics Act of June 1938. This monumental piece of legislation laid the foundation for all commercial air activity during the next four decades. By 1940 a Civil Aeronautics Board (CAB) routinely ruled on airline merger requests, heard appeals for exemptions from antitrust laws, provided special subsidies, opened new cities to some carriers and closed them to others, decided ticket prices, and maintained safety standards. A later CAB chairman called the federal machinery enacted in 1938 a reflection of a national consensus that "the orderly development of civil aviation required that it be subject to public utility-type regulation to promote the development of a nationwide air transportation system capable of meeting the needs of commerce, the postal service, and the national defense."[7]

Thus, just as Robert Six assumed the reins of Continental Airlines, he and his industry entered an uncharted new landscape of federal regulation. Everyone, even the most experienced, found themselves newcomers to the system, a situation which could only help Six's chances of success. A quick study, he grasped the implications of CAB authority almost immediately and found the new system to his liking. The regulatory environment not only offered a measure of protection against the industry giants; it also suited Six's style of management. Six did not run Continental in an iron-fisted or a despotic manner, but he did impose high expectations on his employees and held a tight grip on daily operations. Yet, because he governed his own firm energetically and understood the value of discipline, he rarely chafed at the imposition of directives from Washington. He recognized and respected the CAB's necessary role, regarding it as imperative to the health of air commerce and to the well-being of Continental itself.

Confirmation of his analysis did not take long to materialize. During the year and a half after the passage of the Civil Aeronautics Act, American air carriers pulled out of their nosedive and experienced record returns on investment. Twenty-two airlines received permanent route authority. These awards brought order to the system and resulted in a number of salutary developments: aircraft manufacturers saw a rise in new orders; scheduled flights flew with cargo holds full of mail and seats filled with paying customers; and the period witnessed unmatched safety statistics. During its first decade, the CAB assumed the role of champion of the air carriers, brokering agreements among them and guarding their economic interests. Acting on this precedent, the board played a decisive part in guiding commercial aviation through the turbulence of World War II.[8]

Continental Emerges

Six profited from the brightening prospects of his industry, but not without immense toil and nimble maneuvering. No gambler would have liked the odds of lifting Continental out of obscurity. His workforce had increased, but only numbered twenty-five in all. His hangars housed just six aircraft, three of them outmoded. In January 1938, he essentially operated the same backwater routes flown by Varney. With good reason, the CAB failed to be impressed by his little airline. This situation did more than embarrass Six; laboring under the board's acid test of serving the public's "convenience and necessity," Continental would find it difficult to win new airways. Indeed, when the CAB awarded the baseline (or grandfather) route certificates to the air carriers in August 1938, Continental received only its original Denver–El Paso line.[9]

To prosper, Continental needed new routes. But Six knew that the new regulatory process effectively barred him from other markets until he instituted wholesale improvements in those features which attracted and held paying passengers. Years later he expressed the business credo that originated in the early days: "Competition is what keeps us hopping. And, in a service industry, that is crucial to success. We can only survive by continuing to expand our business. That requires primary attention to presenting a constantly improving product to our customers. Sometimes we are able to improve the product dramatically with a new airplane that is faster or more comfortable. That makes our selling job easy." But when no technical breakthroughs presented themselves, "we have to resort to more subtle changes such as new passenger services or new fares which attract more travelers."[10]

How did Six transform his airline to equal or surpass the industry leaders in reliability, comfort, and safety? "He was a hands-on manager before they coined the phrase," said a fellow airline president. He demanded fresh (if simple) in-flight food, clean planes, well-dressed employees, and strict courtesy to the public. He might explode in rage if

Robert Six enjoyed visiting the flight decks of Continental's aircraft to see the equipment and to chat with his pilots. A flier himself, he felt at home at the controls, although his big frame often filled the cockpit. (Courtesy of the National Air and Space Museum, Smihsonian Institution [SI Neg. No. 98-15890])

the shade of blue on a service ramp did not look to him like a true Continental blue. "You saw him everywhere," one friend recalled. "In the tire shop, in the hostess division. The Harvard Business School never told him how to do anything." His unscheduled visits to hangars, flight decks, and reservation desks sent shivers down the spines of mechanics, pilots, and ticket agents alike. But the constant emphasis on impeccable service, hewn from his ceaseless attention to detail, laid a good foundation for the daring plans to come.

Six began his reforms by making a hard assessment of the equipment parked on the tarmac outside his Denver offices. His conclusion: Neither the dependable Vegas nor the faster Model 12s carried enough passengers to be profitable. To raise money for their replacement, he sold two of the Vegas for a fraction of their $20,000 cost; then he looked for sources of financing. Six persuaded a San Francisco friend in the banking business to introduce him to Robert Lehman of the Lehman Brothers investment house, which agreed to offer the first sale of Continental stock. Lehman waived its commission, and Six realized an infusion of $280,000. The youngest airline executive in America, he already grasped the essential ingredient of the business: "When there have been profits in air transportation . . . built-in obsolescence [of aircraft] . . . forced us to plow the money right back in for newer and better planes." Early in 1939, two new ten-seat Lockheed Super Electras (costing $80,000 each) began to ply the skies between Denver and El Paso. Business on this corridor increased thanks to these speedy aircraft, capable of flying 20 MPH faster than the reigning empress of the air, the DC-3.

Rather than release the Model 12s, Six found a highly profitable role for them. When the CAB granted its grandfather routes, it also opened for bids one entirely new airmail authority running from Wichita, Kansas, to Pueblo, Colorado. After the winning proposal lost in a court decision, the board announced its intention to accept official applications from other carriers. Continental's president hardly contained his enthusiasm when his airline received CAM-43, the prized east-west addition to his existing schedule. "We have the honor," he boasted, "of being the first airline to ever ask the CAB for a new route. Our application was filed so early that it was acknowledged by the new . . . chairman [Ed Noble] . . . on [the] stationery of his former firm, the Life Saver Corporation." Six sold the last Vegas and flew the three Lockheed 12s exclusively for mail and express delivery on the new Wichita to Pueblo line.[11]

Finally, Six initiated profound changes in company staffing. He brought to Continental three top United employees, all of whom he knew in San Francisco during his tenure with Walter Beech. Then he angled for and caught a big fish. Six appealed to Jack Frye, Trans World Airlines president and a recent acquaintance, for the name of someone capable of reorganizing and revitalizing his firm's flight operations. All other positions paled in importance; its incumbent would assume responsibility for the timely and safe arrival of passengers, crew, and cargo wherever the airline flew. But to carry out these duties, the new hire would face a primitive situation in which a part-time accountant appeared only once a month to do the books. No treasurer had been retained, and the entire cockpit staff consisted of four captains and three copilots. Frye agreed to part with his own flight superintendent, one of his most able men, but issued a warning to Six: "He's good, but dammit, Bob, remember I'm just loaning him to you. Unless he's damned fool enough to want to stay with that half-assed outfit of yours."

Oscar R. "Ted" Haueter, the man Frye loaned to Six, served as Continental's vice president for flight operations from 1938 to 1968. Short, stubborn, and hot tempered, Haueter clashed often with the volatile Six but usually got his way. He transformed flight operations and won his spurs by insisting, over the bosses' loud objections, that all crews must be qualified on instrument flying. While tough on his pilots, Haueter also shielded them from Six's legendary short fuse, which he silenced by threatening to return to TWA. Despite their differences, Haueter remained his closest aide and confidant.[12]

Immediately prior to American involvement in World War II, Six continued to tighten and improve the inner workings of his firm. At first prone to choosing friends, family, and needy individuals for job openings, he gradually became an astute judge of talent. He continued to find able new faces like Terrell C. Drinkwater for legal counsel and Braniff's Stan Shatto for chief of maintenance, both of whom joined his inner circle of advisers. These men assumed great importance, but Shatto distinguished himself first. Upon his arrival in 1941, Continental began a program of in-house (rather than contract) repair and restoration. Until then, such activities occurred in a small and inadequate hangar; but Six persuaded the Denver authorities to construct a spacious new one at a cost of $300,000. Maintenance expenses fell quickly under Shatto's watchful eye and he began to evolve a highly effective system of incremental servicing that eventually became Continental's trademark and the envy of the business.

Six also added a few routes and increased the frequency of scheduled service. To support this modest expansion, his payroll rose to 64 in 1939 and by the end of 1940 numbered 102. But the growth hardly seemed excessive, considering that the 15,310 passengers in 1940 represented twice the load of the year before. The quick Super Electras allowed Six to increase Continental's flights by a factor of two; three daily round-trips between Denver and El Paso and one between Pueblo and Wichita, Kansas. The following year Six won some minor east-west extensions to Roswell, Carlsbad, and Hobbs, New Mexico. To accommodate the rising traffic,

Six ordered more planes from Lockheed, and as these sixteen-seat Lodestars arrived, the three Model 12s went on sale. Because the new fleet flew at over 200 miles per hour, the publicity savvy Six dared to call his diminutive airline "America's fastest." But it remained little indeed, despite all the improvements. Continental had only five aircraft when the CAB awarded it a Wichita to Tulsa route in 1941. Although this new artery represented only a modest step, it linked Six's network to oil-rich Oklahoma, prompting him to find buyers for the L-14s and purchase three more Lodestars. The company's all-Lodestar service forced the airline to hire its first stewardesses, who began work in December 1941.

Despite the progress Six had made, and partly because of it, Continental found itself deep in debt due to the constant equipment turnover. Six turned once more to Lehman Brothers for assistance. In March 1941, another public stock offering (of 50,000 shares at $3.75 each) yielded $187,500. Lehman's Fred Ehrman, a director on Continental's board, then introduced Six to bankers at Chase National and they quickly struck a deal to alleviate the firm's $345,000 in red ink. Chase loaned him $425,000 because Six had retired previous obligations on time and predicted future growth accurately and conservatively. Yet, for all of the elaborate measures and costly outlays designed to attract passengers, at the end of 1941 the federal mail subsidy ($491,000) accounted for more than twice the revenue ($218,000) realized from transporting the public for business and pleasure. [13]

Success in War, Stress in Peace

Like many American businesses, Continental Airlines prospered from its contributions to the war effort. Its principal role involved the modification of B-17 Flying Fortresses. In February 1942 the Army Air Forces (AAF) Materiel Command selected Continental's Denver headquarters for bomber retrofits. In exchange for his support, Six received from the AAF two impressive 600 x 400 foot hangars erected at a cost of $5 million. Known thereafter as the Denver Modifications Center, its crews eventually altered more than 1,000 B-17s with such equipment as long-range fuel tanks (for the Battle of Midway) and converted many B-29 Superfortresses for photo-reconnaissance operations. Meantime, Continental's president decided to support the war personally. He joined the

Army Air Transport Command in September 1942 and left Terry Drinkwater in charge as executive vice president. After completing the Thunderbird Flight School in Phoenix, the thirty-five-year-old captain served in air logistics, assigned to Hamilton Field's Sixth Ferry Command in California. Here he earned his multiengine pilot's wings, pinned on his major's insignia, and participated in the site selection of Travis Field, also in the Golden State. Six then undertook his sole operational mission, overseeing the flight of three B-24 bombers to Australia and serving for two months in New Caledonia. When he returned stateside, he received a transfer to Morrison Field in West Palm Beach, Florida, where he took part in a risky venture. American airmen routinely ferried planes from this airfield to Africa via the seaside town of Natal on Brazil's easternmost point and from there across the Atlantic. Recent disappearances of aircraft and personnel in severe weather prompted an expedition to chart an inland route to Natal, rather than the existing one, which followed the Latin American coastline. Acting as copilot and second in command, Six traveled with a meteorologist and a physician, as well as the usual flight crew, and surveyed the Brazilian interior. In a subsequent report to senior air power authorities, he described hazardous conditions involving immense, unmapped mountains and stark terrain. As a consequence, he convinced his superiors to continue the oceanic approaches to Natal but to fly only between dawn and ten in the morning, before the daily storms gathered strength. This strategy reduced significantly the loss of transports and of flying staff. But having discharged his serious duties, Six reverted to his flamboyant style. While most servicemen returned with the usual tourist trinkets, he brought home a jaguar named Whiskey. He allowed the animal to roam his office freely until the safety of his coworkers demanded he confine his pet to a cage.

During Six's absence, Drinkwater displayed solid leadership. The airline saw half of its Lodestars requisitioned by the War Department, taxing to the limit the three that remained and trying the imagination to maintain the daily schedule. But good news also materialized. Airmail rates increased over ten cents a mile. Even better, in 1943 the CAB granted Continental a coveted route between Denver and Kansas City. Unfortunately, not until the Air Transport Command returned one of the Lodestars could the airline open service to this vital midwestern metropolis. Late in the war, Drinkwater inaugurated flights to San Antonio. To meet the escalating demand for cabin space, Stan Shatto flew to the Douglas plant in Santa Monica, California, and placed bids on two of twenty-one C-47 transports released from the inventory of the Army Air Forces. Continental chose ones that had flown in the Africa theater, and in record time he converted them to twenty-one-seat DC-3s. No choice really existed but to buy these planes, since Continental carried more than four times the passengers (52,000) in 1944 than in 1940. Indeed, revenues derived from flying the public finally exceeded those earned by transporting the mail (by almost $160,000), even though rates for moving the nation's letters and parcels jumped in 1942 to an unprecedented 48.5 cents per airplane mile.

Into this bright picture stepped Robert Six, promoted to lieutenant colonel and recently installed as the deputy commander of Morrison Field. He returned to an airline that had grown astonishingly, trebling its route size and about to retire its Lodestars in favor of eleven spacious DC-3s. But none of the wartime gains pleased him. Quite the contrary, Six regarded Continental as his company and felt peeved that others had operated it with such success. Part of his dark mood may have stemmed from a threat to his health. While in uniform he suffered a slight cerebral hemorrhage, perhaps precipitated by a gain in weight to about 235 pounds. Although a minor stroke, it temporarily left the hard-driving executive without power in his legs. He recovered fully and quickly, but the service decided to remove him from active duty, placing him in the reserves before discharging him in May 1944. Almost immediately after arriving in Denver the following month, he learned about a plan conceived by Drinkwater to assume the presidency and relegate Six to chairman. Ill-humored enough because of his premature release from the army and his brush with mortality, Six reacted to Drinkwater's plot with fury, even more so when he discovered that in the process his old mentor, Louis Mueller, would suffer a demotion in the company's hierarchy. "I knew," said one of Six's closest aides, "that Drinkwater couldn't be on a team where Six was boss." Indeed, within weeks of his rival's return, Drinkwater accepted an offer to become vice president at American Airlines. Robert Six resumed full and complete control of his business.[14]

But being back in command proved less agreeable than Six imagined. For all of Terry Drinkwater's sound stewardship of Continental during Six's hiatus, the real source of the airline's wartime success lay in federal largesse: money to modify military aircraft, money for higher airmail rates, and a fortunate allocation of several new routes. During the succeeding decade, with Six in control and postwar retrenchment everywhere, the advances became far harder to achieve. First, the CAB sliced airmail rates in half to 24.8 cents a mile. But even if this subsidy shrank, the award of the all-important Denver to Kansas City service seemed to augur well for the future. Here, too, the period after the war proved to be a time of frustrating reversals. Between 1945 and 1954, Six applied to the CAB for twelve new routes and won only one of consequence. Every other city opened to Continental during this period lay on existing flight paths. The federal regulators felt—with justification—that Continental still lacked the critical mass of financing and equipment necessary to compete as a national carrier. Naturally, Six disagreed strongly. In a daring attempt to expand toward both coasts at once, he peppered the board with applications for authority to fly east from Oklahoma to Memphis and west from Denver to Los Angeles. He lost every battle.

Still, by 1951 Continental's fleet offered air service across 3,000 route miles to cities with a combined population of over 3.5 million. No one could deny that this aggregate represented an astonishing increase both in miles and market since the sun had set on Varney Speed Lines just thirteen years earlier. Recognizing how far his carrier had come, Six concentrated on objectives he could achieve rather than on barriers presented by the CAB. Blocked temporarily from expansion east or west, he undertook a series of internal improvements. Continental, for example, became the first carrier to install terrain-warning radar equipment aboard all its aircraft. Moreover, even though the fourteen DC-3s in the inventory had just entered service in 1946, giants like American and United already flew DC-4s and had placed orders with Douglas for DC-6s. Six could not compete immediately, but he did respond. In the short term he purchased—at a cost of $250,000 each—five Convair 240s, a quantum leap over the DC-3s in size (forty seats) and comfort (pressurized cabins). During 1951 he bought his first sixty-passenger DC-6Bs from Douglas. Again, he found himself immersed in debt and once more contacted his friends at Lehman Brothers, who raised the money for him to stay abreast of his opponents by offering 12,744 new shares of Continental stock.

Six pursued his campaign to circumvent the CAB and to win new clientele by a number of modest but ingenious measures. He paired cities not heretofore linked on Continental's flight paths: Denver and Oklahoma City in 1946; Tulsa and Oklahoma City seven years later. He also resorted to showmanship and price cuts. He named his DC-3s Skystreamers and advertised his routes as the Blue Skyway. Six followed Capital Airlines in breaking the first-class fare structure by offering cheaper, so-called Skycoach seats. Customers could purchase flights from Denver to Kansas City for all of $22.

Six found two other ways to evade the CAB's checkmates of his route requests, both of which proved highly successful and noteworthy. The first, borrowed from railroad practice, became known as interchange agreements. With the growth of many underserved medium-sized markets in the Southwest and elsewhere, the CAB decided to allow carriers to negotiate reciprocal arrangements among themselves in order to transport customers directly from one city to another. For example, before interchange, passengers flew from Houston to Los Angeles by flying Braniff from Houston to San Antonio, Continental from San Antonio to El Paso, and American from El Paso to L.A. Once the three carriers struck a bargain, the public could travel directly—on one aircraft—from Houston to L.A. with each airline operating its own segment. Continental benefited further when Braniff withdrew from the interchange and the CAB bestowed on Six his longest single route to date: from Houston to El Paso via San Antonio. This almost casual award represented Continental's only victory to date in the board's postwar deliberations. Once the sole partnership with American began in 1951, it raised the possibility that an airline capable of cementing a coequal relationship with one of the nation's great carriers might one day transcend its regional niche.

Finally, Six outmaneuvered the CAB and its cautious approach to route assignments by engineering a valuable merger. Pioneer Airlines served the Texas cities of Dallas, Fort Worth, and Austin, all populous, wealthy markets that Six craved. But Pioneer also flew to every Texas city with populations of 100,000 or more. At a cost to Continental of $768,000, the CAB approved the amalgamation, and the two companies joined forces in December 1953. Despite the alarming deficit resulting from the acquisition of Pioneer and the continued purchase of new equipment, Continental retained its fine reputation based on efficient operations, a modern (if small) fleet of aircraft, and a dominant share of the Southwest/

Rocky Mountain regional market. Yet, never content with the status quo, Six added to the existing debt by betting the equivalent of twelve months' corporate gross income to buy seven powerful Convair 340s. In so doing he acted with perfect consistency. Having just won several vital routes, he decided, as always, to serve them in a manner at least comparable to that of his largest competitors.[15]

The Big Leagues

"Continental is a great success story and Continental is Bob Six. What the public conceives of Continental is Bob Six's imagination, personality, and willingness to do the unusual." This praise from Edward Carlson, chairman of United Airlines, really assumed a ring of truth only during the mid-1950s. Until then all of Six's cleverness, attention to detail, and boldness, all of Continental's service, safety, and efficiency still yielded a second-class airline. This changed in 1955 when one route decision by the CAB validated Six's contention that Continental deserved a place among the front-rank carriers. The precipitating case involved the industry's three behemoths—American, United, and Trans World—pitted against each other for rights to a crucial new airway running from Chicago through Denver to Los Angeles, ensuring that the Mile High City would become a pillar of the national air transit system. Six applied, too, as did Western Airlines. It proved to be one of the board's most difficult and important verdicts.

Called the Denver Service Case, it began in 1952 and embroiled the CAB for three years. In this instance the federal regulators found themselves cornered between two of their cherished objectives: to open new routes to the smaller airlines in order to stiffen competition, but to consider only those competitors able to offer full service to the public without bankrupting themselves in the process. The deliberations of the five-member panel pivoted on these very issues. Finally, they announced their ruling in November 1955. The Board concluded that the public's immense appetite for air travel exceeded all expectations, and it decided to satisfy demand by opening a number of new transcontinental airways to the carriers. To achieve the goal of a freer market, each of the Denver applicants received a generous portion of the virgin east-west routes. United gained access to Kansas City; TWA won entry to Denver; American

Late in his career,
Robert Six flashes a
proud smile under
the distinctive
Continental insignia
emblazoned on the
tail of one of his
Golden Jets.
(Courtesy of Con-
tinental Airlines)

received a direct line from Chicago to San Francisco. Starting in January 1956, all three received permission to inaugurate flights from New York to the two big California cities.

The real surprises involved the two smaller applicants. Western won the right to ferry passengers directly from Denver to San Francisco. But the CAB stunned the industry with its award to Continental. In essence, it not only acknowledged Six's seventeen-year struggle to transform his airline, but admitted his success. The outcome represented more than Six had dared to hope for. Henceforth, Continental could fly from Denver headquarters in either direction—to Chicago going east and to Los Angeles going west. More important and completely unexpected, the CAB allowed Six to offer *nonstop* flights between the Windy City and L.A. In a single stroke, Six found himself obligated to provide air transportation between two cities in which his airline had neither presence nor experience, between the second and third largest markets in the country.[16]

Many critics considered these conditions a recipe for failure and denounced Continental's good fortune. They reasoned that even the sharpest rise in demand for air tickets could not support all the carriers the CAB had favored with new routes and that the weaker ones would collapse trying to serve their customers and win their share of the market. Indeed, the CAB itself hardly gave the decision a ringing endorsement, awarding Continental its prize by a tight vote of three to two. Six ignored the doomsayers and plunged ahead with customary optimism and zeal. Recently, he had demonstrated decisiveness in his personal life when he divorced his wife Henriette and married musical comedy star Ethel Merman. But the contest to transfigure Continental dwarfed every project he ever undertook, whether public or private. "All we had to do was buck three of the country's four largest airlines on that route and nobody had ever heard of us. We had to do something to attract attention fast." Six attracted attention by radically refashioning his airline to compete with the industry leaders.

> Our problem was a simple one: We had gross annual sales of $16,000,000, total assets of $14,000,000. We had just been given the opportunity to compete with . . . United, American, and TWA . . . non-stop between Chicago and Los Angeles. We knew full well that a small airline couldn't compete in the Big League without the proper equipment, people or money. We had to be able to prove to the CAB that we could do a creditable job over any routes awarded us. So, we went shopping that year and committed ourselves for $13,000,000 for DC-7Bs with which we planned to offer our first competition; $27,500,000 for 15 jet-powered Viscount IIs, the newest, largest model in a famed series; and $23,800,000 for our four Golden Jet Boeing 707s.[17]

Six thus signed purchase orders for airliners worth almost five times the total assets of his company. Luckily, the entire bill did not come due at once. First, Six persuaded the CAB to let him miss the January 1956 deadline for starting the Los Angeles to Chicago flights; then, he induced Douglas Aircraft to move up on the assembly line two of the five DC-7Bs scheduled for delivery to Continental. Still, it took some time to achieve full service using the new generation of aircraft. The spacious

96-passenger DC-7Bs began operations in spring 1957, the 56-seat Viscount turboprops in mid-1958, and the big 707s late in 1959. Of course, both the Viscount and the Boeing aircraft heralded the jet age and, as such, left some doubts about their production dates and their initial airworthiness. No such uncertainties attended the reliable and tested Douglas propeller-driven airplanes. Six seized on the first ones eagerly and not only configured them for 100 percent coach service but redefined the meaning of the word. With the inauguration of Club Coach, Six offered his customers their choice of seats and a hot (rather than a box) lunch. Moreover, flying a swift 365 MPH, the DC-7Bs transported passengers faster than any of Continental's competitors, which relegated their budget travelers to the slower DC-6s. The new route proved highly successful. Once Six's Viscounts began the first commercial jetliner service in the western states, it took only eight months before Continental carried half of all first-class passengers flying between Chicago and Los Angeles. On the same route, 6,000 customers booked the Golden 707s *before the planes even entered the inventory.* Perhaps sweetest of all for Six, he introduced jet service a year before United. He proclaimed victory with more than a hint of cockiness, saying, "Our improvements forced an upgrading in the industry's products over our routes, because it wasn't long before our competition matched our coach service. Here," he bragged, "was another instance of a small, aggressive firm, not held back by tradition, or the inertia of size, coming up with a better product. We were the first company to offer first class service features to coach passengers in our markets and the other carriers had to follow. Actually, we were just following two of our key principles of doing business—to bring the benefits of air transportation to as many people as possible and to make our product just as fine a one as we're capable of producing."[18]

Six's posturing failed to conceal the company's critical problems. During his first twenty years as president of Continental, the company reported a profit every year. But in 1958 a $132,000 loss appeared in the books. Six's buying spree, designed to lift the airline "by its financial bootstraps," threatened to destroy it. He initially covered the aircraft purchases with loans from Chase Manhattan and other banks. He also issued Continental bonds to the public from which he raised some $16.5 million in 1955 and 1956. But in 1957 these short-term obligations began to come due, and the following year Six's accountants found themselves unable to service $10 million in debts. Once again, Lehman Brothers saved the day. Its financiers persuaded twenty-two lending institutions, including Chase, to pool $22.5 million. They also identified seven insurance companies willing to add another $12.5 million. Finally, Boeing and Viscount, unwilling to lose a prime partner, agreed to loan Continental $3 million and $1 million, respectively. They even postponed repayment until all of the bank and insurance company loans had been redeemed. These agreements, consummated in 1960, averted catastrophe and allowed Six to manage his deficit while continuing to modernize the fleet. He reduced his margin of debt by disposing of fourteen propeller-driven aircraft—the bulk of his piston-engine equipment—yielding a capital gain of $1.1 million.[19]

Despite these imposing fiscal problems, Continental began the 1960s with two important advantages: the increasing respect of the CAB and the unmistakable attention of the media. But, again, Six refused to be satisfied with his new status. Instead, he stepped back briefly to rationalize his company after a period of breathtaking expansion. Continental pioneered an innovative system of progressive (or continuous) maintenance. Rather than removing his airliners from operation for long periods of sustained repair, Six's approach brought them into the hangar on a regular but piecemeal basis, about once every fourth night. The result: his company ran more routes with fewer aircraft than the competition because the planes remained aloft longer—on average twelve hours per day rather than nine for the other carriers. As a consequence, Continental broke even flying only 42 percent capacity; the others required as much as 55 percent before showing a profit. Once Six operated the easier-to-maintain jets, these maintenance techniques squeezed even more savings from the fleet. Yet Continental boasted a safety record unmatched in the business. For twenty-four consecutive years, Six's pilots flew without a single fatality, a feat which extended into the jet age. Only when a 707 crashed in 1962 after a bomb exploded in flight did the streak end. It remained the firm's sole incident during the early turbine engine period despite the infusion of radically new equipment into the inventory.

Finally, to better satisfy the needs of its passengers, Continental designated special check-in agents on the 707 Golden Jets. "Picked," crowed Six, "from supervisors with at least five years seniority, these [directors of passenger service] handle all the ticketing functions on the aircraft, sell tickets, collect for excess baggage, rewrite tickets. They even have a radio-telephone exclusively for their use—the first of its kind in the industry over which they can make advance hotel, rent-a-car, or plane reservations." At the same time this innovation improved the flying experience for customers, the various efficiencies of operation undertaken by Six resulted in a cost per available ton-mile 17 percent lower than the airline average. Even the flight deck was put on notice: fly higher, taxi shorter, and reduce flying time in order to pare fuel costs to the bone.[20]

Just as Continental assumed a role of prominence among the nation's air carriers, Six again experienced turbulence in his personal life. His life with Ethel Merman fell victim to his single-minded crusade to close the chasm between his company and the major carriers. He lived alone for a year before meeting television actress Audrey Meadows, known as Alice Kramden opposite Jackie Gleason in the famed Honeymooners series. In Meadows, Six found the woman to share his ardor for the business, and she accompanied him on most of his travels. His marriage to her proved to be a long and happy one based, he admitted freely, on giving her the attention and priority he failed to show Henriette Ruggles and Ethel Merman. Bolstered by Meadow's presence as well as by Continental's growing reputation, Six decided to play the high-stakes game of national airline politics.

He entered the contest on the strength of a single fact: his firm's unusually low operating costs. Because he could transport passengers for less money than others, he conceived the revolutionary but simple idea of offering sweeping and permanent fare reductions to entice more of the flying public into his new airliners. His biggest competitors, pressed by huge capital outlays to purchase jet-age equipment, denounced Six and his radical scheme. The slowdown in the rate of growth in commercial air traffic—averaging 18 percent between 1950 and 1957 and only 6 percent between 1958 and 1960—persuaded the great companies to demand from the CAB permission to raise their fares, certainly not to lower them. But Six countered with the heretical view that only cheaper seats would lure the vast untapped market of automobile, bus, train, and ship travelers out of their customary modes of transportation and into the golden skies. Would this cure pull every carrier out of the economic malaise? Six made no promises. "They're good for Continental. I'm not running a trade association for the whole industry."

To win broad support, he decided to appeal directly to potential customers. In fall 1961, Continental placed full-page advertisements in the nation's leading newspapers mocking the "loud and angry cries of our competitors." Six also declared an uncharted new fare structure: henceforth Golden Jet passengers could select economy, coach, or first-class service. Economy would be priced one-fourth less than coach, a deep discount offset by more seats in each cabin. Six planned to install the extra seats yet preserve comfort by using new units fabricated of lighter, thinner materials, allowing space to be compressed while reducing the weight of the furniture by 20 percent. Of course, economy class required CAB approval. Six told the regulators that the success of the experiment rested on two numbers: a 16 percent increase in traffic and 20 more seats per plane (based on the more efficient seating). Any rise above 16 percent, he argued, would result in a profit despite the cut in prices. By the same three to two vote that awarded him the Los Angeles to Chicago authority, however, he lost this battle before the CAB. Considering the unanimous and vocal condemnation of his fare proposal by the other airline chiefs, Six could take some comfort in the margin of the loss. At any rate, he enjoyed the controversy and being at its center.

So he tried again and won the opportunity to prove his theory. In summer 1962, he proposed and the board accepted a more sophisticated four-tier plan. On an experimental basis (lasting until October 1963), Continental received permission to offer no frills/no food economy seats for 20 percent less than coach; to offer coach with food and liquor; to offer business class with finer meals, better drink, and more spacious seats for about 13 percent less than first class; and to offer first-class passengers deluxe seats, excellent food, and a full array of beverages. This hierarchy of features aimed to pull first-time fliers into the airports with the advantages of economy travel and to impress coach passengers with the comparative luxuries of business service. Acceptance of the new system grew slowly but steadily. Customer traffic and revenue both increased. Even more important, however, this episode catapulted Six and Continental onto the front pages and established an airline pricing structure still easily recognizable more than a generation later.[21]

A Major Player

Positioned brilliantly at the end of the fare wars as an industry innovator, Robert Six found the wherewithal to capitalize on his airline's reputation as well as on his own notoriety. After twenty-five years in charge of Continental, he started yet another audacious adventure. First, in July 1963 he transported his headquarters from Denver to Los Angeles. This relocation not only recognized the pivotal importance of the vast L.A. market since the Denver Service Case; it likewise reflected Six's conviction that his company's future rested on an Asia-Pacific service. It also suggested a residual attraction to the Orient that Six first acquired as a youthful test pilot with China National Aviation. But western expansion also had its critics. Many feared that as Continental poured resources into the Pacific routes it might sacrifice its hard-won share of the domestic market. But if Six realized his ambition—and he knew that success rested in part on a gamble—Los Angeles would serve as the hinge between travel across North America and travel to the Orient. Once established on the West Coast, Six pursued this majestic reinterpretation of Continental's role. He established himself quickly as a man to be reckoned with in L.A., winning a seat on the board of directors of First Western Bank and being seen and photographed with his wife at Hollywood premieres and parties. Six's reputation as a hunter also burnished his image as a Man of the West. He took to the wild enthusiastically for the annual Grizzly Hunt and the One-Shot Antelope Hunt in Lander, Wyoming. Indeed, he actively cultivated the western image, appearing in the mass-circulation magazine *Parade* wearing a cowboy shirt and hat.

Like most of his other achievements, Six succeeded in the Pacific by quick-footed adaptation and by the capacity to recognize opportunities before his competitors. His first incursion took place during the buildup of U.S. forces in Vietnam. Six responded first when the Military Airlift Command (MAC) announced plans to assemble a massive air armada to supply Southeast Asia. Not yet in possession of a single transcontinental authority, he nonetheless signed a contract with MAC in May 1964 to fly his 707s from California to points as distant as Tokyo. Eventually, Continental operated from McGuire Air Force Base in New Jersey to destinations on the Pacific Rim, all the while providing soldiers the same service as paying customers. By late 1967, Six scheduled ten aircraft for these epic journeys. The airline's military business brought prosperity (contracts worth $60 million in 1968), a hitherto unknown financial stability, and the ranking of fourth largest American carrier operating abroad, second only to Pan American in U.S.–Vietnam transport.

True to past form, Six met success not with complacency but with renewed vigor. Just as the MAC relationship blossomed, he undertook a second transpacific initiative. Having traveled in Southeast Asia, he grasped before his fellow airline executives the necessity of greater air capacity near the war zone. In 1965 Continental opened a subsidiary called Continental Air Services (CAS), the predecessor of which operated from Vientiane, Laos, as William Bird and Son. The Agency for International Development (AID) contracted both with CAS and the Central Intelligence Agency's Air America to ferry supplies into the steep and dangerous Laotian terrain. As many as fifty CAS airplanes—ranging from C-47s to Swiss-made Pilatus Porters—flew to these tiny airstrips. Eventually, this branch of Continental provided airlift for the governments of Vietnam, Thailand, and Cambodia.

The insatiable Six did not rest with the successes germinated by the war in Southeast Asia. The immense South Pacific expanse known as Micronesia beckoned. Six knew he faced long odds to turn a good balance sheet from this vast, underpopulated region. Indeed, early losses totaled $3 million. But he reckoned correctly that when the CAB announced its much awaited decisions on routes to Hawaii, Continental stood a much better chance of being a winner if it showed a convincing record of Pacific service. "What we're trying to do," he admitted, "is convince the CAB that we've got the interest and the capability, rather than just walk in with a piece of paper." The United States governed the 2,000 Micronesian islands under a United Nations mandate declared just after World War II. At first, a small carrier called Transocean operated a schedule in the Trust Territory at the invitation of the Interior Department. Pan American assumed the routes when Transocean filed for bankruptcy. During the late 1960s, the Interior Department decided that Pan Am had failed to serve the area adequately, and it opened the territory to bidders. Pan Am, Northwest Orient, Hawaiian Airlines, and a new carrier competed. The untried entrant—a Continental subsidiary known as Air Micronesia—won a five-year contract in 1968. Six offered the Interior Department some attractive incentives: a promise to hire Micronesians, an offer to construct six new hotels to boost tourism, and a pledge to fly the modern Boeing 727s exclusively. Over time, "Air Mike" served customers from Tokyo to Guam, from the Trust Territory to Honolulu.[22]

Washington recognized Six's Pacific overtures almost immediately.

During the last days of his administration, President Lyndon B. Johnson included Robert Six on his "midnight favors" list. Johnson not only directed the CAB to reverse course on its vote to grant Eastern Air Lines permission to fly to Australia; he told its chairman to award Australia to Continental and to thread the service through Six territory—via Fiji, Samoa, and Micronesia. Two weeks later, Continental received an even greater prize, a Chicago to Hawaii route. A stalwart fund-raiser and Democratic Party activist, Six may have profited from his political affiliations. If so, he lost the advantage just as easily. Richard Nixon no sooner entered the White House than he stripped Continental of its trophies. This reversal dealt a severe blow to the airline's morale. Three of the four new Boeing 747s delivered in anticipation of Hawaiian traffic had to be mothballed in the New Mexico desert awaiting sale. Six visited the company cafeteria just after getting the bad news. "They won't see me bothered," he told his wife. "It's important that [the staff] see just the opposite— that I'm not downcast in the slightest. They've fought and dreamed about a Hawaiian route just as hard as the brass did and they must be just as disappointed as we are." His act lifted the dark mood at headquarters. Finally, after months of deliberations, in July 1969 the CAB restored to Continental the rights to Honolulu via Chicago, Los Angeles, Seattle, and other cities. But it turned out to be less than met the eye. Eight airlines received sanction to fly to Hawaii from the mainland, flooding the market with competitors. Yet Six would not be denied. By offering movies in all classes, serving good food in economy, flying new McDonnell-Douglas DC-10s, and, above all, selling deeply discounted fares midweek, Continental placed second only to United in the contest for Hawaii. Once again, Six's finely tuned instincts for the business and his sheer bare-knuckles hustle won him yet another market for his airline.

> What I'm trying to do is to run the best damn airline I know. A lot of guys think Continental is crazy flying passengers to Hawaii for $85 a head. I don't think so. I look upon it as a temporary loss leader, the kind of merchandising step the department stores take to get customers into the store. Once we get people flying we can gradually upgrade 'em from economy to coach and hopefully even to first class. Besides, what the hell am I supposed to do? Pan Am

and United have been flying the Hawaii-mainland route for years. Suddenly, six other domestic lines are given an okay, with certain restrictions, to share the route. You think I'm going to sit on my big fat duff and let Continental get lost in the shuffle? Hell no. If the other guys don't want to join me in reducing fares . . . nobody's forcing 'em. By attracting new passengers, promoting high density on these long hauls, and by maintaining our low overhead, I think Continental will show a good profit on the run. There's enough business for everyone if they'll only go out and promote. You've got to gamble in this business, try new approaches. I'd rather go for the fast nickel than the slow buck. The carriage trade is not large enough to support the airlines of America. This is not a luxury business. Anyone who tells you that the only way to make money in this business is to charge higher prices to fewer passengers doesn't know his rear end from a hole in the ground.[23]

A Long Decline

Like the faintest star in the evening sky, the forces gathering to dismantle Robert Six's empire appeared distant during the 1960s. The word *deregulation,* which first gained currency during the Johnson administration, as yet had no force of meaning, no cachet. Paradoxically, the president so often associated with Big Government actively pursued efficiencies in the bureaucracy. Indeed, he admired Defense Secretary Robert S. McNamara's cost-based approach to decision making and sought to impose it elsewhere. Johnson found his proving ground in the federal transportation establishment, a diverse collection of entities that seemed likely candidates for deregulation and for open competition. The president initiated a national discussion by proposing legislation to establish a unified Department of Transportation from the many independent agencies and boards. Then his advisors pressed the idea of submerging all of the associated regulatory bodies (Interstate Commerce, the Maritime Commission, and of course the CAB) in the new cabinet-level office. The president finally won his new department in October 1966, but both the Federal Aviation Administration (FAA) and the CAB retained substantial autonomy due to the organized opposition of the aviation community and its congressional allies. Yet, as the debate on transportation unfolded, deregulation entered the national lexicon, and respected institutions like the CAB, until now obscured from public scrutiny, found themselves in an all too public fight for independence.

The conditions required for airline profits soon became highly unfavorable. By 1968, many carriers experienced annual deficits as higher fuel costs and landing fees eroded profits. By 1970 the situation worsened, and the eleven trunk carriers suffered a combined loss of $100 million. A damaging combination of economic inflation *and* recession depressed the demand for air travel just as the first generation of wide-bodies entered service. Already saddled with staggering indebtedness due to purchases of 747s, DC-10s, and L-1011s from Boeing, McDonnell Douglas, and Lockheed, the airlines flew the behemoths half-full. At the same time, labor costs rose disproportionately, up 40 to 50 percent in some categories. True to form, Robert Six weathered the industry's storms better than most. Continental's revenues increased in 1968 and showed modest earnings of $8.4 million in 1971.[24]

Despite Six's continued success, Congress viewed the overall air commerce picture with alarm. Its members reacted to the slump with the hasty suspicion that the issues raised in the 1966 debates on amalgamating federal transportation functions had relevance to the current crisis. Indeed, the House and Senate opened aviation hearings in 1970 and 1971 with the unmistakable presumption that the existing ills corresponded not to factors external to the industry but rather to the unbridled regulatory practices of the CAB. First, the House Committee on Interstate and Foreign Commerce, Subcommittee on Transportation and Aeronautics, heard witnesses in the spring of 1970. The sessions concerned H.R. 16879, "A Bill to Amend the Federal Aviation Act of 1958 to Provide for the Establishment of Mail Rates." Supported by President Nixon and even endorsed by CAB chairman Secor D. Brown, the bill proposed "*to modernize and to simplify* [author's italics] the various provisions of [the] Federal Aviation Act which vest authority in the Civil Aeronautics Board to regulate the rates paid to regulated air carriers by the Post Office Department for the transportation of mail." In other words, this legislation allowed the airlines to compete for postal contracts without the CAB determining whether "each and every mail rate is fair and reasonable." Instead, the carriers merely filed their freight charges with the board, and if the Post Office raised no objections within sixty days, the prices became binding. The U.S. postal authority was undergoing a complete transformation into a quasi-private corporation, and it assumed the corresponding freedom to choose its own shippers.[25]

Before the industry fully comprehended the meaning of the loss of the "fair and reasonable" clause, the Senate heard testimony on a subject of even greater consequence to Six and his colleagues. In February and again in May 1971, the Committee on Commerce, Subcommittee on Aviation, devoted ten days to the subject of the "Economic Condition of the Air Transportation Industry." After the preliminaries on February 2, the proceedings came to order at 10 o'clock the following morning in the New Senate Office Building. At the appointed hour, flanked by his wife, Audrey, and by two senior assistants, sixty-four-year-old Robert Six swept into the chamber with the confidence and sparkle of a presidential candidate. Although he had never appeared before a Senate committee, "the minute he walked in," recalled a seasoned observer, "you could feel the electricity in the room. A lot of people had never seen him before. . . . But here was the legendary Robert Six [and] you knew by looking at him he was going to unload on somebody and it was going to be one hell of a lot of fun." Six did not disappoint. He launched a frontal assault on the five biggest airlines, all of whom advocated some form of deregulation as a means of pulling the business out of its tailspin.

> Everyone interested in the airline industry has been talking a lot recently about the dire plight of the airlines. Most of the statements being made about the ills affecting the industry go beyond gloom. They approach hysteria. I welcome these hearings because this subcommittee has always been a bulwark against panic, and its good sense is badly needed today. I would be the last person to tell you the industry doesn't have serious problems. The management of every airline is experiencing great difficulties and a profit is hard to come by. Times are admittedly bad. But the point I want to stress at this hearing is that the industry can survive without our radically altering the competitive structure of the industry or drastically revamping the regulatory framework. The real cause for worry is the disastrous impact on the industry and the public which would result from adopting some of the solutions being proposed

by the "Big Four" and Pan American. We have serious problems today at Continental. But, frankly, I'm much more worried that the government might accept some of the big carriers' proposals than I am about working my company out of the current earnings slump.[26]

Six laid the industry's funk to four factors, none of which he attributed to basic weaknesses in the CAB's performance or to the ill effects of competition. Rather, he cited (in order of descending importance) the reduction in passenger traffic caused by the sluggish economy, the high business expenses incurred by inflationary pressures, the excess aircraft capacity arising from the biggest carriers purchasing more jumbo jets than they could possibly fill, and the slowness with which the CAB processed requests for fare increases. He almost expressed disdain for the largest airlines, scolding TWA for flying twenty more aircraft than required for its route size. He boasted about his fleet's unusually high rate of utilization (measured in hours aloft per day). He praised the CAB for maintaining open markets in the face of certain monopoly by industry giants chafing under regulatory controls. After holding the chamber rapt with his earthy charisma, he concluded with a plea for the government's continued role in commercial aviation and hinted at a grim future for Continental without the CAB. Six's statement represented thirty-five years in the airline business.

> I personally believe that competition must be encouraged and preserved by government, not destroyed. On the other hand, I have a responsibility to the stockholders of Continental. If all the past efforts of the Congress and its agent, the CAB, to strengthen the smaller airlines like Continental are to be tossed aside, and this industry reduced to two or three supercarriers, then I must make the best deal I can under the circumstances. As much as I would like to see Continental remain an independent, competitive force in this industry, I am not in a position to withstand a tide which flows with the full force of the government behind it. I believe this committee should conduct a careful and thorough study of the true causes of the industry's present dilemma. I am confident the public will be its foremost concern, and will determine whether it sup-

ports the solutions being proposed. I sincerely believe that some of these proposals are designed to benefit the large carriers without regard to their impact on the public, and must be rejected.[27]

For now, Six got his way.

But the deregulation juggernaut continued to gather momentum. It found an unlikely abettor in the Organization of Petroleum Exporting Countries (OPEC), which in 1973 increased the worldwide price of oil to such a degree that the same fuel that once accounted for 10 percent of operating costs rose suddenly to 20 percent. Beset by crushing overhead, the air carriers demanded fare increases from the CAB. But the board responded with one of only 5 percent, too little to quiet the cries for help. At the same time, policy analysts and economists on both sides of the political aisle joined President Gerald Ford in seizing on deregulation as the needed fillip for industries conducting business under tight federal supervision. The reformers trusted in open competition to lower prices and improve customer service. The White House announced in 1974 its intention to submit legislation to curtail the federal role in regulating the creation of new airlines, the distribution of routes, and the cost of fares.

In 1975, Senator Edward M. Kennedy of Massachusetts inaugurated hearings on the CAB in his capacity as chairman of the Subcommittee on Administrative Practice and Procedure. The resulting report praised the efficiency of new intrastate firms such as Texas International and Pacific Southwest, comparing them favorably to the national carriers subject to CAB guidelines. The subcommittee also pointed out that the established companies felt no particular incentive to reduce costs because the board so often acceded to their requests for higher fares. "The CAB," the authors wrote in summation, "has chosen to protect the industry at the expense of the consumer." Obviously, Kennedy and his staff neglected to consult Robert Six before drawing their conclusions.

Six's long career suggested a far different interpretation of the CAB's role. For nearly forty years, efficient performance and passenger service informed his business. Even during the 1970s, when the environment for the airlines proved especially hostile, his company continued to operate in the black. Even in the shadow of the Ford administration's energy proposals to preserve domestic fuel by *doubling* the cost of petroleum for commercial jets, Continental posted profits. Undoubtedly, Six made mistakes; grounding four 747s after realizing that DC-10s better suited his markets cost Continental $650,000 a month in interest. On the other hand, even during the 1973 oil crisis, Continental showed no loss. The following year freight-ton miles rose almost 20 percent, netting the firm $6 million in earnings for the first half of 1974 and the highest quarterly revenue since Six became president. In 1976, profits climbed to $9.2 million on revenues of $540 million.

As Six approached his fortieth anniversary as Continental's leader, he realized his role ought to change. Sensing the public mood, the CAB hierarchy began to speak approvingly of self-imposed deregulation. In 1976, his pilots—whom he always paid well and held in special esteem—went on strike for twenty-five days. "Our communications were poor," he conceded. "Eighty percent of our pilots are under forty and we just didn't realize the gulf that had developed." This unpleasant experience only confirmed a decision Six had made some time before: to yield the leadership of Continental to someone younger. After a lengthy search, he selected Alexander Damm as his successor. Until his appointment, Damm had served as Continental's chief budgeteer, where he practiced a single-minded parsimoniousness and a penchant for order and control. Imagination did not rule Damm's thoughts, so Six decided to remain in proximity by assuming the dual positions of chief executive officer and chairman of the board.[28]

On April 12, 1976, Six again came before the Senate Subcommittee on Aviation, this time for a hearing designated "Regulatory Reform in Air Transportation." The mood of this proceeding contrasted sharply with his last appearance. Now the senators heard witnesses for and against an actual piece of legislation proposed by the White House. The moment of abstract debate had passed. The drumbeat of deregulation had gained more adherents in the interval and Six, older and perhaps tired after tacking against the wind for so long, failed to take the hearing by storm. But his plain talk, backed by unmatched experience, captured the attention of all.

He predicted for the senators the outcome of pursuing the present course.

> In my view, the radical surgery of deregulation will not lead to a more competitive situation. Rather, it is more liable to result in a period of initial chaos and ultimately in a situation in which most

of our air transportation system will be in the control of a few industry giants. In the long run, this would mean higher fares and less
service. I don't mean to suggest that there wouldn't be a number
of small companies entering particular markets, in an effort to find
a limited area in which to make a buck. A few of them might even
succeed. What I am focusing on is who would be providing most
of the service and controlling most of the market.[29]

Six supported his claims with many specifics. Sixteen intrastate carriers opened in California over a period of twenty years. Of that number,
fourteen closed their doors, most within the first twelve months of operation. During their short life spans they served the public erratically at
best. Moreover, in a future dominated by escalating fuel costs, by high
labor costs, and by unknown environmental costs, assertions that deregulation resulted in lower air fares "has no basis in fact and is seriously
misleading." Six conceded that from 1950 to 1969, ticket prices (adjusted
for inflation) did decline. But he blamed this phenomenon on unparal-
leled advances in aircraft technology that appeared to be leveling off
during the 1970s. He recommended that the CAB enact a five-point plan
to revive airline prosperity and to preserve reasonable fares. First, he
proposed expanding service by awarding new routes and by encouraging
companies wishing to enter the airline business. "We can always benefit
from the infusion of new talent," said Six. But "we don't need the scav-
engers." Second, he advised the board to eliminate archaic regulatory restrictions—but on a case-by-case basis. Third, Six suggested the CAB
grant greater leeway in the fares and services offered by air carriers. "The
board need only set the upper limits on fares and cargo rates. Below that,"
he concluded, "we should be completely free to experiment." Fourth, he
urged the board to terminate capacity agreements in international markets. Finally, the Continental boss favored accelerating the CAB's decision-
making process.

In the end, Six addressed himself to the question at the crux of the
hearing: whether a bill to deregulate the industry should be passed by
the Congress. He denounced its essential provisions.

Tearing the certified system apart is no answer. We should try
first to solve these problems by improving what we have carefully

built over the last 38 years. We have the finest air transport system in the world. I say: Let's get on with the task of making it better. I think [the judgment call of whether to embrace deregulation] is one I am qualified to make, based on my intimate knowledge of the industry over almost forty years and my demonstrated commitment to competition. I have never been afraid to face competition, but open entry is a road to monopoly, not competition. It is no solution to the current ills facing the industry. . . . What we need is a return to enlightened regulation designed to provide increased competition over more routes, coupled with less rigid control over rates. Let's see if we can't make the system operate as the Congress intended—which the [CAB] has done for the last five years—before moving to radical solutions. That's the heart of my message today.[30]

This time Six's pronouncements went unheard. The presidential election later that year brought in a new chief executive even more determined to abolish regulations than Gerald Ford. Jimmy Carter appointed a highly able and energetic New Yorker named Alfred Kahn to lead the CAB. The fourth chairman in as many years, Kahn's marching orders coincided with those mandated during his tenure on the New York Public Service Commission: to streamline and to deregulate. His deeds at the CAB represented a complete repudiation of Robert Six's recommendations. Kahn began his task by concentrating on ticket prices; he simply allowed air carriers to charge whatever they pleased. The resulting promotions—Texas International's Peanuts Fares and American Super Savers—swept the industry. He then directed his staff to open airline certification to "all fit applicants." Finally, route certifications, once subject to the CAB's tight-fisted control, now were granted liberally and nonexclusively. His agenda in place, Kahn then lobbied Congress for legislation to deregulate the airlines, a difficult task involving intense opposition from the aviation lobby and the unions. Kahn lavished time on cultivating the press and on winning converts in the House and Senate. His persuasion succeeded. In October 1978, the president signed the Airline Deregulation Act, a law overwhelmingly passed by Congress that codified the administrative reforms enacted by Kahn at the CAB. Robert Six's only comment: "You'll always remember 1977 as the last year of service in the airlines."[31]

At first, the oracle of doom seemed wrong; Continental experienced an Indian summer of prosperity before the hard frost of deregulation set in. It declared its biggest net profit ever—$49.1 million—in 1978. That same year it kept pace with the other airlines in applying for the now open routes and chose eighteen new segments for its domestic network. But 1979 told a different story. Over the decades Six had systematically squeezed out most of the company's inefficiencies so that by the late 1970s not much remained to pare down. On the contrary, high inflation drove up all of his fixed expenses—fuel, labor, advertising, and mainte-nance. At the same time, the cut-rate air carriers, unfettered by the CAB and unbound by Continental's long-standing commitment to quality service, offered fares lower than Six could match. Losses of $13.2 million in 1979 and $20.7 million the next year represented unmitigated catas-trophes for Continental, which, unlike the industry leaders, had always operated on a thin profit margin with no reserves to speak of. Moreover, as the CAB declined in importance, Robert Six's influence declined, too. During his forty-year relationship with the CAB, it seldom favored him with routes or other advantages, although at times its support proved crucial. Rather, for the most part, he extended his airline's reach through his own devices—mergers, mail deliveries, military contracts, interservice agreements, even political influence—and whatever else lay at hand. Six rarely asked the board for fare increases; before the 1960s he preferred to increase profits by internal efficiencies and afterward by discounted tickets. But the CAB *did* offer him an asset far more valuable than routes or price increases: an orderly universe with a finite number of opponents, a world in which Six learned to be a master of the game. After the game folded, his mastery ceased.

The time came for Six to withdraw, and he recognized it. Surprising many in the industry, he resigned as CEO in February 1980 in favor of Alvin L. Feldman, the fifty-two-year-old president of Frontier Airlines. In one year Feldman had transformed the Denver-based Frontier from an unprofitable and ineffectively managed company into one with an envi-able balance sheet. While Six continued as chairman of the board, Feld-man assumed full powers at Continental. But he found little time to work his magic. In February 1981, Francisco "Frank" Lorenzo, president of Texas International Airlines, announced his intention to purchase 49 percent of Continental stock at $13 per share. Seven months later, the government approved the acquisition of 50.9 percent of Continental's shares by Lorenzo. Overwhelmed by record losses of $60.3 million during the year of the takeover, as well as by the daily pressures of countering Lorenzo's offensive, A. L. Feldman took his own life in 1981. As a consequence, Robert Six, on the mend after heart surgery, agreed to manage his company until March 1982, when the Continental shareholders voted in new directors. The firm Six loved and served for over forty-four years then returned to its Texas origins; Frank Lorenzo moved Continental's headquarters to Houston. Six retired from the airline business, disappointed by the outcome of his travails but honored by such distinctions as election to the Aviation Hall of Fame. He lived another four years and died in his sleep at his Beverly Hills home on October 6, 1986, age seventy-nine. One of his closest associates at Continental remembered him as a man who pursued a vocation suited perfectly to his talents.

> If ever there was a guy destined to be in the airline industry it was Bob Six. He fell in love with it when it was kind of hard to love. Too many people have gotten into the business because it was already established; they have no real feeling for it. But he has more going for him than just loving the crazy business. He has a sixth sense—an ability to foresee what's going to happen before it actually does. He's one of the few airline Presidents who never resented regulatory influence but learned to live with it instead, as a way of life. He's a genius when it comes to anticipating economic cycles, when it comes to picking the right equipment, when it comes to knowing what the public will buy.[32]

Perhaps these qualities represent the secrets of his extraordinary success.

Notes

1. For the story of Robert Six's formative years, I am much indebted to Robert Serling's *Maverick: The Story of Robert Six and Continental* (New York, 1974), 15–17. See also William M. Leary, "Robert F. Six," in *The Encyclopedia of American Business History and Biography: The Airline Industry* (New York, 1992), 428; Continental Airlines News Bureau, biography of Robert F. Six, n.d., 1–2, Biographical Files, National Air and Space Museum (NASM), Washington, D.C.

2. Robert F. Six, *Continental Airlines: A Story of Growth* (New York, 1959), 9

(quoted passages); Serling, *Maverick,* 17–18; Edward J. Boyer, "Continental Airlines Founder R. F. Six Dies," *Los Angeles Times,* 7 October 1986; Continental Airlines, biography of Six, 2, NASM.

3. Serling, *Maverick,* 18–21 (quoted passages); "Robert Forman Six," *Current Biography Yearbook* (New York, 1970), 399; Continental Airlines, biography of Six, 2, NASM.

4. Leary, "Robert F. Six," 428, 429 (quoted passage); Serling, *Maverick,* 21–24; "Robert Forman Six," *Current Biography Yearbook,* 399; Continental Airlines, biography of Six, 2–3, NASM.

5. Serling, *Maverick,* 21–32; David D. Lee, "Air Mail Episode of 1934," in *The Encyclopedia of American Business History and Biography: The Airline Industry* (New York, 1992), 25–26; R. E. G. Davies, *Rebels and Reformers of the Airways* (Washington, D.C., 1987), 32; "Robert Forman Six," *Current Biography Yearbook,* 400; Continental Airlines, biography of Six, 3, NASM.

6. Leary, "Robert F. Six," 429, Serling, *Maverick,* 32–36, and Boyer, "R. F. Six," *Los Angeles Times,* 7 October 1986 (quoted passages); Davies, *Rebels and Reformers,* 33; R. E. G. Davies, *Continental Airlines: The First Fifty Years* (Woodlands, Tex., 1984), 11; Six, *Continental Airlines,* 9–10; Continental Airlines, biography of Six, 3–4, NASM.

7. Senate Committee on Commerce, Subcommittee on Aviation, *Regulatory Reform in Air Transportation: Hearings on S. 2551, S. 3364, and S. 3536,* 94th Cong., 2d sess., 1976, 371 (quoted passage); Nick A. Komons, *Bonfires to Beacons: Federal Civil Aviation Policy under the Air Commerce Act, 1926–1938* (Washington, D.C., 1989), 348–66; Donald R. Whitnah, "Civil Aeronautics Board," in *The Encyclopedia of American Business History and Biography: The Airline Industry* (New York, 1992), 105–6.

8. Senate Committee, *Regulatory Reform,* 437; Whitnah, "Civil Aeronautics Board," 105–6.

9. U.S. Civil Aeronautics Authority, *Decisions of the Civil Aeronautics Authority,* vol. 1, February 1939 to July 1940 (Washington, D.C., 1940), 14–17, Docket No. 2–401-E-1, "Continental Air Lines, Inc.—Certificate of Public Convenience and Necessity" [grandfather certificate, Denver, Colorado, to El Paso, Texas], decided 9 March 1939; Davies, *Rebels and Reformers,* 33–34; Davies, *Continental Airlines,* 12; Serling, *Maverick,* 37.

10. Senate Committee, *Regulatory Reform,* 437.

11. U.S. Civil Aeronautics Authority, *Decisions of the Civil Aeronautics Authority,* vol. 1, February 1939 to July 1940 (Washington, D.C., 1940), 182–89, Docket No. 231, "Continental Airlines, Inc.—Mail Rates for Route No. 43" [Wichita, Kansas, to Pueblo, Colorado], decided 15 June 1939; U.S. Civil Aeronautics Authority, *Decisions of the Civil Aeronautics Authority,* vol. 1, February 1939 to July 1940 (Washington, D.C., 1940), 88–104, Docket No. 2–401(E)-2, "Continental

Air Lines, Inc.—Certificate of Public Convenience and Necessity" [certificate to carry mail, passengers, and cargo on Route No. 43, Wichita, Kansas, to Pueblo, Colorado], decided 28 April 1939; "Robert F. Six, Founder of Airline and Aviation Pioneer, Dies at 79," *New York Times,* 7 October 1986, and Six, *Continental Airlines,* 10 (quoted passages); Davies, *Continental Airlines,* 12; Leary, "Robert F. Six," 430; Lloyd H. Cornett Jr., "Continental Airlines," *The Encyclopedia of American Business History and Biography: The Airline Industry* (New York, 1992), 119; Serling, *Maverick,* 37–38; Irwin Ross, "Bob Six's Bag of Tricks," *Fortune,* February 1963, 132; Continental Airlines, biography of Six, 4, NASM.

12. Serling, *Maverick,* 38–43 (quoted passage); Leary, "Robert F. Six," 429; Davies, *Continental Airlines,* 12–13.

13. U.S. Civil Aeronautics Authority, *Decisions of the Civil Aeronautics Authority,* vol. 1, February 1939 to July 1940 (Washington, D.C., 1940), 598–611, Docket No. 265, "Continental Air Lines, Inc.—Amendment of Certificate of Public Convenience and Necessity" [certificate to carry mail, passengers, and cargo over Route No. 29, El Paso, Texas, to Albuquerque, New Mexico, via Carlsbad, Hobbs, and Roswell, New Mexico], decided 8 March 1940; U.S. Civil Aeronautics Board, *Decisions of the Civil Aeronautics Board,* vol. 2, July 1940 to August 1941 (Washington, D.C., 1943), 727–51, Docket No. 192, "Braniff Airways, Inc., et al.—Certificate of Public Convenience and Necessity" [amendment to Route No. 43, extending Continental's service from Wichita, Kansas, to Tulsa, Oklahoma], decided 21 June 1941; Serling, *Maverick,* 52–58 (quoted passage); Davies, *Continental Airlines,* 12–13; Davies, *Rebels and Reformers,* 34; Cornett, "Continental Airlines," 119; Ross, "Six's Bag of Tricks," 194; Continental Airlines, biography of Six, 4, NASM.

14. U.S. Civil Aeronautics Board, *Economic Decisions of the Civil Aeronautics Board,* vol. 4, December 1942 to June 1944 (Washington, D.C., 1945), 1–21, Docket No. 2–401-B-4, "Continental Air Lines, Inc.—Certificate of Public Convenience and Necessity" [certificate for Route No. 60, from Denver, Colorado, to Kansas City, Missouri], decided 10 December 1942; U.S. Civil Aeronautics Board, *Economic Decisions of the Civil Aeronautics Board,* vol. 7, June 1946 to March 1947 (Washington, D.C., 1948), 793–98, Docket No. 2087, "Continental Air Lines, Inc., San Antonio–Hobbs Certificate," decided 7 March 1947; U.S. Civil Aeronautics Board, *Economic Decisions of the Civil Aeronautics Board,* vol. 3, August 1941 to December 1942 (Washington, D.C., 1945), 395–414, Docket No. 670, "Continental Air Lines, Inc.—Mail Rates for Routes Nos. 29 and 43" [mail rates raised to 48.5 cents per airplane mile], decided 6 April 1942; Serling, *Maverick,* 59–61, 72–73 (quoted passage); Davies, *Continental Airlines,* 16–21; Cornett, "Continental Airlines," 119–20; Davies, *Rebels and Reformers,* 34–35; Leary, "Robert F. Six," 430; Continental Airlines, biography of Six, 4–5, NASM.

15. U.S. Civil Aeronautics Board, *Economic Decisions of the Civil Aeronautics*

Board, vol. 6, July 1944 to May 1946 (Washington, D.C., 1947), 97–116, Docket No. 934, "Continental Air Lines, Inc.—Mail Rates" [mail rates cut to 24.8 cents per airplane mile], decided 1 August 1944; U.S. Civil Aeronautics Board, *Economic Decisions of the Civil Aeronautics Board,* vol. 16, July 1952 to February 1953 (Washington, D.C., 1957), 821–42, Docket No. 2936, "Additional North-South Service to Tulsa" [application granted for Continental to extend the Tulsa–Wichita route to Kansas City–Tulsa], decided 19 December 1952; U.S. Civil Aeronautics Board, *Economic and Safety Enforcement Cases of the Civil Aeronautics Board,* vol. 23, January to August 1956 (Washington, D.C., 1960), 162–85, Dockets 6597 and 6749, "Houston-California Interchange Case" [renewal of Continental's authority to serve California via the Interchange Agreement with American Air Lines], decided 9 March 1956; U.S. Civil Aeronautics Board, *Economic and Safety Enforcement Cases of the Civil Aeronautics Board,* vol. 20, February to May 1955 (Washington, D.C., 1959), 323–401, Docket No. 6457, "Continental-Pioneer Acquisition Case" [final approval of the merger after rejection of appeals by Braniff and Central], opinion issued 16 March 1955; Davies, *Continental Airlines,* 22–33; Serling, *Maverick,* 84–85, 88–89, 94–101, 106–107; Davies, *Rebels and Reformers,* 35–37; Leary, "Robert F. Six," 430; Cornett, "Continental Airlines," 120–21.

16. U.S. Civil Aeronautics Board, *Economic and Safety Enforcement Cases of the Civil Aeronautics Board,* vol. 22, November to December 1955 (Washington, D.C., 1959), 1178–1315, Docket No. 1841, "Denver Service Case," opinion issued 14 November 1955; Tom Redburn, "LA's Two Big Airlines: Same But Different," *Los Angeles Times,* 15 May 1977 (quoted passage); Serling, *Maverick,* 111; Davies, *Continental Airlines,* 36; Leary, Robert F. Six," 431.

17. Robert L. Whearley, "The Highflying Robert Six," *Saturday Evening Post,* February 1963, 82 (quoted passages); Six, *Continental Airlines,* 11 (block quotation).

18. Six, *Continental Airlines,* 12 (quoted passage); Davies, *Continental Airlines,* 37–41; Davies, *Rebels and Reformers,* 38–39; Leary, "Robert F. Six," 431; Serling, *Maverick,* 116–17, 130.

19. Ross, "Six's Bag of Tricks," 196; Six, *Continental Airlines,* 11–12; "Continental's Big Six," *Newsweek,* 9 March 1959, 92; Davies, *Rebels and Reformers,* 39; Serling, *Maverick,* 123, 131.

20. Six, *Continental Airlines,* 14 (quoted passage); Davies, *Rebels and Reformers,* 38–40; Ross, "Six's Bag of Tricks," 196; Davies, *Continental Airlines,* 41; Whearley, "Highflying Six," 84; Leary, "Robert F. Six," 432.

21. U.S. Civil Aeronautics Board, *Enforcement and Safety Cases of the Civil Aeronautics Board,* vol. 37, October 1962 to February 1963 (Washington, D.C., 1969), 797–800, Dockets 14310, 14312, 14313, "Continental Air Lines et al., Economy Fares" [Continental won an extension of its economy fares from February to October 1963], adopted 2 February 1963; "Robert F. Six," *New York Times,* 7 October 1986, and Whearley, "Highflying Six," 82 (quoted passages); Serling, *Maverick,*

189–90; Davies, *Continental Airlines,* 47; Ross, "Six's Bag of Tricks," 198; Lloyd Shearer, "Bob Six: Maverick of the Airlines," *Parade,* 12 October 1969, 5; Continental Airlines, biography of Six, 6, NASM.

22.   U.S. Civil Aeronautics Board, *Economic Cases of the Civil Aeronautics Board,* vol. 58, September 1971 to February 1972 (Washington, D.C., 1978), 154–223, Dockets 23666, 17353, 16242, "Pacific Islands Local Service Investigation" [Air Micronesia given authority between Hawaii and Guam; Continental given authority between American Samoa and Okinawa], adopted 27 July 1971; "Six's Big Gamble," *Newsweek,* 14 November 1966, 88 (quoted passage); Davies, *Continental Airlines,* 53–64; Davies, *Rebels and Reformers,* 40–41; Serling, *Maverick,* 235–36, 242–243, 250; Leary, "Robert F. Six," 432; "Six at 61," *Time,* 5 July 1968, 59; Continental Airlines, biography of Six, 6, NASM; Shearer, "Six: Maverick of the Airlines," 4.

23.   U.S. Civil Aeronautics Board, *Economic Cases of the Civil Aeronautics Board,* vol. 51, June to July 1969 (Washington, D.C., 1975), 161–577, Docket No. 16242, "Transpacific Route Investigation: Supplemental Opinion and Order on Reconciliation" [Johnson and Nixon administration decisions on mainland to Hawaii routes], adopted 21 July 1969; Serling, *Maverick,* 253–54, 256–57 (quoted passages); Davies, *Continental Airlines,* 65–68; Davies, *Rebels and Reformers,* 42; Redburn, "L.A.'s Two Big Airlines," *Los Angeles Times,* 15 May 1977; "Six at 61," 59; Shearer, "Six: Maverick of the Airlines," 4–5 (block quotation).

24.   Richard J. Kent Jr., *Safe, Separated, and Soaring: A History of Federal Civil Aviation Policy, 1961–1972* (Washington, D.C., 1980), 169–79; "Six at 61," 59; Donald R. Whitnah, "Airline Deregulation Act of 1978," *The Encyclopedia of American Business History and Biography: The Airline Industry* (New York, 1992), 15; "Six's Shining Promise," *Time,* 15 May 1972, 79; Serling, *Maverick,* 271.

25.   House Committee on Interstate and Foreign Commerce, Subcommittee on Transportation and Aeronautics, *Civil Aeronautics Board Air Mail Rate Authority: Hearings on H.R. 16879,* 91st Cong., 2d sess., 1970, 1, 7–11.

26.   Serling, *Maverick,* 271–72; Senate Committee on Commerce, Subcommittee on Aviation, *Economic Conditions of the Air Transportation Industry: Hearings,* 92d Cong., 1st sess., 1971, 374.

27.   Serling, *Maverick,* 287; Senate Committee, *Economic Conditions,* 374–88.

28.   Whitnah, "Airline Deregulation Act," 15–16, and Redburn, "L.A.'s Two Big Airlines," *Los Angeles Times,* 15 May 1977 (quoted passages); Edmund Preston, *Troubled Passage: The Federal Aviation Administration during the Nixon-Ford Term, 1973–1977* (Washington, D.C., 1987), 253; Harold D. Watkins, "Continental Breaks Through Turbulent Financial Weather," *Los Angeles Times,* 31 July 1974; Edward D. Muhlfield, "Six Sense," *Flying,* September 1975, 5; Harold D. Watkins, "Six Era Draws Near End at Continental," *Los Angeles Times,* 8 May 1975; Rush Loving Jr., "Bob Six's Long Search For a Successor," *Fortune,* June 1975, 95.

29. Senate Committee, *Regulatory Reform*, 425.

30. Ibid., 426–29, 437; "Two Airline Executives Rap Plan to Reduce Regulation," *Los Angeles Times*, 13 April 1976.

31. "Robert F. Six," *New York Times*, 7 October 1986 (quoted passage); Thomas McCraw, *Prophets of Regulation: Charles Francis Adams, Louis D. Brandies, James M. Landis, and Alfred E. Kahn* (Cambridge, Mass., 1984), 258–59, 261, 265–294; Whitnah, "Airline Deregulation Act," 16.

32. Serling, *Maverick*, 109 (block quotation); "Robert F. Six," *New York Times*, 7 October 1986; Boyer, "R. F. Six," *Los Angeles Times*, 7 October 1986; Leary, "Robert F. Six," 433; Davies, *Rebels and Reformers*, 43–45; Davies, *Continental Airlines*, 75–77; Tom Redburn, "Six to Give Up Top Post at Continental," *Los Angeles Times*, 13 December 1979; Michael E. Murphy, *The Airline That Pride Almost Bought: The Struggle to Take Over Continental Airlines* (New York, 1986), 9–11, 21–25, 200–201; Bill Sing, "TIA Battle for Control of Continental Is Over," *Los Angeles Times*, 26 November 1981; "Airline Pioneer Robert F. Six Founded and Built Continental," *Washington Times*, 8 October 1986.

Bibliographical Essay

Despite his unique achievements, surprisingly little has been written about Robert Forman Six. Two reasons may suggest his relative absence from the literature of aviation. First, he ruled Continental for so long and in such a personal manner that he found it possible to act as his own publicist, to control those aspects of his life that he wished to make public as well as those parts that he decided to keep secret. Second, Six took years to raise Continental to prominence. By the time his airline assumed a national reputation, he was in his mid-fifties and had been at the helm for almost twenty-five years. Thus, over all of these formative years he had not attracted much journalistic ink.

Nevertheless, some writers have taken on the formidable Six. The only full treatment, written by Robert J. Serling, is a biography entitled *Maverick: The Story of Robert Six and Continental* (New York: Doubleday, 1974). It is a captivating book that suffers from a lack of source notes or bibliography. Eighteen years later, William M. Leary contributed a thoughtful essay on Six to his book, *The Airline Industry* (New York: Facts on File, 1992), part of the Bruccoli Clark Layman *Encyclopedia of American Business History and Biography*. It should be noted that Leary edited this outstanding volume, which includes essays on such subjects as the Civil Aeronautics Board, the Airline Deregulation Act of 1978, and Continental Airlines. Six offered some testimony of his own in *Continental Airlines: A Story of Growth* (New York: Newcomen Society of North America, 1959). Published from a speech that Six gave to the Newcomen Society's members, the story ends before Continental became a power in the airline industry. A chapter, "Robert Six: The Maverick," in R. E. G. Davies, *Rebels and Reformers of the Airways* (Washington, D.C.: Smithsonian Institution Press, 1987), 31–45, offers a compact and highly favorable outline of Six's career.

A few periodicals attempted to capture the essence of Six. The best are Robert L. Wheatley, "The Highflying Robert Six," *Saturday Evening Post,* February 1963, and Irwin Ross, "Bob Six's Bag of Tricks," *Fortune,* February 1963. A good article on Six's efforts to choose his replacement is Rush Loving Jr., "Robert Six's Long Search for a Successor," *Fortune,* June 1975. Many newspapers, especially the *Los Angeles Times* after Six relocated his airline to southern California in 1963, ran feature stories on Continental's president from 1960 to 1981.

Other literature involves Six, but only incidentally. His congressional testimony is scant, confined only to hearings before the Senate Committee on Commerce, Subcommittee on Aviation, in 1971 and 1976. Six's guiding hand, however, is seen often in the highly informative *Civil Aeronautics Board Reports,* numbering more than one hundred volumes in all and variously entitled *Economic Reports of the Civil Aeronautics Board, Economic and Safety Cases of the Civil Aeronautics Board,* and *Economic Cases of the Civil Aeronautics Board* (1940–1984). R. E. G. Davies's *Continental Airlines: The First Fifty Years* provides a good overview of the history of Six's company. Several of the books in the Federal Aviation Administration History series, notably Nick A. Komons's *Bonfires to Beacons: Federal Civil Aviation Policy under the Air Commerce Act* (Washington, D.C., 1989) and Robert J. Kent, *Safe, Separated, and Soaring: A History of Federal Civil Aviation Policy* (Washington, D.C., 1980), offer detailed background about the operation of the Civil Aeronautics Board. Finally, the tale of Continental's fall into bankruptcy in 1983, which was followed by its resurrection and transformation into the nation's fourth largest airline, is told in Michael E. Murphy's *The Airline That Pride Almost Bought: The Struggle to Take Over Continental Airlines* (New York, 1986).

Fortunate in His Enemies:
George T. Baker, National Airlines,
and Federal Regulators

GEORGE E. HOPKINS

F OR GEORGE THEODORE BAKER, WHO CALLED
himself Ted, the greatest achievement of his life came
near its end. Always "Mr. Baker" to the flight crews, ground employees,
and managerial subordinates who alternately admired and despised him,
this at once pugnacious and charming man took his National Airlines
on a wild ride from a local joke of an "airline" in the 1930s to an "international" carrier by the 1940s (owing to a "stub" route to Cuba), trendy
"Airline of the Stars" in the 1950s, and "transcontinental" carrier status by
the early 1960s.

Baker's pilots in particular carried on a love-hate relationship with
him. They loved the fact that Baker's success had brought them high status as pilots for a "real" airline. But they hated the way Baker treated
them while getting there. "If Ted Baker were here tonight," said retired
DC-8 captain Sid Wilson during a 1979 interview, "he'd charm the socks
off everybody, buy drinks, waltz the ladies, have everybody eating out of
his hand. Tomorrow he'd cut your throat in a second."[1]

Such was the contradictory nature of Ted Baker, at once visionary and
obtuse, stubborn and vacillating, calculating and impetuous. Perhaps it
should not have come as a surprise that, just at the moment of his greatest triumph, he would walk away from it. The 1961 Civil Aeronautics

George T. Baker. (Courtesy Air Line Pilots Association archives, Wayne State University)

Board (CAB) award to National Airlines of a coveted southern transcontinental route was the capstone of his life's work. It allowed Baker to connect Florida to Los Angeles with his DC-8 jets and thus take his place alongside the giants of the airline industry, men like Eddie Rickenbacker and Juan Trippe, who had never considered him their equal. In 1962, with a bright future beckoning National Airlines, Baker unexpectedly sold out to Lewis B. Maytag, lately president of Frontier Airlines, a mere regional carrier. Why did he do it?

Although at the age of sixty-one Baker was a bit young for retirement, his health was failing and he felt the cold breath of mortality upon him. So he sold his interest in National for $6.5 million, and after some second thoughts (during which he tried improbably to control National from a seat on the board of directors), he left on an extended European vacation. While visiting Vienna in November 1963, he died of a heart attack. Obituaries in major newspapers hailed him as an "aviation pioneer."[2]

Baker had indeed left his mark on the history of commercial aviation, but not exactly in the way he would have chosen. Although he saw himself as the prototypical "self-made man," Baker in fact owed everything to the system by which the government regulated the airlines. If anybody made Ted Baker, it wasn't himself but the nearly invisible federal bureaucrats who exercised ultimate control over the industry. The subtext of this situation lay in Baker's response to these regulators, which was occasionally quite maladroit. When it counted, however, Baker conformed to the system of federal regulation quite well.

For four decades, from passage of the Civil Aeronautics Act of 1938 until the Airline Deregulation Act of 1978 ended their dominion, federal functionaries would determine Baker's fate.[3] That these federal "examiners," aviation bureaucrats, and political appointees favored Baker had less to do with who he was than with who he was not. To put it simply, he was not Eastern Air Lines' Rickenbacker, the celebrated World War I combat ace, or Pan American's Trippe, the magisterial ruler of a globe-girdling empire. Herein lay the key to Baker's success. If ever it could be said of a man that he was fortunate in his enemies, Baker was that man.[4]

The Man and His Airline

Like F. Scott Fitzgerald's character Jay Gatsby, Baker cloaked himself in mystery and found it amusing that people suspected him of shady, even ruthless, dealings. Many details of his life are in dispute, mostly because he deliberately misled those who inquired. Take, for example, the most basic facts about that aspect of his life which became central to who he was—aviation. How did Baker become interested in flying? Either he was fascinated by airplanes as a youth and he learned to fly on his own as an adolescent in a neighboring farmer's airplane, or he did not. Either he actually disliked and feared airplanes, preferring boats and automobiles, or he did not. Either he learned the rudiments of flight at Chicago's Midway Airport in the late 1920s merely to puff up his resume so that he could more effectively wheel and deal in the aircraft leasing business, or he did not.[5]

E. J. Kershaw, a pilot who met Baker in Chicago in the early 1920s and later became a lifelong employee and executive at National, thought that he gave Baker his first airplane ride. So did Nemo Black, a legendary Chicago "birdman" and barnstormer. Charles Ruby, a future president of the Air Line Pilots Association, who began flying for National in 1935 and eventually became its chief pilot, remembered Baker talking about developing a lifelong fascination with aviation after getting his first plane ride as a youth at a county fair. Baker told different people different stories over the years. He particularly liked to mislead journalists.[6]

While the specific facts of Baker's life and the rise of National Airlines cannot be confirmed with absolute accuracy, the general outlines are reasonably clear. Baker was born in 1900 to a middle-class family in Chicago.

His father was a newspaperman of some local note, rising to become circulation manager of the *Chicago Daily News*. Baker's education was conventional through high school, after which he claimed to have attended the Montana School of Mines, although no records from that institution confirm it. He claimed service as a tank commander in World War I, but that too is in dispute. In any case, he never made it overseas to fight in the trenches of France.

After the war, Baker worked as a salesman—of almost anything. By the early 1920s he emerged as a somewhat dubious financial operative, first as a strong-armed "repo" man whose stocky build and jutting jaw discouraged protest when he seized cars belonging to the overextended. He parlayed his skills into ownership of a company that dabbled in automobile financing, a calling that bordered on loansharking. Later in the 1920s he earned a reputation as a sharp practitioner in the tricky business of boat leasing. Early in the 1930s he acquired the Chicago franchise of the Eastman Flying Boat Company (nobody is sure quite how), but that venture ended badly. When Eastman's owners discovered that Baker was using their flying boats (which were on consignment to be sold) to ferry Chicagoans to Canada on whisky runs, and possibly (Baker was always coy about this subject) to smuggle bootleg liquor, they canceled his franchise. It was not the last time that Baker would be accused of unethical business practices. As late as 1959, he was subjected to a CAB "enforcement proceeding" aimed at curbing National's excessive overbooking. This practice was common to all airlines because a certain number of passengers holding confirmed reservations inevitably failed to show up. But Baker radically overbooked far beyond what other airlines deemed prudent. Pilots who flew for National still wince when describing scenes involving irate passengers denied seats on overbooked flights. According to these airmen, Baker was directly and personally responsible for this chicanery.[7]

By the early 1930s Baker was all but bankrupt. His only real assets were three decrepit airplanes: an obsolete Butler monoplane and two single-engine Ryans much like the one Charles A. Lindbergh had immortalized by flying nonstop to Paris in 1927. The repeal of Prohibition in 1934 was almost the last straw, because it eliminated the only remaining profitable work to which he could put these aircraft, flying thirsty passengers to offshore destinations not controlled by the United States. Altogether,

Baker's aircraft, if they could be brought up to airworthy condition, could carry a grand total of eleven passengers. Even worse, the Butler monoplane was on the verge of being repossessed and Baker owed hangar rent on the two Ryans. Considering his checkered personal and business past, Baker seemed an unlikely candidate for success in the airline industry.[8]

In 1934, just as his ship seemed to be running aground, Baker got the lucky break he so desperately needed. Alleging fraud and malfeasance in the letting of airmail contracts in 1930, President Franklin D. Roosevelt canceled them and ordered the army to fly the mail. After some crashes and loss of life, the army did a creditable job during the seventy-eight days it substituted for the seemingly disgraced privately owned airlines, but the achievement came at a very high cost in money and bad publicity. With the exception of David L. Behncke, the feisty United captain who headed the then-fledgling Air Line Pilots Association, virtually every prominent aviator in America denounced Roosevelt. Even the usually reticent Lindbergh joined in heaping abuse on FDR. Eastern's Rickenbacker was particularly vitriolic; because a number of army pilots had died flying the mail, he accused the president of committing "legalized murder." As Rickenbacker knew, the only escape from what historian Arthur Schlesinger Jr. called "the New Deal's first great fiasco" was to return the job of flying the mail to private operators.[9]

The Airmail Act of 1934, which returned airmail service to the airlines and restored their main source of revenue, also opened the business to people like Baker. Given the hostility toward Big Business that the Great Depression generated, even minimally qualified parvenus like Baker could have their shot at the main chance.[10] Thus did Baker's grandiosely named "National Airlines Taxi System" win the Tampa–St. Petersburg–Daytona Beach route, a 147-mile segment whose sole purpose was as a "feeder" to connect the west coast of Florida with Eastern Air Lines' north-south service on the Atlantic seaboard. Rumor had it that Eastern's Rickenbacker had failed to bid on the airmail contract that Baker won because he thought nobody else would do so either, owing to its insignificance. Rickenbacker also believed Tampa and St. Petersburg to be "dead-end" towns with no future as airline destinations—a view that did not please local boosters on Florida's "Sun Coast." Baker would soon exploit Rickenbacker's gaffe to his own advantage.[11]

On October 15, 1934, Baker's National Airlines, as the enterprise had now been rechristened, made its maiden flight serving the cross-Florida route to Daytona. Because National's airmail subsidy of 17 cents per mile barely covered operating costs, the airline's prospects were uncertain. But Baker survived, and over the next four years he prospered modestly, almost totally at the expense of Eastern and Rickenbacker. By acquiring secondhand aircraft cast off by other airlines, Baker improved his fleet sufficiently to encourage passenger traffic. With the government covering his basic costs, dollars earned carrying passengers were the margin of survival for National. Baker gradually expanded his service to Jacksonville under a temporary Post Office contract made necessary by the fact that Eastern's DC-2 aircraft often had to overfly Daytona because of the airport's short runways, thus delaying mail deliveries to and from Tampa. Baker eventually enraged Rickenbacker further by stealing the Jacksonville–New Orleans route, which was categorized by the CAB as a "city pair," not merely a "feeder" route like Tampa-Daytona. Because Eastern already served New Orleans through another route, Rickenbacker had apparently gambled on winning that contract with a relatively high bid. This guess made sense, because Baker could not economically serve the new artery, which was a parallel route with no point of connection to National's Tampa-Daytona segment other than the "temporary" authority to fly from Daytona to Jacksonville. Rickenbacker confidently expected to regain that route after airport improvements in Daytona made it possible to accommodate Eastern's DC-2s. But he miscalculated. Perhaps because of Rickenbacker's open opposition to the New Deal, the Post Office allowed Baker to continue serving Daytona-Jacksonville.[12]

Eventually Rickenbacker's need for National's New Orleans–Jacksonville route forced him to bow to the inevitable and offer Baker a buyout. Again, however, Baker outmaneuvered Rickenbacker, countering his buyout tender by publicly offering instead to begin direct Tampa-Miami service should the Post Office open a route between those cities for bids. Thus Baker made Rickenbacker look bad while simultaneously exerting indirect political pressure on federal regulators. An enraged Rickenbacker responded as one might expect, promising to "run over" National and thus making Eastern look like a greedy, monopolistic octopus.

Baker therefore survived, but National was still mostly an all-Florida operation, barely more than an air taxi service. Such success as Baker enjoyed came largely at Eastern's expense, setting a pattern of competition and enmity with Rickenbacker and Eastern that would endure until National disappeared in a merger with Pan American in October 1980.[13]

Baker and His Political Connections, 1934–1938

Politics, in all its manifestations, could not be separated from a business that depended so completely on public money as did the airline industry between 1934 and 1938. But the process was necessarily covert and therefore nearly impossible to detect. Richard Caves, a careful student of the subject, finally gave up trying to describe the "vague and inflexible standards" that characterized the "informal processes" of political influence on airmail-related matters in that era. He finally concluded that, whether indirect or blatant, "political processes acted in systematic ways to affect the regulation of the airlines."[14]

The very fact that Baker won the New Orleans–Jacksonville contract shows that he had some sort of political influence, but its source remains obscure. Roosevelt's postmaster general, James A. Farley, allegedly met with Baker aboard a yacht during a visit to Chicago in 1934 and agreed—perhaps as a favor to politically influential Chicagoans who spoke on Baker's behalf—to consider his airmail bid. All we can know for sure is that eventually Baker won an ill-deserved contract, indicating that political influence cannot be discounted in his gaining a foothold in the airline business.[15]

Something else makes a clear assessment of political influences upon airmail politics in the 1934–38 period almost impossible: the fugitive role of local politics upon national policy. The adage that "all politics is local" might have been coined to characterize the process by means of which businessmen, local boosters, and politicians (from mayors all the way up to senators) competed for Post Office airmail routes. After 1938, a typical CAB hearing would offer formal proof of the realities of local politics. Almost any hearing on any subject, no matter how trivial, that came before the CAB would find long lists of witnesses testifying, often on behalf of municipalities, chambers of commerce, and the like. From 1934 to 1938, under Post Office control, local political pressures were even more direct.[16]

Baker understood this process and played the local Tampa–St. Peters-burg constituency like a virtuoso. As we have seen, Rickenbacker opened the door for Baker by making disparaging remarks about the west Florida cities, but Baker capitalized on the blunder by cementing his relationship with the local business community. His brainiest stroke was to involve his erstwhile competitors, the influential backers of a paper operation called Gulf Airlines, in a "merger" that was little more than a thinly disguised bribe. In effect, Baker bought Gulf's "good will," since it had little else. That National survived infancy under Post Office regulation between 1934 and 1938 is probably attributable to such local political influences. Baker's real challenge would come after 1938, when political pressure, which was easier to apply through local patronage patterns associated with Post Office politics, would have to be filtered through the more indirect channels of a new regulatory system.[17]

The Nature of Government Regulation after 1938

The modern era of airline regulation began with the passage of the land-mark Civil Aeronautics Act of 1938. The survival of Baker's airline would now depend on how he responded to the transformation produced by this legislation. The federal government, acting through the politically appointed members of what became known in 1940 as the Civil Aero-nautics Board, controlled every aspect of airline operations. As it turned out, National Airlines was the CAB's very first "customer."[18]

A look at that first CAB case provides an example of how the new reg-ulatory system worked. As previously noted, National's two major routes, Tampa-Daytona and New Orleans–Jacksonville, connected only via the Daytona-Jacksonville segment and only under "temporary" authority. Un-der Post Office control, the economic regulatory power of government did not extend much beyond giving and withholding airmail contracts. Because virtually no airline could operate without such a contract, it was essential to secure one. Theoretically, Baker could have offered passenger service but not carried mail over the Daytona-Jacksonville "stub" and thus connected his two airmail routes. Under the new post-1938 regulatory system, which divorced airmail subsidies from actual flying, no airline could fly *at all* over a specific route without a CAB Certificate of Con-venience and Necessity. Thus federal regulators could deny any entrepreneur, even one who wished to compete without a subsidy, the right to fly on *any* route. The real purpose of this power was to protect existing "certificated" carriers from competition that paralleled any existing route.[19]

Two historical influences were at work in this system: the desire to regulate "natural monopolies" like public utilities in the public interest, and the desire to protect the general welfare by "regulated competition" among businesses that were not "natural monopolies." The airline business fell somewhere between these two categories. Old "Bull Moose" Progressives (Theodore Roosevelt Republicans) and their ideological counterparts, Wilsonian Democrats, agreed that these regulatory functions were best exercised by independent commissions made up of experts who were free of political influence. The CAB provides a classic example of this type of thinking: a regulatory body of experts who, once appointed, were supposedly beyond direct political control. But CAB members were still subject to political pressure, if only because Congress and the president could let individual CAB members know that if certain decisions displeased them, neither their reappointment nor confirmation would be likely.[20]

Eliminating politics from such a system was clearly impossible. Politics exists as a mechanism for settling conflict. The CAB's "hearings" system, much like the first one set up to "fact find" in the dispute between National and Eastern over the Daytona-Jacksonville "stub" route, invited conflict and hence political maneuvering. The very nature of any government regulatory activity presupposes decision making that will create winners and losers.[21]

The hearings connected with the pioneering first case adjudicated by the CAB took place at the Carlton Hotel in Washington, D.C., and were highly adversarial in nature. Eastern lined up its allies and lawyers to testify, and National did the same. The CAB's examiner heard the facts and then made a decision, which the politically appointed members of the CAB eventually ratified. National was the winner. Effective March 21, 1940, the CAB certificated National to serve the Daytona-Jacksonville segment permanently, thus linking Baker's two separate routes. Shortly thereafter, as the CAB exercised increasing power during wartime, National gained access to the highly profitable New York–Miami route, putting it in direct competition with Eastern. One cannot escape the conclusion that members of the CAB, appointed by New Deal Democrats who controlled both the legislative and executive branches of government, relished seeing Rickenbacker face the kind of market reality that he so often publicly celebrated in theory while doing everything he could, privately, to curtail.[22]

In any case, Baker was the beneficiary of Rickenbacker's high ideological profile. Although no one can either prove or disprove it, Rickenbacker's strident opposition to FDR and the New Deal cannot have helped Eastern's case. In its formal decision, of course, the CAB did not allude to such matters. Instead, acting under its mandate to "regulate the civil air industry . . . in the interest of the United States," the CAB decided that the "national interest" was best served by allowing National to link its two previously separate certificated routes permanently. It would not be the last time that the CAB would favor the "little guy" at the expense of bigger airlines.[23]

The irony of this situation is that, although National arguably benefited from the decisions of federal regulators who came to power owing to the New Deal, Ted Baker was certainly no liberal Democrat. Indeed, he was probably just as extreme in his political conservatism as was Rickenbacker, but craftier. The truth of this assertion can be seen in an episode that showed Baker in his true colors—and almost cost him his airline. He was about to discover that what federal regulators could give, they could also take away.

The National Pilots' Strike of 1948

Baker hated labor unions for reasons both practical and abstract. Practically speaking, Baker hated unions for the same reasons that dynamic, dominating executives have always hated them—because they increase labor costs while limiting management's powers over workers. Baker believed fervently in the "iron law of wages," which held that any worker was overpaid if he or she received more than the most desperately unemployed worker would accept. Abstractly speaking, Baker hated labor unions because, in his essentially laissez-faire worldview, anything that derived its power from the instrumentalities of government was bad. If ever it could be said that any group of workers enjoyed a privileged position because of government intervention, it would be unionized airline pilots in particular and airline labor in general.[24]

Baker allowed unions to gain a foothold at National only under the extreme duress of World War II. At the time the Japanese attacked Pearl Harbor, not one single employee of National Airlines was represented by a union. Since winning a federally supervised representational election early in 1940, the pilots' union, ALPA, had been in almost continuous negotiations with airlines, but National delayed contract negotiations and nothing happened except that Baker contrived excuses to fire the first two Negotiating Committee chairmen that his pilots elected. Sensing that his antiunion stance might deny National a share of the coming bonanza of wartime military contracts, Baker abruptly surrendered to ALPA on December 9, 1941, only one day after the United States declared war on Japan.

World War II saw National expand, both domestically and internationally. National's planes and pilots, under governmental contracts, flew military supply routes all over the Caribbean, through South America, and across the South Atlantic to Africa. The growth of union representation among all categories of National's employees was equally dramatic, but Baker only grudgingly accepted this state of affairs. In 1942 National was the subject of formal CAB investigation into irregular pay practices— a violation of contractual obligations not only to pilots but also to the government. Because a negative finding by the CAB would have resulted in the loss of National's Certificate of Convenience and Necessity, Baker quickly stopped "chiseling," as ALPA president Behncke called it, but not before the union authorized a strike vote—a highly unusual step for ALPA during World War II.[25]

Federal regulators had two primary mechanisms by which they could influence and control airline labor-management relations. First, the Civil Aeronautics Act of 1938 contained explicit guarantees of labor's right to organize and bargain collectively. Within this general guarantee, airline pilots had more specific protections relating to minimum wages and maximum hours, which provided a floor under contractually negotiated wages and a ceiling over flying hours. Second, the so-called 1936 pilots' amendment to the Railway Labor Act of 1926 set up a complicated system of mediation and arbitration designed to resolve labor disputes short of a strike. It also gave the president power temporarily to halt airline strikes so that mediation and arbitration might have a chance to work. This latter system was available to all airline workers, whether unionized or not.[26]

Baker managed to run afoul of both these federal regulatory mechanisms in what one writer has called "the debacle of 1948."[27] How Baker extricated National from this disaster of his own making illustrated the relationship between federal regulators and airline management in all its complexity. It also demonstrated that Baker, for all his boastful posturing, would retreat abjectly from a "principled" fight when circumstances dictated such a response.

The ostensible cause of the strike was Baker's firing of a pilot after a botched landing at Tampa in 1945. The pilot, Maston O'Neal, was almost surely a victim of the then little-understood phenomenon of "hydroplaning." An aircraft "hydroplanes" when a cushion of water insulates the tires from the runway, thus rendering brakes totally ineffective. Because this unpredictable event only occurs under certain conditions of temperature, humidity, and aircraft speed and weight, it could not be duplicated by accident investigators. It therefore brought an end to the careers of many airline pilots who were guilty of nothing more than being unlucky. Until the early 1960s, when runway grooving finally solved the problem, accident investigators repeatedly declared the "probable cause" of a runway "overshoot" to be "pilot error," ignoring bewildered pilots' explanations that they had indeed touched down in the proper landing zone but could not make the brakes work. Pilots knew that something was wrong in this category of accidents but lacked technical proof, so there was little they could do about it through formal accident investigating channels. The accident in question at Tampa was relatively trivial (no one was injured), and it might otherwise have been forgiven but for a long history of irritations between the pilots and Baker. Because Baker and his pilots were at odds over other issues, nobody was willing to back down.[28]

The real reason for the pilot strike of 1948, which lasted from February 3 to November 24, was that Baker wanted to get rid of his unions. Specifically, he wanted to emulate Delta Air Lines, which had resisted unionization of its workers more successfully than other carriers. Aside from its pilots, who were ALPA members, Delta enjoyed a largely nonunion, docile workforce. But Delta avoided unions by paying nonpilot workers rather generously, given the lower wages that prevailed across the southern states in the 1940s.[29]

Voluntarily paying higher-than-union wages was a policy that the notoriously tight-fisted Baker found both unappealing and unnecessary. He knew that there were large numbers of semiskilled people who could easily be trained to function as baggage handlers, ticket agents, and the like. The problem for Baker was that his pilots and mechanics were both highly skilled and tightly organized. With large numbers of ex-military pilots and mechanics available after World War II, Baker saw an opportunity to break these princes of organized labor, and all of his other unions as well, by replacing them with equally competent, low-wage employees. Had it not been for federal regulators, he might have succeeded.[30]

The presidential election of 1948, pitting Democrat Harry S Truman against the Republican governor of New York, Thomas E. Dewey, dramatically affected the outcome of the pilots' strike. Baker was an outspoken Dewey supporter who, according to many pilots, contributed money to his campaign. When Truman upset Dewey, Baker knew that he was in trouble. Even before the election, ALPA and other unions had prevailed upon the Democrats to bring a CAB "dismemberment" case against National. Baker had little reason to worry about the outcome of this case, known as CAB Docket 3500, because he expected it to be dismissed after a Dewey victory brought new, presumably antilabor Republicans to the CAB. In fact, Baker had already won the purely economic aspects of the strike well before the presidential election. National's ALPA pilots had been completely "scabbed out," and Baker was once again operating a full schedule.[31]

The CAB "dismemberment" case rested on the fact that National was losing money. How could it not, considering its pilots' highly effective "Don't Fly National" campaign? Questions about the competence of "scab" pilots and mechanics raised ugly fears among potential passengers who took competing airlines whenever possible. Baker filed a $5 million slander suit against ALPA over this tactic. Needless to say, ALPA countersued, providing a field day for lawyers and more expense for Baker. Additionally, Baker negotiated "package" deals with Miami Beach hotels, which, although approved by the CAB, subverted the basic purposes of the regulated system by effectively shifting airline revenues to lodging costs. The CAB had to know that permitting this type of "cost shifting" damaged other carriers; indeed, Eastern protested furiously. Even worse for the ALPA, when Baker asked the CAB to increase his subsidy midway through the strike, it did so. There seems little doubt, although it cannot be conclusively proved, that during this whole episode the CAB was intimidated by the antilabor Republicans who controlled Congress (Truman's fabled "do nothing 80th"). With an antilabor reaction running at full tide, the CAB's bureaucrats were obviously tolerating behavior from Baker that they disliked but feared to challenge. Truman's startling victory changed all that.[32]

Operating under its mandate to "promote" civil aviation, the CAB had statutory authority to revoke National's certificate and award its routes to competitors. The CAB's power lay in the notion that since the taxpayers subsidized the airlines, the airlines must serve the public. With a pro-labor Democrat returning to the White House, the bureaucrats at the CAB, after months of dawdling and waiting to see which way the political winds would blow, took up Docket 3500, the "dismemberment case," with alacrity. There seemed little doubt that Baker's stewardship of the taxpayers' dollars would be found wanting.[33]

But it never came to that. In one of the more bizarre episodes in aviation history, Baker beat a retreat on all issues. The "cover" he used was a professed religious conversion. Allegedly, Baker had fallen under the spell of Dr. Frank Buchman's "Moral Rearmament" movement, which enjoyed a sudden vogue among business executives during the early cold war period. Buchman had formerly found moderate success as a conventional evangelist, heading a so-called First Century Christian Fellowship. By adapting preacherly techniques to the currently more trendy anticommunist movement, Buchman soared. At the height of cold war enthusiasm, Buchman's Moral Rearmament crusade found a significant following.[34]

Shortly after Truman's victory, Baker abruptly dropped out of sight. Nobody knew where he had gone. This behavior was very unusual for Baker, who seldom took vacations. As it turned out, Baker had slipped away to attend one of Buchman's retreats, called "House Parties," on Mackinac Island, Michigan. From there he began calling pilots individually, begging their forgiveness, swearing to mend his ways, and blaming all of the bad things that had happened on the "power of Satan." Baker sent a DC-4 to pick up fifty carefully chosen National employees—a cross-section of pilots, stewardesses, mechanics, and ground personnel—and flew them north to Michigan, where they shared in their employer's "religious conversion through the sweet healing power of Jesus." For four days the selected group of employees prayed with Baker and Buchman.

They were then asked to return to Miami to spread the word among their colleagues that Baker was a "changed man" who wanted to "let bygones be bygones."[35]

In fact, Baker had ready allies in his pilots, who had more at stake in the survival of their airline than did he. "Dismemberment" of National Airlines would have ended their careers, for National's routes—but not its planes and pilots—would in all likelihood have been parcelled out to Eastern and Pan American. Baker was really setting up a plausible public rationale for the CAB to end its "dismemberment hearing." He understood that his pilots had more political influence at this point than he did, so he turned over the fate of his airline to them. Baker was beaten, and he knew it. If he must grovel to survive, he would do so. Hearing of this revivalistic love feast between previously bitter opponents, even hardened bureaucrats at the CAB must have been touched. Scenes of mutual filial devotion and cooperation between labor and management were sufficiently unusual to get their attention. In any case, the CAB finally withdrew Docket 3500 (in 1951; CAB cases always moved slowly), sparing National from dismemberment.[36]

The Southern Transcontinental Service Case, 1961

Confronted by powerful opponents and with an overwhelming need to revive his fortunes—National had lost nearly all of its net worth during the 1948 strike—Baker buried his resentments in order to survive during the 1950s. After at first irritating the CAB with some poststrike harassment of his returning pilots, who had to "requalify" because of their long absence from flying during the ten-month work stoppage, Baker seems to have realized that another misstep would end his career. In any case, he rather quickly began accommodating himself more willingly to the federal regulatory system. Perhaps he decided that it was no worse than surrendering to his labor unions. So Baker curbed his occasionally intemperate *ex cathedra* criticisms of the CAB and the examiners who worked for them. Instead, he concentrated strictly on business for the next few years and became a model citizen in the regulated airline community. This reversal came as no surprise to the pilots who worked for him, because they had already seen him shift ground abruptly. Baker's new conformist posture would eventually pay off for National.[37]

But bureaucracies have long memories, and at first Baker paid for his transgressions with a stay in the CAB's version of purgatory. Except for a piddling route extension from New Orleans to Houston in 1957, the CAB blocked all of National's attempts at expansion during the 1950s. The CAB also awarded lucrative new routes between Florida and major Midwest markets to other airlines, in one case overruling an examiner's recommendation favoring National. Veteran pilots recall Baker uncharacteristically commiserating with them, all the while voicing dark suspicions of a hostile regulatory system out to ruin him. National's failure to gain new routes seemed to Baker proof of bias against him. He often urged pilots to use their influence on National's behalf, perhaps overestimating their "clout" with Eisenhower-era officialdom. For obvious reasons of self-interest, National's pilots and other unionized employees willingly used what limited influence they had on behalf of their employer.[38]

By far the worst blow came when the CAB opened National's profitable New York–Florida routes to Northeast Airlines in 1956. The CAB hoped that by permitting Northeast to enter the Florida market, it could reverse that carrier's deteriorating financial situation so that it could either become viable or be a suitable merger partner for a stronger airline. But with three airlines now competing for the New York–Florida vacation traffic, including powerful Eastern, Baker feared that National might sink into the same morass as Northeast. Financial failure in the era of regulation usually meant a forced merger with a stronger carrier—something Baker would not contemplate.[39]

As National's route structure remained generally stagnant throughout the 1950s, at a time when the airline badly needed to increase its revenues, Baker tried innovations such as "interchange" agreements with other carriers in order to give National the semblance of a larger system. What this tactic meant, in practice, was that National could sell tickets over routes it did not actually fly. A passenger, for example, could purchase a National Airlines ticket to fly from Florida to California but would not actually fly on a National aircraft—although it might be flown by National pilots. In 1958, owing to such an interchange agreement with Pan Am, the first airline to acquire the Boeing 707, National pilots were first to fly this pure jet transport, in Pan Am livery, on a regular domestic route.[40] The CAB, driven by its need to reduce domestic subsidies, permitted Baker this kind of latitude. All the while, Baker searched circumspectly, or appeared to, for ways of achieving a voluntary merger with a partner of whom both he and the CAB might approve. At various times he explored mergers, stock swaps, and outright purchases with Colonial, Northeast, Continental, and, most important, Pan American. Over the years, however, all such merger attempts fell through, primarily because Baker could not bring himself to join any other airline executive as an equal—let alone relinquish control.[41]

For many years, a National–Pan Am merger seemed to most airline industry observers to be the perfect fit for each airline. National needed to expand and Pan Am was a strictly international airline that needed domestic routes. Many of the two carriers' routes converged in Miami. Owing to National's Cuban route, its pilots were experienced in international flying. In 1958, Baker and Juan Trippe arranged a stock swap that made each airline the largest individual shareholder in the other. To howls of protest from competitors fearful of Pan Am gaining access to the domestic market, the CAB nullified the transaction in 1960. This decision hurt Pan Am far more than it did National, and played a role in the long, steady decline of what had once been the world's greatest airline. Pan Am was paying the price for its success and for Trippe's attempt to monopolize America's role in international aviation. The CAB's steady diminution of the protected domestic routes of the "Big Four"—American, Eastern, TWA, and United—after World War II had put Trippe's efforts to make Pan Am the "chosen instrument" of the country's presence in world air routes on the wrong side of history. For years Trippe had used his political influence in Washington to deter overseas competition by airlines based in the United States, the quid pro quo being that Pan Am would stay out of the domestic market. When the CAB began opening Pan Am's international routes to competition after World War II, however, it refused to allow the "magnificent cripple" access to American domestic markets.[42]

The essence of National's problem during these years lay not just in its lack of new routes but in the inadequacies of its existing route structure. Put simply, National served too many small markets across the South which, by their very nature, were unprofitable. This problem grew worse during the 1950s, just as the CAB's preferred method of subsidizing unprofitable routes underwent a change. Even in the 1930s (actually from the time when the first truly "modern" commercial airliner entered service—the legendary DC-3), it was apparent that any airline could make money on *certain* routes.[43] Between major cities, high passenger demand for air transportation meant automatic profits. But between lesser cities ("city pairs," in CAB terminology), and particularly between outlying cities and major cities ("feeder routes"), *no* airline could make money, because passenger demand was simply insufficient, no matter what quality of service an airline might offer. Accordingly, in order to connect these intrinsically unprofitable markets to the national air transportation system, which was the CAB's mandate, taxpayers would either have to subsidize service directly or do so indirectly by permitting airlines grossly to overcharge passengers traveling between major "city pairs" in order to make up the shortfall on "feeder" routes.[44]

CAB thinking on the subsidy issue underwent a change after President Eisenhower began appointing Republicans to the CAB. Instead of forcing major airlines to serve unprofitable markets by rationing out profitable "city pair" markets, by the late 1950s a "market-oriented" CAB began rethinking the subsidy problem. Northeast Airlines won access to the Miami–New York route and the right to compete directly with National and Eastern because of this new approach to subsidies.[45]

This variation on the original system actually began shortly after passage of the Civil Aeronautics Act of 1938. On the eve of World War II, the CAB decided to allow the development of a new category of carriers to serve regional markets that the "trunks" served grudgingly and often poorly. In the Essair Case of 1939, the CAB determined that the Houston-Abilene market would be served best by a small airline, devoted to it exclusively and flying smaller aircraft tailored to that route's specific needs. Although some trunk airlines resisted these changes (Braniff protested the Essair Case strongly), most trunks thought they would be well rid of troublesome local routes. World War II delayed implementation of the Essair decision, but the principles embodied in it resulted in the establishment of "feederlines" early in the postwar era.[46]

These feederlines were for the most part heavily dependent on "flow through" traffic destined for the trunk carriers. By the mid-1950s, when feederlines had become known officially as "local service carriers," there were thirteen of them. Such "locals" (including Mohawk and Piedmont) joined the eleven trunks as the stable basis for an integrated system of government-regulated airlines. But the "locals," as originally conceived, were never intended to be self-sustaining. On the other hand, if they were given access to major "city pair" markets, the new CAB reasoning went, and if they could compete effectively on such routes, then at least their subsidies might be reduced. In another change of nomenclature, several of the "locals" were now officially redesignated as "regional airlines" and permitted to enter markets previously reserved for the trunks.[47]

A "domino effect" now forced the CAB into further action. If the newly designated regionals took market share from the smaller trunks, like National, which had been allowed to fly on Eastern's primary New York–Florida routes merely in the interest of "competitiveness," the logical redress would be to permit the smaller trunks to enter the major airlines' last preserve, the transcontinental routes. Driven by the need to reduce subsidies, all distinctions between the "Big Four" (American, Eastern, TWA, and United) and the "minor trunks" (Northwest, Delta, Western, Continental, Capital, Northeast, Braniff, and National) ceased to exist by the early 1960s. It would be only a matter of time—the mid-1960s—when the ultimate *reductio ad absurdum* transpired and a former feeder-line upgraded to the status of a "regional"—Frontier—received CAB permission to fly transcontinentally. In utter disregard of the theory that had given rise to them, the former "local service carriers" were now becoming "junior trunklines."[48]

Out of this swirling controversy, with aspiring "junior trunks" competing for favors from a CAB determined to reduce subsidies, emerged airline regulation's Battle of Armageddon—the Southern Transcontinental Service Case. Its origin lay in the unsatisfactory nature of transcontinental airline service across the burgeoning "Sunbelt" stretching from Florida to Texas. While transcontinental service existed, most of it involved a stop in Texas and often a change of planes, with resulting inconvenient schedules for passengers wishing to board in Texas itself. Owing to complaints from several Texas cities, the CAB announced in 1958 that it would consolidate several smaller cases into a single gigantic one directly affecting the futures of eleven airlines.[49]

Two of the original "Big Four"—TWA and American—had the most to lose in this case, because they already enjoyed a substantial position in Florida to California routes. Both for ideological and practical reasons, the CAB had allowed a steady encroachment by lesser airlines into their domains over the years. It was therefore unlikely that they would get much out of the case. Eastern, widely considered a powerful player, was hungry for western routes. Its primary New York–Florida market, while still lucrative, showed signs of weakening, partly due to declining Cuban traffic after Castro's 1959 revolution. Rickenbacker participated personally in the case, using his high profile to line up support from civic groups, veterans' organizations, and municipalities.[50]

The CAB announced its decision in March 1961. National won big, getting the Miami-California route. Delta, the other big winner, got Atlanta-California. Baker's victory surprised almost everybody. Other contestants, like Delta, had put on far more impressive exhibits and witnesses. Baker's subordinates, charged with presenting National's case, were (even in the estimation of his pilots) second-rate. Their calculations, arguments, and witness lists lacked the sophistication of other airline representatives, and Baker himself was no match for Rickenbacker as a celebrity. Why, then, did National win?

In a CAB proceeding like the Southern Transcontinental Service Case, with its reams of documents, testimony, statistics, and arguments, no analyst can ever be entirely sure what specific issue resonated most importantly with members of the CAB. But we can draw general conclusions based upon historical trends. The CAB wished to reduce subsidies by allowing smaller airlines into more lucrative markets. National had been a relatively successful and well-behaved player among the second tier of airlines for a decade. If it had not received some kind of route expansion, National would almost certainly have been forced into a merger. The logical merger partner was Pan American, a special airline that was perceived historically as even bigger than the "Big Four." Bias against bigness, and perhaps lingering animosity toward Rickenbacker personally, ruled out Eastern, while fear of Pan Am, perceived as both mighty and Machiavellian, motivated the CAB to strengthen National in order to save it from Juan Trippe.

Conclusion

The CAB's 1961 certification of National to offer single carrier service across the southern transcontinental route between Florida and California was the fruit of long-standing CAB policy. The language of the award

A Lockheed L-18 "Lodestar" operated by National Airlines. Note "The Buccaneer Route" on the fuselage. (Courtesy of Air Line Pilots Association archives, Wayne State University)

was in the familiar bureaucratese of a well-established regulatory system. It laid out the reasoning behind its finding that the "public convenience and necessity" dictated the choice of National. Typically, the CAB left to "managerial discretion" the choice of timing, schedules, and specific equipment that National would use to service the route, but it was understood that Baker would use his new DC-8 jets. The fact that National had fewer such planes than unsuccessful airlines made little difference. For Baker, it was an improbable hour of triumph.[51]

Baker saw himself as a swashbuckling rebel, fighting the big guns of his competitors, pioneering Eastern Air Lines and gigantic Pan American World Airways, with a guerilla's guile and evasiveness. In the 1940s he even went so far as to emblazon "The Buccaneer Route" as a logo on his twin-engine Lockheed "Lodestar" aircraft—an indirect tweaking of Eastern's giant nose. Baker's seventeen-seat Lodestars carried barely half the passengers of the DC-3s flown by Eastern in that airline's salad days, nor could the Lockheeds fly from New York to Florida nonstop. Why not turn this liability into a Pimpernellian advantage, appealing to the traditional American admiration for the underdog? Baker's retired pilots thought it such a good idea that they named their organization "The Buccaneers."[52]

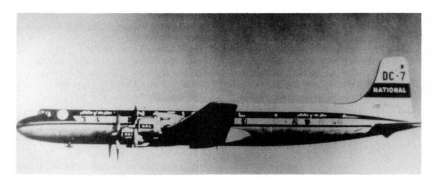

National Airlines Douglas DC-7. (Courtesy of Air Line Pilots Association archives, Wayne State University)

However, Ted Baker should be remembered less as a self-sufficient outsider than as a man who benefited beyond all measure from the decisions of government regulators. He achieved this success less through overt courting of federal bureaucrats than by virtue of the simple fact that he was not Eddie Rickenbacker or Juan Trippe. Yet, at the end of his active career, Baker rubbed shoulders on equal terms with both men and the other great names of the airline industry. His little National Airlines had exceeded all expectations, probably including even his own. Federal regulators midwifed National and wetnursed it to the mountaintop not because of who Ted Baker was but because of who he *was not*.

Notes

1. Quoted in George E. Hopkins, *Flying the Line: The First Half Century of the Air Line Pilots Association* (Washington, D.C.: Air Line Pilots Association), 127. Throughout this essay I will attribute certain information and comments to a series of oral history interviews that I conducted with retired and active National Airlines pilots in 1979. These interviews were conducted under the auspices of the Air Line Pilots Association (AFL-CIO), as part of the work cited above. For reasons of brevity and clarity, I will cite my own published work when these sources appear. The purpose of the interviews was to explore the 1948 pilot strike covered later in this essay, but they also include a wealth of information pertaining to National's overall history. Whenever I use "outtakes" that do not appear in *Flying the Line,* I will cite them as "oral history interview, 1979," with the subject's name.

2. George E. Hopkins, "George T. Baker" and "National Airlines," in William M. Leary, ed., *The Airline Industry* (New York: Facts on File, 1992), 47–51, 302–4.

3. Phaseout of the CAB, or "sunset," finally came on January 1, 1985.

4. Brad Williams, *The Anatomy of an Airline* (Garden City, N.Y.: Doubleday, 1970), 3–4. This journalistic history is an essential tool for any historian writing about National Airlines. Lacking footnotes and other scholarly features, it is in effect a primary source, being based on Williams's personal observation and interviews with Baker. Wherever possible, to avoid confusion, I will attribute information to specific page citations in *Anatomy*. But if ever there was a source that warranted the citation "passim," it would be Williams's immensely readable and entertaining book.

5. Williams, *Anatomy*, 19–24; Hopkins, "George T. Baker" and "National Airlines," 47–51, 302–4. Curiosity about Baker's behavior often led ALPA negotiators to speculate about his obscure past. Late in 1943, for example, ALPA president David Behncke and Baker were required by the Air Transport Command, which regulated airline contract operations in World War II, to meet and discuss contractual problems specific to National. Behncke held several meetings with pilots who knew Baker to discuss with them how to deal with Baker's "SOB attitude." These discussions were filled with speculations about Baker's shadowy past. See ALPA Central Executive Committee, minutes, January 6, 1944, 107–15, in ALPA Archives, Reuther Library, Wayne State University, Detroit.

6. ALPA Executive Committee minutes, 107–15; George E. Hopkins, "Charles H. Ruby," in Leary, *Airline Industry*, 417–18; oral history interview, 1979, Charles H. Ruby. For a further example of the evolution of Baker's deliberate evasiveness about his past, see also the article on Baker in *Current Biography*, 1953, 37–39, containing information conflicting with sources previously cited.

7. CAB Order Serial No. E-15614, August 4, 1960, National Airlines, Inc., Enforcement Proceeding, Docket No. 8761; Williams, *Anatomy*, 21–24; Richard E. Caves, *Air Transport and Its Regulators: An Industry Study* (Cambridge: Harvard University Press, 1962), 243; oral history interview, 1979, Captain E. P. McDonald.

8. Williams, *Anatomy*, 21; Hopkins, "George T. Baker," 48.

9. George E. Hopkins, *The Airline Pilots: A Study in Elite Unionization* (Cambridge: Harvard University Press, 1971), 107–10; Samuel B. Richmond, *Regulation and Competition in Air Transportation* (New York: Columbia University Press, 1961), 2–9; Donald Dale Jackson, *Flying the Mail* (Alexandria, Va.: Time-Life Books, 1982), 159–68; George E. Hopkins, *Pan Am Pioneer: A Manager's Memoir from Seaplane Clippers to Jumbo Jets* (Lubbock: Texas Tech University Press, 1995), 183–84; R. E. G. Davies, *Airlines of the United States since 1914* (Washington, D.C.: Smithsonian Institution Press, 1988), 160.

10. ALPA president Behncke, who had received a good deal of national exposure in the news media owing to his support of FDR's decision to cancel existing

airmail contracts, warned Congress that people like Baker would, upon gaining
a foothold in the industry, inevitably "tear down standards." House Committee
on the Post Office and Post Roads, 73d Cong., 2d sess., *Hearing on HR 3, HR
8578, and Other Air Mail Bills,* February 15, 1934, 160.

11. Williams, *Anatomy,* 46. For reasons of brevity, I will hereafter refer to the
Tampa–St. Petersburg–Daytona Beach airmail route as "Tampa-Daytona."

12. R. E. G. Davies, *Pan Am: An Airline and Its Aircraft* (McLean, Va.: Paladwr Press, 1987), 44–47; Carroll V. Glines and Wendell F. Moseley, *The Legendary
DC-3* (New York: Van Nostrand Reinhold, 1979), 40–46. The DC-2 ("Douglas
Commercial") was the lineal predecessor of the DC-3, the first truly successful
airliner. It greatly resembled the DC-3 except that it was smaller, carrying fourteen passengers instead of twenty-one for the DC-3. Douglas built 220 DC-2 aircraft in 1934–35.

13. Hopkins, "National Airlines," 302–4; Davies, *Airlines of the United States,*
169, 197; Williams, *Anatomy,* 31–32, 41–46.

14. Caves, *Air Transport and Its Regulators,* 5, 283–84.

15. Williams, *Anatomy,* 19–23; Hopkins, *Airline Pilots,* 152–60. Although Farley's acceptance of Baker's low bid was technically within the law, he had to ignore Baker's lack of experience in flying routes as long as the one from Jacksonville
to New Orleans. The law gave Farley discretion in this area, but its intent was to
limit bidding to real airlines. Put simply, successful bidders for the New Orleans–
Jacksonville artery were supposed to have demonstrated their ability actually to fly
the route, which Baker had not done. Williams's account of the Farley-Baker political connections cannot be proved, but it is suspect for several reasons. For one
thing, Williams described Farley, a New York politician, as a former mayor of
Chicago, which he was not. Williams is surely correct, however, in surmising that
Baker's connections with Chicago politicians played at least some role in placing
him at the putative meeting aboard the yacht *Zenith,* and his credibility is enhanced
by his admission that "no one can remember precisely when the meeting occurred."

16. See, e.g., Florida-Texas Service Case, Docket 5701, CAB *Reports* 24 (September 1956–March 1957): 307. This case saw not only the usual lineup of lawyers
and company executives from the airlines themselves but also representatives from
the following local chambers of commerce: Corpus Christi, Texas; Lafayette and
Baton Rouge, Louisiana; and Pinellas County and St. Petersburg–Clearwater,
Florida. National won this case, thereby extending the Jacksonville–New Orleans
route, which the CAB had permitted Baker to "steal" from Rickenbacker in 1939,
from New Orleans to Houston. It is small wonder that CAB hearings held before
an "examiner" often produced documents running to thousands of pages.

17. Williams, *Anatomy,* 25–32, 42. This "Gulf Airlines" should not be con-
fused with an earlier airline of a similar name, St. Tammany–Gulf Coast Airways,
Inc. See Davies, *Airlines of the United States,* 105–6.

18. For concise historical analyses of the developments summarized here, see Nick A. Komons, "Civil Aeronautics Administration," and Donald R. Whitnah, "Civil Aeronautics Board," in Leary, *Airline Industry*, 101–4, 105–8. For purposes of brevity and clarity, I will refer to the Civil Aeronautics Board (CAB) and its predecessor, the Civil Aeronautics Authority (CAA) as a single entity. On National's status as the first airline to have a case adjudicated by the CAB, see Williams, *Anatomy*, 54.

19. Richmond, *Regulation and Competition in Air Transportation*, 1–20. The Air Mail Act of 1934 was modified in 1935 to give the postmaster general more control over "off route" competition, empowering him to prohibit an airline holding a mail contract from flying over any route that another subsidized carrier already flew.

20. Caves, *Air Transport and Its Regulators*, 270–71; House Committee on Interstate and Foreign Commerce Subcommittee, 85th Cong., 2d sess., *Hearing on Investigation of Regulatory Commissions and Agencies* (Washington, D.C.: Government Printing Office, 1958), 14–73.

21. William A. Jordan, *Airline Regulation in America: Effects and Imperfections* (Baltimore: Johns Hopkins University Press, 1970), xiv.

22. Davies, *Airlines of the United States*, 290; W. David Lewis, "Edward V. Rickenbacker," in Leary, *Airline Industry*, 403–4.

23. A good case in point is CAB, *The New York–Florida Case*, Order No. E-10645, Docket No. 3051, September 28, 1956, 31. See also Williams, *Anatomy*, 52–57; Lewis, "Edward V. Rickenbacker," 403–5; Caves, *Air Transport and Its Regulators*, 270ff.; Richmond, *Regulation and Competition in Air Transport*, 43–44.

24. Williams, *Anatomy*, 52, 64–72, 81; Hopkins, *Flying the Line*, 126–48. Baker's extreme parsimony was legendary. He was so dilatory paying his fuel bills that one major oil company briefly cut off his credit, forcing pilots on several occasions to pay for fuel out of their own pockets rather than strand passengers. Afterwards, Baker delayed reimbursing them for months. Veteran National pilots now tell such tales with humor, but the situation was no laughing matter at the time. Williams recounts a famous story of Baker's refusing to buy proper drapes for his headquarters, describing them as "old-fashioned." In fact, real shades, no matter how old-fashioned, were used only in National's executive offices. In the rest of the company's offices, Baker used brown butcher paper taped to the windows. Oral history interview, 1979, Charles H. Ruby.

25. Williams, *Anatomy*, 63; Hopkins, *Flying the Line*, 131–32. The issues were ultimately settled after a face-to-face meeting between Behncke and Baker in Washington. ALPA Central Executive Council minutes, February 5, 1944, 136.

26. Hopkins, *Airline Pilots*, 178–88. For Behncke's anger at nonunion airline workers who benefited from this law, see ALPA Central Executive Council minutes, February 5, 1944, 138.

27. Williams, *Anatomy,* 208. Williams's otherwise enjoyably breezy history of National misses the mark in its account of this labor disturbance. The firing of pilot Maston O'Neal was merely a pretext, not the reason, for the strike of 1948.

28. Hopkins, *Flying the Line,* 126–38; George E. Hopkins, "The Strange Career of Hydroplaning," *Air Line Pilot: Journal of the Air Line Pilots Association,* February 1989, 22–25.

29. W. David Lewis and Wesley Phillips Newton, *Delta: The History of an Airline* (Athens: University of Georgia Press, 1979), 136.

30. George E. Hopkins, "Awakening: ALPA's First Contract with Delta," *Widget,* June 1991, 1, 4–5; Hopkins, *Flying the Line,* 126–38; Williams, *Anatomy,* 67, 205. The *Widget* is the monthly magazine of the Delta Master Executive Council (MEC), ALPA's union local in Delta Air Lines. I wrote "Awakening" for the Delta MEC to commemorate the fiftieth anniversary of the signing of Delta's first, and at that time only, union contract. Back in 1941, National's pilots were encouraged that Delta's pilots, who had a generally nonunion orientation, had succeeded in obtaining a contract, spurring them to redouble their own efforts in this regard. Oral history interview, 1979, Captain Mac Gilmour.

31. Hopkins, *Flying the Line,* 126–38; Williams, *Anatomy,* 65–72. Again, Williams's admiration for Baker makes his account of the strike suspect. Williams's view is that the ALPA forced the strike on Baker, which is not entirely accurate. The pilots, who were not fools, knew that many well-trained military pilots, recently demobilized, were eager to take their jobs and already had their own "union," which they called the Military Pilots Association. The National Mediation Board (NMB), which was involved in the strike under the terms of the Railway Labor Act, issued a scathing report on Baker's "lack of good faith bargaining."

32. Hopkins, *Flying the Line,* 136–38; Williams, *Anatomy,* 82–83; oral history interview, 1979, Charles H. Ruby.

33. Hopkins, *Flying the Line,* 136–38.

34. William H. Harris and Judith S. Levey, eds., *The New Columbia Encyclopedia* (New York: Columbia University Press, 1975), 386. Buchman (1878–1961) was a controversial figure, largely owing to some early, ill-considered enthusiasm for Adolf Hitler, which, of course, Buchman later disavowed.

35. Hopkins, *Flying the Line,* 136–37; oral history interviews, 1979, Captains Ed McDonald and Charles H. Ruby. Ruby, who was MEC chairman at the time of the strike and who had kept the National pilots together during the arduous months of picketing, refused to go to Mackinac. Not only did Ruby doubt that Baker's religious conversion was genuine but he also feared Baker's powers of persuasion.

36. Hopkins, *Flying the Line,* 136–38; Williams, *Anatomy,* 83.

37. Lewis and Newton, *Delta,* 153–54; Hopkins, *Flying the Line,* 217. The

most visible sign that Baker wanted no further trouble with ALPA was his appointment of Charles Ruby, who had led National's pilots throughout the strike, as National's chief pilot.

38. Oral history interview, 1979, Charles H. Ruby.

39. Lewis and Newton, *Delta*, 283–85; Davies, *Airlines of the United States*, 344; Williams, *Anatomy*, 97–99; Hopkins, *Flying the Line*, 251–53 for a discussion of the impact of the CAB's merger policy in the Capital Airlines case of 1961; oral history interview, 1979, Captain Robert Rohan.

40. T. A. Heppenheimer, *Turbulent Skies: The History of Commercial Aviation* (New York: John Wiley, 1995), 184–85. This lightly documented survey of the history of commercial aviation contains some interesting speculations about Baker having "snookered" Juan Trippe on this deal, pursuant to a merger that never took place. Unfortunately, the only sources for these speculations are articles in popular business magazines.

41. Williams, *Anatomy*, 63, 87–101, 159–60, 169–70; Davies, *Pan Am*, 68; oral history interview, 1979, Charles H. Ruby.

42. Marilyn Bender and Selig Altschul, *The Chosen Instrument* (New York: Simon and Schuster, 1982), 9–16; Leary, *Airline Industry*, 346; Hopkins, *Pan Am Pioneer*, 227. For a discussion of the disabilities under which Pan Am labored during much of its later history, see George Hopkins, "Maybe We Should Help Pan Am," *Washington Monthly*, September 1976, 53–61.

43. Glines, *The Legendary DC-3*, 40–46.

44. Caves, *Air Transport and Its Regulators*, 123–269 passim; William M. Leary, introduction to Leary, *Airline Industry*, xvii–xix.

45. "Audit Report to the Congress of the United States on Civil Aeronautics Board, October, 1955," reprinted in *Department of Commerce and Related Agencies Appropriations*, House Committee on Appropriations, 84th Cong., 2d sess., *Hearings* (Washington, D.C.: Government Printing Office, 1956), 754–811; Caves, *Air Transport and Its Regulators*, 123–269 passim. The movement toward a more "market-oriented" use of airline subsidies originated in Congress when, for a variety of reasons, congressional opinion on the use (or misuse) of subsidies began to shift. Critics of the CAB's approach had forced a full-scale review of the issue by 1955.

46. George C. Eads, *The Local Service Airline Experiment* (Washington, D.C.: Brookings Institution, 1972), vi, 1–5; Davies, *Airlines of the United States*, 388–93.

47. Eads, *The Local Service Airline Experiment*, vi, 1–5; Davies, *Airlines of the United States*, 388–93; William M. Leary, "Pioneer Air Lines," in Leary, *Airline Industry*, 370. *The Transportation of Our Nation*, message from the president of the United States, 87th Cong., 2d sess. (1962), H. Doc. 384, clearly shows the increased political pressure on the CAB to "do something" about the subsidy issue.

48. CAB, Docket 18022, 6–10; William M. Leary, "North Central Airlines" and Lloyd H. Cornett Jr., "Northeast Airlines," in Leary, *Airline Industry,* 316–18; Eads, *The Local Service Airline Experiment,* vii, 1–5.

49. Lewis and Newton, *Delta,* 288–89.

50. Ibid., 294.

51. CAB *Reports* 33, *Southern Transcontinental Service Case* (January-May 1961).

52. Hopkins, "National Airlines," 302–4.

Bibliographical Essay

Secondary works on the history of commercial aviation are abundant. Henry Ladd Smith's pioneering *Airways: The History of Commercial Aviation in the United States* (New York: Knopf, 1944) and Elsbeth E. Freudenthal, *The Aviation Business: From Kitty Hawk to Wall Street* (New York: Vanguard, 1940), must still be consulted. More recent surveys, such as Carl Solberg, *Conquest of the Skies: A History of Commercial Aviation* (Boston: Little, Brown, 1972), also offer a useful starting point.

An important source for this essay has been my own previous work, *Flying the Line: The First Half Century of the Air Line Pilots Association* (Washington, D.C.: Air Line Pilots Association, 1982), and the associated oral history interviews I conducted with retired and active National Airlines pilots in 1979. I was also able to use significant parts of my other published work, including *The Airline Pilots: A Study in Elite Unionization* (Cambridge: Harvard University Press, 1971), which originated in my doctoral dissertation at the University of Texas at Austin, and a memoir I edited, Sanford B. Kauffman's *Pan Am Pioneer: A Manager's Memoir from Seaplane Clippers to Jumbo Jets* (Lubbock: Texas Tech University Press, 1995). Both of these projects allowed me to conduct interviews with professional airline pilots whose knowledge of the history of National Airlines and George T. Baker proved useful.

Brad Williams's *Anatomy of an Airline* (Garden City, N.Y.: Doubleday, 1970), a journalistic account, is an essential tool for any historian writing about National Airlines. It is, in effect, a primary source because it is based on a good deal of personal observation and first-person interviewing by Williams with many people who are now deceased. Although Williams's book is not without errors of fact, it is nevertheless immensely readable and entertaining.

Two reference works, William M. Leary, ed., *The Airline Industry* (New York: Facts on File, 1992), which is part of the Bruccoli Clark Layman *Encyclopedia of American Business and Biography,* and R. E. G. Davies, *Airlines of the United States since 1914* (Washington, D.C.: Smithsonian Institution Press, 1988) are indispensable for any historian working with this subject. Samuel B. Richmond's *Regula-*

tion and Competition in Air Transportation (New York: Columbia University Press, 1961) and Richard E. Caves, *Air Transport and Its Regulators: An Industry Study* (Cambridge: Harvard University Press, 1962), are pioneering and essential to this subject. T. A. Heppenheimer, *Turbulent Skies: The History of Commercial Aviation* (New York: John Wiley, 1995), although lightly documented, surveys the history of commercial aviation and contains some interesting speculations about Baker's business maneuvers.

W. David Lewis and Wesley Phillips Newton, *Delta: The History of an Airline* (Athens: University of Georgia Press, 1979), is among the best of specific airline histories and is a model for scholars working with this subject, particularly because of its sophisticated use of documentary sources in Delta and federal records. For clarity of narrative covering a spectacularly complex subject, no other airline history compares in thoroughness, attention to detail, reliance on original sources, and sureness of analytical judgment. For the history of Delta Air Lines, this book well merits the often-used accolade "definitive." Marilyn Bender and Selig Altschul's magisterial study of Pan American and Juan Trippe, *The Chosen Instrument* (New York: Simon and Schuster, 1982), also deserves mention in this category.

The *Reports* of the Federal Aviation Administration, arranged by "docket" and subsidiary "enforcement proceedings," contains exhibits introduced before federal regulators by interested parties. Although these "document sets," available in most research libraries, are useful, they do not contain the record of regulators' behind-the-scenes deliberations. But the sheer bulk of the transcripts contained in these bound volumes offers scholars almost unlimited access to the atmosphere of decision making at the federal level.

A Man Born out of Season:
Edward V. Rickenbacker, Eastern Air Lines,
and the Civil Aeronautics Board

W. DAVID LEWIS

HAD EDWARD V. RICKENBACKER LIVED ONLY A few more years, he could have celebrated the passage of the Airline Deregulation Act of 1978 by having dinner at one of his favorite Manhattan restaurants, the "21" Club on West Fifty-second Street between Fifth and Sixth Avenues. Tracing its origins to the Prohibition era, when it was one of New York's classiest speakeasies, it had a well-deserved reputation for superior food and drink and would have made an ideal setting in which to savor a moment of triumph.[1] Because Rickenbacker believed that federal regulation rewarded inefficiency and wasted public funds on needless subsidies, deregulation was squarely in line with ideas he had preached throughout his life. Above all, he would have enjoyed cheering the death sentence that the act imposed on the Civil Aeronautics Board, with which he had repeatedly crossed swords as chief executive of Eastern Air Lines.[2]

Under Rickenbacker's autocratic but benevolent leadership, Eastern became for a time the most profitable airline in America. Ultimately, however, its fortunes declined, forcing him into unwilling retirement in 1963. Rickenbacker's involuntary departure from a great industry he had helped to build resulted partly from physical problems caused by the lingering effects of traumas he had suffered more than two decades earlier, when he had nearly died in a plane crash near Atlanta. Soon thereafter, in 1942, he spent three weeks marooned on a raft in the Pacific Ocean while conducting a secret mission in World War II. By the time he and his companions were rescued, he was dehydrated and had lost fifty-four pounds. After these two terrible experiences, his business judgment was less dependable, resulting in a series of unfortunate decisions.

There was a more fundamental reason, however, why Eastern's board of directors reluctantly dismissed Rickenbacker in 1963. His political and economic views were out of step with the age in which he lived, seriously complicating the company's dealings with federal regulators. Rickenbacker was a throwback to an earlier era of unbridled free enterprise. His fierce entrepreneurial spirit and dedication to the work ethic made him a living symbol of the American Dream, but his passionate individualism, grounded in traditions of self-help that had once been dominant in a nation that he loved as a bastion of human liberty, put him at odds with the New Deal and everything it stood for. Robert J. Serling, who has written a history of Eastern Air Lines, aptly called Rickenbacker "a nineteenth-century American trying hard to cope with the twentieth century—a task in which he achieved both magnificent success and dismal failure."[3]

Rickenbacker's fate is ironic because he survived long enough to witness the beginning of a new cycle in government-business relationships, one that would have been much more consistent with his outlook than the phase through which he lived. The fact that airline deregulation came within five years of his death indicated that a new era was about to begin when he died of pneumonia in 1973. Nine years earlier, he had sensed that the political tide was turning when Barry Goldwater, a man whom he greatly admired, won the Republican presidential nomination. The Reagan Revolution probably would have disappointed Rickenbacker because it did not erase the legacy of the New Deal, but he would have felt vindicated by the conservative leadership of the Great Communicator. He certainly would have been no friend of the Clinton administration, but he would have savored the spectacle of a Democratic president proclaiming that the era of big government was over.

Rickenbacker had a hard role to play. He was a classic example of a man born out of season. As a product of an old order who found it increasingly hard to cope with a new age, and as a prophet of developments that took place in the late twentieth century, he deserves more attention than historians have yet paid him.

A Hero's Journey Begins

Rickenbacker was born to poor, hard-working Swiss immigrants in Columbus, Ohio, on October 8, 1890. He soon displayed strong entrepreneurial tendencies and a deep commitment to rugged individualism.[4] His business career began at age five, when he was already smoking. Needing money to buy tobacco for hand-rolled cigarettes, he collected rags, bones, and rusty nails and sold them to a junk dealer named Sam. Bones had market value because they could be made into fertilizer when treated with sulfuric acid. Finding that the bones he gathered weighed more when soaked in water, Rickenbacker swished them in mud puddles before selling them to Sam. Suspecting that Sam had improperly set his scales to short-weigh him, he brought his own scales to make sure the wily dealer did not cheat him out of a single penny.[5]

Young "Edd," as his family called him, was deeply committed to the work ethic. He got his first steady job selling newspapers when he was only ten years old. He rose early each morning and walked two miles to get copies of the first edition of the *Columbus Dispatch* so he could get on the street ahead of competing newsboys. Four years later, when his father was killed by an assailant, he dropped out of seventh grade to support his mother. He never forgot the thrill of giving her his first pay envelope, containing three one-dollar bills and a fifty-cent piece he had earned at a factory by working six twelve-hour days. His income rose steadily as he became increasingly resourceful. Getting a job cleaning passenger cars at the Pennsylvania Railroad shops in Columbus for one dollar a day, he doubled and tripled his income by finding loose change that had fallen behind seat cushions. He never understood why anybody could not succeed by developing the traits of initiative and perseverance that came naturally to him.

The frugality with which Rickenbacker managed Eastern Air Lines was based on his earliest experiences. In childhood he saw that the only way his parents managed to survive was by raising as much of their own food as possible, planting every available square inch of their tiny property with fruits and vegetables, keeping a goat for milk, and raising chickens for eggs. They dressed their children in hand-me-down clothes that his mother patched and mended until they were too threadbare to be worn, and warmed their house with chunks of coal that fell from freight cars along nearby railroad tracks. After Rickenbacker became his mother's main source of income, the value of money became even more apparent to him because of the long hours and hard work it took him to earn it. The gospel of thrift preached by such historical figures as Benjamin Franklin never had a more fervent exponent than Rickenbacker, who became a model of the self-made man. His fierce ambition to succeed and his deep commitment to self-improvement carried him far beyond the humble circumstances of his birth.

Rickenbacker had to overcome many handicaps in his rise to fame. His father, a harsh disciplinarian, subjected him to frequent beatings that left him with an abiding inner rage he could never expunge. Throughout his business career he subjected subordinates to fierce tirades that were the verbal equivalent of "lambastings" he had experienced at his father's hands. His crusty outward behavior, however, concealed a warm, compassionate heart that his employees and advisers recognized and treasured. He was both greatly feared and deeply loved.

Cultural attitudes prevailing in Rickenbacker's youth forced him to hide significant aspects of his personality. His desire to display a tough masculine image at a time when manliness was associated with hardness and emotional insensitivity masked an artistic temperament that manifested itself in a talent for watercolors. A postcard-sized sample of his work, showing an Italian shoreline that he sketched during his honeymoon in 1922, reveals a grasp of perspective and exquisiteness of detail belying his conventional image as an aerial Marlboro Man. It is characteristic of gifted, highly sensitive people to devalue their innermost selves, often because of a mistaken sense of being flawed by the very traits that make them exceptional. Rickenbacker was a case in point.[6]

Rickenbacker's sensitive nature never recovered from humiliations he endured in his youth. Friends teased him unmercifully because of his thick Germanic accent and poor command of English; nothing but the Swiss-German dialect was spoken in his home until he was about ten years old. His obvious poverty exposed him to endless taunts; particularly painful to him was the ribbing he took for having to wear a mismatched pair of shoes, one brown and the other tan, one square-toed and the other pointed, that his father cobbled together.

Rickenbacker was a thrill-seeker. He learned early in life that subjecting himself to mortal danger and coming out alive gave him ecstatic feelings that he learned to crave. The opening pages of his autobiography describe close brushes with death that energized his will. His need for the overpowering sensations he derived from successfully facing danger, along with his sense of the aesthetic beauty of mechanical technology, led him to become an automotive engineer after a car salesman gave him an terrifying but exhilarating ride in a Ford runabout. Long a center of carriage making, Columbus played an important role in the early history of the American automobile. Forty brands of motor cars were produced in the city between 1895 and 1923.[7] Frustrated by the menial and stultifying work he had to do after his father died, Rickenbacker set out to learn a profession through on-the-job training.

Rickenbacker started as a handyman at the Evans Garage, a small shop that repaired bicycles and horseless carriages. Feeling stultified with the job after learning everything he could from such routine tasks, he moved on to the Oscar Lear Company, which made a car, the Frayer-Miller, named after two of the firm's partners. When Rickenbacker's first attempts to get a job with the company were rebuffed, he badgered the owners into hiring him by grabbing a broom, sweeping the floor, and asking for nothing in return. After he was hired, he displayed phenomenal zeal to learn as much as he could about anything having to do with cars. Saving as much from his wages as possible, he paid $60 in installments to International Correspondence Schools for a mail-order course in automotive technology. He rose at 4 a.m. to study the lessons and spent his lunch hours poring over engine diagrams.

Rickenbacker's determination to succeed caught the attention of Lee Frayer, a partner in the Oscar Lear Company who had earned an engineering degree at Ohio State University. Frayer, a designer of innovative air-cooled engines and builder of race cars, became Rickenbacker's mentor and surrogate father. Under Frayer's instruction, Rickenbacker mastered basic engineering principles and showed an intuitive feeling for gasoline motors. Rickenbacker had an uncanny ability to diagnose what was wrong with a malfunctioning engine merely by feeling peculiar vibrations or listening for telltale sputters pointing to underlying problems.

Edward Rickenbacker (left of pilot and copilot) poses with passengers and crew at Chicago Municipal Airport for inauguration of Douglas DC-2 "Florida Flyer" service between Chicago and Miami in late 1934. The inscription on the fuselage relates to a speed record of 12 hours, 3 minutes, set by the plane on its delivery flight from Los Angeles to New York on November 8, 1934. (Courtesy of the Auburn University Archives)

Frayer not only built racing cars but also drove them. In 1906 he took Rickenbacker to the Vanderbilt Cup Race, a prestigious international meet held on Long Island. There, Rickenbacker served as Frayer's riding mechanic, a dangerous assignment requiring steady nerves and quick reflexes. Sitting beside the driver as a racecar hurtled around a twisting course at breakneck speed, a riding mechanic pumped oil, checked fuel consumption, monitored tire wear, and used hand signals to warn the driver about impending hazards or to indicate that other cars were about to pass. Because riding mechanics could not brace themselves with the steering wheel, they were three times more likely than a driver to be thrown out of a car and killed if it overturned.

Frayer had spent an entire year preparing for the race. Rickenbacker never forgot his mentor's reaction when the engine overheated and Frayer had to leave the course in his first trial run. Taking the setback calmly,

Frayer turned to Rickenbacker and said, "We're through." Repression of emotions considered unworthy of a man were part of the stern masculine code of behavior prevailing in America at the time.

Soon after the Vanderbilt race, Frayer left Oscar Lear to become chief engineer of a much larger enterprise, the Columbus Buggy Company, whose sprawling plant occupied a city block. Taking Rickenbacker with him, he gave him charge of the testing department, where, at age seventeen, he supervised fifteen or twenty workers who were older and more experienced than himself. His ingenuity and zeal came to the attention of Clinton Firestone, chief owner of the Buggy Company and a relative of the famous rubber-manufacturing family in Akron.[8] Impressed by Rickenbacker's intuitive mechanical abilities and the flair for salesmanship he demonstrated at automobile shows, Firestone sent him to Texas and Arizona as a troubleshooter for dealers who sold cars bearing the Buggy Company's "Firestone-Columbus" marque and found that their engines overheated in the hot southwestern environment. Within two years he was a district manager, in charge of sales in five midwestern states. Headquartered in Omaha, Nebraska, with six salesmen working under him, he made $150 per week, a remarkable salary for a person his age.

But being a salesman did not satisfy Rickenbacker's craving for excitement. Stripping the fenders from a Firestone-Columbus and installing a bucket seat, he began advertising its power and speed by entering it in races on dirt tracks at county fairs. Because he took risks shunned by other drivers, his winnings mounted and Frayer invited him back to Columbus to take part in a race against Barney Oldfield, the most famous driver in America. In 1911, Frayer entered the first running of the Indianapolis 500, taking Rickenbacker along as his relief driver. A year later, Frayer retired from racing and loaned Rickenbacker his "Red Wing Special" to drive in the second Indy classic. Forced off the track by a mechanical breakdown, Rickenbacker retreated to the stands and watched Ralph de Palma meet a stunning defeat after running one of the most courageous races in the history of automobile racing. The sportsmanship that de Palma displayed after his powerful gray Mercedes broke down in the final laps powerfully reinforced lessons in Rickenbacker's mind that Frayer had already taught him about meeting adversity without complaint.

Bored by selling automobiles and dissatisfied with the management of the Buggy Company, which resisted changing models to compete against more progressive firms, Rickenbacker quit his position at Omaha in 1912. Securing a license from the Contest Board of the American Automobile Association (AAA), which regulated motor sport at the time, he joined the "Flying Squadron," a second-rate racing team that competed at county fairs in Nebraska and Iowa. Within a few months, the Contest Board suspended Rickenbacker's license because the team's promoters entered unsanctioned events and did not observe mandatory safety precautions. Undaunted, Rickenbacker spent the winter in Des Moines, Iowa, working as a mechanic for Frederick and August Duesenberg, who had designed a promising new racing car and were destined for future greatness in the American auto industry. In the summer of 1913, after the Contest Board lifted his suspension, Rickenbacker joined the Duesenberg Racing Team as a driver.

Rickenbacker's gutsy style and flashing grin made him a crowd favorite on the American racing tour. His first big victory came on the Fourth of July in 1914 when he won a 300-mile race at Sioux City, Iowa. During the race Rickenbacker was pelted with "gumbo," racing slang for loose stones buried under the surface of the dirt track, which flew in his face and temporarily knocked his riding mechanic unconscious. Rickenbacker took such danger in stride. In the next two years he won additional championships at Omaha, Providence, Brooklyn, Tacoma, and Los Angeles and became one of the country's greatest racing stars.

As his fame grew, Rickenbacker moved from one sponsor to another seeking more and more powerful vehicles. When one of his backers, the Maxwell Motor Company, abandoned auto racing in 1915, he bounced back by making a profitable deal with Carl G. Fisher, a prominent manufacturer of carbide headlights who was also chief owner of the Indianapolis Speedway, and James A. Allison, one of Fisher's financial associates. Buying Maxwell's fleet of race cars, Fisher and Allison hired Rickenbacker to manage a newly constituted "Prest-O-Lite Racing Team," with a guaranteed share of its winnings. Rickenbacker was now not merely a racer but an up-and-coming businessman in his own right.[9]

As a racer-entrepreneur, Rickenbacker displayed traits he would later show as an airline executive. He paid careful attention to detail and compiled a long list of instructions to be followed by members of the Prest-O-Lite team. He pioneered in shipping race cars around the country by rail, multiplying potential winnings by devising a schedule permitting two separate fleets to compete in widely separated events at the same time. He hired Harry Van Hoven, an Iowan who was expert in time-and-motion study, to manage his pit team. Shaving seconds off the time it took to change tires or make repairs swelled Rickenbacker's victory total.

Rickenbacker's personal winnings and his share of the team's profits made him the third leading money-winner on the 1916 racing tour, with earnings of $40,000 after expenses. His grease-smeared face, poor command of the English language, and unrefined manners betrayed his lower-class background but did not prevent rich, well-educated young sportsmen who competed against him from admiring his courage and ability. His army of fans included wealthy and powerful people who would help him at opportune times throughout his life.

Rickenbacker's racing experience was a fitting prelude to his later career as an airline executive because it intensified the competitiveness in his makeup. Relationships that he established with influential business leaders, culminating in his association with Fisher, also solidified his self-identification with market capitalism. Rickenbacker was well aware that auto racing was not merely a sport. It was an industry, and he excelled in playing the game.

From the Roaring Road to the Perilous Sky

A fateful chain of events unfolded for Rickenbacker at the end of the 1916 racing season. Glenn Martin, one of America's pioneer aircraft manufacturers, took him aloft for his first plane flight, which powerfully stimulated his imagination. At about the same time, Rickenbacker came upon a stranded pilot with a disabled aircraft, diagnosed what was wrong, and fixed the plane's engine on the spot. The flyer was Townsend F. Dodd, a major in the Army Air Service. Aviation began to enter the fabric of Rickenbacker's life and would never let go.

After Rickenbacker won his last victory of the season at Los Angeles, William Weightman III, a wealthy sportsman from Philadelphia, commissioned him to go to England to help the Sunbeam Motor Company design a new racer. Weightman planned to enter it on the American tour in 1917, with Rickenbacker as its driver. While in England, Rickenbacker worked closely with Sunbeam's world-famous shop engineer, Louis Coatalen, deepening his already comprehensive knowledge of motor vehicle technology. He also visited the Brooklands Speedway near London. The oval-shaped infield was being used as a base for British combat pilots training to fight in France. Captivated by the idea of becoming a fighter pilot, Rickenbacker decided that when he returned home he would try to organize a team of racing drivers who would learn how to fly and form an aerial squadron modeled on the Lafayette Escadrille, an American volunteer unit that had become famous by fighting in the French Air Service. His plan, however, was rejected by military officials in Washington because he lacked the social background, manners, and education thought necessary for an officer.

As usual, obstacles did not prevent Rickenbacker from achieving his dreams. After the United States entered World War I in 1917, Burgess Lewis, an officer on General John J. Pershing's staff who also happened to be a racing fan, offered Rickenbacker a chance to become one of Pershing's drivers. Hastily withdrawing from a major race in Cincinnati, Rickenbacker took a train to New York City and enlisted the next day as a sergeant. By nightfall he was aboard Pershing's troopship, the *Baltic,* bound for the front. Dodd, whose airplane engine Rickenbacker had recently repaired, was on the ship as Pershing's aviation adviser.

When the advance party of the American Expeditionary Force got to France, Dodd made Rickenbacker his own personal chauffeur, but lost him when a Packard used by Billy Mitchell, operational chief of the Army Air Service, broke down and Rickenbacker repaired it on the spot. "He found that the needle valve had bent," Mitchell recalled, "and in less time than it takes to tell he cleaned it, put it back, and had the engine going. I had never seen a man do anything so quickly with a gasoline engine, or who knew more about what he was doing."[10] Mitchell immediately pulled rank and made Rickenbacker his personal chauffeur. Together they toured the front as Mitchell made logistical and operational plans. Again, Rickenbacker had demonstrated his knack for making powerful friends.

Soon afterward, while strolling down the Champs-Élysées, Rickenbacker was hailed by James Miller, a wealthy New York banker, airplane pilot, and racing enthusiast who had enlisted in the Army Air Service and been given charge of building a large training base at Issoudun. With Mitchell's consent, Miller appointed Rickenbacker chief engineer at the new installation, an assignment that permitted him to undergo training as a pilot. After winning his wings, Rickenbacker supervised construction of the Issoudun base, where recruits from social backgrounds far superior to his own dug latrines under his direction. When the base had been completed, Rickenbacker, unwilling to stay in an administrative post while graduates of the training program went off to fight, persuaded his commanding officer, Carl Spatz, to have him posted for gunnery training at Cazeau.[11] By March 1918, Rickenbacker had qualified to become a combat pilot and was assigned to the 94th ("Hat-in-the-Ring") Pursuit Squadron.

The swift reflexes, competitive instincts, timing, sense of distance, and depth perception that Rickenbacker had demonstrated in auto racing served him equally well in aerial combat. There was a crucial difference, however, between what he was doing now and what he had done in the past. "Fighting in the air is not a sport," he said. "It is scientific murder."[12] As he stalked enemy aircraft, he combined bravado with rational calculation, carefully estimating his chances of surviving an encounter before committing himself to it. In less than six months, he became America's Ace of Aces by shooting down twenty-two German airplanes and four observation balloons.

True to form, Rickenbacker soon moved into a position that demanded managerial skills as well as fighting instincts. During the summer of 1918, American pursuit squadrons switched from the Nieuport 28, which had a relatively simple rotary motor, to the Spad XIII, which had a complicated Hispano-Suiza V-8 engine. Ground crews were baffled by the new ships and their puzzling power plants, which seriously complicated maintenance operations and made it hard for commanding officers to keep enough planes in the air to carry out their orders. Desperate for help, Colonel Harold E. Hartney, who led the 1st Pursuit Group, turned to Rickenbacker, whose leadership qualities and mechanical skills made him a logical choice to take charge of his squadron. Instinctively understanding the Hispano-Suiza engines, he taught ground crews how to service them. Just as he had meticulously coached drivers on the Prest-O-Lite racing team, Rickenbacker drilled his pilots in the intricacies of formation flying and won their loyalty by never asking them to undertake anything, however hazardous, that he was unwilling to do himself. On his first day in command of his unit, he took on seven German planes singlehanded, shot down two, and scattered the rest. He later received the Medal of Honor for his valor in this engagement.

Rickenbacker's promotion showed how the exigencies of war could catapult a person with a humble background and a lack of formal education into a position he could not have won in peacetime. Flying was still a rich man's activity, and pilots with college backgrounds winced at his faulty grammar when he conducted briefings. But there was no questioning his courage and ability, and the dispirited squadron rallied to his leadership. His innovative spirit once again became manifest. Just as he had broken new ground by introducing time-and-motion study in automobile racing, he became a pioneer in what later became known as "calculated risk management," minimizing casualties by teaching his men that it was no disgrace for a pilot to withdraw from a combat situation if he faced impossible odds. By war's end the 94th had the best record of any American aerial unit and was honored by being assigned to the army of occupation in Germany. Shortly thereafter, Rickenbacker resigned his command and came home as a charismatic national hero with a chestful of medals.[13]

Like his racing career, Rickenbacker's wartime experiences further reinforced his competitive instincts. The "scientific murder" of aerial combat was the deadliest game of all, with no quarter being asked or given. Later, Rickenbacker would take this conditioning into his career as an aviation executive.

The Hero's Trials and Frustrations

By 1918 Rickenbacker had become a living embodiment of one of America's supreme role models, the self-made man who rises from poverty to fame. Modest, handsome, seemingly unaffected by his meteoric ascent, he was cheered in the spring and summer of 1919 by millions of admirers who lined the streets of New York, Columbus, Detroit, Chicago, and Los Angeles to pay tribute to him. Unfortunately, he quickly learned that, as one writer has aptly stated, "Fame's radiance burns."[14] Rickenbacker was unprepared for the media pressures that came with being a celebrity, and he had nightmares as he crossed the country in Pullman cars. Waving to crowds in Los Angeles "in a mock-up of an airplane covered completely with flowers" made him "feel like an idiot." At one point in the tour he returned temporarily to Columbus after having a reported "nervous breakdown." He "wondered which was worse, combat or the onslaught of well-wishers, hero-worshippers, and fast-buck operators."[15]

Rickenbacker did not want to return to the racetrack after having tasted the thrills of a much more dangerous arena. He wanted to hone his entrepreneurial skills by becoming an industrialist. Well aware of his lack of formal education, his rough edges, and his awkwardness as a public speaker, he studied etiquette manuals, took lessons in elocution, and gradually became more and more at ease in the spotlight. But his outward self-assurance concealed emotional strains that he could not admit in public. It is hard for any combat veteran to resume civilian life and mingle with people who have not experienced the horrors of war, and being constantly in the public glare only made things worse. Deprived of the camaraderie he had experienced on the front, Rickenbacker felt lonely and insecure.

Rickenbacker had fallen in love with flying. He wanted to devote his life to the aviation industry. Confident that Billy Mitchell, who was now a brigadier general, would succeed in establishing a separate air force, Rickenbacker and three former comrades made plans to establish an aircraft-manufacturing company that would profit from government orders for up-to-date warplanes. But Mitchell met fierce resistance in the military establishment, and his abrasive manner ultimately led to his being court-martialed. Meanwhile, the aviation market was saturated with surplus Curtiss Jennies and de Havilland DH-4s that could be bought cheaply and used in barnstorming and flying federal airmail routes, the only occupational activities open to veterans of the Air Service.[16]

Seeking solitude in a remote area of New Mexico, Rickenbacker pondered what to do. Reluctantly, in one of the most crucial decisions of his life, he fell back on what he knew best—the automobile industry.

Byron F. "Barney" Everitt, a Detroit millionaire who had once produced a car called the EMF and wanted to get back into the automobile business, capitalized on Rickenbacker's popularity by offering to back him in manufacturing a motor vehicle that would bear the hero's name. While waiting in California for Everitt to acquire a factory site in Detroit, Rickenbacker gained sales experience by promoting the Sheridan, a car that had just been acquired by a rapidly rising industrial conglomerate, General Motors.[17] The zeal with which he organized dealerships and launched an energetic sales campaign captured the attention of Pierre S. duPont, William C. "Billy" Durant, and Alfred P. Sloan, who were transforming GM into an American colossus.[18]

Rickenbacker's ties with GM were strengthened when he renewed an earlier acquaintance with Adelaide Frost Durant, whom he had met briefly in California before the war. Adelaide, a physically alluring woman with a beautiful singing voice, was the estranged wife of Billy Durant's son, Clifford, a playboy and race driver with a reputation for wild behavior. When Rickenbacker met her again after the war, she was living in New York City and had been separated from her husband for several years. After Rickenbacker moved to Detroit he began going to New York to visit her and what had started as a casual relationship soon became romantic.[19]

In July 1921 Adelaide secured an interlocutory divorce decree from Clifford, which became final a year later. On September 16, 1922, she and Rickenbacker were married and left immediately on a European honeymoon. During the trip, which lasted three months, Rickenbacker visited automobile shows and manufacturing plants in England, France, Germany, and Italy, studying the latest European innovations in automotive technology.[20] After the newlyweds returned home, they set up housekeeping in Detroit, where Everitt had acquired a factory in which to manufacture the Rickenbacker. It would be advertised as "a car worthy of its name."

Billy Durant, who was fond of Adelaide and realized that she had not been at fault in her failed marriage to his son, had established a trust fund for her in 1918 based on 4,200 shares of General Motors and United Motors stock valued at $120,000. He remained generous to her after the divorce, giving her blocks of GM stock as Christmas and birthday presents. As the stock appreciated in value, Adelaide's growing wealth made it possible for Rickenbacker to maintain the lifestyle expected of an industrial executive.[21] He and his bride settled in a luxurious residential complex, Indian Village Manor, on the Detroit River overlooking Lake St. Clair, Belle Isle, and Windsor, Ontario.[22] Dissatisfied with the Rickenbacker Motor Company's first production facility, a converted glass factory, Everitt acquired a twenty-seven-acre site at 4815 Cabot Street and erected a sprawling plant complete with a two-story office building. Known by admiring residents of the city as "the Ty Cobb of the clouds," Rickenbacker was well on his way to becoming an automotive titan.

Just as he had been bored by selling cars in Omaha, however, Rickenbacker was not fulfilled by making them in Detroit. For a while he sublimated his frustrations by taking prototypes of his new car on 80,000 miles of test drives over some of the most grueling terrain in the United States while Everitt worried that valuable time was being lost in putting the vehicle into production. Rickenbacker also barnstormed around the country establishing dealerships. The first production models were put on the market in 1922, in which 2,262 cars were made. Output gradually rose to a peak of 8,049 in 1925. Designed as "a mid-priced car with many advanced features," the six-cylinder vehicle was a remarkable value at prices ranging from $1,485 for a touring model to $1,995 for a sedan. Taking advantage of the ideas Rickenbacker had brought back from his European honeymoon, it had a low center of gravity, a virtually vibration-free engine with two tandem flywheels, a heated interior, a lockable steering wheel, and many other features, including a chrome "Hat-in-the-Ring" ornament on the radiator hood. Advertisements declared of its frame that, comparatively speaking, "Brooklyn Bridge does not provide such a factor of rigidity and strength." Rickenbacker's commitment to dependability foreshadowed a similar emphasis that he would observe as an aviation executive. But his experience as an automobile manufacturer would also teach him the dangers of trying to combine quality and mere frills.

After the planning and organizational stage had been completed, Rickenbacker's imagination was not sufficiently stirred by administering what he had created. His heart was still in the sky. Even before he left California to move to Detroit, he made a hair-raising trip across America from San Francisco to Washington to attend a reunion to which Billy Mitchell had invited him. Flying a de Havilland DH-4, he crashed the plane at Cheyenne, Wyoming, survived without a scratch, took a mail plane to Chicago, picked up another DH-4, encountered a terrible storm over the Allegheny Mountains, was forced down in a muddy field in Maryland, and still managed to make the reunion on time. After settling in Detroit, he used a notoriously fire-prone plane, the Junkers 14 (known in America as the Larsen JL-6), to fly around the country while organizing dealerships. During one trip to the West Coast, the plane was struck by lightning while it was on the ground. Rickenbacker made emergency landings in Indiana and Iowa, and crashed while trying to take off with overloaded fuel tanks in Omaha. He had to go the rest of the way by train.

Such junkets were like manna to a hero with a burning need for adrenaline rushes. Being an automobile manufacturer could not satisfy him for long.

Despite his frustrations, Rickenbacker did not neglect the automobile that bore his name. He poured his energy into making it notable for artistic styling and technological innovations, including the first four-wheel brakes in an American production car. This innovation, however, backfired when competitors launched an advertising campaign claiming that such brakes were unsafe. Rickenbacker later blamed such propaganda for the demise of his company, but a more fundamental cause was the fact that its advanced features were ill-conceived for the market niche he and his associates were trying to fill. His basic weakness as an entrepreneur was that he was trying to make too much car for too little money. Sales fell when a recession struck in 1925, and morale deteriorated when prices were lowered at a time when dealers were overstocked with cars that they had already accepted at a higher cost. In 1926, trying to boost sales, the company compounded its problems by creating a high-powered, boat-tailed, eight-cylinder "Super Sport Roadster," with "a torpedo rear deck, aerofoil bumpers, cycle fenders made with laminated mahogany, bullet-shaped headlamps, safety glass all the way around, and no running boards." Upholstered with Spanish leather and painted canary yellow with green trim, it sold for a premium price, $5,000. After being displayed for the first time at the New York Automobile Show, it was sold only by a few favored dealers. More bickering resulted between Rickenbacker and Everitt. This bitter experience strongly conditioned the no-frills strategy Rickenbacker later pursued at Eastern Air Lines, but the lesson he had learned was a poor guide to success in a service-oriented industry in which government regulators and passengers alike expected amenities that cost more than he thought it prudent to pay.

In September 1926, a year in which production fell to 4,050 cars, Rickenbacker decided to quit his automotive career. "Here's where I get off," he wrote in his letter of resignation. "I can't go along any further because I don't want to be a party to losing any more money. The Rickenbacker company is in a ditch and out of the race, and the best way I can let people know that we're out of the running is to walk away with the wreck." After he left, the directors tried to keep the company alive, but it went out of business in 1927, leaving Rickenbacker $250,000 in debt. Honorably refusing to take refuge in bankruptcy, he seized every possible means of making an honest dollar and paid off his obligations, preserving a reputation for fidelity to his financial supporters.

Showing unbounded faith in free enterprise, Rickenbacker plunged into new ventures. Even while the Rickenbacker Motor Company was still in business, mirroring his dissatisfaction with ground-based transportation, he had created a subsidiary to develop an automobile that would not only fly but also be amphibious. The project diverted effort he could have devoted to the company itself but for his frustrated longing to be an aircraft manufacturer. Working with Glenn Angle, a gifted engineer, Rickenbacker helped create a lightweight five-cylinder radial engine to power the vehicle. An airplane designer, Ivan Driggs, helped Rickenbacker develop the body, which had foldable wings. Like the parent Rickenbacker Motor Company, however, this venture was unsuccessful. It assets were sold to the Detroit Aircraft Corporation, an over-capitalized enterprise that collapsed during the Great Depression.[23]

Plunging ahead, Rickenbacker borrowed $90,000 to acquire the Allison Engineering Company, which he sold to Fisher Brothers at a profit that helped him retire some of his debts. A Detroit bank helped him buy the Indianapolis Speedway, which was in run-down condition. He developed the Speedway into a major testing ground for automotive innovations and remained owner until 1945. He enjoyed presiding over the annual running of the Indy 500. In a neat turn of fate, he also became chairman of the AAA Contest Board, which had suspended his racing license in 1912.

No ground-based activities, however, could satisfy Rickenbacker. The roar of the road simply could not compete with the lure of the sky. In 1926, together with a wartime comrade, Reed Chambers, he founded Florida Airways, planning to fly airmail between Atlanta and Miami under a contract with the Post Office Department. Wealthy financiers like Richard F. Hoyt and Percy A. Rockefeller invested in the venture, but it got off to a bad start when three of its planes were damaged in a freak ground accident at Nashville while being ferried to Tampa. Because of a scarcity of passengers, the collapse of the Florida real estate boom, and inability to secure a connecting route from Atlanta to New York, the enterprise failed in less than a year and went into receivership. It was acquired by

Harold Pitcairn, a member of a Pittsburgh family that had made a fortune in the plate glass industry. Ultimately the disaster paved the way for Eastern Air Lines, which would play a crucial role in Rickenbacker's future. For the present, however, it was merely another failure among many into which Rickenbacker's restless spirit had impelled him.[24]

Falling back on his ties with GM, Rickenbacker became a sales executive in its Cadillac division. Once again, with what must have been a growing sense of disillusionment, he was back selling automobiles. In 1928 he promoted the LaSalle, a luxury car intended as Cadillac's version of the Rolls-Royce Bentley. Visiting dealerships throughout the country, he valiantly gave motivational speeches that had more to do with his wartime experiences than with automotive matters. Airplanes haunted his mind. In 1929, under his prodding, GM acquired the Pioneer Instrument Company, which became better known as Bendix Aviation, and Fokker Aircraft Corporation of America, which made passenger planes. The finder's fees he earned in these transactions finally got him out of the financial hole into which he had fallen with the demise of his automobile company. More important, however, the acquisition of Fokker opened another door through which he could reenter aviation. Leaving Cadillac, he moved to New York and became Fokker's vice president for sales.

The United States had now entered the worst depression in its history, but Rickenbacker was happier than he had been for a long time, and he showed it by dreaming about the future of aviation instead of being discouraged by the financial adversities under which the country was reeling. In 1932, when GM decided to move Fokker from Hasbrouck Heights, New Jersey, to Dundalk, Maryland, Rickenbacker refused to leave the New York City area. Resigning a secure post at a time when the national economy was in shambles, he became vice president of the Aviation Corporation (AVCo), an ill-coordinated holding company whose air routes ran mainly from east to west.[25] AVCO was losing money and had dubious prospects, but Rickenbacker, with his faith in free enterprise unimpaired, proposed a merger with Eastern Air Transport, another ailing company whose routes ran mostly north and south. Trying to implement the idea, AVCO's chief stockholders, Averell Harriman and Robert Lehman, got into a proxy fight with one of the country's shrewdest financiers, Errett L. Cord. Rickenbacker picked the losing side by backing Harriman and Lehman and was once again unemployed.[26]

As always, Rickenbacker fell back on GM, scouting for investments that might interest the giant firm. In a move fraught with profound consequences for his future career, he persuaded GM to acquire North American Aviation, a bankrupt conglomerate that had been built by Clement M. Keys, a Canadian-born financial analyst who had made a fortune on Wall Street. Among North American's assets was Eastern Air Transport, which flew airmail on the Washington-Atlanta-Miami route pioneered by Harold Pitcairn. In July 1931, Eastern acquired New York Airways, gaining access to Atlantic City. In 1933, it bought a passenger line between New York, Philadelphia, and Washington that had been established by wealthy Philadelphians, the Ludingtons, who had failed to secure an airmail contract. As a result of these acquisitions, Eastern now had a potentially lucrative vacation route from New York to Miami.[27]

Challenge and Response

In 1934, after GM had taken control of North American, Franklin D. Roosevelt responded to an investigation of the way in which the Hoover administration had allocated airmail routes by canceling all existing airmail contracts with privately owned carriers and ordering the Army Air Corps to fly the mail. Knowing that army pilots were poorly trained and unfamiliar with airmail operations, Rickenbacker foresaw that crashes would occur, and he angrily declared Roosevelt guilty of "legalized murder." In a gesture of defiance aimed at demonstrating the quality of new aircraft that had recently been developed for the airline industry, Rickenbacker and William J. "Jack" Frye, president of TWA, flew a revolutionary new airliner, the Douglas DC-1, across the country with a load of mail on the last day of normal airmail operations. Taking off from Los Angeles and racing against a severe storm closing in on the East Coast, they arrived at Newark, New Jersey, in thirteen hours and two minutes, setting a transcontinental speed record. Because Rickenbacker had not obtained a pilot's license after the federal government mandated them in 1926, Frye did all or most of the flying, but Rickenbacker got the lion's share of the publicity.[28]

Rickenbacker's characterization of Roosevelt as a murderer widened a breach between the two men that never healed. After voting for Roosevelt in 1932 because FDR ran on a platform emphasizing fiscal respon-

Rickenbacker (in hat) at Lockheed air terminal in Burbank, California, before inaugural flight from California to New York on May 17, 1948, of the first of fourteen Lockheed L-649 Constellations acquired by Eastern Air Lines. A replica of a Spad XIII, one of the fighter planes Rickenbacker flew in World War I, is nestled under the nose of the new airliner to emphasize the Constellation's much larger size. When it was delivered, the airliner set two commercial speed records, flying from Burbank to Miami in 6 hours, 55 minutes and from Miami to New York in 3 hours, 29 minutes, 45 seconds. (Courtesy of the Auburn University Archives)

sibility and a scaling back of governmental interference with the economy, Rickenbacker had become increasingly disenchanted with the New Deal and made common cause with the Liberty League, organized by Pierre S. du Pont, John J. Raskob, and other financiers with whom Rickenbacker was allied through his close connections with GM.[29] Long before he locked horns with the Civil Aeronautics Board, Rickenbacker was on a collision course with the approach to government that it represented.

As Rickenbacker had foreseen, a series of crashes, many of them fatal, followed the beginning of airmail flights in 1934 by army pilots in what turned out to be an abnormally severe winter. As the toll continued to mount and public outrage intensified, new airmail legislation was hastily introduced, and Postmaster General James A. Farley reopened bidding for new contracts pending its passage. Airline executives who had attended "spoils conferences" in 1930, at which Hoover's postmaster general, Walter F. Brown, had restructured the nation's airmail system, could no longer remain in charge of airlines holding mail contracts. Ironically, in view of Rickenbacker's animosity toward the Roosevelt administration, this prohibition would soon make it possible for him to become the powerful aviation executive he had long dreamed of being.

The government also ordered that no airlines represented at the spoils conferences would be eligible for new mail contracts. Recognizing that chaos would result from strict implementation of this policy, Farley allowed existing airlines to circumvent it by changing their names. After making minor name changes to comply with FDR's demands—Eastern Air Transport, for example, now became Eastern Air Lines—carriers that had formerly held airmail contracts won back most of their old routes, albeit with lower rates. In the ensuing reorganization of the industry, under the Air Mail Act of 1934, air transport was separated from aircraft manufacturing and airmail contractors were forbidden to hold conflicting interests in enterprises that made commercial planes. These provisions had important consequences for GM, which sold its holdings in several airlines, including TWA, which was part of North American. GM also tried to sell Eastern, but the deal fell through. Under a technicality in the new airmail act, taking advantage of the fact that North American made only military aircraft, GM retained control of Eastern.

These developments had dramatic consequences for Rickenbacker. Because Eastern's president, Thomas B. Doe, had attended the spoils conferences, he had to be removed, and Ernest R. Breech, a GM executive who had been in charge of North American, took control of Eastern. Breech, however, did not want to run Eastern's day-to-day affairs because he had greater responsibilities in the GM hierarchy. In December 1934, while remaining president of Eastern, Breech asked Rickenbacker to take administrative charge of the airline as general manager. Jumping at the offer as the opportunity of a lifetime, Rickenbacker took the position on January 1, 1935. For the next three decades he would zealously devote himself to Eastern's interests.

The Hero in His Prime

Eastern was an unimpressive enterprise when Rickenbacker took over. In 1934 it had lost $1.5 million. Its fleet, composed of Curtiss Condors, Pitcairn Mailwings, and other weary birds, was antiquated. Apart from the experience and loyalty of its employees, its main assets were two routes from New York City and Chicago to Miami via Atlanta. Both of these arteries had outstanding potential in the winter vacation trade. Plunging vigorously into his new duties, Rickenbacker sold Eastern's old planes and acquired new Lockheed L-10 Electras and Douglas DC-2s, which he proudly christened "The Great Silver Fleet." Firing old and jaded executives and station managers, he recruited fresh managerial talent, reorganized the traffic department, instituted a stock-option plan to enhance employee morale, and established pioneering medical, radio, and meteorological departments. By acquiring the Wedell-Williams Transport Corporation late in 1936, he added Houston to Eastern's expanding route structure.

Although Rickenbacker was opposed to labor unions in principle, he had no choice but to deal with the AFL-affiliated Air Line Pilots Association (ALPA), which was protected by federal airmail legislation. In any case, the ALPA avoided direct collective bargaining, preferring to reach its goals through governmental agencies.[30] Being an aviator himself, Rickenbacker felt a bond with Eastern's pilots and treated them sympathetically. He put down a strike among the company's mechanics that began late in 1937, but soon thereafter invited the International Association of Machinists (IAM) to organize Eastern's maintenance workers. He established a forty-hour week, increased wages, offered paid vacations, and gave Eastern's employees group insurance and pension benefits.

Rickenbacker's aggressive program paid off. Eastern, which had lost $1.5 million in 1934, made a modest profit of $38,000 in 1935 and was soon firmly in the black.[31] Rickenbacker's performance was all the more impressive because conditions in the airline industry generally deteriorated whereas Eastern's fortunes improved. In 1938, however, Rickenbacker learned that Breech had decided to sell Eastern for $3 million to a syndicate headed by car rental magnate John Hertz. Knowing that Eastern could not have been offered to Hertz for such a price but for the hard work he had done in rebuilding the carrier, Rickenbacker was enraged. Going to GM's chief executive, Alfred P. Sloan, over Breech's head, Rickenbacker secured an option to retain control of Eastern contingent on his raising $3.5 million within thirty days. Aided by Smith, Barney and Company and the Kuhn-Loeb banking interests, Rickenbacker arranged enough stock subscriptions to implement his plan. Laurance S. Rockefeller, who was at the beginning of his career as a venture capitalist, was among the investors. By quickly raising his stake in Eastern to $250,000, Rockefeller became the company's dominant stockholder. In April 1938, Rickenbacker became president and chief executive officer.[32]

The takeover engineered by Rickenbacker coincided with the passage of the Civil Aeronautics Act of 1938, which brought about momentous changes in government regulation of commercial aviation.[33] Rickenbacker scored a notable triumph just before the new law went into effect. In one of its last actions before yielding control of airmail contracts, the Post Office Department opened bids on service between Houston, San Antonio, and Brownsville, Texas. Because the winner would be in a good position to gain a route to Mexico City, two carriers, Eastern and Braniff, fought furiously to get the contract. Finding that Eastern planned to bid one cent per mile, Braniff bid less than one mill. Learning about Braniff's plan, Rickenbacker won the battle by offering to carry mail on the new route for nothing.[34] The victory demonstrated his capacity for decisiveness.

Despite his animosity toward Roosevelt and the New Deal, Rickenbacker initially supported the Civil Aeronautics Act on the grounds that it would prevent unfair competition from "wildcat" airlines threatening chaos in the industry. Eastern's annual report for 1938 anticipated "sound regulation" under the statute. Relations with the CAA and CAB were temporarily amicable as Eastern won several new routes. St. Louis, added to Eastern's system in 1939, was a particularly welcome prize.[35]

But Rickenbacker's antipathy toward the New Deal was too great for the honeymoon to last long. In 1939 the CAB instituted a proceeding to determine whether the airmail rates paid to Eastern and several other airlines were "fair and reasonable." At the time, Eastern received $1.20 per ton-mile, the lowest rate earned by any domestic carrier. Despite Rickenbacker's protests, CAB examiners recommended a 50 percent reduction in Eastern's mail rates and asked for a recapture of fees for the previous three years that would have cost the company $2.5 million. Reporting to the stockholders that the proposal "completely failed to recognize the efficiency and economy of your Company's operations," Rickenbacker won a major concession when the CAB dropped the recapture demand. Nevertheless, the CAB cut Eastern's mail rate in half, dealing it a serious blow.[36]

Despite such problems, Eastern flourished as world conditions worsened in the last few years leading to American involvement in World War II. Symbolic of the company's pride was the steady expansion of its Great Silver Fleet, which began switching from DC-2s to 21-passenger DC-3s in December 1936. By the end of 1940, the company's aircraft included thirty-four DC-3s and four Douglas DSTs, the 14-passenger sleeper version of the DC-3. The superb condition in which these planes were kept aroused the admiration of Donald W. Nyrop, a young attorney who was beginning a rapid ascent in the Washington bureaucracy regulating commercial aviation.[37] In 1940, Eastern's profits exceeded $1.5 million, the largest net income in the industry. Its route system spanned 5,782 miles, mostly east of the Mississippi River, making it the second largest air carrier in the country. In July 1940, Eastern moved its headquarters from the Chrysler Building to 10 Rockefeller Plaza, which was part of a splendid new complex, Rockefeller Center. The high-rise structure in which Rickenbacker had a sixteenth-floor office was proudly named the Eastern Air Lines Building. Eastern now carried 346,593 passengers, up from 162,246 only two years before, and transported nearly 5 million pounds of mail.[38]

The six-year period from 1935 to 1941 marked the apex of Rickenbacker's career. Never again would he flourish as he was doing at this time. Photographs taken as he traveled throughout Eastern's system showed a tall, smiling, dapper man who looked younger than his years. Employees regarded him as a father-figure and appreciated the heroic aura he brought to the airline. On Memorial Day, he took pride in presiding over the annual running of the Indy 500, wearing a straw hat that was his trademark during seasonable weather. Although Charles A. Lindbergh had

*Rickenbacker at his desk at Rockefeller
Center after World War II. (Courtesy of
the Auburn University Archives)*

now become the nation's most famous aviator, Rickenbacker was revered
by the public as a symbol of the values that made America great. Count-
less newspaper and magazine articles proclaimed his fame.

The Hero in Extremis

Two harrowing ordeals soon changed Rickenbacker's life forever. On February 26, 1941, a Douglas DST on which he was flying crashed near Atlanta, leaving him with multiple injuries including a crushed hip socket,
a broken pelvis, and a fractured knee.[39] Initially given up for dead, he
clung to life and was walking again, with a permanent limp, by early summer. He was still recuperating in December when the Japanese attack on
Pearl Harbor plunged the United States into World War II. Despite his
shattered condition, he volunteered for special missions for General Henry
H. "Hap" Arnold, chief of the Army Air Corps, starting with an inspection tour of American domestic military bases in March and April 1942.
He then conducted another mission in September to inspect installa-
tions in England and reported back to Arnold on how American planes
could be improved.

Rickenbacker's second ordeal began in October 1942, when Secretary
of War Henry L. Stimson asked him to take a secret message—a stern
reprimand—to General Douglas MacArthur, who was then stationed in
New Guinea and had been making public statements denouncing the

Roosevelt administration's war policies. On October 21, en route from Hawaii to a refueling stop at Canton Island, a Boeing B-17 on which Rickenbacker was flying had to be ditched in the Pacific Ocean because of a navigational error that led it off course and caused it to run out of fuel. For three weeks, Rickenbacker and seven companions, one of whom died, drifted through shark-infested waters and suffered from hunger, thirst, and exposure to the elements. By the time the party was finally rescued in mid-November, Rickenbacker had lost fifty-four pounds and was severely dehydrated. Showing phenomenal resilience, he went to New Guinea after being briefly hospitalized at Samoa and gave Stimson's message to MacArthur. He then visited Guadalcanal, where bitter fighting was taking place between U.S. marines and Japanese troops, and came home to a frenzied welcome at Bolling Air Force Base in mid-December.[40]

After recovering from his raft experience, Rickenbacker went on two more missions for Stimson. One of these assignments took him to North Africa, Iran, India, China, and the Soviet Union in 1943; the other, to the Aleutian Islands in 1944. While he was gone, two subordinates, Paul Brattain and Sidney Shannon, ran Eastern. Like other American carriers, the airline gave up most of its planes to transport military supplies while maintaining its domestic schedules with a reduced fleet and shrunken staff. The planes it turned over to the Air Transport Command, painted olive drab and jokingly called "The Great Chocolate Fleet," transported approximately 130,000 passengers and 45 million pounds of supplies, logging more than 33 million miles. Flying over virtually impenetrable jungles in Brazil and long stretches of uninterrupted water in the South Atlantic, they carried cargo and military personnel between outposts like Trinidad, Natal, Ascension Island, and Accra. Pilots from Eastern who served with the ATC never canceled an assignment, and they lost only one plane during the entire war.[41]

Rickenbacker's wartime experiences reinforced his heroic stature in the eyes of his fellow Americans. He received thousands of letters and telegrams after his ordeal in the Pacific. *Life* published a three-part series of articles about the episode, and put his picture, plainly showing the effects of his harrowing ordeal, on its cover on January 25, 1943. His book, *Seven Came Through,* also dealing with the raft episode, became a best-seller. An article, "When a Man Faces Death," that he published in

American magazine in November 1943, created such a sensation that 1.5 million copies were reprinted, mostly with a liberal subvention by John D. Rockefeller Jr., and given to members of the armed forces who embarked for distant theaters of war. Admirers tried unsuccessfully to persuade Rickenbacker to run for president in 1944. Early in 1945, Twentieth Century Fox released a film about his life, *Captain Eddie.* Starring Fred MacMurray, implausibly cast as Rickenbacker, and Lynn Bari, who gave a more convincing performance as Adelaide, it had a syrupy plot that distorted Rickenbacker's life by turning it into a Hollywood melodrama.[42]

The Hero in Decline

Returning to Eastern from his wartime missions, Rickenbacker presided over the nation's most profitable airline. Setting a good example for the rest of the industry, he hired hundreds of disabled veterans and found ways for them to fit into the company's operations. Stories abound about the compassion he showed in helping ease the problems of returning employees, some of them still recuperating from their wounds, in adjusting to civilian life. Birdie Bomar, widow of an airman who became one of Eastern's senior pilots, recalled how Rickenbacker visited her husband in a hospital near the end of the war and gave him an envelope before leaving the room. Upon opening it, the Bomars found that it contained a generous sum of cash.[43]

As always, Rickenbacker traveled incessantly throughout Eastern's system, calling all of his employees by name and showing interest in their everyday lives as well as their professional concerns. He personified a paternalism that was still deeply entrenched in the airline industry. Successful executives like Delta's C. E. Woolman and Continental's Robert Six practiced it and received the same veneration from their employees. To demonstrate his determination to become involved with as many members of Eastern's rank and file as possible, Rickenbacker instituted staff meetings, attended by hundreds of junior executives and supervisors, at which he explained company policies, identified problems, and heard oral reports on various aspects of the carrier's operations.[44]

During the late 1940s, Eastern's earnings sometimes exceeded those of the rest of the industry put together. But the seeds of its later decline were already present, and Rickenbacker was at least partly responsible for its problems. Although his phenomenal vitality remained as strong as ever, his body had been ravaged by what he had gone through earlier in the decade. Years of hero-worship had subtly affected his self-image; his interactions with powerful world leaders had inflated an already powerful ego, intensifying his tendency to be overbearing and abrasive. His temper was too quick, and his judgment was too hasty. He made costly decisions based on emotion and sentiment rather than sound business judgment.

An early indication of tendencies that would lead to unfortunate results for Eastern occurred when Rickenbacker gave a speech at a conference in Havana in 1945 after the death of Franklin D. Roosevelt. Too candid to hide his true feelings, he said he was glad FDR had died. Rickenbacker's remarks created such a furor that he had to leave the meeting. His forthrightness, however admirable in itself, was a business liability that could not help but hurt Eastern's chances in important route cases conducted by the CAB, whose members continued to be chosen by a Democratic president, Harry S Truman. Writing about this phase in Rickenbacker's life, Robert Serling aptly stated that "Eastern entered the postwar era . . . with a time bomb buried in the inflexible personality of the man who ruled the Great Silver Fleet."[45]

Rickenbacker also poured huge amounts of energy into speeches and radio broadcasts that took time from his responsibilities at Eastern Air Lines. During the war, immediately after he returned from his raft ordeal and only weeks away from observing frightful suffering among American troops on Guadalcanal, he stumped throughout the country accusing labor leaders of treasonous behavior by fomenting strikes, encouraging featherbedding, and otherwise impeding the war effort. After coming back from the Soviet Union in 1943, he started a foreign policy debate by saying that Stalin and other Russian leaders were not really communist fanatics but simply nationalists with whom the United States should cooperate in reaching an amicable postwar settlement. In 1945 he traveled widely to promote showings of *Captain Eddie*. He was often away from his desk.

Religion became increasingly important to Rickenbacker, who was haunted by questions about why God had seen fit to spare his life in so many close brushes with death. Surely, he reasoned, God had a higher purpose for him, and he did his best to find it. Trying to find a mission larger than himself or the role he played with Eastern, he allied himself with Norman Vincent Peale, for whom he wrote "Why I Believe in Prayer," the first article ever to appear in Peale's magazine, *Guideposts*. Rickenbacker also spent much time supporting ecumenical causes in which members of the Rockefeller family were involved. He invested himself heavily in secular crusades, giving vehement speeches in which he condemned the legacy left by the New Deal and the continuation of liberal policies he abhorred. As relations with the Soviet Union worsened, he abandoned the accommodationist stance toward Stalin that he had once advocated and became a stalwart cold warrior, preaching passionately against communism. During the early 1950s, he strongly supported Senator Joseph McCarthy. Later, he publicly opposed President John F. Kennedy's conduct in the 1962 Cuban missile crisis, accusing him of appeasing the Russians and subverting the Monroe Doctrine by allowing the Castro regime to stay in power. His deepening need to devote his life to transcendent causes led him to become a John the Baptist crying in the wilderness of a liberal society that in his view had gone morally soft and was departing from the fundamental principles on which the country was founded. In the process, he damaged the reputation of his airline among many of the passengers it served. Business leaders whose firms have large numbers of customers with varied points of view do well to avoid controversy, but Rickenbacker was too sincere to avoid speaking his mind.

It might have been better for Eastern, and for Rickenbacker, had he retired, but he could not bear to leave the airline and its people, whom he regarded as his family. He had endured too much frustration finding a role to play in aviation to give it up. His love affair with the sky was as strong as ever. Remaining at Eastern's helm, he became increasingly involved in combat with the CAB, which he saw as part of a New Deal conspiracy against free enterprise.

During the war, the CAB had awarded Eastern a lucrative route from St. Louis to Washington and extended its Miami–New York route to Boston. Soon after Rickenbacker returned to his post, however, the CAB issued Eastern and three other well-established airlines a show-cause order asking why their mail rates should not be cut, this time from 60 to 32 cents per ton-mile. Infuriated, Rickenbacker charged that the CAB was ignoring Eastern's "superior economy and efficiency." The new rate advocated by the CAB, he stated, would eliminate any incentive for the carrier to excel. The CAB finally settled for a 45 cent rate, but Rickenbacker felt aggrieved.[46]

Anticipating a dramatic growth of air travel after the war, the CAB decided to encourage competition on routes formerly limited to one-carrier service. Because fares could not be changed without CAB approval, only service competition was possible. Partly because of his unfortunate experience as an automobile manufacturer, Rickenbacker was ill-equipped to thrive in a regulatory environment based not simply upon giving passengers safe and dependable service but upon offering them every possible amenity to make flying a luxurious experience despite its inherent discomforts. In Rickenbacker's unvarnished words, the business of an airline was "to put asses in seats" and keep them there as often as possible to maximize aircraft utilization. Service meant getting passengers where they wanted to go at reasonable prices that would yield profits to Eastern without federal subsidy. To the CAB, it meant indulging the public with amenities designed to make flying as pleasant as possible, whether or not subsidies had to be paid for this purpose—unless, of course, an airline happened to be big and successful, in which case it would be held to the smallest possible mail payments. Aided by federal subsidies, smaller carriers that the CAB admitted to routes Eastern had formerly flown alone wooed passengers in ways that Rickenbacker, who hated subsidy as a matter of principle, could not and would not emulate. He was playing by one set of rules while they played by another. Under such circumstances, Eastern was bound to be hurt.

In 1944, the CAB authorized National Airlines to fly from New York to Miami, ending Eastern's exclusive control of that route. In August 1945, it broke Eastern's single-carrier hold on flights from Chicago to Miami by giving Delta the right to compete with Eastern in that market. Though avowing that he favored fair competition, as he defined it, Rickenbacker resented the fact that Eastern would now have to share two important vacation routes with much smaller carriers that would need generous subsidies to develop them.

In 1946, the CAB denied Eastern permission to inaugurate a potentially lucrative vacation route from Florida to Cuba, Jamaica, Colombia, and the Canal Zone.[47] Instead, the routes went to airlines that would incur higher costs in serving them. Rickenbacker became increasingly indignant because of such decisions. At one point he stormed into the office of CAB chairman L. Welch Pogue and launched a tirade, pounding Pogue's desk with his fist while sweeping a row of books onto the floor with his other hand. But he also winked slyly at Pogue's secretary as he left.[48] At least in part, he had been putting on an act.

But he was also seriously upset, and his rage overflowed at Eastern's headquarters as he vented his wrath on staff members and business associates. One of his sons, Bill, remembered sitting outside his father's office listening to him administer a fierce tongue-lashing to Brad Walker, a public relations executive who was probably trying to change Eastern's image with advertisements that were more in tune with the service competition desired by the CAB. The rumblings coming from behind the closed door reminded Bill of the lurid atmosphere that gathered ahead of a violent electrical storm. As his father grew increasingly angry, profanity resounded and the walls reverberated with verbal thunder and lightning. Soon, however, the two men emerged arm in arm as if nothing had happened. After Rickenbacker had temporarily discharged his rage, the soft side of his personality asserted itself and he showered kindness on Walker, who was too accustomed to dealing with his famous client to take offense about what he had said.[49]

Rickenbacker's dilemma persisted as other carriers, including Capital, Colonial, and Chicago and Southern, were permitted by the CAB to compete with Eastern on routes it had once controlled. As Pogue stated later, one of the reasons why the CAB authorized such competition was because it received a growing number of complaints about the quality of service Eastern provided.[50] However well-merited some of the criticism may have been, it was unrealistic in Rickenbacker's view to expect too many amenities from an airline forced to compete with carriers that could cover their losses with mail rates far higher than those Eastern received. Moreover, much also depended on how service was defined. Because Rickenbacker placed so much emphasis on dependability, for example, Eastern's gate crews worked under strict rules to get planes off the ground on schedule and give no consideration to passengers who reached a gate even a few seconds late.[51] Such policies benefited persons already aboard a plane by increasing the chances that they would reach their destinations on time, but last-minute arrivals who were unceremoniously turned away could, and did, complain loudly to the CAB, which was unfailingly sympathetic.

Eastern's alleged deficiencies in service competition were especially damaging because its foremost rivals not only operated under different rules but took full advantage of their favored situation. Delta (whose cabin attendants, unlike Eastern's, were not unionized) took pride in giving passengers sugar-coated southern hospitality. National, which stayed in business chiefly because the CAB needed it as a way to discipline Eastern, did its best to make flying a glitzy experience while its president, George E. Baker, shaved costs by resorting to unfair labor practices and using butcher paper instead of window curtains in his corporate office building. Meanwhile, Eastern had the sad distinction of being the only carrier in the industry whose passengers formed an organization to vent their hostility toward it. Its acronym was WHEAL, for "We Hate Eastern Air Lines."[52]

Rickenbacker was by no means indifferent to passenger welfare, which in his eyes began with providing travelers safe, well-maintained aircraft. Because of his emphasis on reliability, he was also extremely concerned about dependable handling of luggage. Before one general staff meeting, for example, he made elaborate preparations to impound the baggage of hundreds of the personnel who attended it so they would learn firsthand how passengers felt upon reaching their destinations and finding that their belongings had been lost or mishandled. He also preached endless sermons about courtesy at staff gatherings. On the other hand, courtesy was a two-way street as far as he was concerned, and he expected passengers to be polite to his crew members. In his autobiography, talking about his early flights throughout Eastern's far-flung system, he took pride in relating episodes in which he upbraided passengers who were rude to cabin attendants. This attitude, however, much as it may have endeared Rickenbacker to his corporate family, was out of step with a service-oriented industry governed by the idea that "the customer is always right."

Despite inspiring affection among Eastern's employees, Rickenbacker also made unfortunate decisions that damaged personnel relations. As four-engine airliners began to be used throughout the industry in the postwar era, the Air Line Pilots Association (ALPA), the Airline Flight Engineers Association (AFEA), and the militant Transport Workers Union of America (TWUA) pushed the Civil Aeronautics Authority to require three persons—two pilots and a flight engineer—to staff the cockpits of large planes like the Boeing 377 Stratocruiser, Lockheed L-649 Constellation, and Douglas DC-6. Against strong opposition from airline leaders and aircraft manufacturers, federal regulators adopted the idea but provided leeway for airlines in failing to stipulate that the flight engineer be trained solely in that restricted capacity. Taking advantage of the loophole, Delta's C. E. Woolman decided to use "pilot-engineers" who belonged to the same union that pilots and copilots did and would in due course be promoted into their ranks. In Woolman's words, it was unwise to "put a board on a man's head," meaning that a flight engineer with no chance for advancement would naturally feel resentful. Delta's policy was expensive; after absorbing Chicago and Southern in a merger in 1952, settlements with flight engineers who declined to be trained as pilot-engineers cost Woolman an estimated $250,000. Not surprisingly, many airlines, including Eastern, chose to fill the third cockpit seat with a flight engineer solely trained to work in that capacity. It is possible that Rickenbacker followed this policy not merely because of his characteristic frugality but also because he was thinking about the days in which two persons of highly unequal status, drivers and riding mechanics, once rode together in race cars. In any case, Eastern experienced bitter jurisdictional disputes between ALPA and AFEA members who were forced to share the same cockpit, leading to a series of costly strikes from which Delta escaped.[53]

Eastern also experienced problems from choices Rickenbacker made in aircraft selection. Shortly after the war, when the industry was looking for a somewhat larger twin-engine replacement for the DC-3, Eastern narrowly averted a potentially serious blunder when Rickenbacker decided to acquire the Curtiss C-46 Commando, which was too slow to be an effective passenger liner. Besides being more concerned about dependability than speed, he was also motivated by his close friendship with Guy Vaughan, president of Curtiss-Wright. Fortunately for Eastern, the plan fell through when Curtiss-Wright, which shifted its manufacturing facilities from one place to another, failed to deliver planes on schedule, forcing Rickenbacker to cancel the order. The C-46 proved to be an excellent cargo plane in the postwar era, but would have been at a serious disadvantage in a period of service competition when speed was a key selling point.

Eastern had another close call when Rickenbacker chose to acquire the Martin 2-0-2 for short-haul passenger flights, partly because of his sentimental attachment to Glenn L. Martin. Luckily for Eastern, Northwest introduced the plane and had disastrous results when its lack of airworthiness resulted in a series of fatal crashes. Passengers and pilots alike refused to fly in the aircraft, and federal regulators grounded it. Rickenbacker hastily arranged emergency financing that permitted Martin to retool and develop a much better plane, the 4-0-4, which Eastern operated successfully after introducing it in 1952. Meanwhile, at Delta, Woolman listened to advisers who warned him about the deficiencies of the 2-0-2. He saved money by using DC-3s with expanded seat configurations until superior Convair airliners became available for short-haul service.

Eastern also got off to a slower start than Delta and National after the war in using large aircraft for nonstop service on long-haul routes. Rickenbacker had his eye on the four-engine Lockheed L-049 Constellation, which had been designed in 1939 for Howard Hughes and saw service in World War II as the C-69 military transport. Rickenbacker was understandably attracted by the fact that the Constellation was pressurized, had a range of more than 3,000 miles, and could cruise at speeds exceeding 300 miles per hour. But he had no way of anticipating teething problems that the Connies would have in their first postwar use with Hughes's airline, TWA. Tendencies to catch fire in midair plagued the L-049, and the CAB grounded it in July 1946. While Hughes had the ship redesigned, Rickenbacker shrewdly persuaded him that it would be wise not to restrict the plane to TWA but instead share it with Eastern. Rickenbacker regarded the deal as a coup, but had to wait until the new model was available.

Fortunately, Rickenbacker had leased a number of R5D transports, the naval equivalent of the DC-4, to cushion the impact of the delay in securing the Connies. But the Douglas ships were not ready for commercial service in February 1946, when National's chief executive, Baker, put DC-4s in service on the route between New York and Miami that Eastern had previously monopolized. Eastern hastily deployed DC-4s on an interim basis pending arrival of its L-649, and Baker soon became embroiled in labor disputes that prevented him from exploiting the lead he had gained. But the reprieve was only temporary, because Delta was better prepared to compete vigorously with Eastern when Woolman started providing nonstop service with DC-4s between Chicago and Miami in

November 1946. Even by this time, Eastern still had received no Connies. Eastern had already introduced DC-4s on the route, but was not providing nonstop service with them and soon lost heavily to Delta until Rickenbacker added nonstop flights in January 1947.

It is possible that Rickenbacker, looking down from his lofty eminence in Rockefeller Center, had underestimated Baker and Woolman by allowing these rivals to steal a march on him, forcing him to scramble to recover. If so, Rickenbacker soon learned that both executives, particularly Woolman, were worthy adversaries. Beginning in 1947, Rickenbacker and Woolman fought one of the classic battles in the history of aircraft selection, in which a spunky Delta gradually gained ground on its mighty adversary and ultimately overthrew it.

The battle started well for Eastern. In June 1947, Rickenbacker finally inaugurated service with his new L-649 Constellations and Delta's share of the Chicago to Miami market plummeted. In September 1948, Eastern transported 1,377 persons between the two cities, while Delta carried 189, mostly travelers who could not get tickets to fly on the Connies. Facing disaster, Woolman acquired a fleet of Douglas DC-6Bs and met Eastern's subsequent switch to L-1049 Super Constellations by adopting Douglas DC-7s. Rickenbacker thereupon upped the stakes by securing an improved model, the DC-7B.[54]

Meanwhile, Woolman fought to gain access to major cities on the East Coast, which he liked to call "America's Main Street." He achieved his goal in 1955 when the CAB awarded Delta a route connecting Atlanta to Charlotte, Washington, Baltimore, Philadelphia, and New York City. By absorbing a slightly smaller airline, Chicago and Southern, in a 1952 merger, Delta also gained long-haul routes linking Houston, Detroit, Chicago, New Orleans, and several Caribbean markets, enabling Woolman to make increasingly effective use of four-engine airliners.[55] Whereas Delta had existed in the 1930s mainly to feed traffic into Eastern's much larger route system, the struggle between the two carriers became increasingly a war between near-equals. Delta's reputation for southern hospitality, appreciated by both passengers and the complaint-conscious CAB, played some part in the advances it scored against Eastern. Above all, however, Delta adroitly played a shrewd political game by nurturing its contacts with powerful Democratic senators and representatives at a time when Eastern, even under the Republican Eisenhower administration, was on less than ideal terms with the CAB. For this state of affairs, Rickenbacker's curmudgeonly behavior was at least partly to blame.

In the 1960s, Delta gradually pulled ahead of Eastern, partly because of mistakes made by Rickenbacker in aircraft selection as the industry entered the jet age. Fearing that jet engines were ill-suited for Eastern's route system, still penalized by its preponderance of short-haul routes, Rickenbacker chose to acquire Lockheed Electra turboprops while Delta purchased Douglas DC-8 and Convair CV-880 jetliners. Again, history repeated a pattern similar to the experience of the ill-fated Martin 2-0-2. Although the Electra became an outstanding plane that Eastern's pilots liked to fly, it initially had a serious flaw causing wing flutter, leading to a public relations disaster when Electras owned by Braniff and Northwest crashed soon after entering service. Amid the resulting clamor, the Federal Aviation Administration, successor of the CAA, imposed speed restrictions on the plane that hobbled Eastern's ability to compete with Delta's DC-8s and CV-880s. Delta's pilots delighted in telling passengers to look out their windows at one of Eastern's lumbering Electras and then zooming triumphantly past them amid cheers and guffaws. Ironically, Eastern could have had DC-8s like the ones owned by Delta, but Rickenbacker had decided to wait for a later model with more powerful engines.

Meanwhile, Eastern was also suffering the long-range results of a decision made by the CAB in the late 1940s to sanction the creation of "feederlines" to provide air service to small cities. Earlier, Eastern had won permission from the CAB to serve such destinations as Brunswick, Georgia, Muscle Shoals and Dothan, Alabama, and Spartanburg, South Carolina. After the CAB authorized feederlines, Rickenbacker was obliged to continue serving these small markets while competing with newly established companies that received much larger airmail compensation from the federal government than Eastern did. The CAB followed the same strategy in the 1950s when it favored smaller trunklines like Delta and National in key route decisions and denied most of Eastern's applications. The only way Rickenbacker could significantly expand Eastern's route system was by acquiring small carriers like Colonial in mergers. But this solution was hazardous. Although Eastern did manage to gain a few large markets like Bermuda and Montreal in the Colonial merger,

it also inherited a hodgepodge of smaller northeastern communities like
Malone, New York, Rutland, Vermont, and Lancaster, Pennsylvania, that
could not be effectively integrated with larger cities in Eastern's route
structure. Some of these cities were reassigned to smaller carriers with
the CAB's consent, but Eastern was still plagued by a chronic problem
of short-stage operations that prevented it from using its equipment efficiently. As a result of acquiring Colonial, Eastern was also saddled with
obsolete DC-3s and DC-4s that were outmatched in short-haul markets
by newer Convair CV-330s and -440s that Delta had purchased. Eastern
badly needed to extend its route system west of the Mississippi in order
to make efficient use of its planes, particularly its large four-engine airliners. But the CAB refused to give the company any transcontinental
routes.[56]

Having to compete with smaller carriers that had much higher costs
per route-mile, and therefore received federal subsidies, was particularly
galling to Rickenbacker because Eastern was well known to be the most
frugal airline in the industry. As Pogue admitted, "Eastern's costs were
simply on a different plateau" when compared to those of its competitors.[57] In 1949, Rickenbacker's rage spilled over in a well-publicized letter to the Senate Finance Committee in which he offered to operate the
entire domestic systems of Delta, National, Chicago and Southern, Capital, and Colonial for sixty-five cents per ton-mile instead of the subsidy
rates, averaging $4.45, that they were actually receiving. He estimated that
Eastern could transport 2.7 million tons of mail, for which these five
firms had received $12 million in 1948, for only $1.6 million, saving the
taxpayers $10.4 million. He professed surprise that the five carriers "did
not accept this generous offer."[58]

As he fumed about CAB policies, Rickenbacker became more and
more vehement in speeches blasting the continuing legacy of the New
Deal and the shortcomings of a bloated federal bureaucracy. As a veteran
CAB counsel later stated, Rickenbacker and his corporate lawyers did
not mince words with members of the CAB's staff. They told them to
their faces that they were incompetent. In Rickenbacker's view, which he
did not hide, the fact that such men worked for the government instead
of going into private enterprise showed plainly that they lacked the
ability to succeed in the business world. In turn, CAB staff members
gave stern lectures to Eastern's Washington representatives, saying that

the company should be more respectful to federal officials and that it was damaging its own interests by alienating them. Rickenbacker's inability to control his tongue was all the more unfortunate because CAB members leaned heavily on their staffs for advice.[59]

Eastern took a critical blow in 1961 in a hotly contested transcontinental route case in which the CAB gave Delta and National access to San Diego, Los Angeles, San Francisco, and other western cities while denying Eastern's application to serve those markets. Rickenbacker did nothing to strengthen Eastern's chances by giving a scathing speech in Atlanta attacking John F. Kennedy, who had recently become president. Once again, Rickenbacker's tendency to speak his mind resulted in politically inadvisable behavior. The decision in the transcontinental case was a major setback for Eastern, which could not fly west of Texas and increasingly needed long-haul transcontinental routes for efficient aircraft utilization as the cost of airliners spiraled upward.[60]

Labor problems continued to haunt Rickenbacker in the late 1950s and early 1960s as members of the pilots' and flight mechanics' unions waged internecine warfare in the cockpits of Eastern's planes. Bitterness became so pronounced that lines were drawn on cockpit floors to mark jurisdictional boundaries. By contrast, Delta reaped the advantage of having its pilots and flight mechanics under the same union umbrella. Eastern's ability to serve what few long-haul routes it had was compromised by a series of strikes. One such walkout, in 1958, took place at the peak of the normally profitable winter vacation season, lasted thirty-nine days, and provided a temporary bonanza to Delta, which was unaffected by the strike. Although the work stoppage clearly indicated the extent to which Rickenbacker had miscalculated by choosing to mix pilots and mechanics in the first place, he ended it by agreeing to put not three but four persons in the cockpits of the jet planes that Eastern was now beginning to acquire, resulting in serious cost increases.

Throughout these labor problems, Rickenbacker displayed the warm human characteristics that endeared him to his many admirers at Eastern. During work stoppages, while fulminating about union activities, he rose early on bitterly cold mornings to serve hot coffee to strikers on picket lines. As always, he acted in a paternal manner, stern and punitive at one moment and tenderhearted the next. His behavior at the large staff meetings he continued to hold was typical of a style that was deeply rooted in an earlier period of the nation's history but now seemed increasingly anachronistic, particularly to younger persons who could not understand where his attitudes came from. Rickenbacker believed that the oral reports he required his subordinates to give at staff conclaves would help them learn to "think on their feet," but many persons who gave them were terrified as they stood at a microphone beside the podium, knowing that the boss was ready to pounce on them at any moment to justify whatever they were saying. Occasionally, using his cane, he would reach out and give one of them "a good hard rap on the leg," as he stated in his autobiography. Najeeb Halaby, a young naval intelligence expert who had won the confidence of Laurance Rockefeller and later headed both Pan American and the Federal Aviation Administration, attended a staff meeting at Miami Beach as a fact-finder for Rockefeller and was appalled by what he saw. "I had never seen a more dictatorial example of centralized management nor such public humiliation of employees," he wrote.[61] Halaby, who came from a younger generation, could not comprehend how some of the same persons who suffered indignities at Rickenbacker's hands could at the same time idolize the old hero who was making a public spectacle of them—as he thought, for their own good.

The Hero in Defeat

Concern began mounting among Eastern's directors as danger signs appeared under Rickenbacker's leadership. In 1953, one of his subordinates, T. F. Armstrong, became president and Rickenbacker moved up to chairman of the board. But Armstrong was merely a figurehead, and Rickenbacker continued to dominate the decision-making process. In 1958, Armstrong took a newly created post of executive vice president, and Eastern's increasingly frustrated directors appointed a new president, Malcolm MacIntyre, an attorney who had been undersecretary of the U.S. Air Force. Although MacIntyre was designated chief executive officer, Rickenbacker, who remained board chairman, could not give up the control he had held for so long, and he interfered constantly with MacIntyre's attempts to run the company. Increasingly, cleavages appeared in Eastern's executive hierarchy as old-timers continued to take orders from Rickenbacker and newer appointees sided with MacIntyre, who tried to solve some of the airline's problems by instituting a novel but highly successful shuttle service between New York and Washington.[62]

One incident above all indicated the extent to which Rickenbacker's judgment was deteriorating during this heartbreaking period. Over the years, airmen who had fought in World War I had held reunions of their old units throughout the country. Responding to an initiative taken by Royal D. Frey of the Air Force Central Museum (now the U.S. Air Force Museum) and other persons, Rickenbacker sponsored a preliminary meeting in New York City to hold a grand reunion of all World War I airmen at Wright-Patterson Air Force Base, form a single organization, and create an Air Force Museum Foundation. At the time, more than 1,200 American veterans of the world's first air war were still living. After strenuous preparations, 340 of them, along with 200 wives, showed up for the big meeting in Dayton on June 24, 1961. Over the next few days, enthusiasm grew to form a Reunion Association, and an Organizing Committee worked far into the night to prepare a charter to be presented at a final banquet. Five hundred copies were placed on the tables prior to the banquet, at which welcoming addresses were given by dignitaries and the charter was brought up for discussion. Logically, Rickenbacker was asked to speak about the subject.

The result was one of the greatest debacles of Rickenbacker's career. Instead of speaking about the proposed charter, and apparently oblivious to the fact that he was preaching to the already converted, he launched into what James J. Sloan, one of the organizers of the function, called a "diatribe" about communism and the deficiencies of the new Kennedy administration. The speech was interminable, lasting for almost an hour and a half. Nearly six hundred persons were in the hall when Rickenbacker started speaking. Less than fifty remained by the time he stopped. At one point, as a group got up to leave, Rickenbacker tried to wave it back, prompting one of its members to thumb his nose at America's Ace of Aces as the party left the room. On the next day, the veterans and their wives went home. A few organizers tried to mobilize what spirit was left for passing the charter, but it was decided that it was useless to make the attempt.[63]

As Eastern went through what became a never-ending ordeal, Laurance Rockefeller decided that the only way out of its problems was to work out a merger with one of the country's two largest carriers, American Airlines. Again, however, the need to secure CAB approval stymied Eastern's hopes. Led by Delta, the rest of the industry strongly attacked the plan. Meanwhile, it became clear that John F. Kennedy's brother, Robert, would veto the merger on antitrust grounds in his capacity as attorney general, even if the CAB did not. The merger plan was therefore scuttled.[64] Rockefeller had hoped that the attempted consolidation would permit him to replace Rickenbacker and MacIntyre with American's chief executive, C. R. Smith, whose managerial abilities were legendary. When the merger plan died, Rockefeller appointed a search committee to find a new CEO.

After the committee chose Floyd D. Hall, an executive at TWA, MacIntyre was fired and Rickenbacker was summoned to a meeting with the committee at which he was told to retire. Rickenbacker, who sensed what was going to happen and arrived after fortifying himself with alcohol, flew into a rage, shaking a finger at each of the directors in turn, dressing them down for being disloyal to him, and refusing to yield his post. A second meeting, this time with Rockefeller and one of his chief lieutenants, Harper Woodward, had to be held before the embattled executive finally agreed to step down. Showing great class, he graciously relinquished command to Hall, whom he respected as a fellow pilot. Then, leaving his office, he never set foot again in the Eastern Air Lines Building.[65]

Although he tried not to show it, Rickenbacker was devastated by what had happened. Moving to an office that Eastern provided for him elsewhere in Rockefeller Center, he retreated behind an unmarked door. The self-praise in the autobiography that he commissioned a freelance journalist, Booten Herndon, to ghostwrite at this time (one veteran aviation writer called it an "exercise in conceit")[66] must be seen in the light of the humiliation he felt at having been relieved of command. It was a wounded lion whom Herndon interviewed in the summer of 1965. Herndon was so deeply offended by Rickenbacker's abrasive manner that he spent his evenings at the New York Athletic Club swimming repeated laps to work off his anger and frustration. One day, when Rickenbacker raged at him and red-penciled some lines in Herndon's account of the 1943 mission to Russia, Herndon started to leave, ready to pull out of the project. After reaching the door, however, he came back, having asked himself, "Who would win if I walked out—he or I?" After the two men made up, they found that the tape recorder had been left running during Rickenbacker's explosion. With Rickenbacker's acquiescence, Herndon decided to leave it as it was, "for posterity." Herndon wrote: "I never lost sight of the fact that he was an authentic hero with a story to tell and that I was a dedicated journalist with the mission to tell it. From then on I took the abuse without answering back."[67]

In retirement, Rickenbacker corresponded with friends and admirers, gave public speeches in which he denounced left-wing doctrines, and dreamed of a future in which the United States would impose its will on the rest of the planet with the aid of space technology and nuclear weapons, destroying any nation that dared to "threaten world peace." Periodically he would have lunch at the "21" Club with Hall, who would report on developments taking place at Eastern. Listening attentively, Rickenbacker refrained from asking questions or making suggestions. As a token of his regard for Hall, he gave him a battered gray hat that he had worn throughout the raft episode in 1942.

As always, Rickenbacker maintained an active interest in world affairs, traveling to far-off places with Adelaide. He went to Germany, saw the Berlin Wall, and had lunch with two surviving combat pilots against whom he had fought many years before. With the consent of East German officials, he visited the Hero Veteran Graveyard and paid homage to three of the German Empire's greatest World War I aces, Otto Boelcke, Ernst Udet, and the "Red Baron," Manfred von Richthofen. He was denied permission, however, to have his picture taken in front of a monument honoring the Red Baron.

Despite such diversions, life became increasingly barren for Rickenbacker. Unable to bear the thought of leaving his beloved New York, he continued to live there even after Adelaide, feeling isolated as more and more of her friends died, moved to Florida. While visiting her there, just before his eighty-second birthday, Rickenbacker suffered an encephalitic aneurysm and underwent emergency surgery. Hall visited him at the hospital, talked at length about how things were going at Eastern, and got no response. Thinking that Rickenbacker was in a coma and that communication was futile, Hall excused himself and headed out of the room, only to have Rickenbacker get out of bed and accompany him to the door, dragging an intravenous feeding pole with him. "I'll take good care of your airline, Eddie," Hall said. Looking solemnly at him, Rickenbacker replied, "It's *your* airline now, Floyd."[68]

Incredibly, Rickenbacker recovered to a point at which he took Adelaide, who was losing her eyesight, to Switzerland for treatment by an ophthalmologist in July 1973. Not long after they arrived in Zurich, Rickenbacker's longtime secretary, Marguerite "Sheppy" Shepherd, who had also made the trip, noticed that he was breathing with difficulty and she summoned a physician. He was diagnosed as having pneumonia and taken to a hospital. After enduring much pain, he died in his sleep on July 23. His ashes, enclosed in a metal container, were flown to the United States in one of Eastern's DC-8s, which had been sent by Hall with a full crew of pilots and cabin attendants. A memorial service was held at the Key Biscayne Presbyterian Church on July 27, with General James H. "Jimmy" Doolittle as the eulogist. Not long afterward, Rickenbacker's remains were interred in Columbus as a group of jet interceptors from the 94th Fighter Squadron roared overhead in the "missing man" formation in final tribute to America's Ace of Aces.

Epitaph

Rickenbacker's failings are obvious. Every human being has them. Rickenbacker should be remembered for his many achievements. As one of the greatest fighter pilots in the history of aerial warfare, and as one of a small cadre of pioneers who dominated the formative years of American commercial aviation, rightfully described by R. E. G. Davies as "giants among a band of intuitive executives who counted few pygmies in their numbers," Rickenbacker merits an honored place in the history of the American airline industry. As Davies has said, it is no small tribute to Rickenbacker's stature that he took a struggling airline in 1938 and "almost single-handed, made it one of the biggest . . . without the benefit of either a transcontinental or a transoceanic route."[69]

Rickenbacker was a tragic hero. Had he lived in ancient Greece, a Homer or a Sophocles might have seen in him a fitting subject for a work of poetry like the *Iliad* or a drama like *Oedipus Rex*. There is about him the same quality of nobility that one finds in a Hamlet or a King Lear; he was an epic figure who was larger than life. He can also be seen as a mirror image of traits deeply embedded in American civilization. Passionately individualistic, he personalized everything with which he came into contact, was guided by his emotions, and saw things in black and white that members of a later generation came to see in various shades of gray. Whatever mistakes he made in his business career should be seen in this light and in the context of his seriously debilitated condition after the Atlanta crash in 1941 and the raft ordeal in 1942.

One of Rickenbacker's closest associates described him to Robert Serling as a person who was "mentally unequipped to move into an era when air transportation was on the verge of becoming mass transportation."[70] But was he simply an anachronism? Despite all of his shortcomings, it would be more accurate to say that he was born out of season, not only *after* his time but also *before* an era in which his talents and abilities would have been more appropriate. Had he been able to move boldly into new markets, as he could have done after deregulation, his record might have been different despite his limitations. Temperamentally unable to deal with the imperatives of service competition, he might have thrived at the helm of a no-frills airline after 1978, when his zeal for low costs would have been an asset in fare wars that the CAB would not have allowed.

Lowell Thomas, one of the foremost news commentators of the era in which Rickenbacker lived, called him "one of the towering figures of the twentieth century."[71] Many would disagree; Rickenbacker's name is conspicuously absent from lists of eminent persons in books and magazines looking back at one of the most turbulent centuries in history. But Thomas, an inveterate globetrotter who had met many world leaders, was a seasoned judge of character. Repeatedly, in interviews that I conducted in my research, distinguished business leaders and federal regulators—men of the stature of Laurance Rockefeller and L. Welch Pogue— would criticize Rickenbacker's leadership and personality and end by admonishing me to remember that he was "a great man and a great American." Whatever the merits of Thomas's assessment, it is time to pay Rickenbacker the attention he deserves, both as a casualty of the age in which he lived and as a prophet of an era that was yet to come.

Notes

1. Kenneth T. Jackson, ed., *The Encyclopedia of New York City* (New Haven: Yale University Press, 1995), 1207.

2. For a brief account of the nature and significance of this statute, see Donald R. Whitnah, "Airline Deregulation Act of 1978," in William M. Leary, ed., *The Airline Industry* (New York: Facts on File, 1992), 15–16.

3. Robert J. Serling, *From the Captain to the Colonel: An Informal History of Eastern Airlines* (New York: Dial Press, 1980), 309.

4. His surname at birth was Rickenbacher; he retained that spelling until 1918, by which time he was a combat pilot on the Western Front. Writing to a friend back in America at some point in that year, he signed the letter "Eddie Rickenbacker," drawing attention to the "k" by bracketing it. See W. David Lewis, "Edward V. Rickenbacker," in Leary, ed., *Airline Industry,* 398.

5. The basic details of Rickenbacker's life in this essay are based largely on *Rickenbacker: An Autobiography* (Englewood Cliffs,N.J.: Prentice-Hall, 1967), hereafter cited as *Autobiography*. I have also made use of Hans C. Adamson, *Eddie Rickenbacker* (New York: Macmillan, 1946), and Finis Farr, *Rickenbacker's Luck: An American Life* (Boston: Houghton Mifflin, 1979). Because one or more of these sources could be mentioned in virtually every one of the endnotes that follow, I have chosen not to multiply such references to no good purpose. Other sources on which I have relied include a manuscript, "Life Story of Captain Edward V. Rickenbacker," at Ohio State University Library, compiled from a series of interviews conducted by Eureka Pictures, Inc., in 1943 in connection with the making of a film, *Captain Eddie,* released in 1945 by Twentieth Century Fox; and typescripts of seventy-eight reels of interviews at the U.S. Air Force Museum, Wright-Patterson Air Force Base, Dayton, Ohio, made in 1965 in connection with the ghostwriting of Rickenbacker's autobiography by Booten Herndon, a freelance writer from Charlottesville, Virginia.

6. For a perceptive analysis of the behavioral expectations pervading the "Boy Culture" in which Rickenbacker grew up, see E. Anthony Rotundo, *American Manhood: Transformations in Masculinity from the Revolution to the Modern Era* (New York: Basic Books, 1993), 31–55. On tendencies among highly sensitive people to devalue the very traits that make them exceptional, see Elaine N. Aron, *The Highly Sensitive Person* (Secaucus, N.J.: Carol, 1996), 3–22.

7. Richard E. Barnett, *"Made in Columbus" Automobiles* (Columbus, Ohio: Columbus Historical Society, 1994).

8. Charles E. Tuttle, "Columbus Buggy Company," parts 1 and 2, in *Carriage Journal* 15 (spring 1978): 386–91, and 16 (summer 1978): 7–14.

9. For a synopsis of Rickenbacker's racing career, see Edward V. Rickenbacker Papers, Library of Congress, Washington, D.C. (hereafter cited EVRP), folder marked "Racing Data," box 23.

10. William Mitchell, "Rickenbacker—The Ace of the American Expeditionary Force," in Frank C. Platt, *Great Battles of World War I* (New York: Weathervane Books, 1966), 90.

11. Later to become famous as Carl Spaatz, this officer then spelled his surname with only one *a*.

12. "Eddie Rickenbacker Discusses Flying," newspaper clipping in Rickenbacker Scrapbooks, Auburn University Archives (hereafter cited as AUA), scrapbook 1 (1913–22).

13. On the history of the Ninety-fourth Aero Pursuit Squadron and Rickenbacker's role in it, see "Gorrell's History of the American Expeditionary Forces Air Service, 1917–1919," M990, series E, vol. 12, National Archives, Washington, D.C. For Rickenbacker's own account of his wartime experiences, see his book *Fighting the Flying Circus* (New York: Frederick A. Stokes, 1919).

14. For historical perspective on this phenomenon, see Clive James, *Fame in the Twentieth Century* (New York: Random House, 1993).

15. Numerous newspaper accounts pertaining to events honoring Rickenbacker in 1919 are contained in "Clippings, 1913–1922," the first of twenty-six Rickenbacker scrapbooks at the AUA.

16. For a good example of a remarkable business career built with great difficulty on barnstorming, stunt flying, and aerial racing by an entrepreneur whose social and educational background was similar to Rickenbacker's, see Carroll V. Glines, *Roscoe Turner: Aviation's Master Showman* (Washington, D.C.: Smithsonian Institution Press, 1995).

17. On the brief history of this vehicle, see Nick Baldwin, G. N. Georgano, Michael Sedgwick, and Brian Laban, *The World Guide to Automobile Manufacturers* (New York: Facts on File, 1987), 198, 247.

18. On the history of the Rickenbacker Motor Company, see Beverly Rae Kimes, "Hat in the Ring: The Rickenbacker," *Automobile Quarterly* 13, no. 4 (1975): 418–35, and Stephen G. Ostrander, "A Car Worthy of the Name," *Michigan History Magazine,* January–February 1992, 25–27, on which the discussion that follows is largely based.

19. "Rickenbacker Material Collected by Isabel Leighton," AUA. Leighton interviewed numerous persons who knew Adelaide Rickenbacker for Eureka Pictures in 1943 before the making of *Captain Eddie.*

20. California divorce decree of 10 July 1922 and a diary kept by EVR during his three-month honeymoon, both in AUA.

21. Articles of indenture between William C. Durant and Guaranty Trust Company of New York, 31 December 1918, AVA; interview by author of William Frost Rickenbacker, October 6, 1994.

22. For detailed information on Indian Village Manor, see "Detroit—Apartment Houses H-J," folder in Burton Historical Collection, Detroit Public Library, Detroit. Before leaving Detroit, Rickenbacker and his wife also lived in a large house in Grosse Pointe. Farr, *Rickenbacker's Luck,* 166.

23. Newspaper clippings and magazine articles about this vehicle and the engine designed to power it are in a Rickenbacker scrapbook, "Clippings 1920–1935," AUA.

24. Albert LeShane Jr., "Florida Airways," *Journal of the American Aviation Historical Society* 22, no. 2 (2d quarter, 1977), 123–35.

25. On AVCO's tangled history, see Henry Ladd Smith, *Airways: The History of Commercial Aviation in the United States* (New York: Knopf, 1942), 147–55, and Davies, *Airlines of the United States,* 99–101.

26. On this episode, see esp. Robert J. Serling, *Eagle: The Story of American Airlines* (New York: St. Martin's/Marek, 1985), 42–44, and Rudy Abramson, *Spanning the Century: The Life of W. Averell Harriman, 1891–1986* (New York: Morrow, 1992), 186–208.

27. For a detailed account of Eastern's development before and after its acquisition by General Motors, see "History of Eastern Air Lines," typewritten document at Rockefeller Archives Center, North Tarrytown, N.Y. (hereafter cited as RAC), Rockefeller Family Archives, Record Group 2.

28. See esp. Smith, *Airways,* 249–58. In addition to biographical works already cited, see Robert J. Serling, "Unsung Hero: Frye of TWA," *Airways* 3 (May–June 1996): 24–26. As Serling says, Rickenbacker "went along for the ride" and "hardly touched the controls" during the flight.

29. For a perceptive analysis of related developments, see Douglas B. Craig, *After Wilson: The Struggle for the Democratic Party, 1920–1934* (Chapel Hill: University of North Carolina Press, 1992). A close reading of this book is indispensable to understanding Rickenbacker's fervent opposition to the New Deal.

30. See esp. George E. Hopkins, *The Airline Pilots: A Study in Elite Unionization* (Cambridge: Harvard University Press, 1971).

31. On Eastern's gains in this period, see esp. "History of Eastern Air Lines," RAC, 22–27, and North American Aviation, Inc., annual report, 1937, at National Air and Space Museum (NASM).

32. In addition to the account of this episode in Rickenbacker, *Autobiography,* 190–94, see also Alfred P. Sloan Jr., *My Years with General Motors* (Garden City, N.Y.: Doubleday Anchor Books, 1972), 427–28. On Laurance S. Rockefeller's involvement as a venture capitalist in Eastern Air Lines and other aerospace enterprises, see Peter Collier and David Horowitz, *The Rockefellers: An American Dynasty* (New York: Holt, Rinehart and Winston, 1976), 217–18, 292–303.

33. Smith, *Airways,* 301–9; Nick A. Komons, "Civil Aeronautics Administration" and Donald R. Whitnah, "Civil Aeronautics Board," in Leary, *Airline Industry,* 101–8. For the best study of the evolution of federal policy toward the airlines throughout this entire period generally, see Nick A. Komons, *Bonfires to Beacons: Federal Civil Aviation Policy under the Air Commerce Act, 1926–1938,* reprinted ed. (Washington, D.C.: Smithsonian Institution Press, 1989).

34. Serling, *From the Captain to the Colonel,* 148–51.

35. Eastern Air Lines, Inc., annual reports, 1938, 9, and 1940, 6.

36. Ibid., 1941, 5–6, and 1942, 1–2.

37. Interview by author with Donald W. Nyrop. The favorable impression given me by Nyrop of Rickenbacker's administrative ability, coming from a person who had a unique career as chairman of the Civil Aeronautics Board and chief executive of a major airline, had a major impact on the interpretation advanced in this essay.

38. Eastern Air Lines, Inc., annual report, 1940, 3–8; *The Great Silver Fleet News* 5, no. 3 (1940): 1, and 6, no. 4 (1940): 7.

39. The Rickenbacker scrapbooks at AUA contain hundreds of clippings relating to the crash. For an official analysis, see *Report of the Civil Aeronautics Board . . . Released June 13, 1941.*

40. In addition to the account of the raft ordeal in *Autobiography,* 296–339, see also Rickenbacker's *Seven Came Through* (Garden City, N.Y.: Doubleday, Doran, 1943). For a recent article on the episode based on a wealth of previously unknown or unexamined evidence, see W. David Lewis, "The Rescue of Eddie Rickenbacker," *Air and Space/Smithsonian* 13 (August-September 1998): 64–71.

41. Lewis, "Edward V. Rickenbacker," 408. For a listing of Eastern Air Lines aircraft surrendered for military use during the war, see Arthur Pearcy, *Douglas Propliners DC-1–DC-7* (Shrewsbury, England: Airlife, 1995), 78–79. For a detailed account of Eastern's contribution to the war effort, see Robert J. Serling, *When the Airlines Went to War* (New York: Kensington Books, 1997), 162–70.

42. "Eddie Rickenbacker's Own Story," *Life,* January 25, 1943, 19–26, 90–99; "Pacific Mission," *Life,* February 2, 1943, 79–92, and February 9, 1943, 95–106; "When a Man Faces Death," *American,* November 1943, 20–21, 117–19; Folders, "*Captain Eddie* Movie Picture" and "E. V. Rickenbacker Magazine Articles," EVRP, Boxes 9, 20. The Ohio Historical Society in Columbus has a script of the film. The motion picture itself is privately owned and unavailable for public showing, but AUA has a taped copy supplied by John F. Barrek, a survivor of the raft episode.

43. Interview by author of Birdie Bomar.

44. Information supplied to author by V. E. Gouldener on December 30, 1998. Gouldener, who joined Eastern in 1940, started as operations agent/radio operator and advanced to supervisor, station manager, and regional director, serving at fourteen locations on the airline. I am pleased that Gouldener, who read the manuscript of this essay, endorses my interpretation of Rickenbacker's managerial career.

45. Serling, *From the Captain to the Colonel,* 204.

46. Eastern Air Lines, annual reports for 1944, 5, 10 and 1945, 5.

47. Eastern Air Lines, annual reports for 1946, 6–7 and 1947, 7–8.

48. Interview of L. Welch Pogue by author.

49. Interview of William F. Rickenbacker by author.

50. Interview of L. Welch Pogue by author.

51. Interview of William M. Leary by author. Leary, now a distinguished historian of commercial aviation, once worked for Eastern as a flight dispatcher.

52. Serling, *From the Captain to the Colonel,* 277.

53. For a comprehensive account of the postwar rivalry between Eastern and Delta, see W. David Lewis and Wesley Phillips Newton, *Delta: The History of an Airline* (Athens: University of Georgia Press, 1979), 109–15, 120–31, 251–61, 283–346.

54. For detailed information on aircraft that Eastern adopted in the postwar era and the dates they were put in service, see George W. Cearley Jr., *Eastern Air Lines: An Illustrated History* (Dallas: privately published, 1983, 1985), 25–57.

55. For an account of the merger, see W. David Lewis and Wesley Phillips Newton, "The Delta–C&S Merger: A Case Study in Airline Consolidation and Federal Regulation," *Business History Review* 53 (summer 1979): 161–79.

56. Serling, *From the Captain to the Colonel,* 244–51; see also map in Eastern Air Lines, annual report, 1954.

57. Interview by author of L. Welch Pogue.

58. "Comments on Air Mail Subsidy and Competition," April 4, 1949, attached to Eastern Air Lines, annual report, 1949; Rickenbacker, *Autobiography,* 402.

59. Interview of Irving Roth, Washington, D.C., by author. On the reliance of board members upon their staffs, see Marylin Bender and Selig Altschul, *The Chosen Instrument* (New York: Simon and Schuster, 1982), 412–13.

60. Lewis and Newton, *Delta,* 251–61, 283–302; Serling, *From the Captain to the Colonel,* 323. For the text of the decision made by the CAB, see *CAB Reports* 33 (1961): 701–69.

61. Najeeb E. Halaby, *Crosswinds: An Airman's Memoir* (Garden City, N.Y.: Doubleday, 1978), quoted in Lewis, "Edward V. Rickenbacker," 413.

62. An account of this shakeup appeared in the *Miami Herald,* September 1, 1959. The copy at my disposal was accompanied by a letter to Rickenbacker on the same date from Eastern employee Ned Aitchison in which Aitchison stated, "To me, Eastern Air Lines always has, and always will, mean just one individual, Captain Eddie." Edward V. Rickenbacker Papers, Library of Congress, box A. This letter epitomizes the difficult position in which MacIntyre found himself in trying to assert his authority as chief executive officer, and the reason why Eastern's board of directors finally felt reluctantly impelled to force Rickenbacker to retire.

63. James J. Sloan Jr., *Wings of Honor: American Airmen in World War I* (Atglen, Penn.: Schiffer, 1994), 14–15.

64. On these developments, see esp. Serling, *From the Captain to the Colonel,* 310–47. On the failure of the merger with American, see also Lewis and Newton, *Delta,* 343. Rockefeller, in an interview with the author, indicated that he wanted to have Smith take command of Eastern.

65. Serling, *From the Captain to the Colonel,* 383–85; interviews of James E. Elkins, Floyd D. Hall, and Laurance S. Rockefeller by author. Elkins, a Houston banker and developer, was a member of the search committee that replaced Rickenbacker with Hall. Elkins attended the stormy meeting described here.

66. Letter from Robert J. Serling to author.

67. Typewritten report by Booten Herndon on his experience in ghostwriting Rickenbacker's autobiography, Virginia Commonwealth University Archives.

68. Interviews by author of William F. Rickenbacker, Marcia Rickenbacker, and Floyd D. Hall. Marcia Rickenbacker is a granddaughter of EVR by his son David.

69. R. E. G. Davies, *Airlines of the United States since 1914* (Washington: Smithsonian Institution Press, 1988), 532–33.

70. Serling, *From the Captain to the Colonel,* 305.

71. Lowell Thomas, *Good Evening, Everybody: From Cripple Creek to Samar-kand* (New York: Avon Books, 1976), 49.

Bibliographical Essay

An admirable character study of Rickenbacker is contained in Robert J. Serling, *From the Captain to the Colonel: An Informal History of Eastern Air Lines* (New York: Dial Press, 1988). Edward V. Rickenbacker, *Rickenbacker: An Autobiography* (Englewood Cliffs, N.J.: Prentice-Hall, 1967), ghostwritten by Booten Herndon, remains the most satisfactory book-length account of Rickenbacker's life, but contains misstatements of fact and must be used with caution. For an extended essay on Rickenbacker's life and career, see W. David Lewis, "Edward V. Rickenbacker," in William M. Leary, ed., *The Airline Industry* (New York: Facts on File, 1992), 398–415. Finis Farr, *Rickenbacker's Luck: An American Life* (Boston: Houghton Mifflin, 1979), lacks sufficient scope to do justice to its multifaceted subject but contains valuable insights about Rickenbacker's strengths and limitations. Hans Christian Adamson, *Eddie Rickenbacker* (New York: Macmillan, 1946), is well written but uncritical. Because of Adamson's role as Rickenbacker's aide in 1942, it contains much firsthand information about the raft episode that occurred late that year. One of its major limitations is that it was written too early to cover Rickenbacker's career after World War II.

Information about specific phases of Rickenbacker's life is available in his World War I memoir, *Fighting the Flying Circus* (New York: Frederick J. Stokes, 1919), which was ghostwritten by Laurence LaTourette Driggs, and *Seven Came Through* (Garden City, N.Y.: Doubleday, 1943), Rickenbacker's account of the 1942 raft episode. An abridged version of *Fighting the Flying Circus* was published in 1997 under my editorship in R. R. Donnelley and Sons Company's Lakeside Classics Series (Chicago: Lakeside Press, 1997), with a historical introduction, annotations, and epilogue. For an explanation of Driggs's role in ghostwriting the book and its limitations as a source of dependable factual information, see my article, "Ghostwriting for the Ace of Aces: Laurence LaTourette Driggs and the Authorship of Eddie Rickenbacker's *Fighting the Flying Circus,*" in *W.W.1 Aero: The Journal of the Early Aeroplane,* no. 160 (May 1998): 20–28. For an up-to-date account of the 1942 raft episode, see W. David Lewis, "The Rescue of Eddie Rickenbacker," in *Air and Space/Smithsonian* 13 (September 1998): 63–71.

Serling, *From the Captain to the Colonel,* is the best available history of Eastern Air Lines up to 1988, the date of its publication. For an essay carrying the history of the company up to its ultimate bankruptcy in 1991, see W. David Lewis,

"Eastern Air Lines," in Leary, ed., *Airline Industry,* mentioned above. Also see George Walker Cearley Jr., *Eastern Air Lines: An Illustrated History* (Dallas: privately published, 1983, 1985), for detailed information on airliners, timetables, logos, and company advertising.

There are four large manuscript collections relating to Rickenbacker at Auburn University, the Library of Congress, the Ohio State University Library, and the U.S. Air Force Museum. The Auburn University collection is particularly notable for twenty-six scrapbooks full of newspaper clippings pertaining to every phase of Rickenbacker's life. It also includes letters, diaries, interviews, photographs, and four bound volumes of Rickenbacker's staff presentations. Materials of great value at the Ohio State University Library include a long typescript, "Life Story," of Rickenbacker based on interviews conducted in connection with the making of *Captain Eddie,* a film released in 1945 by Twentieth Century Fox. The Edward V. Rickenbacker Papers at the Library of Congress include 130 boxes of materials pertaining to his life and career, including taped interviews with Booten Herndon, the ghostwriter of his autobiography, conducted in 1967. The U.S. Air Force Museum has diaries kept by Rickenbacker in 1918 and 1919, orders and other documents connected with his military career, a large collection of photographs, and a duplicate set of transcribed copies of Rickenbacker's taped interviews with Booten Herndon in 1965.

The Rockefeller Archives Center, North Tarrytown, N.Y., has a large collection of letters, memoranda, and other materials related to the role Rickenbacker played as chief executive of Eastern Air Lines. The Eleutherian Mills Historical Library, Wilmington, Delaware, has valuable materials relating to Eastern Air Transport and Rickenbacker's connections with General Motors. Other collections and newspaper files relating to specific periods in Rickenbacker's life are at the editorial offices of *Automobile Quarterly,* Kutztown, Penn., the Herbert Hoover Presidential Library, West Branch, Iowa, the Iowa State Historical Society, Des Moines, the National Air and Space Museum, Washington, D.C., and the National Archives, Washington, D.C.

Robert E. Peach and Mohawk Airlines: A Study in Entrepreneurship

WILLIAM M. LEARY

OHAWK AIRLINES STANDS IN THE FOREFRONT of the local service or feeder airlines that emerged in the United States after World War II. Under the aggressive and dynamic leadership of Robert E. Peach, Mohawk grew from a tiny air taxi service that carried 1,200 passengers in 1945 between Ithaca and New York City to a major regional airline that transported 2.7 million passengers in 1969 along an extensive network of routes in the northeastern United States. During these years, Mohawk became known as a pioneer in the industry. It was the first local service carrier to introduce pressurized aircraft. Later, it was the first to purchase and operate jet transports. It was the first airline in the country to adopt a Telepak telephone communications and reservations system in combination with a Univac computer reservations center. And it was the first airline in the United States to hire an African American stewardess.

Mohawk's growth took place during an era in which the Civil Aeronautics Board (CAB) exercised broad authority over U.S. air carriers. Under the Civil Aeronautics Act of 1938, the CAB had the power to issue certificates of convenience and necessity and thereby control the entry of aspiring companies into the world of U.S. scheduled airlines. It decided routes, prescribed rates, paid subsidies, and performed other functions to promote and stabilize the nation's air transport industry.

*Mohawk executives inspect Convair 240 at Grand Central Airport, Glendale,
California, 1955: (left to right) Robert Peach Jr., Robert Peach, E. A. Butterfield,
Remington Taylor, Carl Benscoter. (Author's collection)*

The relationship between Mohawk's Peach and the CAB could most
charitably be termed dynamic. Ambitious for the success of his airline,
Peach constantly pushed for longer routes and better airplanes. The CAB,
however, saw Mohawk—along with the other local service carriers—as
occupying a modest niche in the nation's air transport system, enabling
people in smaller cities to connect with the established trunk carriers.
Although the CAB resisted Mohawk's efforts to compete with these major trunk carriers on heavily traveled routes, it wanted the airline to be
sufficiently profitable so that subsidy would not be necessary. But operating only short routes that carried few passengers meant that Mohawk
could never turn a profit. Unable to resolve this dilemma, the CAB failed
to adopt a consistent policy in dealing with the airline. An ambivalent
CAB and a determined Peach made for a volatile situation.

The story of Mohawk Airline and Robert Peach can be viewed as a case study of the clash between the imperatives of free enterprise and the demands of a regulated economy. It sheds considerable light on the dynamics of the pre-deregulation era of the U.S. airline industry.

The Birth of an Airline

On December 12, 1941, five days after the Japanese attack on Pearl Harbor plunged the United States into World War II, the Civil Aeronautics Board suspended action on requests for new routes. The CAB obviously believed that a period of wartime emergency was no time to be considering any expansion of air service. By mid-1943, however, with over 400 applications pending for new domestic and international routes, the CAB decided to end its restrictive policy. There was an "urgent need" to start the administrative machinery in motion, the CAB pointed out, "not only to prepare for aviation's future but to prevent the calendar of the Board from growing to insurmountable proportions."[1]

Even before the CAB began to consider the flood of applications for new service, it had responded to pressure from local communities and their political representatives by instituting a general investigation into the possibility of providing air service to the nation's smaller cities. On March 22, 1943, the CAB opened docket no. 857, "Local-Feeder-Pickup Air Service," with hearings held between September 28 and October 25, 1943.

The CAB's examiners submitted their report and recommendations on February 9, 1944. After receiving comments and hearing oral arguments, the CAB rendered its opinion on July 11, 1944. While recognizing that the air traffic potential of smaller cities was "not encouraging," the CAB nonetheless decided to authorize a new category of feeder or local service airlines on an experimental basis. Applicants that could meet the test of public convenience and necessity would be granted temporary certificates and would be eligible for subsidy in the form of mail pay.[2]

One of the many aspirants for the new certificates was C. S. Robinson, an inventor and businessman from Ithaca, New York. Robinson had been an aerial photographer before World War II. When taking pictures from high altitudes, he found that the rubber mounting for his camera became hard and caused vibration. Robinson invented and patented a cushioning device that was made from spun stainless steel. After the war broke out, he expanded the operations of Robinson Aviation to Teterboro, New Jersey, where he built a factory to provide the military services with shock mounts for their radios and instruments.[3]

Robinson often flew a Fairchild F-24, with seats for three passengers, between Ithaca and Teterboro. Encountering a constant stream of fellow Ithacans who wanted to hitch a ride, he recognized a business opportunity and began to charge the hitchhikers. Aware of the traffic potential on the route from upstate New York to the New York metropolitan area, on April 1, 1945, he filed an application with the CAB for a feeder certificate to serve Buffalo, Rochester, Ithaca, Binghamton, Albany, New York City, and Washington, D.C. In order to demonstrate his ability to conduct air services along the proposed route, Robinson established the airline division of Robinson Aviation and on April 6 began a scheduled air taxi service between Ithaca and New York City.[4]

Robinson initially operated two Fairchild F-24s on the route. Traffic proved so encouraging, however, that he bought two four-passenger Cessna T-50s and hired additional pilots. One of the new pilots, Robert E. Peach, turned out to be more important to the company's success than the quickly outmoded Cessnas.

Pioneering Executive

Born in Syracuse, New York, on March 9, 1920, Peach graduated from Hamilton College in 1941. He entered law school at the University of Chicago in the fall of 1941, but left to join the navy early in 1942. Following pilot training, he saw action in the Pacific, where he commanded a squadron of patrol planes. Peach compiled a distinguished war record, rising to the rank of lieutenant commander and winning two Distinguished Flying Crosses and other decorations for valor.[5]

Following his release from active duty in the fall of 1945, Peach resumed the study of law at Cornell University. When Robinson came looking for a part-time pilot for his expanding air taxi business, Peach seized the opportunity to return to the cockpit and add to the income that he was receiving under the Servicemen's Readjustment Act ("GI Bill of Rights").

Within a short time—in Peach's own words—Robinson Airlines clearly had "a bear by the tail." By the end of 1945, the airline had carried 1,200 passengers. On January 22, 1946, service began to Buffalo. With passenger volume increasing, the airline on April 1 purchased the first of four seven-passenger twin-engine Beechcraft D-18s. The route system—confined to New York State and therefore not requiring the blessing of the CAB, as long as no subsidy was involved—continued to expand, with Binghamton added on May 23 and Albany on July 1. On December 1, 1946, Robinson formed the Robinson Airline Corporation to handle an air transport enterprise that would carry 12,000 passengers annually. By this time, Peach had become so impressed with the potential of the airline that he had quit school to become traffic manager of the company.[6]

As Robinson grew, it developed the infrastructure of a proper airline, with a company radio system, teletype circuit, flight control procedures, and regular maintenance schedules. Passenger traffic continued to increase, reaching 28,700 in 1947. Despite the growth, or perhaps because of it, the airline lost money, registering a $264,000 deficit in 1947. Clearly, a subsidy would be necessary.

Achieving Feederline Status

The problem that faced C. S. Robinson and Peach was to keep the airline in business while waiting for the Civil Aeronautics Board to act on the company's application for certification. If granted, the airline would be eligible for the needed subsidy. But the CAB was not to be rushed.

Flooded with applications for feeder service, the CAB consolidated the requests into eleven regional cases. The first decision came in March 1946. In the Rocky Mountain Air Service Case, the CAB set forth the guiding principles for feeder services. "Certificates for local feeder service," the CAB observed, "are issued only to such operations as show a justifiable expectation of success at a reasonable cost to the government." The certificates would be limited to an "experimental period" of three years. The CAB authorized a temporary subsidy rate of 25 cents a mile (increased to 35 cents in 1947).[7]

Action on Robinson Airlines, part of the Middle Atlantic Air Service Case, remained painfully slow, however. Not until March 12, 1947, did the CAB's examiner report favorably on the company's application. It then took another three months before C. S. Robinson was called before the CAB to present his brief and financial statements.

While the wheels of the bureaucracy ground slowly, C. S. Robinson searched for financial backing to keep his airline flying—and with some success. Ithaca Enterprises, a nonprofit organization responsible for bringing new businesses to Ithaca, agreed to purchase $12,000 of the airline's stock. The Cooperative Grange League Federation Exchange took a similar amount, and Cornell University signed up for $10,000. In all, C. S. Robinson hoped to raise $40,000 to $50,000 from local industries.

Robinson was especially anxious to obtain the backing of Edwin A. Link, the inventor of the widely used "Link Trainer," who had a factory in Binghamton. In April 1947, following receipt of the favorable report from the CAB examiner, Robinson wrote to Link and outlined the financial status of the airline. He had sold 24,000 shares of stock at $3 a share. Robinson proposed to sell 65,000 additional shares, raising $195,000. These funds would enable the airline to sustain operating losses while awaiting certification and to purchase or lease two DC-3s.[8]

While Link was prepared to invest in the company, he wanted assurances with regard to control of the airline. No doubt tales of C. S. Robinson's casual managerial practices had reached him. More than once, Robinson had walked into the airport ticket office in Ithaca and simply scooped out all the cash in the drawer and put it in his pocket.[9] In June 1947, Robinson and Link reached an agreement. Link purchased 16,700 shares of stock for $50,100 ($3 a share). In return, Robinson agreed to assign voting rights of sufficient airline stock to a neutral third party so that he and his family would not control more than 49 percent of the stock. Decisions by a majority of the airline's board of directors would be binding despite stock ownership.[10]

Link also came to the company's rescue as it struggled to meet rising passenger demands for its services. In the summer of 1947, he lent the airline $75,000 to purchase the first of three secondhand 21-passenger DC-3s to replace the D-18s.

On February 20, 1948, the CAB finally announced the awards for the Middle Atlantic Air Service Case. Three companies received certification for air routes for the first time, including Robinson Airlines. The CAB's three-year certificate authorized Robinson to fly from New York City to Binghamton via Middleton, and from Binghamton to Albany via Elmira, Ithaca, Syracuse, Auburn, Geneva, Rochester, and Batavia. The certificate included the prized airmail contract without which, Peach emphasized, "an airline cannot exist."[11]

By the time Robinson Airlines received the long-awaited certificate, the company's debt had reached $461,000. Before certificated operations could begin, additional financing had to be found. The promise of subsidy, however, made it possible to sell $500,000 in convertible debentures (later converted to common stock) to Endicott-Johnson, International Business Machine, National Cash Register, and other leading industries in upstate New York that would benefit from the air service.[12]

Certificated flight operations began on September 19, 1948. By this time, three former wartime pilots held the key managerial positions with the airline. Peach had become general manager and was in overall charge of the company. His top assistants were operations manager Carl A. Benscoter and John R. Carver, who handled legal and financial matters.

Challenge and Response

The three men faced a difficult challenge as the airline—in Peach's word's— "suffered badly from growing pains." Keeping the three DC-3s in the air was no easy task. All maintenance had to be conducted outdoors, and there was a minimum of spare parts. Cash flow was a constant headache. At one point, Charles Johnson of Endicott-Johnson came to the airline's rescue and advanced enough money so that Peach could meet his payroll. In return, Johnson accepted free flying for his company's executives as repayment for the loan. It came as no surprise to Peach to learn that the airline had suffered a net loss of $184,000 for 1948; it could have been worse![13]

Traffic continued to grow as upstate New Yorkers, mainly businessmen, took increasing advantage of the new air service. In 1949, with the airline now operating five DC-3s with a total seating capacity of 105, 43,000 passengers flew on Robinson Airlines. Peach struggled to reduce costs. For example, male flight attendants replaced stewardesses on the DC-3s; the men could handle mail and baggage. But it proved a losing fight. Although revenue for 1949 soared to $500,000, double the figure for 1948, the net loss for the year increased to $200,000.[14]

C. S. Robinson, who had taken little part in the company's day-to-day operations since certification, decided that the airline business was not for him. In June 1949, he resigned as a director of the company. In the reorganization that followed his departure, E. Victor Underwood, president of the Cooperative Grange League Federation Holding Company, became chairman of the board of directors and Peach became executive vice president as well as general manager of the airline.[15]

Peach had hoped that federal subsidy would cover the airline's losses and provide a source of working capital. He soon learned, however, that the CAB proceeded at a glacial pace in providing the money. By the end of 1949, the airline had received nothing from the CAB for the first sixteen months of operations. Peach wanted $190,000 in mail pay and a rate of 70 cents per plane mile. Not until March 1950 did the CAB authorize retroactive mail pay of $155,000 and a rate of 50 cents per mile. Although the mail rate staff at the CAB had favored Robinson's request, the legal department had decided—"arbitrarily," according to Peach—that the airline's costs had been too high. The airline accepted the award "under protest."[16]

As Peach struggled to hold down costs, the CAB seemed to be sending mixed messages to the local service operators. In November 1950, Peach complained to CAB chairman Delos W. Rentzel that a recent examiner's report had favored high pay for local service pilots. Peach pointed out that the salaries for Robinson's top four executives in 1949 had been $10,000, $9,500, $9,200, and $7,200. At the same time, the *average* pay for the airline's captains had been $8,953, with two captains making more money than Robinson's chief pilot and operations manager.

"Although I can assure you that the subsidy stigma is repugnant to all the local service carriers," Peach wrote to Rentzel, "our own company has regretfully decided that attaining economic self-sufficiency is impossible unless the Civil Aeronautics Board is willing to take a firm stand with regard to the presently excessive demands of organized labor." Should the CAB give in to organized labor, Peach warned, "the unions can and may well put us out of business."[17]

Peach had more than rising labor costs to worry about in 1950. On September 4, Robinson suffered its first fatal accident. Flight no. 31, a DC-3 flown by Harold L. Carter, had just lifted off from Oneida County Airport with twenty passengers for Newark when a cylinder on the left engine exploded. Carter feathered the engine's propeller and tried to continue his climb, but the left wing hit the tops of trees, causing the aircraft to cartwheel into a nearby pasture. Thirteen passengers and three crew members died.[18]

Mohawk DC-3 used for successful "Gas Light Service" in the early 1960s. (Author's collection)

Peach received some good news, however, in February 1951, when CAB examiner Edward T. Stodola reported his investigation into the renewal of Robinson's three-year temporary certificate. Stodola noted that Robinson, which carried over 100,000 passengers in 1951, had made "steady progress" in developing daily passenger traffic. At the same time, the airline had been equally successful in reducing operating costs. Robinson's total operating expenses for 1949 had been $1.82 per revenue ton-mile. During the first two quarters of 1951, this figure had fallen to $1.00.

Robinson's record of successful operations, he concluded, "leaves no doubt that it is fit, willing and able to perform the services herein found required by the public convenience and necessity." Stodola recommended a extension of Robinson's certificate for an unprecedented period of ten years. The airline, he emphasized, "now badly needs a longer breathing space from the uncertainties of recertification to help it do the best job possible."[19]

While not willing to grant the full ten years, the CAB did authorize a renewal of seven years, the longest period ever granted a local service carrier. To celebrate the CAB's ringing endorsement, Robinson's management decided to conduct a contest to rename the airline. Employees submitted some 2,200 entries, with the top three names Mohawk Airlines, Atlantic Airlines, and Yankee Airlines. In June 1952, Robinson's board of directors voted for Mohawk Airlines.[20]

The Problems of Growth

The newly renamed Mohawk saw a continued increase in passenger traffic. With nine DC-3s in operation, the airline flew 106,000 passengers (18 million passenger-miles) in 1952, and 162,000 passengers (27.1 million passenger-miles) in 1953.

Financial problems, however, continued to plague the airline's management. Working capital, Peach reported to the airline's board of directors in 1952, remained "critically short." The company had been undercapitalized since its inception. As the airline expanded its operations, replacements for the DC-3s would become necessary, and this would require new equity capital.[21]

Another theme that runs consistently throughout the airline's history involves costs and subsidy. On December 13, 1953, CAB chairman Oswald Ryan wrote to the presidents of all local service carriers and expressed his concern over rising mail payments. Subsidy for local service carriers had increased from $11.6 million in 1948 to $21.5 million in 1952. Ryan pointed to the airlines' spiraling costs, noting that 55 percent of these costs represented wages. Two days later, Ryan met with the presidents of the local service airlines and reiterated the CAB's concern about rising wage costs. Higher wages for pilots and other employees, he stressed, should be tied to increased revenue rather than the scale of trunk carrier employees.[22]

The pilots of the local service carriers, members of the Air Line Pilots Association (ALPA), had a different point of view. They believed that they were entitled to wage parity with their trunk carrier peers. In November 1953, Mohawk's pilots began negotiations with the company for a new contract. The pilots wanted a base pay increase of $10 a month and a mileage pay increase amounting to $35 a month. They also argued that newly promoted captains should be paid as though they had been captains since first employed.

Peach balked at the union's demands. The total dollar costs to Mohawk, he informed his board of directors, could amount to $80,000 a year. This sum would have an adverse impact on the company's ability to continue operations.

Mohawk's management applied to the National Mediation Board on December 3, 1953; they were told that a mediator would not be available until March. While the pilots flew without a contract, which expired on January 1, 1954, the airline's management received mixed signals about its hold-the-line position on wages. While Frontier Airlines and Piedmont Airlines refused to grant high wage increases in contracts negotiated with their pilots in March, Allegheny Airlines signed a contract with ALPA that gave their pilots everything they wanted. As Peach pointed out, the Allegheny contract "represented a substantial victory for the pilots." Shortly thereafter, Allegheny applied to the CAB for increased subsidy.

In the wake of the Allegheny settlement, the CAB restated its opposition to increased labor costs. On March 19, 1954, the new CAB chairman, Chan Gurney, wrote to the presidents of the local service carriers and again voiced the CAB's concern over rising costs. He urged the presidents to pay close attention to reducing their subsidy needs, warning that certificate renewal, route extensions, and other vital factors affecting their future depended upon the trend toward lower mail pay.

Mohawk's pilots, not surprisingly, saw the Allegheny contract as setting a precedent. When mediation began in late March 1954, they demanded equal treatment, with wage increases that ranged from $90 to $648 a month. The airline's management countered with an offer that was similar to the union's recently signed contract with Frontier and Piedmont; it fell short of the Allegheny agreement by at least $25 a month per pilot. The two sides deadlocked. Negotiations broke off on April 5 and mediation was terminated.

Peach expressed his frustration when he reported to the board of directors on April 19. In 1953, he pointed out, pilots comprised 10 percent of the airline's employees and accounted for 26 percent of its payroll. The average captain made $10,000. Only the company's top three executives were paid more money that the *average* captain. Given the costs of running an airline, he emphasized, the demands of the pilots were excessive.

Short-haul transportation, Peach reminded the board, always had to deal with small margins of profit. Furthermore, uncontrolled labor costs and featherbedding had nearly destroyed the nation's railroads, merchant marine, and urban bus transport. "I firmly believe, as do the other officers and executive personnel, that here is the place to draw the line."[23]

Mohawk's directors agreed. On May 14, they endorsed management's policy, even if it resulted in a strike.[24]

ALPA seemed equally determined and called for a strike to begin at midnight on July 12, 1954. Three weeks before the scheduled work stoppage, Peach met in Chicago with ALPA president Clarence N. Sayen and representatives of Mohawk's pilots in a last minute effort to settle the dispute. With the assistance of Frank O'Neill, chairman of the National Mediation Board, the two sides narrowed their areas of disagreement to $5 a month and several months of retroactive pay. Despite a 21-hour session between Peach and Sayen, the two sides could not bridge the gap.

Peach reported the results of his negotiations to Mohawk's board on July 10. The board voted to maintain management's position. On Monday, July 12, Peach informed the CAB that the airline would shut down at midnight. At 11:15 p.m., after eight hours of continuous telephone contact with chairman O'Neill of the National Mediation Board, ALPA caved in and accepted the same contract that Peach had offered in Chicago the previous week. It gave the pilots a pay scale of approximately $10 a month below the Allegheny contract level. As Peach pointed out, "This marks one of the few times a local carrier has signed a pilot contract at a lower wage level than the preceding ALPA contract settlement in the industry."[25]

Although management could claim victory in the dispute, it had not been achieved without a price. The direct costs of eight months of negotiation had amounted to $25,000. Loss of passenger revenue because of the publicity about the proposed strike was estimated at another $25,000. Wage costs under the new contract, including across-the-board percentage increases for all employees, would amount to more than $50,000 a year. Finally, the lengthy and frequently acrimonious negotiations produced an atmosphere of bitterness and distrust between the pilots and management that would linger for years to come.

The Politics of Permanent Certification

The contract dispute with the pilots came as Peach was deeply involved in the political battle over permanent certification for local service carriers. The presidents of the feeder airlines—and their many supporters in Congress—believed that the experimental period of operations had amply proved the necessity for the air service. Local service carriers, they pointed out, had a route structure by 1953 that totaled 30,000 miles and served 440 cities in forty-two states. The airlines carried nearly 2 million passengers in 1953, while generating $24.3 million in revenue. In 1954, legislation was introduced in Congress "to assist and stabilize" the operations of local service carriers by issuing permanent certificates of convenience and necessity.[26]

The local service airlines had a powerful and effective advocate during the hearings before congressional committees in April and June 1954. Donald W. Nyrop, the Washington counsel of the Conference of Local Airlines, had been head of the Civil Aeronautics Administration in 1950–51, and CAB chairman in 1951–52. While noting the substantial growth of the local service carriers, Nyrop pointed to the continuing problems of the industry. Short-term certification made it difficult for the airlines to attract equity capital and to secure loans. Permanent certificates would not only alleviate these problems but enable the management of the carriers "to devote their full time and energy toward building their airlines instead of fighting a rearguard action in protecting the routes they have developed."[27]

Sinclair Weeks, secretary of commerce in the Dwight D. Eisenhower administration, opposed the legislation. A change in the duration of the route certificates, he believed, would be "unsound policy." CAB chairman Chan Gurney agreed. "Personally," he told Congress, "I like the local service carriers." The CAB also liked them, he said. "We think they are doing a great service." However, Gurney noted, the CAB continued to regard local air service as in the "developmental stage." The CAB did not consider the future of the local service carriers "sufficiently predictable with respect to routes, type of service, or manner of operation to warrant permanent certificates at this time on an industrywide basis."[28]

Despite the opposition of senior officials in the Eisenhower administration, the political support in Congress for permanent certification proved overwhelming. As Representative Lloyd M. Bentsen Jr., Democrat from Texas, argued: "Local service airlines have been beneficial to the economy and welfare of our smaller communities. They have helped us by more rapid transportation to more closely integrate our economy and further the development of our country." Bentsen dismissed Gurney's arguments against permanent certification. "Obviously what should be paramount," he observed, "is the economy and stability of local airlines rather than what happens to suit the administrative convenience of the CAB." Bentsen's colleagues obviously agreed. Both houses of Congress passed the bill by unanimous vote. President Eisenhower signed it into law on May 19, 1955.[29]

Expansion

Four months before permanent certification became official, Mohawk Airlines took a major step toward modernizing its flight equipment. The airline had reached a point of maximum efficiency with its fleet of ten DC-3s in 1954, registering a passenger load factor of 62.1 percent, the highest in the local service industry. Although the airline modified the DC-3s to seat twenty-eight passengers, the need for more seating capacity became urgent. As Carl A. Benscoter, vice president for operations, observed, "We have squeezed every bit of cubic capacity out of the DC-3 cabin."[30]

Peach had anticipated this problem and in 1953 had hired a consultant to study possible replacements for the DC-3s. The consultant's report covered six different transports that might be compatible with Mohawk's route system; however, the airline's limited financial resources placed them all out of reach.

The possibility of finding a bargain seemed dim until 1954 when General Clair L. Chennault offered to sell five Convair 240s that had been recovered from the communist Chinese government after a lengthy legal battle in Hong Kong. The modern airliners, in superb condition, were part of a fleet that had been claimed by the Peking regime after it had come to power in 1949. While oil companies purchased two of the aircraft from Chennault, Mohawk obtained the right of first refusal on the remaining three.[31]

Peach lusted after the aircraft. These practically brand-new pressurized twin-engine transports could seat forty passengers. When fully loaded, Peach estimated that a Convair would earn a net profit of $432 per hour beyond direct flight costs; this compared with $211 for a DC-3. He planned to use the airplanes on Mohawk's heaviest traveled route segments: Buffalo to New York via Rochester, Syracuse, and Utica-Rome; and Buffalo to New York via Rochester, Ithaca, and Binghamton. He predicted that passenger traffic would increase by 26,000 a year. This would enable Mohawk to attain subsidy-free operations "within the next few years."[32]

Mohawk needed more than $1 million for the purchase. The three aircraft would cost $630,000. Another $200,000 would be required for modifications, plus $140,000 for spare parts. Costs for personnel training and a runway extension at Ithaca brought the total package to $1,050,000. On February 2, 1955, Mohawk's board of directors approved the purchase of the Convairs. The airline planned to cover the costs by raising new equity capital through stock sales and with a loan from the Chase Manhattan Bank. No doubt encouraged by the airline's pending permanent certification, Chase agreed to the loan in March 1955.[33]

The three Convairs went into service on July 1, 1955. Passenger response was enthusiastic. "Things are not humming at Mohawk," Board chairman Underwood wrote to Ed Link in September, "they are jumping." The airline would carry over 30,000 in September, averaging 1,000 a day for the first time. Passenger traffic had increased so rapidly that the airline had purchased another Convair from Northeast Airlines for $525,000. "It is a big price to pay," Underwood acknowledged, but Mohawk had had no choice.[34]

Mohawk's success with the Convairs continued. The first year's operating results with the new airplanes, Peach reported, had been "extremely gratifying." The four Convairs had carried 116,076 passengers during the first twelve months in service, with the fourth Convair available only during the last quarter. The load factor had been 55.5 percent. During the same period, Mohawk's ten DC-3s had carried 207,904 passengers, with a load factor of 58.8 percent. The purchase of the Convairs, Peach later observed, had marked "a turning point in Mohawk's coming of age as a truly regional carrier."[35]

So impressive had the public response been to the new equipment that in February 1956 Mohawk had taken an option on seven additional Convair 240s. The airplanes, owned by Swissair, were in excellent condition. The price, however, seemed daunting. The total package—including airplanes, nine zero-time engines and propellers, and the entire Swissair Convair parts inventory—amounted to $3,320,000. This was about the same as Mohawk's total assets, which in 1955 had totaled $3.8 million.[36]

Despite the high cost, Mohawk's board of directors promptly approved the purchase. The airline immediately secured a loan of $307,000 from the Chase Manhattan Bank for the down payment of the airplanes, due on March 12. The bank also agreed to refinance Mohawk's entire loan on existing and additional flight equipment if the company could secure new equity capital. By the summer of 1956, the airline managed to raise $3.5 million by issuing stocks and debentures and obtaining loans. "This is the largest flight equipment program ever undertaken by a small carrier," Peach noted with pride, "and will make Mohawk the second largest Convair-240 operator in the world." The Convairs went into service beginning in August 1956.[37]

Crisis and Reequipment

The CAB initially opposed Mohawk's new equipment purchases and dragged its heels in establishing a permanent rate for subsidies. In June 1957, Peach vented his frustration to the airline's board of directors. Mohawk, he pointed out, had the highest load factor in the local service industry and carried the second largest number of passengers on the smallest geographical route system. "As a reward for this relative efficiency," he noted, "the Civil Aeronautics Board has allowed our cash position to deteriorate through inadequate mail payments to an alarming degree, and it has paid us less than half the dollars in mail pay paid to the average local carrier."

The previous year, Peach continued, the CAB had paid Allegheny Airlines $2 million on a temporary mail rate. This was $600,000 more than Mohawk was seeking on a permanent rate. And Allegheny, with a load factor ten percentage points less than Mohawk's, was hardly a model of efficiency. "I pass this along to you," Peach concluded, "mostly so that you can share management's frustration."[38]

While waiting for the CAB to act, the airline's cash position continued to deteriorate. By July 1957, the situation had become so critical that Mohawk placed one of its Convairs up for sale. The next month, Peach informed CAB chairman James R. Durfee that the airline was in "a critical financial position." However, not until December 25, 1957, did the CAB grant Mohawk an increase in subsidy of $696,714, covering the period July 1, 1955, to December 31, 1957. This brought Mohawk's total subsidy payment for 1957 to $2.7 million. At the same time, the CAB directed the airline to submit within five days "a complete operational plan" designed to reduce subsidy requirements for 1958.[39]

Peach promptly produced a scheme that would increase service on densely traveled—and highly profitable—routes, while sharply reducing flights on less traveled routes to smaller communities. As he expected, the CAB rejected the plan on the grounds that the airline had an obligation to serve all communities on its route system. Mohawk and the CAB then began a series of lengthy negotiations. "Mohawk had to play for time," Peach later explained, "to let traffic results and moderating unit costs prove it was right."[40]

While these discussions were taking place, the CAB in 1958 embarked on a long overdue review of the entire local service industry. "It was apparent that the needs for expanded local air transportation from smaller communities to important metropolitan terminals would increase within the next few years," the CAB observed, "as trunkline carriers acquired more and faster aircraft in long-haul services." While the trunklines were moving toward jet transports, "certain local service carriers" were adding larger and improved twin-engined equipment to their DC-3 fleets. The time had come to determine the overall needs for local air transportation and the extent to which local carriers could fulfil these needs.[41]

The results of the investigation confirmed what Mohawk already had discovered: the economics of DC-3 operations favored reequipment. It cost the typical local service carrier $1.10 to $1.25 a mile to operate a DC-3. At current fare levels, the CAB observed, the airlines would have to carry an average of eighteen passengers per flight on a DC-3 to operate without subsidy. During 1957, however, the average passenger load was eleven. The problem, Mohawk knew well, stemmed from the fact that most short-haul routes did not generate enough traffic. Withdrawal of service from the low traffic routes, the CAB pointed out, would produce savings in subsidy. On the other hand, withdrawal would "so curtail local service as to render such service not more than an empty gesture."[42]

To carry out the mandate of Congress with increasing subsidy payments, the CAB decided to allow local service carriers to fly more lucrative routes in direct competition with the trunk carriers. Furthermore, the CAB acknowledged that no local service airline could become self-sufficient while flying only DC-3s. The American traveling public was entitled to local air service with faster, larger, more modern equipment. And the CAB agreed to underwrite, at least to a limited extent, the purchase of this new equipment.

With regard to Mohawk, in September 1958 the CAB proposed that the airline receive an annual subsidy of $2,074,706 (later set at $2.3 million). At the same time, it increased the allowable rate of return on investment, and it permitted a salary increase for the airline's chief executive from $20,000 to $25,000 a year.[43]

By 1960, the local service airlines had attained the size achieved by the domestic trunk carriers in 1940. Mohawk led the way. The airline in 1960 flew 116 million passenger-miles and had an operating revenue of $13.1 million. With a booming economy and a general increase in passenger traffic for the nation's airlines, Mohawk was poised for seven years of unprecedented growth.

Mohawk at Its Peak

In the late 1950s and early 1960s, the CAB rendered a series of decisions that substantially expanded Mohawk's route system. The airline gained access to a number of major cities, including Detroit, Cleveland, Pittsburgh, and Boston. The CAB also permitted Mohawk to fly nonstop between Syracuse and New York City, competing directly with American Airlines on this heavily traveled route.

In 1961 Mohawk underwent the largest route expansion in its history. As the trunk carriers acquired jet equipment and concentrated on profitable routes between major cities, they agreed to transfer shorter route segments to local service carriers. Mohawk acquired from Eastern Airlines the routes in eastern New York and Vermont that previously had been operated by Colonial Airlines before its acquisition by Eastern in 1956. This transfer increased Mohawk's operations by 45 percent. It meant new service to eight cities and a major nonstop route between Albany and New York City.

Mohawk needed additional equipment to handle the increased traffic. In 1960, it purchased five new 54-passenger Convair 440s. The following year, it bought fourteen Martin 404s from Eastern, primarily to use on the newly transferred routes. These acquisitions joined a fleet of fourteen Convair 240s and four DC-3s. The DC-3s, which had been flying a popular "Gaslight Service," with "Gay Nineties" decor, were retired in 1962.[44]

Peach, who was always thinking ahead, already had his sights set on grander equipment acquisitions. In the summer of 1961, he and Benscoter

Mohawk's first BAC One-Eleven rolls off the assembly line of the British Aircraft Factory at Bournemouth, March 21, 1965. (Author's collection)

traveled to Europe to investigate two new short-haul jets, the British Aircraft Corporation's BAC One-Eleven and Sud Aviation's Caravelle. On October 27, 1961, Mohawk's board agreed with Peach that the airline should provide jet service by the spring of 1965. It authorized him to negotiate with the British Aircraft Corporation for four jets and agreed to a $100,000 payment to the company upon signing a letter of intent.[45]

The BAC One-Eleven seemed ideal for Mohawk's route structure. It could carry sixty-nine passengers at 550 miles per hour and operate from most of the smaller airports that Mohawk used. In February 1962, Peach raised the possibility of purchasing the jets with CAB chairman Alan S. Boyd. Boyd assured both Peach and Sir George Edwards, managing director of the British Aircraft Corporation, that the purchase seemed "a sound business decision" and represented "the only reasonable course Mohawk could follow."[46]

With the appearance of a green light from the CAB, Peach concluded an agreement to purchase four BAC One-Elevens on July 24, 1962. This $17 million program, $2 million more than Mohawk's total assets in 1962, would be financed by issuance of $6 million in convertible debentures (at 5.5 percent interest), bank loans, and internally generated funds.[47]

Despite chairman Boyd's assurances, the CAB's staff seemed less inclined to go along with the plan to bring jet equipment into the short-haul market. In 1962, they made several attempts to force Mohawk to produce an entire forecast for system operations in 1966. Peach resisted these efforts. Mohawk was not obliged to provide this kind of information, which would immediately become known to its competitors, especially American Airlines. On December 14, 1962, the staff released to the press a letter from Boyd to Mohawk that threatened dire consequences should the airline acquire jets. Both Peach and Sir George Edwards immediately protested to Boyd. The CAB chairman said that he was "surprised and chagrined" to learn that the letter had been released to the press. "He is obviously embarrassed," Peach informed Mohawk's board. "I imagine we will survive this attack." One thing was for sure, Peach concluded. "This business is never dull."[48]

While awaiting the arrival of the new jets, Mohawk had a series of outstanding years that surpassed even Peach's most optimistic traffic projections. In 1962, the airline flew 206 million passenger-miles, the highest total in the local service industry. In 1966, Mohawk recorded a record 423 million passenger-miles. During the same five-year period, the rapidly growing airline posted total operating profits of $10.6 million. And this came at a time when subsidy payments decreased from $4.3 million in 1962 to $3.2 million in 1966. As Peach later remarked, these were Mohawk's "golden years."[49]

Robert Peach certainly was enjoying these golden years. His bold decision to acquire jet aircraft had thrust him into the forefront of air transport executives. In 1964, he received a signal honor from his peers when he was asked to address the Newcomen Society of North America on the history of Mohawk. The following year, Syracuse University awarded him the prestigious Salzberg Memorial Medal.

Peach used the occasion of the Salzberg award to reflect on the nature of managing a regional airline in a regulated environment. Privately owned and managed, he observed, regional airlines should be viewed as "aggressive, competitive, and new examples of free enterprise." They are in many ways comparable to public utilities that are franchised to serve a given territory. Although telephone, gas, and electric power companies are fully regulated with respect to charges, rate of return on investment, and quality of service, they all properly regard themselves as "champions of free enterprise."

An airline, on the other hand, is "an enfranchised public utility thrown open to competition." Governed by a rigid set of rules under which it must operate, it is bound to perform many unprofitable elements of public service, yet it is obligated to its stockholders to provide a maximum return on investment. This leads to the touchy question of subsidy.

It is important to understand, Peach emphasized, that subsidy "is not in any sense a guarantee of profit." On the contrary, it is a negotiated settlement between the airline and government over the cost of furnishing a service which the government orders and which both the government and the airline agree will not be profitable. "It is, therefore, in no sense an airline subsidy," Peach argued, "but is, instead, a community subsidy."

On the whole, Peach observed, the CAB has acted appropriately in the areas of route development and safety. However, the CAB has tended to use its subsidy power to interfere in areas that are more properly left to the airline's management. Congress has denied the CAB authority over the method by which an airline develops its financial structure and chooses its flight equipment. With regard to Mohawk, the most blatant example of the CAB's use of its subsidy power to exert pressure on management came with the decision to order Convair 240s. Over a three-year period, Peach recalled, the CAB imposed massive administrative disallowances of Mohawk's expenses when computing its "community subsidy." He stressed: "Under less enthusiastic public response and less determined and aggressive ownership and management, the company would have necessarily been liquidated."

The function of the CAB, Peach emphasized, is not to manage. It must refrain from second-guessing. He welcomed "fairly and consistently applied regulation." On the other hand, Peach deplored "governmental management by hindsight without the assumption of corollary management and ownership responsibility."

Mohawk, he noted with pride, had become the largest regional airline in the United States and one of the twenty-five largest scheduled airlines in the world. By the 1970s, he expected Mohawk to be operating an all-turbine-powered fleet with hourly shuttle service between New

York City and Albany and Syracuse. Dedicated to the earliest possible elimination of subsidy, the company had no desire to become a trunk-line. "We expect to remain a hungry airline devoted to first-rate, short-haul service," Peach concluded. "We expect fair competition but not destructive competition."[50]

The first BAC One-Eleven, christened *Ohio*, went into service on June 25, 1965. Three additional jet transports joined *Ohio* by the end of the year. With traffic booming, Peach not only increased Mohawk's orders for the British jet but also placed orders for Fairchild-Hiller FH-227 twin-engined turboprop transports to serve the airline's less heavily traveled routes. Mohawk took delivery of four more BAC One-Elevens in 1967. By the end of the decade, it was operating a fleet of twenty BAC One-Elevens and seventeen FH-227s.

All went well for Mohawk at first as it made the transition to an all turbine-engine fleet. In 1966, Peach reported to its stockholders, the airline "enjoyed a good traffic year." Revenue passenger-miles rose 22.4 percent over 1965, with new service to Washington and Philadelphia. Mohawk posted an operating profit of $2.3 million and a net profit of $1.2 million at the same time that subsidy decreased by $1 million.[51]

The following year, 1967, began well enough when the airline received what Peach termed "the most promising single route award in Mohawk's 22-year history." The CAB gave Mohawk permission to fly nonstop between Detroit and all upstate New York cities, nonstop between Cleveland and Albany, and two-stop between Detroit and Boston. In fact, if not yet in name, Mohawk had become a *regional* airline.

Mohawk in Decline

The 1967 year-end economic picture, however, raised some warning flags. Although Mohawk posted operating profits of $2.3 million, interest expenses of $2.8 million led to a net loss of $274,000. Even more worrisome, perhaps, was the general reversal of the economic fortune of the local service airlines as a whole, which recorded a $4.5 million loss for the year.[52]

The bottom fell out for Mohawk in 1968. The beginning of the end, symbolically at least, came with the loss of a BAC One-Eleven named *Discover America* on June 23. Shortly after taking off from Elmira, New

York, en route to Washington, D.C., the aircraft crashed into a heavily wooded area near Blossburg, Pennsylvania. Thirty passengers and four crew members died in the accident. An investigation revealed that a non-return valve from the auxiliary power unit had failed, causing a fire that led to structural damage in the tail of the aircraft.[53]

Less than two weeks later, on July 3, 1968, the Professional Air Traffic Controllers Organization (PATCO) announced the beginning of "Operation Air Safety." Founded on January 3, 1968, by a small group of controllers in the New York City area, the organization had grown to over 5,000 members by the summer. Under the aggressive leadership of Michael J. Rock, PATCO took its first job action—Operation Safety—to protest what the group saw as inadequate staffing levels and excessive overtime.[54]

With controllers working "by the book" at major air traffic chokepoints throughout the country, delays quickly mounted. By August, the situation in the New York City area had degenerated into chaos. Along with other airlines, Mohawk suffered financial losses because of increased costs for fuel, labor, and overtime. "Under today's air traffic control situation," Peach reported in September, "we can't make a profit."[55]

Although the restrictions on air traffic eased during the fall, the slow-down contributed to Mohawk's growing financial woes. As noted in the airline's *Annual Report,* the year had been "a disappointing one from both a traffic and financial point of view." Mohawk suffered a net loss of $4.3 million, with interest payments on its debt increasing from $2.8 million in 1967 to $4.1 million in 1968. While management expressed its disappointment with the company's financial results, it assured Mohawk's stockholders that the trend "can and will be reversed," and the company would return to profitability at an early date. After all, management concluded, "We have the plant, tools, equipment, and most important of all, the employee know-how to accomplish this."[56]

But the situation did not improve in 1969. A general economic slow-down produced a sluggish passenger growth rate for all the nation's airlines, including Mohawk. The company's interest debt continued to soar, reaching $5.4 million. At the same time, subsidy payments decreased. The result was another "disappointing year," with a net loss of $4.7 million.[57]

The year also saw major changes in the airline's management. In 1968 Peach had moved from president to chairman of the board and chief executive officer (CEO); Russell V. Stephenson had replaced him as president. During 1969, Peach suffered from a series of personal and emotional problems that led to his removal from active management of the airline. Stephenson took over as CEO. At the same time, William P. Tolley, chancellor of Syracuse University, replaced Peach's longtime ally, Victor Underwood, as chairman of the board.[58]

Mohawk's financial situation became critical in 1970. With the economy now in a full-blown recession, total airline domestic passenger traffic declined for the first time in twelve years. As a result, the nation's air carriers suffered their first net operating loss since 1947. Mohawk shared in this misery. Revenue passenger-miles declined from 641 million in 1969 to 575.9 million in 1970. At the same time, an operating profit of $591,000 in 1969 turned into a loss of $5.4 million in 1970.[59]

Mohawk also faced a crippling strike by its pilots. The dispute centered on the trend by local service carriers to turn over to commuter airlines its less profitable routes. As the local service carriers acquired jet aircraft and matured into regional airlines, they became less eager to serve the shorter, less traveled routes. Between 1966 and 1970, the local service airlines turned over routes serving seventy cities to commuter airlines. The CAB approved this arrangement, provided that the local service carriers agreed to reenter the market if commuter airline service proved unsatisfactory.

The local service airlines facilitated this process of route abandonment by developing special relationships with commuter lines. Allegheny Airlines led the way, entering into a partnership in the late 1960s with several commuters to operate its sparsely traveled routes. Commuter aircraft were painted with Allegheny colors and shared codes and joint fares. Mohawk had followed Allegheny's lead, concluding agreements with Northern Airways, Executive Airlines, and Command Airways.[60]

Mohawk's pilots saw this trend as a threat to their jobs, as lower paid commuter pilots began to fly Mohawk's less heavily traveled routes. In negotiations with the company, they demanded the right to veto agreements to take over routes between Mohawk and the commuter lines. This demand, Stephenson asserted, amounted to an effort by the pilot union to usurp management's "right to manage the company."[61]

Because the issue was so fundamental, negotiations proved difficult. The pilots, who had been working on an expired contract, went on strike one minute after midnight on November 12, 1970. Mohawk's management shut down the company, removing 2,000 nonunion workers from the payroll.

Three weeks later, on December 1, Mohawk told a group of insurance companies that held $10 million of 7.5 percent senior subordinated notes that it would be unable to make a scheduled interest payment. Shortly thereafter, the airline announced that it had obtained the services of Jet Capital Corporation to assist in developing a program for obtaining new capital funds and restructuring a debt that had reached $81.8 million.[62]

Although everyone expected bad news, the announcement on March 19, 1971, that the airline had lost $11.9 million in 1970 still came as a shock. Two days later, the airline's pilots dropped their demand for a veto over subcontracted services and agreed to binding arbitration if the dispute could not be settled by March 25.[63]

Negotiations again failed, and the dispute went to arbitration. On March 31, the arbitrator rendered a decision that represented a compromise settlement on economic issues. Service resumed on April 14 after what the *New York Times* labeled "one of the longest [154 days] and most bitter disputes in airline history." That same evening, Mohawk's management, which had twice deferred debt obligations during the preceding three months because of a shortage of cash, announced that an agreement in principle had been reached to merge with Allegheny Airlines. Allegheny, which agreed to advance Mohawk $4 million as interim working capital, would be the surviving carrier.[64]

On April 20, 1971, Peach, who had long feuded with Allegheny's management, was found dead from a self-inflicted gunshot wound. He was fifty-one years old.[65]

The End of an Airline

The pilots' strike was the most immediate reason for Mohawk's demise, but a more fundamental cause had been the decision to reequip the airline with BAC One-Elevens and Fairchild-Hiller FH-227s. Peach had gambled. The airline had taken on a huge debt. If the economy had remained strong and passenger traffic had continued to grow as it had in the mid-1960s, the airline could have met the heavy interest payments on its debt out of operating profits. Between 1968 and 1970, however, a weakening economy had resulted in operating losses of $5.3 million. At the same time, interest on Mohawk's debt had totaled a staggering $14.9 million.

The CAB had no intention of underwriting Peach's gamble. Subsidy payments, which had reached a peak of $4.7 million in 1963, had continued to decline during the remainder of the decade. Between 1968 and 1970, the airline received $7.3 million in subsidy. In a sense, the CAB, which had so often punished Mohawk's past attempts to upgrade its equipment, finally acted as Peach had always desired. The function of the CAB, he had stressed repeatedly, was not to manage. It was not responsible for the consequences of misjudgments by management.

Free enterprise involves risk. Peach had taken his chances; he had led the way. In the end, he failed. But without Peach's vision and determination, Mohawk would have languished as a small feeder airline. If he had adopted a cautious and conservative approach to the management of the airline, Mohawk would probably have made only limited progress— and Peach would not have been remembered by historians of the airline industry.

Notes

1. Civil Aeronautics Board, *Annual Report for 1943* (Washington: Government Printing Office, 1944), 7.

2. Civil Aeronautics Board, *Annual Report for 1944* (Washington: Government Printing Office, 1946), 20. See also George C. Eads, *The Local Service Airline Experiment* (Washington: Brookings Institution, 1972).

3. Leary interview with Elwood A. Butterfield, February 14, 1996.

4. Robert E. Peach, *"Four-Seaters to Fan Jets": The Story of Mohawk Airlines, Inc.* (New York: Newcomen Society in North America, 1964).

5. "Robert English Peach," *National Cyclopedia of American Biography*, vol. 56 (Clifton, N.J.: James T. White, 1975), 414–15.

6. Peach testimony, April 27, 1954, Senate Committee on Interstate and Foreign Commerce, *Hearings: Provide Permanent Certificates for Local Service Air Carriers*, 83d Cong., 2d sess. (Washington: Government Printing Office, 1954), 29–36.

7. Civil Aeronautics Board, *Annual Report for 1946* (Washington: Government Printing Office, 1946), 3–4.

8. Robinson to Edwin A. Link, April 28, 1947, Link Papers, State University of New York at Binghamton.

9. Leary interview with Butterfield, February 14, 1996.

10. Robinson to Link, June 4, 1947, Link Papers.

11. *New York Times,* February 21, 1948; Robinson Airlines, board of directors' meeting, February 8, 1950, Link Papers.

12. Peach testimony, April 27, 1954, Senate Committee on Interstate and Foreign Commerce, *Hearings,* 29–36.

13. Ibid.; Peach, *"Four-Seaters to Fan Jets."*

14. Peach, *"Four-Seaters to Fan Jets."*

15. Robinson Airlines, annual stockholders' meeting, February 7, 1950, Link Papers.

16. Robinson Airlines, board of directors' meeting, March 27, 1950, Link Papers.

17. Peach to Rentzel, November 27, 1950, Link Papers.

18. *New York Times,* September 5, 1950.

19. Excerpts from report of Edward T. Stodola, examiner, Robinson Airlines Corporation, renewal application, docket no. 4947 et al., Link Papers.

20. Robinson Airlines, board of directors' meeting, June 28, 1952, Link Papers.

21. Robinson Airlines, board of directors' meeting, April 3, 1952, Link Papers.

22. Peach to the Civil Aeronautics Board, July 21, 1954, citing Ryan's letter of December 13, 1953, Link Papers.

23. Peach to the Board of Directors, Mohawk Airlines, "Status of Pilot Union Negotiations," April 19, 1954, Link Papers.

24. Mohawk Airlines, board of directors' meeting, May 14, 1954, Link Papers.

25. Peach to the Civil Aeronautics Board, July 21, 1954, Link Papers.

26. For the background of the fight for permanent certification, see Eads, *Local Service Airline Experiment.*

27. Nyrop testimony, June 23, 1954, House Committee on Interstate and Foreign Commerce, *Hearings: Permanent Certificates for Local Service Air Carriers,* 83d Cong., 2d sess. (Washington: Government Printing Office, 1954), 38.

28. Ibid., 13–14, 61–64.

29. Ibid., 91.

30. Peach, "Convairs for Mohawk," *Flight Magazine* 43 (June 1955): 32–34, 54–56.

31. On the Chennault Convairs, see William M. Leary, "Aircraft and Anti-Communists: CAT in Action, 1949–52," *China Quarterly* 52 (1972): 654–69.

32. Peach, "Convairs for Mohawk."

33. Mohawk Airlines, board of directors' meeting, February 2, 1955, Link Papers.

34. Underwood to Link, September 30, 1955, Link Papers.

35. Peach, "Convairs for Mohawk," and *"Four-Seaters to Fan Jets."*

36. Peach to the Board of Directors, Mohawk Airlines, February 17, 1956, Link Papers.

37. Mohawk Airlines, board of directors' meeting, April 12, 1956, Link Papers.

38. Peach to the Board of Directors, Mohawk Airlines, June 23, 1957, Link Papers.

39. Peach to Durfee, August 5, 1957, Link Papers; Peach, *"Four-Seaters to Fan Jets."*

40. Peach, *"Four-Seaters to Fan Jets."*

41. Civil Aeronautics Board, *Annual Report for 1958* (Washington: Government Printing Office, 1958), 11.

42. Ibid., 18–20.

43. *New York Times,* September 2, 1958.

44. Peach, *"Four-Seaters to Fan Jets."*

45. Mohawk Airlines, board of directors' meeting, October 27, 1961, Link Papers.

46. Peach to the Board of Directors, Mohawk Airlines, July 20, 1962, Link Papers.

47. Mohawk Airlines, *Annual Report for 1963.*

48. Peach to the Board of Directors, Mohawk Airlines, December 15, 1962, Link Papers.

49. *Newsday* interview with Peach, September 9, 1968, Link Papers.

50. Peach, "Free Enterprise in a Regulated Economy," November 8, 1965, the 1965 Salzberg Lecture, Syracuse University.

51. Mohawk Airlines, *Annual Report for 1966.*

52. Mohawk Airlines, *Annual Report for 1967.*

53. *New York Times,* June 24, 25, 26, and 27, 1968; Leary interview with Butterfield, February 14, 1996.

54. *New York Times,* July 21, 1968. For the background on PATCO, see Nick A. Komons, "Professional Air Traffic Controllers Organization," in William M. Leary, ed., *Encyclopedia of American Business History and Biography: The Airline Industry* (New York: Facts on File, 1992), 382–85.

55. *Newsday* interview with Peach, September 9, 1968, Link Papers.

56. Mohawk Airlines, *Annual Report for 1968.*

57. Mohawk Airlines, *Annual Report for 1969.*

58. Leary interview with Russell V. Stephenson, May 3, 1996.

59. Mohawk Airlines, *Annual Report for 1970.*

60. On the rise of commuter airlines, see R. E. G. Davies and I. E. Quastler, *Commuter Airlines of the United States* (Washington: Smithsonian Institution Press, 1995).

61. *New York Times,* December 23, 1970.

62. *New York Times,* December 1 and 18, 1970.

63. *New York Times,* March 20 and 22, 1971.

64. *New York Times,* April 15, 1971.

65. *New York Times,* April 21, 1971.

Bibliographical Essay

The Mohawk Airlines Collection at Syracuse University and the Papers of Edwin A. Link at the State University of New York at Binghamton contain the essential primary materials for the study of Robert E. Peach and Mohawk Airlines. Twice, Peach reflected on the history of Mohawk and its place in the regulated airline industry: *"Four-Seaters to Fan Jets": The History of Mohawk Airlines, Inc.* (Newcomen Society, 1964) and "Free Enterprise in the Regulated Economy," the 1965 Salzberg Lecture at Syracuse University.

For a brief account of Mohawk's history, see R. E. G. Davies, *Airlines of the United States since 1914* (Washington, D.C.: Smithsonian Institution Press, 1982). George C. Eads, *The Local Airline Experience* (Washington, D.C.: Brookings Institution, 1972) is a detailed study of the regulatory context within which Mohawk operated.

A biography of Peach and a scholarly history of Mohawk Airlines remain to be written.

Right Man, Right Place, Right Time? Orvis M. Nelson and the Politics of Supplemental Air Carriers

ROGER D. LAUNIUS

IF EVER AN AIRLINE PROMOTER WAS THE VICTIM of a subtle form of aviation apartheid that permeated the minds of those in control of commercial aviation in the United States during the first two decades following World War II, that man was Orvis Nelson."[1] In this statement, airline historian R. E. G. Davies echoed the official position of the class of airlines Nelson belonged to, the so-called nonscheduled or supplemental carriers. The leaders of these air carriers in the post–World War II era convinced many senior politicians of the unfriendly nature of the regulatory arm of the federal government and the internecine warfare of the largest airlines to bar them from competition. This is a provocative thesis that conjures up images of conspiracy and cover-up at the highest levels of government and business, collusion between the regulators and the regulated, and victimization of the weak and defenseless but nonetheless important supplemental air carriers by a far from benign airline industry elite and by the regulatory infrastructure of the Civil Aeronautics Board (CAB).

The Senate Select Committee on Small Business endorsed this theory as early as 1951:

Beginning in 1948 the Board [CAB] apparently commenced a program of strict enforcement . . . the certificated carriers took an active interest in these efforts to eliminate the nonscheduled air carriers. . . .

To the extent that the "nonskeds" still exist today, they have managed to survive since 1948 in spite of constant harassment. . . .

In view of the Board's responsibility for the route pattern and the determination of mail pay allowances, it is only reasonable to expect that the five Board members would generally view air transportation problems in very much the same way as they are viewed by members of the industry. . . .

The nonscheduled industry has kept alive and developed technical skill and administrative know-how which has proved to be of great value in defense emergencies. . . .

These carriers offer a flexible airlift capacity that can be brought into military use far more rapidly than the certificated airlines whose equipment is obligated by commitments and scheduled to service regularly appointed routes.[2]

Senator Wayne Morse (D-Oregon) summarized well the details of this perspective in 1962: "We have the picture of the aviation industry arriving at a state of total monopoly, coming to this state through the machinations of the major trunk carriers. A pliant Civil Aeronautics Board has historically responded to their bidding . . . and has functioned as their . . . devout champion over the years."[3]

Orvis Nelson certainly believed this position as a matter of faith because of the fate of Transocean Air Lines (TAL). He told a Senate committee in 1976 that "the CAB has abused the power given it by Congress to regulate and promote the well-being of American commercial air carriers by giving preferential treatment of the highest order to the so-called Grandfather airlines operating when the Aviation Act of 1938 was passed. For the past thirty years, ever since the supplemental and feeder airlines took their challenge to the skies, the CAB has maintained these privileged scheduled airlines on a pedestal of gold, and defended and protected them with every means at its command."[4] Clearly, Nelson believed the demise of TAL in 1960 was the result of conspiracy.

Orvis M. Nelson in a DC-4 at the Oakland, Calif., headquarters of Transocean Airlines. (Courtesy of the National Air and Space Museum, Smithsonian Institution [SI Neg. No. 99-40057])

Nelson based his observations about the industry on his direct experience with Transocean Air Lines, which he headed between 1946 and 1960 with sometimes spectacular success and flashy brilliance. He also ran it on the edge of safety, flying old and inefficient war surplus aircraft and suffering a series of high-profile accidents that called its operations into question. Nelson admitted that he was rarely far from bankruptcy during the company's history, living hand-to-mouth on government defense contracts and unusual foreign activities that betrayed the firm's relationship to intrigues of the CIA around the globe. The result was a unique airline with an interesting operational style that proved marginally profitable during the immediate postwar era when cold war crises cropped up every few months and then collapsed as a result of the economics of the airline industry, not because of the machinations of any entity, regulatory or otherwise.[5]

Origins of an Air Transport Entrepreneur

The story of Orvis Marcus Nelson and Transocean Air Lines began in Tamarack, Minnesota, a small town fifty miles west of Duluth, where Nelson was born on 18 March 1907.[6] Growing up in the lumbering region of the upper Midwest, Nelson helped his parents, Marcus and Mamie Barnett Nelson, operate the general store and post office in Tamarack. As the store prospered, Marcus, the son of Norwegian immigrants every bit as stoic and hardworking as the stereotype, branched out into the lumbering business that dominated the local economy and eventually purchased large plots of timber land and several small sawmills. From the time Nelson was old enough to control an ax, he contributed to the family business. Before age ten he "was driving a team in the Tamarack yard and skidding logs up into the pile-up for the mill. At twelve, Orvis was operating the big chain-driven hoists which hauled the logs up into the mill and spilled them down on to the rollways where they went on to the saw carriage."[7] Logging was grueling work by anyone's account, but through it Nelson learned the values of hard work, diligence, and patience. He also had burned into his psyche his parents' drive and devotion, attributes he would draw upon in his TAL career.

Because Tamarack had no secondary schools, Nelson did not attend school regularly. He and his siblings traveled thirty-five miles to Aitkin for what formal education they received as children, but when the time came for them to attend high school, their father, who valued education as a means of advancement in America, moved the family to Minneapolis for the winters so the children could take advantage of the public schools.

When Charles Lindbergh made his epic transatlantic flight in 1927, Nelson, like so many other Americans, became enamored with aviation. After an unproductive semester at Hamline University in Minneapolis, he left Minnesota and joined the Army Air Corps, serving as a technician on the aerial survey of the Philippines. He was unhappy with this assignment because he was not able to fly as much as he wanted, however, and in 1929 he opted out of his commitment. Nelson then attended tiny Franklin College in Indiana and received a degree in mathematics in 1932. While in college he tried to satisfy his thirst for aviation by doing aerial photography, but it was not enough. When Nelson completed his degree, he reenlisted in the Army Air Corps and entered flight training, graduating from Kelly Field in October 1933.

Nelson was a military pilot for almost two years, serving much of that time with the 11th Bombardment Squadron at March Field, California. He told journalist Richard Thruelsen in 1953 that he sought out bombers to fly because they were the largest aircraft available.

> In those days everybody who went through the flying cadet course was sweating out a regular commission in the Air Corps, and I wanted to fly the big airplanes so that I'd have a chance to get a job with the airlines in case the regular commissions didn't come through. What we flew then as big airplanes would, of course, look comical today. Our training aircraft were two-engined Keystones which made about 90 miles an hour wide open and stalled like a brick at 80. We flew right out in the open because we didn't have any closed cockpits in those days. The Keystones had high-speed propellers and they'd make a terrific noise. The damn things would hardly move, but they surely would shake the earth.[8]

Nelson flew the mail with the Army Air Corps in 1934, but on 1 July 1935 he resigned his commission and went to work for United Air Lines.[9] Flying in DC-2s and DC-3s, Nelson built a reputation as a reliable, capable, and conscientious pilot.

Protected from immediate recall into the military during World War II because he was in a critical support field, Nelson was sent by United to fly defense-related missions in Alaska under contract to the Air Transport Command (ATC), the single manager for strategic airlift services for the government.[10] Later he transferred to the California-Hawaii route for United. As Nelson recalled in 1976, "Here a whole new world of flying opened for me and over the years that I was with United I flew its whole system as well as on United's wartime Air Transport Command operations to Alaska and across the Pacific." By the end of the war, United had flown almost 20,000 tons of military personnel and equipment more than 21 million miles using 77 United crews. The company had made more than 1,700 trips across the Pacific and another 1,800 on the Alaska run.[11]

While engaged in these flights in 1942, Nelson was elected first vice president of the Air Line Pilots Association (ALPA).[12] He quickly became its chief representative in discussions with management and government officials. Among the issues he negotiated was the viability of the continued use of civilian pilots under contract on government routes rather than their commissioning in the Army Air Forces. It was decided that they should remain airline employees.

Nelson recalled in 1976 his experience with ALPA and its importance to his future career: "Active in the Air Line Pilots Association contract negotiations with UAL I gained a considerable insight into the business side of running a major airline. As a member of United's Pilot System Board of Adjustment, as Master Chairman of United's ALPA Councils, as Chairman of the 3 man ALPA Committee that represented all of America's pilots during WWII and as First Vice President of the ALPA for four years, I gained invaluable experience in working productively with people that effectively prepared me for heading Transocean."[13]

For the first time, as a result of this experience, Nelson saw the airline industry from some other vantage point than a flight deck, and it fundamentally altered his perspective. For example, as much fun as flying truly was, he realized that pilots were essentially hired help and that the entrepreneurs were in board rooms rather than behind flight controls. He had to make that transition as well in order to achieve the type of ambitions his parents had inculcated into him.

Nelson and the Birth of Transocean Air Lines

It was in mid-August 1945, on a flight for United in the central Pacific, that Nelson first began to consider creating his own airline. He was waiting out a typhoon at Okinawa with some fellow commercial pilots, and over several bottles of liquor they began to talk about the future. Holed up in a tent as torrential rains and high winds swirled around them, Nelson opined that it would be years before the Japanese would be able to run their own airline and that it would be lucrative for United to extend

its operations to the Orient. If United was unwilling to take this chance,
Nelson added, he and some other enterprising men should do so them-
selves. The United men at this session—Sid Nelson, Harry Hulking,
Sherwood Nichols, and Nelson—all agreed to this plan.

Although the idea might have been dreamed up over liquor during
a Pacific typhoon, Nelson was serious about pursuing it. When he returned to the United States, Nelson met with United leaders and pled
the case of opening up a Far East department. He had no success, however. Nelson returned to domestic air routes for United over the winter
of 1945–46, and by his own account he spent a miserable winter flying
United's Denver–San Francisco route. Each time he made the trip, he
fumed about the possibilities present in the Pacific. "When you're flying," he recalled, "you don't just sit there and fly—you think."[14]

As Nelson ruminated about the promise of aviation for the Pacific,
he also thought a lot about the economic opportunity that starting an
airline in the region held. As Nelson told Richard Thruelsen: "There was
a lot of talk all around the subject of what was going to happen to aviation after the war and I finally sold the boys on the idea that, if United
wasn't interested in extending its routes, we ought to go on our own and
try to get a contract to set up the airlines in Japan. I knew it would be a
long time before the Japs would be allowed to have their own domestic
air service. As for the longer routes—we all felt that there would be a lot
of flying across the Pacific in connection with rebuilding the bases on
Okinawa and Guam. It seems to me that this would offer a wonderful
opportunity for a profitable new business."[15] Clearly, Nelson understood the necessity of continued involvement by the United States in the
international community of the Pacific Rim. He also realized that serv-
icing the American establishment in the region would provide a stunning
opportunity for investors.

Nelson could not have been more correct in sizing up the situation
at the end of World War II. First, for all intents and purposes, the airline industry had been nationalized during the war and operated mostly
for military and diplomatic purposes. This state of affairs ensured that its
private sector market stagnated during the war. From a national perspective, however, this approach had worked quite well. "Such an operating
fleet serves peacetime commerce and industry," the Aviation Policy Board
concluded in 1948, "while remaining available for military use in an emer-

Transocean Airlines DC-4 on ramp in Agana, Guam, in late 1940s. (Courtesy of the National Air and Space Museum, Smithsonian Institution [SI Neg. No. 99-40058])

gency."[16] At the same time, flying in World War II brought about a shift in the national mind-set toward the use of aircraft for transportation. By 1945, flying in commercial airplanes, one could leave home in the early morning and be in the nation's capital for a meeting and back home that evening. The opportunity for movement manifest in this system had never been so great, and it acclimated those who experienced it to demand the rapid growth of the air transport sector when peace came so that it could serve their private needs.[17] This situation virtually assured that the airlines, while limited by what they could do during the war because of government restrictions and priorities, would not only quickly recapture their prewar market but also rise rapidly as soon as the fighting ceased.

Second, as a result of the Allied victory in 1945, the United States acquired a large number of international dependencies and conquered provinces that demanded governance. The far-flung nature of this American "empire" ensured that the maturing air transportation system had to expand radically as a means of linking the realm. The Truman administration at war's end quickly awarded permanent international routes to the domestic carriers that had been so prominent in the early 1940s. These routes were mostly the same ones the carriers had flown under military auspices during the conflict. In so doing, Truman overturned a long-standing policy of using Pan American Airways as the "chosen instrument" for overseas air transport in favor of certificating several U.S. carriers for regional flights and in so doing creating a climate of moderate and healthy, but not cutthroat, competition.[18]

Third, the commercial carriers certificated for these routes by the Civil Aeronautics Board could not begin to satisfy the sudden explosion of demand for air transport between 1945 and 1948. The early postwar experience prompted the Civil Aeronautics Board to forecast an increase in demand for the decade after the cessation of hostilities to an unprecedented one billion ton-miles per year. And while the actual demand for air transportation did not meet expectations, everyone agreed that the burgeoning demand for services far exceeded the 1945 airlines' capabilities.[19]

Enter the nonscheduled carriers such as Transocean Air Lines and young entrepreneurs such as Orvis Nelson. Tremendous opportunity awaited those who could get organized, acquire aircraft, and negotiate contracts with government agencies for air transport to and within defeated provinces. The impediments to entry into the air transport business were also exceptionally low during the first couple of years after the war. The CAB used a loophole in the Civil Aeronautics Act of 1938 to certificate the operations of "irregular" air carriers without fixed schedules and routes, intended to license the activities of bush pilots, crop dusters, and various other small operators, to validate companies flying large transport aircraft. Those airlines could not help but compete with the regulated industry, but they had a significant advantage in that they were not held to the same requirements for safety and service.

Moreover, thousands of pilots, trained by the military and suddenly unemployed as a result of the postwar demobilization, could be hired at nominal wages. Stockpiles of virtually new aircraft were available as war surplus from the government for a pittance. One would-be operator bought nine twin-engine C-46s for $221,550, the normal government purchase price of one aircraft.[20] Those unable to secure the financing could lease government aircraft by the month for as little as $2,000 for a four-engine C-54 and $300 for a C-46. The federal government also did everything possible to make financing available, instructing the Reconstruction Finance Corporation and the War Assets Administration to help secure loans for new airline companies.[21]

Because of this situation, the number of nonscheduled airlines founded during the bonanza years immediately after World War II cannot be determined with accuracy. The Civil Aeronautics Board tried to register each of them in 1946, but turnovers in leadership, name changes, mergers, quiet entry and exit in the industry, and the general chaos reigning in the field prompted the CAB not to place much confidence in this method of accounting. The CAB estimated that 3,600 firms started operations before 1949. At best, these firms accounted for less than 8 percent of the air transportation market, so the result was that a very large number of companies competed for a very small piece of the industry. The Department of Defense (DOD), furthermore, supported virtually all of that market through its contracts, so the business opportunity in reality was monolithic and tied to very specific U.S. interests overseas.[22] It also had the potential to be a somewhat short-term opportunity, for everyone recognized that while demand might exceed capacity at present, the larger carriers would quickly expand their operations to take up as much of the expanded contract market as possible.

Perhaps because of this situation, Nelson failed to convince United of the Pacific's potential for air transport, but his entreaties, it appears, had not fallen on completely deaf ears. On 9 March 1946, Jack Herlihy, United's vice president for operations, knowing Nelson's goal of establishing a new airline, asked if he could organize a military airlift route between San Francisco and Hickam Field, near Honolulu. Herlihy offered Nelson this route as a subcontract under United from the Army Air Forces provided he could get himself organized within ten days. Nelson jumped at the opportunity, and on 18 March 1946, his company got its start as an unincorporated firm by flying the missions with surplus C-54s leased from the U.S. government. Nelson's airline venture was assured solvency with this contract, at first making as much as $2,000 per day in profits. Later, on 1 June 1946, Nelson incorporated his company as Transocean Air Lines with its base in Oakland, California. Nelson became by far the largest shareholder with 27 percent of TAL's stock, but he had reasonable contributions from some of his flying buddies and,

A DC-4 N-90915 in Oakland, Calif., in May 1952. (Photo by W. T. Larkins)

because he had the United subcontract, a rush of investment from venture capitalists. At the end of the first official day of operation in 1946,
TAL had some $190,000 in its treasury.[23]

Orvis Nelson proved an air transport entrepreneur with considerable
imagination and flair during Transocean's formative years. His first important actions involved hiring personnel and acquiring equipment. His
approach to hiring was ad hoc at best and the stuff of which legends
are made. Samuel L. Wilson, a veteran pilot and later a member of
TAL's board of directors, liked to tell the story of his hiring. While still
in an Army Air Forces uniform in March 1946, he had gone to United
to inquire about civilian opportunities. Hearing that Nelson was hiring
pilots for TAL, he immediately called him at his home:

> "I hear you're looking for pilots," said Wilson.
> "Yes," replied Nelson. "You looking for a job?"
> "Maybe," said Wilson cautiously.
> "O.K.—you're hired."

This seemed a little abrupt to Wilson. "Don't you even want to see my logbook?" he asked.

"Hell, no—I know all about you."

"Well . . . say, Nelson, there's another fellow here who's looking for a pilot's job—name of Wally Simpton."

"Is he O.K.?" asked Nelson.

"Yes . . . "

"O.K.—he's hired."

Wilson and Simpton both thought this method of hiring strange. When they discussed it with another pilot, Bill Word, who had been chief of training at the Army Air Forces' West Coast Hamilton Field, they found that he had just signed on with Nelson after a similarly weird conversation. They decided to drive over to Nelson's house in San Lorenzo, a suburb of Oakland, California, to see this entrepreneur for themselves. After he had kept them waiting for half an hour while talking on the phone to other prospective employees, Nelson asked, "What the hell are you guys doing here? You're hired, and I told you I'd let you know when to go to work." He shooed them out after telling when and where to report for operations.[24]

Because of the press for pilots, Nelson began in 1946 the first of several subsidiary businesses, the Taloa Academy of Aeronautics at the Oakland Airport, to train both his own and other companies' pilots. Taloa, a takeoff of the TAL acronym, became something of a "cash cow" for the parent corporation for more than a decade as its training services found demand within the air transport industry. Winning contracts from government agencies and foreign nations for pilot training, the academy gained fame for the quality of its graduates. It proved so successful that in 1950 it opened a branch site at Bakersfield, California. Beginning in 1951, Taloa expanded its training to flight attendants.[25]

Nelson acquired aircraft with similar bravado. He bought two Douglas DC-4 four-engine transports that had been used extensively during the war and were familiar to virtually all Transocean pilots under their military designation, C-54. He purchased them for $90,000 each—they had a price tag now of more than $500,000 each—with 15 percent down and the balance to be paid off within three years. Nelson sank another $150,000 into modifications to make them acceptable for commercial operations per the CAB's requirements. He groused about these regulations, the first but not the last time he would complain about the government regulators charged with managing the airways, but he had no choice if he wanted his own airline. By the summer of 1946, Nelson recalled, TAL was "flying 12 of the government-owned planes on the San Francisco–Honolulu run and had two of our own being readied for business. Now we had to go out and look for business for those two airplanes. And it was then that the fun and the trouble began."[26]

Nelson proved himself an able salesman of air services during those early years after World War II. His instinct for finding business seemed uncanny to all and spooky to some. One competitor recalled, "Every time I'd hear of a piece of business and go after it, there would be Nelson just departing, shaking hands in the doorway, the contract in his pocket." He gloried in the moniker assigned to him and his band of vagabond pilots and war surplus airplanes: "sky tramps," "carpetbaggers of the skies," and "air gypsies." It was an exciting time, and Nelson and those who worked for him at Transocean claimed always to enjoy high morale and optimism for the future.

But TAL could not survive solely on government subcontracts. The first airlift that did not support the U.S. military was a contract to fly a Filipino newspaper publisher, a Dr. Yap, and his party from the United States to Manila for the Philippines' Fourth of July celebration. Unable to meet the contract because aircraft in conversion were not ready in time, Nelson arranged for Philippine Air Lines to transport Dr. Yap's entourage. Transocean then subcontracted with PAL for regular charter flights between San Francisco and Manila. On 23 July 1946, a Transocean DC-4 named *Taloa–Manila Bay* began the first mission, with Nelson at the controls and his fiancée serving as flight attendant. Aboard were thirty-five passengers and a small amount of cargo. Island-hopping across the Pacific, Nelson encountered difficulties at every turn. There were problems with clearances for the flight, maintenance and other support had to be pried out of personnel at Pacific stops, and aircraft security never ceased to be a concern. Nelson later recalled: "Whether the difficulties could be laid to obstructionism by some of our competitors in the Pacific or just the usual official red tape, I can't say, but I do know that when the *Taloa–Manila Bay* showed up on its return trip in Honolulu we still had no permission to use the islands."[27] These roadblocks were only the beginnings of the difficulties encountered by Nelson and his upstart airline.

Nelson reflected on those heady first months of operation thirty years later before a Senate Committee on Small Business investigating airline regulation in 1976:

> While the ATC operation of 1946 was keeping some 12 C54s busy, aircraft provided by the Air Corps on bailment, we were actively seeking out commercial business. Opportunity came along with the first DC-4 we bought from the War Assets Administration. In August we started scheduled flights for Philippine Air Lines under a wet lease and management program. Using DC-4s we started flying from California to Manila and Shanghai with DC-4s. Meanwhile a Transocean team was heading up the interisland operation of PAL, using DC-3s donated by the U.S. Army. Within a year we extended PAL's international operations to Hong Kong, Bangkok, Calcutta, Karachi, Lydda, Rome, and Madrid.[28]

The company looked like a success, and nothing Nelson experienced over the next year really seemed to contradict that position.

A major change to Nelson's company came near the end of 1946 when United decided to give up its contract with the military for service between San Francisco and Hawaii. As the subcontractor operating this service, Transocean decided to bid on it, but for a variety of reasons, some of them political, it lost the bid to the Flying Tiger Line. This subcontract had ensured Transocean operating capital, and its loss forced Nelson to search desperately for other business. To compensate, Nelson entered into a contract to run the part of Philippine Air Line's East Asian operations that had been contracted to TWA.

Nelson also aggressively sought charter flights throughout the world. In 1947, for example, his company flew several missions between Great Britain and Canada, hauling about 7,000 English immigrants to Toronto. Of this operation, Nelson recalled: "This Canadian job was our first contract for what you might call the mass movement of people by air and the lessons we learned from this project served us well on later jobs of similar nature—such as the transportation of the workers to the Pacific islands and the movement of refugees from China and the carriage of religious groups in the Middle East."[29] Working for the International Refugee Organization, a Division of the United Nations, this was the first movement of more than 25,000 persons Transocean flew for that organization over the next several years. In every case it relocated people displaced by World War II, with the bulk of them flying between Europe and South America or Australia. Nelson commented, "This became a daily service that headed westward from Munich and Rome."[30]

In so many ways over the years, the cold war was good for American business. Certainly it was good for Orvis Nelson and TAL. An overwhelming percentage of the airline's work was directly related to the conduct of U.S. foreign policy associated with dislocations of war and the resulting superpower rivalry between the United States and the Soviet Union. In many respects TAL became an instrument for the furtherance of national policy in the 1940s and 1950s. The same situation was also true for the other nonscheduled, supplemental carriers that emerged after World War II in response to the sudden requirements for airlift to support the nation's intercontinental obligations. And the leadership of the Department of Defense was Nelson's and his fellow supplemental carriers' greatest supporter. In 1958 DOD officials publicly announced, "The preservation of those airlines . . . is of genuine concern to us. In any future military action, your group would unquestionably make a vital contribution."[31] In 1961, Assistant Secretary of the Air Force Joseph Imrie restated the same position: "The continued existence of the irregular air carrier fleet is of real value in terms of national defense and it is evident that the future of the irregular air carriers to service the military, as they are doing now and have done so ably in the past, depends upon their ability to operate their planes in commercial activities when not engaged in service for the military."[32]

This position as a core tenet of the DOD grew because of the response of the supplemental carriers to calls for contract airlift during the Berlin crisis of 1948–49 and the Korean War of 1950–53.

Like his fellow supplementals, Nelson's company picked up some of the other routes of the Military Air Transport Service when it was dedicating virtually all of its resources to Berlin, which was blockaded for more than a year by the Soviet Union.[33] TAL and the other carriers that helped with the Berlin crisis received excellent publicity for what the media reported as an act of generosity and patriotism. Perhaps those ingredients existed in Nelson's case, but TAL was well paid by the DOD for its contract work. The supplementals also entered myth in the halls of Congress with what circulated about their service in this, the first full-fledged crisis of the cold war. Senator Joseph C. O'Mahoney (D-Wyoming) stated the myth in this way in 1953: "I am sure every American thrills with pride over the fact that American carriers were able for more than a year to feed and fuel and supply the beleaguered city of Berlin in the face of the Communist threat. . . . The Kremlin was sure that we would not have the courage to go through, and in the period from July 1, 1948, to December 1, 1949, irregular carriers flew 25 percent of the cargo that was flown."[34] Other members of Congress picked up this assertion and used it repeatedly thereafter.

In reality, supplemental carriers flew no cargo or passengers into Berlin. It was entirely a military operation, and it had to be to ensure success because the rhythm of the airlift dictated clockwork precision best accomplished in a military structure. General William H. Tunner, who directed the airlift and was America's most accomplished and thoughtful airlift commander, wrote, "The actual operation of a successful airlift is about as glamorous as drops of water on stone. There's no frenzy, no flap, just the inexorable process of getting the job done. In a successful airlift you don't see planes parked all over the place; they're either in the air, on loading or unloading ramps, or being worked on."[35] Commercial carriers, no matter how competent, would have thrown Tunner's airlift system into an uproar, and he rightly kept them far away from it. Instead, the Air Force used TAL and the other supplementals to fill in on other routes stripped of military airlift for the Berlin operation. Nonetheless, this myth about the supplementals' performance in Berlin persisted for more than a quarter century whenever discussions surfaced over the fate of these carriers.[36]

When it came to the Korean War and the supplementals, the positive media image remained but became more justified. Indeed, it rescued from bankruptcy many of the supplemental carriers by providing much-needed business at a critical time. Several, and Transocean was the first, immediately volunteered to supplement organic military airlift by contracting to carry critical war materiel and personnel from the United States to Asia. To make up the airlift deficit, the Air Force chartered about sixty four-engine contract transports to fly the transpacific route full-time. Nelson's enterprising Transocean Air Lines was the first commercial carrier to fly Korean airlift missions for the emergency. On 30 June 1950, he began Transocean's first flight with a planeload of 3.5 inch bazooka rockets. As a measure of the Air Force's dependence on its commercial contractors, Transocean used seven DC-4s, the commercial version of the C-54, to handle nearly 14 percent of the entire Korean strategic airlift. Throughout the conflict, Nelson's airline hauled more than 20,000 military passengers, 7,112 litter patients, and 9.6 million pounds of cargo on 673 flights. In all, during the Korean airlift civil air carriers flew more than 40 percent of the missions on the United States/Japan shuttle. Of that total, TAL's share was 14 percent.[37]

Nelson also aggressively marketed TAL elsewhere and found success in several charter flights. In 1949, the Department of the Interior took over from the Navy's administration of the American trust territories of Micronesia and two years later contracted operations in that area to Transocean. Beginning scheduled operations on 1 July 1951, Nelson used a fleet of four PBY5A flying boats supplied by the Navy to provide regular service throughout Micronesia from its base on Guam. This same period saw the great expansion of oil production in the Middle East, and Nelson soon branched out into contract work in that region as well. He also contracted with the Army Corps of Engineers and the Navy to fly construction workers between the United States and Guam, Okinawa, and the Aleutians; the total number moved in five years exceeded 25,000. He also established and operated major service and support bases at Wake Island and Guam, including a facility at Wake built by Transocean Engineering, a TAL subsidiary. This complex could sleep 900 people and serviced all of the military transpacific flights for many years plus scheduled and supplemental airlines flying the Pacific. Nelson also got involved in numerous refugee airlifts. In August 1948, for example, he contracted to carry fifty Eastern European Jewish refugees from Paris to Australia. When China fell to Mao Zedong's communist forces in 1949, Nelson evacuated thousands of White Russians from Shanghai to the Philippines and then flew them to South America for resettlement. In addition, in 1956–57 he airlifted several Hungarian refugees fleeing a Russian invasion from West Germany to the United States.[38]

In addition to this type of airlift activity, a diverse array of other operations followed for Nelson and Transocean. As one example, Nelson actively courted filmmakers in California and got more than his share of contract work for movies. In 1953, Nelson leased aircraft and crews to Hollywood to make two John Wayne movies, *Island in the Sky*, about a World War II transport aircraft downed in Labrador, and *The High and the Mighty*, a classic airplane film about an in-flight disaster during a passenger flight from Hawaii. Nelson also operated seven DC-4s carrying $6.2 million worth of gold bars from Japan to New York City in the early 1950s. Finally, in a 1954 operation called "Noah's Ark," TAL flew a DC-4 containing 550 rabbits, thirty goats, and two million bees from California to Pusan, South Korea, on a church-supported project to rebuild the wartorn nation.[39]

Nelson worked extremely hard hawking airlift around the world during those years. By 1953 he had built Transocean into the largest of the supplemental carriers, possessing a fleet of 114 aircraft, more than 3,000 employees, and twenty-eight operating offices scattered throughout the world. It had also diversified, branching into a number of support operations. Richard Thruelsen, who published a history of Nelson's airline in 1953, listed several additional enterprises. He noted that Transocean

> . . . owns and operates one of the country's largest aircraft and engine plants in Oakland.
> . . . staffs a string of its own bases which stretch around the world.
> . . . operates two airport restaurants.
> . . . runs a hotel—on Wake Island.
> . . . owns and operates a printing plant in Oakland.
> . . . has a heavy construction company engaged in road- and bridge-building on the West Coast.
> . . . operates a barber shop.
> . . . owns and operates a chemical plant.
> . . . has a crop dusting operation working at home and abroad.
> . . . runs an automotive sales and service company on Okinawa.
> . . . has a world-wide trading division which deals in such diverse items as Afghanistan fish-meal and Swiss watches.
> . . . has an industrial development division which manufactures aircraft components for Navy fighters.

... is busy supervising the reactivation of Japanese domestic airlines.

... owns and operates the Taloa Academy of Aeronautics.

... runs the 3,000,000-square-mile interisland air transport system for the Department of the Interior in the Trust Territory of the Pacific Islands.

... flies approximately 10 percent of the U.S.–to–Korea airlift.

... owns an interest in the Philippine Air Lines, which it reactivated on a world-wide basis after the war.

... flies a "vittles" airlift from Africa to the desert oil outposts of the Middle East.[40]

It was an impressive list of operational accomplishments and fully deserving of credit. TAL was also directly helpful to the goals of the United States in supporting the nation's widespread international commitments after World War II and in combating the threat of communism worldwide by transporting humanitarian relief, projecting technological might, and assisting allies.

Collusion between Established Air Carriers and the CAB?

While Nelson expanded and diversified operations, so the traditional story goes, Transocean began to run into all manner of opposition from competitors and government officials. As a nonscheduled carrier without clear sanction from the CAB—also under intense pressure from the larger carriers to safeguard their prerogatives—and essentially renegade status in financial circles, Transocean had a most difficult time during the 1950s. A dean of aviation history, R. E. G. Davies, suggested that Nelson was caught in a classic Catch-22 situation: "Without the blessing of the C.A.B. an airline lacked respectability in the eyes of the financiers, but the C.A.B. would not provide the respectability unless the airline was well financed."[41]

Nelson was constantly strapped for cash to operate as a result, and the Civil Aeronautics Board refused to address repeated formal requests for certification of the supplemental carriers. This lack of clear status in the government's aviation policy, which seemed to be largely the result of lobbying by established competitors, desperately hurt Transocean. In addition, Nelson found that the CAB threw constant restrictions against the supplemental carriers that prohibited him from flying as many missions over established routes as he would have liked. As Nelson sank into a quagmire during the decade, he needed money to update his aircraft and CAB legitimacy to increase his potential customers. He could get neither.

By 1957 Nelson was in serious financial trouble. As a last-ditch effort to save Transocean, he agreed to sell 40 percent of the company's stock to the Atlas Corporation, a New York investment consortium. By the next year, Atlas had stripped Transocean of most of its diversified operations and Nelson saw his business empire crumble. To a very real extent, Transocean suffered from corporate raiders who sold off profitable divisions of the company for all the cash they could obtain. All the while government and financial leaders interested in aviation watched and did nothing, or according to Nelson in a few cases actually helped weaken Transocean. By January 1960 Nelson's enterprise was all but dead. On 11 July 1960, Transocean's last remaining business, the Department of the Interior contract for airlift in Micronesia, terminated operations and the company declared bankruptcy. The obituary for Transocean was written on 3 September 1960 when the *New York Times* published this note about the disposal of its fleet: "Fourteen double-deck stratocruisers once valued at $14,000,000 were sold as scrap yesterday for $105,000. The airliners, once the pride of Transocean Airlines, were bought at auction by the Airline Equipment Company of Newark. Transocean went out of business early this year."[42]

But the demise of Transocean Air Lines is both more complex and sublime than the rather straightforward account usually given to punctuate the myth of CAB/airline collusion in driving down supplemental carriers. Rightly or wrongly, until the Airline Deregulation Act of October 1978 the airline industry was a heavily subsidized and regulated industry. The Civil Aeronautics Act of 1938 put in place a regulatory organization, known after 1940 as the Civil Aeronautics Board, charged with the explicit authority not only for the supervision of the air transport industry but also for its promotion and development. The goals of CAB were to provide the American public with the safest, most efficient, least expensive, and broadest air service possible. The CAB accomplished these objectives by regulating entry into and exit from individual markets (essentially by dictating the route structure between cities and the frequency of flights), rates charged for passengers and cargo, safety measures, finance, subsidies to carriers flying on low income-producing routes, mergers and acquisitions, intercarrier agreements, and quality of service.[43]

Proponents of regulation asserted that the CAB appropriately used its power to mandate carriers to fly routes of high traffic volume (and therefore high profit) as well as those with low traffic and profit. Without this policy, advocates urged, the airlines would concentrate on flying routes between high volume and high profit routes while out-of-the-way communities would be deprived of air transport altogether. Moreover, concentration of airlines on lucrative routes could easily create a business climate of cutthroat competition, as the carriers competed for traffic on such airways. In the process the carriers would undercut the economic stability of the industry and possibly, even probably, cut corners on safety and maintenance of aircraft in an effort to reduce costs to compete more effectively with the other carriers. The fear of cutthroat competition had especially motivated members of Congress, because of the possibility of large numbers of bankrupt companies, costly products, and disorganized service, to vote for the Civil Aeronautics Act of 1938. Regulation also ensured that no one company could dominate the market in a particular region and therefore be in a position to dictate excessive rates because of the lack of competition.

These concerns were not without foundation. The railroad industry in the latter half of the nineteenth century had experienced each of the problems advocates of airline regulation wanted to guard against. Vertical integration by such men as Jay Gould had enabled control of markets between two points, with disastrous consequences for consumers whom he could charge anything he wanted. Rate wars between competing railroads had also wrecked companies, followed by a long, slow climb out of receivership. Piecemeal attacks on these problems from various state legislatures created a patchwork quilt of regulations that varied from jurisdiction to jurisdiction, but since the problems were inherently interstate in focus, these efforts failed to bring resolution. The consequence was that by the 1880s many officials of both the railroad industry and the federal government were advocating national regulation to bring order out of chaos. It came with the creation of the Interstate Commerce Commission in 1887 and found refinement thereafter.[44]

Air transportation offered essentially the same challenges and resolutions posed by the railroads a half century earlier. Federal regulation was a natural means of ensuring that the industry operated efficiently and with the greatest good for the greatest number of Americans. The Civil Aeronautics Act of 1938 brought relative stability, without a doubt, but one could question whether the price of subverting the free market was too high. Certainly, Orvis Nelson and the leaders of the other supplemental carriers thought so.

The real problem Nelson faced throughout TAL's life was that in the regulatory environment just described, there was no room for nonscheduled carriers. The administrations of presidents Harry S Truman and Dwight D. Eisenhower in the 1950s realized this problem early on and sought to address it through a series of studies and regulatory and legislative reforms. Nelson's problem with the CAB was best articulated by Brigadier General R. B. Landry, Truman's air adviser, in a memorandum of 14 January 1952 written to the president: "In its simplest form, I think the problem boils down to this: Are the non-scheduled air carriers essential to our air transportation needs, and do they provide a public service consistent with the long-range interest of our national and international air commerce? If the answer is 'Yes,' the Government should provide the means by which the non-scheds can conduct efficient, business-like operations. If the answer is 'No,' then appropriate action should be taken to terminate this type of operation."

Landry urged appropriate study and consideration of recommendations before implementing any new approaches.[45] A CAB study sent to the president six months later observed that as a class the supplemental carriers were much less safe than the scheduled airlines, with more than twice the rate of fatalities. Many such carriers routinely violated CAB regulations allowing them to operate within certain specified bounds. While some of the supplementals scrupulously observed the regulations allowing them to operate on an air charter basis—and there is every reason to believe that Nelson was one of those supplementals, since there is no record of legitimate discipline from the CAB upon TAL for any violations—as a whole the supplementals represented an exceedingly troublesome sector of the air transportation industry. To many people inside the federal government, these companies seemed to be more trouble than they were worth.[46]

A series of studies ensued following World War II aimed at defining a niche for the supplementals in the airline industry. Early on, the CAB had created a nether world for the supplementals that permitted them to fly as many charter flights as they desired wherever they wished and to fly up to ten frequencies per month between fixed points of their own choosing. The supplementals were also exempted from economic regulation and from many of the safety rules governing the industry. The charter aspect of the supplementals' operating stricture never enjoined debate, and Nelson exploited it through his contract work for other agencies. The "ten frequencies" business looked a lot like commercial airline service provided by any number of companies where passengers purchased tickets for a ride on an airplane.[47] Nelson always wanted to expand that portion of his business, while certificated airlines wanted to limit this competition.

The most sophisticated study of the air transport industry was the comprehensive "Role of the United States Government in the Development of the Air Transportation System," a serious attempt to define a comprehensive national aviation policy in 1954 and 1955. It found that "bona fide charter operations of the larger irregular carriers represent a supplemental type of service which should be encouraged. A new type of certificate should be developed for such operations, providing suitable flexibility in terms of routes and areas to be served." Nelson's TAL received such a certificate, and its charter activities were never questioned. But the operation of what amounted to regular flights between geographical points on which one could buy a ticket had to end. "In the future there should be no general use of the exemption authority as a basis for authorizing common carrier transportation to individually ticketed passengers on larger transport planes," the study recommended.[48]

Charter service was one thing, but for supplemental carriers to prosper, perhaps even to survive, they had to make the transition from essentially offering airplanes for hire to haul anything to any place at any time into airlines with established routes where passengers could buy tickets and cargo could be shipped in something less than full planeloads. There was simply not enough charter business, and Nelson and the smartest of his colleagues heading other supplemental carriers realized that to survive they had to enter the ranks of the scheduled airlines and obtain permission to fly regular routes between set points on established schedules. Nelson proposed doing so early on, and he consistently sounded a drumbeat for CAB permission, seeking a certificate of public convenience and necessity granted by the CAB to airlines as licenses for specific routes. Of course, Nelson and his fellow supplemental carrier CEOs erred in asking only for permission to fly on routes viewed as plums by the industry, ones that enjoyed high traffic volumes and the expectation that their markets would expand rapidly in the near term.

Nelson advocated certification for Transocean to fly regular schedules on transpacific and transatlantic routes in the later 1940s, but in both instances the CAB denied the request. These cases involved more than five years of effort before they were finally decided, and then they only found resolution in the White House as seemingly round after round took place in the dance of Washington bureaucratic politics and interest group lobbying. At every point Nelson failed to gain CAB certification to fly regular routes.[49] He appealed the CAB's decision to the president and offered this rationale to Ike's aide for overturning the CAB's recommendation: "I just can't believe that President Eisenhower is for a 'status quo' in a growing and expanding industry. You personally know that the certificated carriers need a competitive spur and that many of the innovations and developments in the public interest in our industry have been due to the ingenuity and resourcefulness of the irregular carriers, but it is only a matter of time until the present policy of letter of registration and temporary exemptions will cause even the strongest of the irregulars to fall by the wayside or embark on a policy of flaunting the existing regulations."

Nelson also played the political card by reminding the White House of his long-standing support of the Republicans and of his connections with members of Congress from California. "We believed then and believe now that this country has not stopped going, that we are on the threshold of even greater things," he added, "and we have even deeper and stronger faith in the absolute need for the maintenance of a free competitive economy in this country, particularly in an industry which, if it is not an infant, is in the early stages of adolescence."[50]

Nelson's plea to the White House neither fell on deaf ears nor brought Transocean a positive outcome in the cases. In February 1955, Eisenhower sided with the CAB decision concerning Transocean and stated, "As you know, I believe in the strength of competitive enterprise if based upon sound economic considerations, but it must not be wasteful duplication at the expense of the Federal Government." The CAB had believed that Transocean's entry into these markets, all quite lucrative routes generating excellent returns for the carriers already on them, would cut into their profits. This would force the government under law in that regulated industry to pay those carriers additional direct subsidies to off-set those losses. The cost to the taxpayer, therefore, would be greater, and Eisenhower decided that such expenditure represented "wasteful dupli-cation." As a fiscal conservative (and no one could seriously challenge his commitment to the free enterprise system), Eisenhower viewed Trans-ocean's intrusion into the market as inappropriate because of the havoc it would create elsewhere in the air transportation system.[51]

Nelson did not give up quietly. He mobilized the strength of the en-tire California congressional delegation to reverse this decision. In a joint letter to the president, these members of Congress urged reconsideration, since the present decision "adversely affects the continued operation of Transocean Airlines." They also noted that the CAB's original examiner had accepted Nelson's position, at least to a point, and had recommended certificating TAL to "conduct nonsubsidized, nonscheduled transporta-tion of persons and property in the Trans-Pacific areas for a period of seven years" but that the CAB had decided not to support this recom-mendation. Reversal of the present decision, they argued, would therefore validate the original examiner's recommendation and appropriate posi-tion, since he had the most detailed understanding of the case after his years of study and reflection on the problem.[52]

Nelson ultimately succeeded in reversing this decision, although some members of the CAB and a few on Ike's staff recommended yielding to the pressure and certificating Transocean.[53] The best Nelson could do was to persuade the Eisenhower administration to ensure that the issue become a part of the CAB's "Large Irregular Carrier Investigation Case," published in early 1956. This study stipulated that the supplemental car-riers be allowed to make a maximum of ten flights each month between any pair of cities. The CAB did not restrict the total number of flights permitted Transocean and the other supplementals, but the ten-flight rule between city pairs limitation ensured that they would not set up a per-manent schedule. The CAB also revalidated its long-standing policy of relaxed regulation over the supplementals' safety and operations.[54]

The certificated airlines, assisted by interest groups dedicated to air safety and passenger welfare, challenged this CAB decision in the courts. When finally decided, the court ruled that the Civil Aeronautics Board had violated the Civil Aeronautics Act of 1938 by unlawfully relieving the supplemental carriers of the normal licensing process and by shirking its responsibilities to regulate the industry on behalf of the American people.[55] Taken altogether, the Civil Aeronautics Board had sought a niche in the air transportation system in the 1950s that allowed Nelson and his colleagues a full range of operations as contract carriers and as limited scheduled airlines. The CAB even aided the supplementals by relaxing operating and safety regulations for the companies. The president and key members of his administration agreed with these efforts. The federal government's executive branch, therefore, actively encouraged a modicum of, but not cutthroat, competition in the air transportation industry. These efforts, never enough to satisfy Nelson and his fellow supplemental carrier CEOs, probably represented the most favorable policies that could have been expected in the environment of heavy regulation then in place over the industry. Indeed, the courts determined that the Eisenhower administration had been overly salutary in its handling of the supplemental carriers and their place in the air transport system. One might fault the aviation policy process as flawed; one might ridicule the CAB for its drawn out deliberations; one might condemn the courts as unfair; one might even challenge the necessity of industry regulation altogether. But one is hard pressed to conclude that Nelson, Transocean Air Lines, and the other supplemental carriers were run out of business because of a diabolical conspiracy between members of the CAB and heads of the airlines.

But such a conspiracy thesis remained the only way to secure a future in the regulated air transport industry, and the supplementals played it for all it was worth as a means to pressure government for increased expenditures for airlift contracts and as a way to ensure a continuation of lax regulation. The supplemental carriers' very existence, however, was contradictory to the national and international regulatory apparatus and could not survive long-term without redefinition. After a series of scandals over safety, service, and reliability that emerged in the latter 1950s, Congress determined that it had to restructure the industry. Although TAL was out of business by this time, Nelson took heart in the fact that Public Law 87–528, passed by Congress on 10 July 1962, partially vindicated his

arguments by establishing the permanent role of the supplemental carriers as a legitimate part of the United States' air transport system. This
legislation enabled the CAB to set specific standards for the supplementals, to restructure that segment of the industry, and to ensure a place for
them as charter carriers fenced off from the scheduled airlines. Many of
the supplementals that survived this process became giants in the industry, and companies like the Flying Tiger Line and World Airways have
become well known since 1962.

But it was, at least for Nelson, a case of too little, too late. After the
collapse of Transocean in 1960, Nelson worked as a pilot with other companies, but in 1966 he moved back to Minnesota. After a few years he
returned to California, and from there he worked as an air transport consultant for several firms. He died of a heart attack on 2 December 1976.

Nelson also spent the rest of his life lobbying for the complete deregulation of the airline industry. On 6 October 1976, he asked Congress
to "take the necessary steps to force deregulation by the Board to the
greatest extent possible. Start with cancelling control over air fares, give
unlimited right of entry into the airline business domestically and right
of entry and departure from points served." Always optimistic, he concluded, "We have people standing by, many of the Transocean originals,
eager to get Transocean back in the air."[56] It is ironic that he died before
the passage of the Airline Deregulation Act of October 1978. Had he lived
to see it, he might well have enjoyed the comeuppance such airlines as
Eastern and Pan American received, since within a few years they went
into receivership. He most assuredly would have cringed at the chaotic
situation that has resulted in the present airline industry, however, with
cutthroat competition prompting scandalous corporate decisions to reduce costs at the expense of service, reliability, and safety.

Conclusion

Was Nelson the right man in the right place at the right time? No crys-
talline answer emerges from the historical record. He enjoyed enormous
success for a considerable period, and his ability to take advantage of the
short-term situation at the end of World War II certainly sustains the
"right man" ideal. Had he been operating TAL in the latter 1970s, he would
have had no excuse had he not been able to succeed in the deregulated
environment following the 1978 act. Perhaps he would have done so

spectacularly, but he might just as easily have failed, as did many air transport entrepreneurs. Certainly, had he tried to enter the marketplace just a few years later, the barriers would have been too high to succeed with the meager capitalization and connections available to him when he started in 1946. What can be concluded about Nelson's legacy is that he was an enormously ambitious and talented individual who took advantage of the opportunities that presented themselves in the latter 1940s, and that he played the string out during the 1950s as market, cold war, and domestic political forces struggled for the emergence of coherency in policies related to the airline industry. Unfortunately, Nelson's TAL did not survive that very natural sorting out of U.S. aviation policy.

Notes

I wish to acknowledge the research assistance of Gail Culler, Richard Faust, Mark Kahn, and Andrew Pedrick at the NASA headquarters and David Haight, archivist at the Dwight D. Eisenhower Library in Abilene, Kansas, in preparing this article.

1. R. E. G. Davies, *Rebels and Reformers of the Airways* (Washington, D.C.: Smithsonian Institution Press, 1987), 101.

2. Senate Select Committee on Small Business, *Report on Role of Irregular Air Carriers in United States Air Transportation Industry,* 82d Cong., 1st sess., 1951, S. Rept. 540, 5, 8, 17.

3. Offprint of speech from *Congressional Record,* 11 April 1962, Wayne L. Morse Papers, Special Collections, University of Oregon Library, Eugene.

4. Testimony of Orvis M. Nelson, 6 October 1976, in Senate Select Committee on Small Business, *The Decline of Supplemental Air Carriers in the United States,* 94th Cong., 2d sess., 1976, "Hearings before the Subcommittee on Monopoly," 104.

5. I tend to agree with the argument that the nonscheduled carriers as a group were not economically viable from at least the late 1940s when the major airlines had recovered from wartime restrictions. This has been advanced by Frederick C. Thayer Jr. in *Air Transport Policy and National Security: A Political, Economic, and Military Analysis* (Chapel Hill: University of North Carolina Press, 1965), 90–113. The CIA connection is related in Anthony Sampson, *Empires of the Sky: The Politics, Contests and Cartels of World Airlines* (New York: Random House, 1984), 85; William M. Leary, *Perilous Missions: Civil Air Transport and CIA Covert Operations in Asia* (University: University of Alabama Press, 1984), 100–106; John Marks and Victor Marchetti, *CIA and the Cult of Intelligence* (New York: Dell Books, 1980), 129–36.

6. Biographical information on Nelson contained in this article is based on

Roger D. Launius, "Orvis M. Nelson," in William M. Leary, ed., *Encyclopedia of American Business History and Biography: The Air Industry* (New York: Facts on File, 1992), 309–13; Richard Thruelsen, *Transocean: The Story of an Unusual Airline* (New York: Henry Holt, 1953); Arue Szura, *Folded Wings: A History of Transocean Air Lines* (Missoula, Mont.: Pictorial Histories, 1989).

7. Thruelsen, *Transocean*, 24–25.

8. Ibid., 31.

9. In 1934 President Franklin D. Roosevelt canceled all commercial air mail contracts because of possible illegalities in the manner in which they had been awarded by the preceding Republican administration. On this episode see Benjamin D. Foulois and Carroll V. Glines, *From the Wright Brothers to the Astronauts: The Memoirs of Benjamin D. Foulois* (New York: McGraw-Hill, 1960), 237–38; John F. Shiner, "General Benjamin Foulois and the 1934 Air Mail Disaster, *Aerospace Historian* 25 (winter 1978): 221–30; Mauer Mauer, *Aviation in the U.S. Army, 1919–1939* (Washington, D.C.: Office of Air Force History, 1987), 299–317; Paul Tillett, *The Army Flies the Mails* (Tuscaloosa: University of Alabama Press, 1956).

10. The War Department entered a service arrangement with United through contract no. WD 535 ac-27360, 24 March 1942. For information on these flight operations, see Betty R. Kennedy, ed., *Anything, Anywhere, Anytime: An Illustrated History of the Military Airlift Command, 1941–1991* (Scott AFB, Ill.: Office of Military Airlift Command History, 1991), 15–17, 36; Roger D. Launius, "World War II Military in the Rockies: From Natural to National Resource," *Journal of the West* 32 (April 1993): 86–93; Robert H. Jones, *The Roads to Russia: United States Lend-Lease to the Soviet Union* (Norman: University of Oklahoma Press, 1969), 24–25, 35, 162; Deanne R. Brandon, "ALSIB: The Ferrying of Lend-Lease Aircraft from Great Falls, Montana, to the War Fronts of the Soviet Union, September 1942–September 1945," in Stan Cohen, ed., *The Forgotten War: A Pictorial History of World War II in Alaska and Northwestern Canada* (Missoula, Mont.: Pictorial Histories, 1991), 2:34–49; Daniel L. Haulman, "The Northwest Ferry Route," in Fern Chandonnet, ed., *Alaska at War, 1941–1945: The Forgotten War Remembered* (Anchorage: Alaska at War Committee, 1995), 319–25; Edwin Remmen Carr, "Great Falls to Nome: The Inland Air Route to Alaska, 1940–1945," Ph.D. diss., University of Minnesota, 1946, 142–77.

11. Nelson testimony, Senate Select Committee, *Decline of Supplemental Air Carriers,* 109; R. E. G. Davies, *Airlines of the United States since 1914,* vol. 2 of *Airliners from 1919 to the Present Day* (London: Putnam, 1972), 274.

12. On the activities of the Air Line Pilots Association, which remains important to the present, see George E. Hopkins, *The Airline Pilots: A Study in Elite Unionization* (Cambridge: Harvard University Press, 1971) and *Flying the Line: The First Half-Century of the Air Line Pilots Association* (Washington, D.C.: Air Line Pilots Association, 1982).

13. Nelson testimony, Senate Select Committee, *Decline of Supplemental Air Carriers,* 109.

14. Thruelsen, *Transocean,* 45–53.

15. Ibid., 47–48.

16. Senate Congressional Aviation Policy Board, *National Aviation Policy,* 80th Cong., 2d sess., S. Rept. 949 (Washington, D.C.: Government Printing Office, 1948), 15.

17. This contention is very difficult to prove, and I have no wish to overstate my case, but such sociological studies as William F. Ogburn, *The Social Effects of Aviation* (New York: Houghton Mifflin, 1946); J. Parker Van Zandt, *America Faces the Air Age,* 2 vols. (Washington, D.C.: Brookings Institution, 1944); Hall Barlett, *Social Studies for the Air Age* (New York: Macmillan 1942); and George T. Renner, *Human Geography in the Air Age* (New York: Macmillan, 1943), support these contentions and in some cases go much further.

18. The story of Pan Am's special relationship with the prewar federal government has been detailed in Marilyn Bender and Selig Altschul, *The Chosen Instrument* (New York: Simon and Schuster, 1982). The change in policy is clearly described in Thayer, *Air Transport Policy and National Security,* 68–75; Sampson, *Empires of the Sky,* 78–83; John R. M. Wilson, *Turbulence Aloft: The Civil Aeronautics Administration amid Wars and Rumors of Wars, 1938–1953* (Washington, D.C.: Federal Aviation Administration, 1979), 196–204; and Nawal K. Taneja, *The Commercial Airline Industry: Managerial Practices and Regulatory Policies* (Lexington, Mass.: D. C. Heath, 1976), 170–17.

19. Richard Malkin, *Boxcars in the Sky* (New York: Import, 1951), 234; House Committee on the Judiciary, *Monopoly Problems in Regulated Industries,* Hearings before Subcommittee, 84th Cong., 2d sess., 1956, 1:183, 189.

20. Malkin, *Boxcars in the Sky,* 98; Alfred Goldberg, ed., *A History of the United States Air Force* (Princeton, N.J.: D. Van Nostrand, 1957), 8; Thayer, *Air Transport Policy and National Security,* 105–6.

21. Senate Select Committee, *Report on Role of Irregular Air Carriers,* 4; Senate Select Committee on Small Business, *Role of Irregular Airlines in United States Air Transportation Industry,* Hearings before Subcommittee, 82d Cong., 1st sess., 1951, 9.

22. John H. Frederick, "American Air Cargo Development," *Air Affairs* 2 (autumn 1947): 93; U.S. Department of Commerce, Civil Aeronautics Administration, *Statistical Handbook of Civil Aviation, 1948* (Washington, D.C.: Government Printing Office, 1949), 37; Thayer, *Air Transport Policy and National Security,* 90–93.

23. Thruelsen, *Transocean,* 62; Robert Hotz, "Transocean Makes Money," *Aviation Week,* 30 August 1948, 39.

24. Thruelsen, *Transocean,* 56–57.

25. Szura, *Folded Wings,* 98–104, 142.

26. Thruelsen, *Transocean,* 63–64.

27. Szura, *Folded Wings,* 11; Thruelsen, *Transocean,* 74.

28. Nelson testimony, Senate Select Committee, *Decline of Supplemental Air Carriers,* 110.

29. Thruelsen, *Transocean,* 91.

30. Nelson testimony, Senate Select Committee, *Decline of Supplemental Air Carriers,* 110.

31. Senate Committee on Commerce, *Study of Military Transport Service,* Hearings before Subcommittee, 85th Cong., 2d sess., 1958, 166; Richard E. Caves, *Air Transport and Its Regulators* (Cambridge: Harvard University Press, 1962), 278.

32. Letter from Assistant Secretary of the Air Force Joseph Imrie, in House Committee on Commerce, *Supplemental Air Carriers,* 87th Cong., 1st sess., 1961, H. Rept. 1177, 59.

33. On the details of the airlift, as well as the role of the commercial carriers, see Roger D. Launius, "The Berlin Airlift: Constructive Air Power," *Air Power History* 36 (spring 1989): 8–22; Roger D. Launius, "The Berlin Airlift—Refining the Air Transport Function, 1948–1949," *Airlift: The Journal of the Airlift Operations School* 10 (summer 1988): 10–17; Roger D. Launius and Coy F. Cross, *MAC and the Legacy of the Berlin Airlift* (Scott AFB, Ill.: Office of Military Airlift Command History, 1988).

34. Senate Select Committee on Small Business, *Future of Irregular Airlines in United States Air Transport Industry,* Hearings before Subcommittee, 83d Cong., 1st sess., 1953, 267–68. A similar mythical statement was made by an industry spokesman in his testimony before the same committee; see 115–16.

35. William H. Tunner, *Over the Hump* (New York: Duell and Sloan, 1984), 162.

36. Thayer, *Air Transport Policy and National Security,* 102–3.

37. Civil Aeronautics Board, "Brief of the Independent Military Air Transport Association to Examiners Ralph L. Wiser and Richard A. Walsh, in the Matter of the Irregular Air Carrier Investigation," 25 October 1954, CAB Irregular Air Carrier (1) folder, White House Official Files, OF62, Box 265, Dwight D. Eisenhower Library, Abilene, Kans.; Roger D. Launius, "Forty Years Ago: MATS and the Korean War Airlift," *Airlift: The Journal of the Airlift Operations School* 12 (summer 1990): 16–21; Roger D. Launius, *Significant Airlift Events of the Korean Conflict, 1950–1953: A Brief Chronology* (Scott AFB, Ill.: Office of Military Airlift Command History, June 1990).

38. "Flying Handyman," *Time,* 22 November 1948, 92, 96; Nelson testimony, Senate Select Committee, *Decline of Supplemental Air Carriers,* 112–14; Roger D. Launius, "Operation SAFE HAVEN: MATS and the Hungarian Airlift," *Airlift: The Journal of the Airlift Operations School* 11 (winter 1989): 17–21.

39. Szura, *Folded Wings,* 35–37.

40. Thruelsen, *Transocean,* 4–5.

41. Davies, *Rebels and Reformers,* 114.

42. *New York Times,* 3 September 1960, 36.

43. D. Daryl Wyckoff and David H. Maister, *The Domestic Airline Industry* (Lexington, Mass.: D. C. Heath, 1977), xlv–lix.

44. This story has been magnificently related in Gabriel Kolko, *Railroads and Regulation, 1877–1916* (Princeton: Princeton University Press, 1965).

45. Brig. Gen. R. B. Landry, memorandum for the president, 14 January 1952, CAB 1953(1) folder, General Advisory Committee, White House Central Files, Office File OF 61-A, Box 254, Eisenhower Library.

46. Brig. Gen. R. B. Landry, memorandum for the president, 21 July 1952, with additional memoranda and a study, "Report on Status of Large Irregular Air Carriers" attached, CAB 1953(1) folder, General Advisory Committee, White House Central Files, Office File OF 61-A, Box 254, Eisenhower Library. There was a run-in between the CAB and TAL in 1949 over the nature of some of Nelson's overseas operations. While he asserted that his flights were charters, the CAB argued that they were "actually common carrier in nature even though a contract may have been signed." They reached an agreement wherein TAL changed some of the details of its practice and the CAB ended its investigation. See Charles Adams, "Contract Flight Ban Weighed," *Aviation Week,* 17 October 1949, 50–51; Orvis M. Nelson to Charles F. Willis Jr., 14 July 1954, CAB 1954(3) folder, White House Central Files, OF62, Box 255, Eisenhower Library.

47. William Kroger, "Unscheduled Carriers Determined to Fight Full Federal Control," *Aviation News* 5 (17 June 1946): 7; Civil Aeronautics Board, Regulations, Serial Number 184, "Temporary Exemption of Non-Scheduled Operations from Certain Provisions of Title IV of the Civil Aeronautics Act of 1938, as Amended," 17 May 1946, FAA History Office, Washington, D.C.; Ivor P. Morgan, "Government and the Industry's Early Development," in John R. Meyer and Clinton V. Oster Jr., eds., *Airline Deregulation: The Early Experience* (Boston: Auburn House, 1981), 22–23. There was some modification and CAB regulation of this policy beginning in 1949, the details of which are explained in Thayer, *Air Transport Policy and National Defense,* 94–96.

48. Air Coordinating Committee, "Review of National Aviation Policy—Air Transport—Non-Scheduled Airline Operations," 12 April 1954, White House Central Files, Subject Series, Air Coordinating Committee, Eisenhower Library.

49. "Examiner Vetoes Ocean Cargo Bids," *Aviation Week,* 4 September 1950, 47; "Brief to the Civil Aeronautics Board on Behalf of Transocean Air Lines, in the Proceeding Known as the Trans-Pacific Certificate Renewal Case," 17 May 1954, CAB 1954(2) folder, White House Central Files, OF62, Box 255, Eisenhower Library; Civil Aeronautics Board, "Docket No. 3041, et al., Transatlantic Cargo

Case," 19 May 1954, CAB 1957(2) folder, White House Central Files, OF62 1957, Box 258, Eisenhower Library; Civil Aeronautics Board, "Docket No. 5589, et al., West Coast-Hawaii Case," 26 November 1954, and "Docket No. 5031, et al., Trans-Pacific Certificate Renewal Case," 15 December 1954, both in White House Central Files, Subject Series, Air Coordinating Committee, Eisenhower Library; "Policy for Aviation," *Washington Post,* 5 June 1954; "Nonskeds Awaiting Legal Rulings," *Aviation Week,* 15 March 1955, 157, 161; Wayne W. Parrish, "Reckless . . . and Irresponsible," *American Aviation,* 5 December 1955, 11.

50. Nelson to Willis, 14 July 1954, CAB 1954(3) folder, White House Central Files, OF62, Box 255, Eisenhower Library.

51. Civil Aeronautics Board, "Docket No. 5589, et al., West Coast–Hawaii Case" and "Docket No. 5031, et al., Trans-Pacific Certificate Renewal Case," 8 February 1955, White House Central Files, Subject Series, Air Coordinating Committee, Eisenhower Library.

52. Rep. John J. Allen Jr. to the President, 5 February 1955; George P. Miller and the entire California delegation to Congress, 14 February 1955; Sen. William F. Knowland to the President, 15 February 1955; Rowland Hughes, Director of the Bureau of the Budget, to Gov. Sherman Adams, 16 February 1955; L. Jack Martin, Administrative Assistant to the President, to Hon. John J. Allen Jr., 18 February 1955, all in White House Official Files, OF62, Trans-Pacific Certificate Renewal Case(4), Box 272, Eisenhower Library.

53. ·Hughes to Adams, 16 February 1955; Martin to Allen, 18 February 1955, both in White House Official Files, OF62, Trans-Pacific Certificate Renewal Case(4), Box 272, Eisenhower Library; Hughes to the President, February 1955, White House Central Files, Subject Series, Air Coordinating Committee, Eisenhower Library.

54. Chairman, Civil Aeronautics Board, to the President, 9 January 1956; Hughes to the President, 17 February 1956, both in White House Official Files, OF62, Irregular Air Carriers, Box 265, Eisenhower Library.

55. Testimony of CAB chairman Alan Boyd, in House Committee on Commerce, *Supplemental Air Carriers,* 87th Cong., 1st sess., 1961, H. Rept. 1177, 4–6.

56. Nelson testimony, Senate Select Committee, *Decline of Supplemental Air Carriers,* 146.

Bibliographical Essay

Archival information on Orvis M. Nelson and Transocean Air Lines is in the Civil Reserve Air Fleet Records, 1948–89, Office of History, Military Airlift Command, Scott Air Force Base, Illinois. For other primary sources, see particularly Testimony of Orvis M. Nelson, 6 October 1976, in Senate Select Committee on Small Business, *The Decline of Supplemental Air Carriers in the United States,* 94th

Cong., 2d sess., "Hearings before the Subcommittee on Monopoly" (Washington, D.C.: GPO, 1976). Important materials pertaining to the Civil Aeronautics Board's deliberations on nonscheduled carriers in the 1950s are in the White House Official Files, Boxes 265 and 272, of the Dwight D. Eisenhower Presidential Library, Abilene, Kansas.

For biographical information and interpretive articles on Nelson, see Roger D. Launius, "Orvis M. Nelson," in William M. Leary, ed., *Encyclopedia of American Business History and Biography: The Airline Industry* (New York: Facts On File, 1992), 309–13, and "Orvis Nelson: Mr. Transocean," in R. E. G. Davies, *Rebels and Reformers of the Airways* (Washington, D.C.: Smithsonian Institution Press, 1987), 101–17. On Transocean itself, see Richard Thruelsen, *Transocean: The Story of an Unusual Airline* (New York: Henry Holt and Company, 1953), and Arue Szura, *Folded Wings: A History of Transocean Air Lines* (Missoula, MT: Pictorial Histories Publishing Company, 1989).

On federal regulatory policy in the period in which Transocean's history took place, see particularly Richard E. Caves, *Air Transport and Its Regulators* (Cambridge, MA: Harvard University Press, 1962); Frederick C. Thayer Jr., *Air Transport Policy and National Security: A Political, Economic, and Military Analysis* (Chapel Hill: University of North Carolina Press, 1965); Nawal K. Taneja, *The Commercial Airline Industry: Managerial Practices and Regulatory Policies* (Lexington, MA: D. C. Heath, 1976); John R. M. Wilson, *Turbulence Aloft: The Civil Aeronautics Administration amid Wars and Rumors of Wars, 1938–1953* (Washington, D.C.: Federal Aviation Administration, 1979); and Stuart I. Rochester, *Takeoff at Mid-Century: Federal Civil Aviation Policy in the Eisenhower Years* (Washington, D.C.: Federal Aviation Administration, 1976). On military airlift in general, see Betty R. Kennedy, gen. ed., *Anything, Anywhere, Anytime: An Illustrated History of the Military Airlift Command, 1941–1991* (Scott AFB, Ill.: Office of MAC History, 1991).

Contributors

Roger E. Bilstein is professor of history at the University of Houston–Clear Lake, where he teaches courses in twentieth-century American history, technology, and foreign relations. He has written numerous articles on aerospace history and several books, including *Flight in America: From the Wrights to the Astronauts* (1994) and *The American Aerospace Industry: From Workshop to Global Enterprise* (1996).

Donna M. Corbett spent several years on the curatorial staff of the Smithsonian Institution before entering private industry. Her writings have explored a variety of topics related to the air travel industry, from an evaluation of postderegulation airline executive performance to an interpretation of gender role stereotypes in airline crew uniforms.

Michael H. Gorn is research historian for the NASA Flight Research Project. He is also a research collaborator at the National Air and Space Museum, Washington, D.C., and associate editor of the Smithsonian History of Aviation book series. Gorn's publications include *Hugh L. Dryden's Career in Aviation and Space* (1996), *Prophecy Fulfilled: Toward New Horizons and Its Legacy* (1994), and *The Universal Man: Theodore* *von Karman's Life in Aeronautics* (1992). He is currently at work on two books: "NASA's Bright Star: Hugh L. Dryden's Life in Aviation and Space-flight" and "Flight Research at the NACA and NASA."

George E. Hopkins is professor of history at Western Illinois University. He is the author of *The Airline Pilots: A Study in Elite Unionization* (1971) and *Flying the Line: The First Half-Century of the Airline Pilots Association* (1982). His research interests center on the history of airline labor relations, and he is a leading expert on the history of pilot unionization.

Roger D. Launius is chief historian of the National Aeronautics and Space Administration, Washington, D.C. He has written or edited several books on aerospace history, including *NASA and the Exploration of Space* (1988), *Frontiers of Space Exploration* (1998), *Spaceflight and the Myth of Presidential Leadership* (1997), edited with Howard E. McCurdy, and *NASA: A History of the U.S. Civil Space Program* (1994).

William M. Leary is E. Merton Coulter Professor of History at the University of Georgia. He has written histories of the China National Aviation Corporation, Civil Air Transport, and the U.S. Air Mail Service. He also has edited a volume on the U.S. airline industry for the *Encyclopedia of American Business History and Biography* and a collection of proceedings from the International Conference on the History of Civil and Commercial Aviation, which was held at the Swiss Transport Museum in Lucerne in 1992.

W. David Lewis is Distinguished University Professor of History at Auburn University. He has written *Delta: The History of an Airline* (1979) with Wesley Phillips Newton; *The Airline to Everywhere: A History of All-American Aviation* (1988) with William F. Trimble; and *Sloss Furnaces and the Rise of the Birmingham District: An Industrial Epic* (1994), which was nominated for a Pulitzer Prize in U.S. history. He also edited Edward V. Rickenbacker's World War I memoirs, *Fighting the Flying Circus* (1995). He is currently writing a biography of Rickenbacker.

W. F. Trimble's books include *Admiral William A. Moffett: Architect of Naval Aviation* (1994), *High Frontier: A History of Aeronautics in Penn-*

sylvania (1982), and *The Airway to Everywhere: A History of All American Aviation, 1937–1953* (1988) with W. David Lewis. He is Charles A. Lindbergh Professor of Aerospace History at the National Air and Space Museum, where he is completing a biography of aeronautical engineer Jerome C. Hunsaker.

Index

Page numbers for illustrations are in italics.

Historical Perspectives on Business Enterprise Series

Mansel G. Blackford and K. Austin Kerr, Editors

The scope of the series includes scholarly interest in the history of the firm, the history of government-business relations, and the relationships between business and culture, both in the United States and abroad, as well as in comparative perspective.

BFGoodrich: Transition and Transformation, 1870–1995
Mansel G. Blackford and K. Austin Kerr

Capitalism, Politics, and Railroads in Prussia, 1830–1870
James M. Brophy

Regulated Enterprise: Natural Gas Pipelines and Northeastern Markets, 1938–1954
Christopher James Castaneda

Managing Industrial Decline: Entrepreneurship in the British Coal Industry between the Wars
Michael Dintenfass

Werner von Siemens: Inventor and International Entrepreneur
Wilfried Feldenkirchen

Siemens, 1918–1945
Wilfried Feldenkirchen

Henry E. Huntington and the Creation of Southern California
William B. Friedricks

Making Iron and Steel: Independent Mills in Pittsburgh, 1820–1920
John N. Ingham

Eagle-Picher Industries: Strategies for Survival in the Industrial Marketplace, 1840–1980
Douglas Knerr

Wolf Creek Station: Kansas Gas and Electric Company in the Nuclear Era
Craig Miner

A Mental Revolution: Scientific Management since Taylor
Edited by Daniel Nelson

American Public Finance and Financial Services, 1700—1815
Edwin J. Perkins

A History of Accountancy in the United States: The Cultural Significance of Accounting
Gary John Previts and Barbara Dubis Merino

Courts and Commerce: Gender, Debt Law, and the Expansion of the Market Economy in Eighteenth-Century New York
Deborah A. Rosen

The Passenger Train in the Motor Age: California's Rail and Bus Industries, 1910–1941
Gregory Lee Thompson

Rebuilding Cleveland: The Cleveland Foundation and Its Evolving Urban Strategy
Diana Tittle

Daniel Willard and Progressive Management on the Baltimore & Ohio Railroad
David M. Vrooman